# LEAN MASTERY COLLECTION

## 6 BOOKS IN 1

The Ultimate Collection Guide to Agile Project Management, Scrum, Kanban, Six Sigma, Lean Analytics and Enterprise

**By Adam Ross**

© Copyright 2020 By Adam Ross - All rights reserved.

This content is provided with the sole purpose of providing relevant information on a specific topic for which every reasonable effort has been made to ensure that it is both accurate and reasonable. Nevertheless, by purchasing this content, you consent to the fact that the author, as well as the publisher, are in no way experts on the topics contained herein, regardless of any claims as such that may be made within. As such, any suggestions or recommendations that are made within are done so purely for entertainment value. It is recommended that you always consult a professional prior to undertaking any of the advice or techniques discussed within.

This is a legally binding declaration that is considered both valid and fair by both the Committee of Publishers Association and the American Bar Association and should be considered as legally binding within the United States.

The reproduction, transmission, and duplication of any of the content found herein, including any specific or extended information will be done as an illegal act regardless of the end form the information ultimately takes. This includes copied versions of the work both physical, digital, and audio unless express consent of the Publisher is provided beforehand. Any additional rights reserved.

Furthermore, the information that can be found within the pages described forthwith shall be considered both accurate and truthful when it comes to the recounting of facts.

As such, any use, correct or incorrect, of the provided information will render the Publisher free of responsibility as to the actions taken outside of their direct purview. Regardless, there are zero scenarios where the original author or the Publisher can be deemed liable in any fashion for any damages or hardships that may result from any of the information discussed herein.

Additionally, the information in the following pages is intended only for informational purposes and should thus be thought of as universal. As befitting its nature, it is presented without assurance regarding its prolonged validity or interim quality. Trademarks that are mentioned are done without written consent and can in no way be considered an endorsement from the trademark holder.

# BOOKS

| | |
|---|---|
| AGILE PROJECT MANAGEMENT | 5 |
| KANBAN | 155 |
| LEAN ANALYTICS | 297 |
| LEAN ENTERPRISE | 429 |
| LEAN SIX SIGMA | 541 |
| SCRUM | 689 |

# AGILE PROJECT MANAGEMENT

*The Beginner's Step-By-Step Guide to Learn Agile Methodology to Save Resources At Work and Help Deliver a Successful Project on Time and Within Budget*

By Adam Ross

# Table of Contents

Introduction .................................................................... 9

Chapter 1: The Basics of Agile ............................................... 11

Chapter 2: The Benefits of Agile Project Management .................................................................. 18

Chapter 3: Understanding the Agile Lifecycle ..................... 28

Chapter 4: The Difference Between Agile Project Management and Traditional Project Management ............ 35

Chapter 5: Agile Methodologies ............................................. 38

Chapter 6: The Authenticity of Agile Management ............. 43

Chapter 7: Common Misconceptions About Agile Project Management .................................................................. 47

Chapter 8: Agile Project Management in Practice ................ 51

Chapter 9: How to Create a Product Vision ......................... 53

Chapter 10: Roadmap to Agile Fluency ............................... 57

Chapter 11: How to Create an Agile Team ........................... 60

Chapter 12: How to Lead an Agile Team ............................. 66

Chapter 13: Tools for Greater Team Effectiveness in Agile Project Management ........................................................... 72

Chapter 14: Managing Risk in Agile Project Management.... 77

Chapter 15: Common Challenges Faced When Using the Agile Method .................................................................. 82

Chapter 16: Understanding Agile Programming Practices .. 88

Chapter 17: Examples of Agile Project Management Software 91

Chapter 18: Techniques of Agile Software Development..... 94

Chapter 19: How to Implement Agile Project Management Effectively ........................................................................ 98

Chapter 20: Monitoring the Progress of an Agile Project ... 106

Chapter 21: Tools for Quality Control in Agile Project Management .................................................................. 110

Chapter 22: Key Metrics to Measure Agile Success ............ 115

Chapter 23: Closing and Evaluating Project Success ........................................................................ 122

Chapter 24: How Agile Can Easily Fail ............................... 126

Chapter 25: How to Apply the Agile Project Management Method Effectively ........................................................... 130

Chapter 26: The Need for Agile Project Management in Today's Market ................................................................ 133

Chapter 27: Tips and Tricks to Make Your Agile Project Management System Efficient .......................................... 140

Conclusion ....................................................................... 151

# Introduction

When it comes to the field of management, everyone is involved in managing projects. Whether one has a certificate in project management or not, at one point or the other they will be saddled with the responsibility of handling a project, ensuring that every part of the project works as it should, and that the requirements of the customer are met.

One of the most popular industry techniques used by project managers is known as Agile Management. Essentially, Agile Management is an interactive and incremental approach to a job. This form of management means that each person has a complex role that will eventually fit together with others to create one cohesive team. Each member of the team is "agile" and has an agile role. This is a management technique perfect for those who want to increase communication and organization within a project team.

This book helps you learn about Agile Project Management with the complete involvement of every person and process necessary to build an understanding of how crucial it is to follow the trends of the market, to stay up to date, and retain that competitive edge needed in business. You cannot expect a huge success suddenly unless you put in the hard work and Agile Project Management requires consistent hard work with complete focus on the project. There are ways for you to get through any project with the guidance in this book, along with instructions on the entire implementation of the Agile lifecycle. Each phase is explained in full detail which can help you to head in the right direction, even if you feel lost somewhere in-between while developing your Agile Project Management skills.

In this book, you can learn more about the basics of Agile Project Management including sections on how to encourage each employee to own the project and take responsibility for its success. You can find out what material to employ, how much of it to employ, and even when to employ it – all without waiting for instructions from above! This book includes a step by step explanation on how you do your planning in Agile Project Management, and you will see how different this planning method is from the traditional project management methods. This book clearly shows you that you can oversee a project to its successful completion, and all the time remain friends with your team members while maintaining a close relationship with your customer.

You will realize that working on a project, and particularly managing it, does not have to be a stressful undertaking. In Agile Project Management, every participant – your employees, your product owner, and the scrum master – all work hand in hand and enjoy their work. When working within Agile, you are can be certain that what you are developing is going smoothly from the onset, through all iterations, to the time for the customer to take it away. In short, Agile is a great cost saver as you do not risk your final product being rejected by the end-user.

The sooner you start applying the principles as well as practices of Agile Project Management the quicker you can reduce the risk of losses emanating from rejected goods, lost man-hours from stressed workers taking sick-days, and other losses that crop up when the working environment is unfriendly. If you want to keep up with the modern management styles and maintain a good relationship with both your employees and your customers, Agile Project Management is the way to go. You will see your profits shooting up as a result. The Agile method is one of the best choices that you can make when it comes to helping with new products and software.

# Chapter 1:
# The Basics of Agile

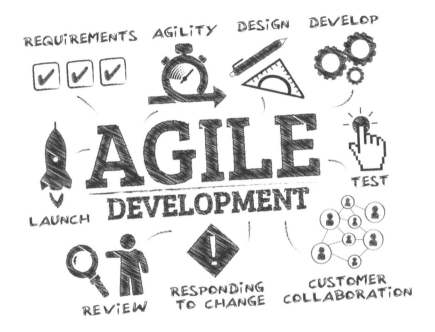

Agile Project Management is basically a way of handling a project in order to help fulfill the goals of that project. This could include things such as early delivery of a specific task, or even a continuous development process of the project processes and products. In addition, Agile is going to focus a bit on creating a scope that is more flexible to ensure that the products the company makes and tests are going to reflect all of the needs of the customer.

Everyone understands that a big project for a company is going to require total attention, time, and the correct amount of planning. Without all of these factors in place, there is very little chance that a new project is going to be successful. The successful software projects, the ones that make it to market and do well, are going to have a goal and an objective set from the beginning. In addition, they will also have a defined deadline to ensure they get the project done.

Agile Project Management comes with a lot of techniques, and we will talk about them more through this guidebook to help improve the way that you can manage a project. Being the leader of a project means that you must always be up to date on all of the latest approaches with Agile so that your project is managed smoothly and efficiently.

## What Is Agile Project Management and how does it work?

Before deciding if this type of style is for you and your team you should explore it in-depth. This will give you a better idea of what it is and how it should work.

Agile Project Management is a popular phenomenon developed by software project managers. It aims to deliver on projects at a lower cost while producing more effective results over a period of time. Customers are asked to plan ahead, indicating future needs before they wish to start the project so that there is a minimum delay in adapting to these. Agile Project Management helps in making such changes easier for the projects, even if there are some new requirements in the later stages.

Agile Project Management involves the activities and features of delivering added value work while keeping the three important factors of any project: scope, time and cost. These three factors are managed in real-time to ensure that value is created in the project. It reduces complex situations, by breaking the project lifecycle into separate portions so that every portion can be completed before the deadline. It highlights critical segments and then tests the processes which need to be done for these to be achieved within a time frame of two to four-week cycles.

With Agile Management a project and deliverables are done in stages, ensuring that each piece is done correctly and efficiently before moving on. This enables mistakes to be spotted right away and allows progress to continue. Once an agile project is finished, there should not be any unwanted or unexpected surprises or faults that stall the project's implementation.

The concept is simple: members of a team are given specific and complex instructions and tasks. The project manager aims to be interactive with the other members and help guide them. The entire project is worked on by stages or milestones and delivered to the client as such. The stage is then either improved or denied. If denied, the team can figure out what went wrong and fix it right away. This helps from keeping a team backtracking to find old mistakes. Instead, if a stage is denied right away, the team can easily find what is wrong and fix it. This style of project management is convenient and can reduce stress for the project team, manger, and the client.

By breaking a project into specific stages and milestones in this way, each member is given their personal set of detailed instructions and they can focus solely on one step at a time. Other types of management allow a team member to focus on more than one step at a time. This often leads to an increase in errors and can jeopardize a project's success. It can also cause costly delays. Agile Project Management prevents these problems. A team member works on only one piece of the puzzle at a time and then puts it together with other pieces. This gives team members an amount of work they can easily handle and creates a full and complete step that is more likely to be what a client wants, with few (if any) errors to deal with.

This type of management technique and the breaking up of a project into stages also makes each member of a team and their task "agile." But, what does this mean? This style allows managers to deliver high-quality and high-performance work to a client by ensuring that each person on the team is value-oriented. They should love what they are doing and be looking toward the short-term goal instead of that which is long-term. This helps to streamline the entire approach.

Turning a standard team into an agile one is not always easy. To become agile means that the manager in charge must embrace change. When working with software, changes are constant and clients may believe they want one thing and then, once tested, find that they want something very different. By being agile, a team and manager embrace changes made by clients or by the process and apply them correctly. Being agile also means that you do not try and do many steps at one time. You break up long term projects into small, weekly milestones or stages.

Agile Project Management is a way that managers can hit key milestones in a project, eliminate flaws or errors, and deliver an overall project that a client will love. So, is it time for you to ditch the classic Waterfall Management Technique?

## THE 12 PRINCIPLES OF AGILE MANAGEMENT

Agile management principles support the concept of teams and their implementation in the project, which includes streamlining the tasks and responsibilities to get the project completed easily.

- It ensures customer satisfaction by delivering consistent value and leads to the retention of clients. This is built around a continuous improvement process aimed at giving customer value to every segment of the cycle without any interruptions or delays.
- Agile management works on the shortest possible timescale for the delivery of results.
- People on the business side and project developers must work hand in hand to give the most effective results.
- Have regular face-to-face conversations with all parties to tackle any issues and work as a team to help solve any problems as they arise.
- Make sure to work within the software for progress and keep monitoring changes in the market.

- All the team members need to pay complete attention to the project with a focus on good design and agility in enhancing technical excellence.
- There is a need to maintain the simplicity of the objectives without any deviations or complications.
- A self-organizing team working together as good architects producing attractive designs.
- The team behavior may need to be modified, with regular tuning in and reworking to achieve effective results.
- Meetings on a daily basis. Daily meetings can be held, keeping the communication easy and open between the workers and the upper management for a smoother workflow.
- Demonstration. Delivering live demonstrations to allow the work to be understood by all while showing the progress in reaching the final product.
- Sharing feedback. The Sharing of feedback with team members, from both the stakeholders and the customers who are a part of this project and help the team work enthusiastically for the next iteration.
- Stay agile. Make changes to the project where needed to ensure it will be more effective and bring about any improvements by monitoring every step of the way.

## WHY SHOULD I LEARN HOW TO USE AGILE?

Let's say that you have heard about Agile in the past and you have decided to get started with some of the practices of Agile. But as you get going, you find that it is complex and maybe things aren't working out the way that you would like. In this case, it is best for you to inspect the various processes that you are using with implementation. Implementation of Agile can be difficult, but doing it in the right way is going to help create more success when it comes to the delivery process.

Even if you are having difficulties with working in Agile, you will find that it is worth your time. It can prove to be a struggle for some companies because they have to work to get everyone on the team in line and onboard with this idea.

There are so many things that you will enjoy when it comes to using the Agile system. It can help you to get constant feedback on a new software, which ensures that you are making the right products that your customers want. It helps you to control costs and it ensures that everyone on the team can work together and get the best results, sharing their ideas and more. While it takes some time to start and implement, you will be able to see results right away when your company implements Agile.

## WILL AGILE PROJECT MANAGEMENT WORK FOR YOU?

The biggest thing about finding if this type of management will work for you is determining if your company and team is agile.

To give you a better idea of if your company is agile or not there are factors that help define "being agile." Rate your company (and team) from 1 to 5; 5 being that it is nothing like your company and 1 being that it sounds just like it.

- You use mostly email communication. There is little face-to-face interaction and the "forward" button is your best friend.
- "Test-driven" is a phrase not uttered in the workplace. In fact, you have only ever really heard it when referring to a car, not a product.
- You have no idea what PHB stands for.
- You do not know if your office has whiteboards or no one uses them very often.
- You know about CPM and rely on it.
- Someone still believes in the Gantt Chart.
- Everyone has one rigid assigned role.
- You try to manage project dependencies, not remove them.

- A change control board may meet. You don't really know.

- Simplicity means something is simple.

If you scored a majority of these between 1 and 3 your company is not an agile company or is only partway there. At this point and time, Agile Project Management may not be the best option for you. If, on the other hand, you rated each bullet point between 4 and 5 then your company is agile or almost agile. This means, Agile Management is already in place or you have a better chance of applying it and being successful.

# Chapter 2: The Benefits of Agile Project Management

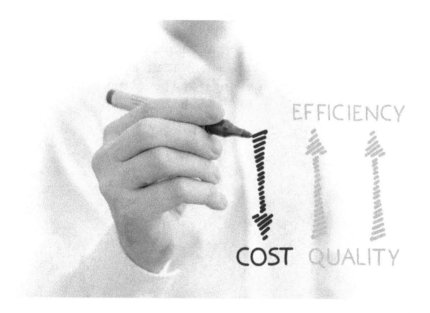

## QUALITY CONTROL

A main feature of Agile is the assurance of a high-quality outcome. Because tests are integrated throughout a project's lifecycle, you can regularly inspect the working product while it undergoes development. And thus, the product owner can incorporate necessary adjustments.

It doesn't lean towards a sequential development process. Sometimes, even if one stage hasn't been completed as the original plan suggests, another stage can begin.

## An Approach for Improved Risk Management

Agile also helps in risk reduction. Due to the increase in visibility of product problems during the early stages, managers and developers can eliminate virtually all chances of project failure by rectifying every problem.

## Improved Predictability

The improved predictability of a project is also Agile's benefit over traditional methods. Despite its disregard for careful planning at the initial stage, Agile's predictable nature is traceable to its flexible control process. With the ability to control processes during product development, the outcome is shaped, and thus, it becomes predictable.

## Increased Customer Satisfaction

This technique also leads to higher customer satisfaction. Because the project is submitted in stages, it gives the customer or client the ability to see everything before it is in its final stages. This allows changes to be made along the way. This is especially important when stage changes or even larger scope changes are requested. By informing the team earlier, fewer changes will have to be made to the entire project; instead of making the changes as the team progresses.

## Increased Team Morale

Higher team morale has also been found within teams whose manager practices Agile Management. This style allows members of a team to feel more comfortable in their part of a project and gives them the ability to take things slowly and review instructions several times. Agile Management also allows those who do their job correctly and to the best of their ability to be honored for it. This is because it is easier to pick out who did what when software is being worked on in milestones or stages.

## Customized Team Structure

Agile projects are made of several scrum teams and decisions normally made by a manager can be delegated to these teams. This increases the productivity of self-management. There are also size limitations that provide opportunities for customization and accountability.

## More Collaboration

Agile Management allows for more collaboration throughout the project process. All of the top members of a team such as the manager, scrum master, and client work on a daily or weekly basis to discuss what has been done and where the software project is going. It allows a client to see what roadblocks are happening and how they are being handled by the team. It also allows for scrum teams to meet with those above them to discuss their progress on a certain stage or milestone.

## Better Values

Certain values or metrics are used within management to measure cost, efficiency, and time. By measuring these things on a daily or weekly basis, it provides more exact values to help a team stay on track and see their progress first hand. It also allows for time, cost, or performance quality to be refined as a team works; instead of stopping and restarting when something needs to be adjusted.

## Efficiency of Delivery

It can seem as if time is standing still and you are transported to another dimension. The band that is in tune and in sync can bring about a transformation in the hearts and ears of their listeners. The team that is acting as though they are reading each other's minds leaves the opponent in the dust as though they never showed up to the game - so it is with an Agile team running on all cylinders. What is delivered with this kind of team is far greater than what each individual can contribute individually. A definite synergy is created that increases the efficiency of delivery.

## Stakeholder Engagement

One of the biggest benefits of Agile is the fact that, from the beginning, you have the customer involved. There is no guessing as to whether what the team is producing is what the customer wants because the customer or stakeholder is engaged from the start. Why is this important? It is because of change. If you've been managing projects for any length of time, you'll know that change can not only derail a project, but it will bring to a halt any kind of momentum that may have been created. By having your client engaged every step of the way, you minimize the changes that may come about.

## Improved Communication

Communication improves when there is a great connection between the individuals communicating. You've seen this in your own life. It is easier to communicate with someone when they are right in front of you, and you've built some kind of connection with them. If you have this kind of interaction on a daily basis, it is normal for a deeper connection to be created, and thus communication will improve.

## Quick Identification of Incorrect Approaches

Using the agile method advocates for the fail-fast strategy. This is an approach whereby the product developers aim at getting fast feedback from customers or end-users. After getting a response, changes are rapidly made to ensure that the product meets customer demands in every way.

## Quick Decision Making

An agile environment brings together individuals in an organization to realize that their joined efforts help to realize project goals that have been set. Quick decisions can be made in daily meetings. Team members are fully aware that the agile method demands that face-to-face interactions are highly valued.

## Collaborations Lead to Numerous Benefits

The idea of working in a collaborative environment has benefits for the entire organization. In this case, by people working together toward a common goal, they also have a shared desire to succeed. People and technological resources get to interact together to meet the project's goals fast. With the quickly changing environment, using agile tools comes in handy.

## Change is Embraced

Working in an agile environment also fosters the quick adaptability to change. During the product development process, the importance of adapting quickly to change is promoted by the agile method. Ideally, the push for change is one of the core values of the agile method. Therefore, as teams learn to make changes more often, they develop a culture where change is embraced regardless of the development stage.

In this case, people understand that change leads to an improved product being delivered to consumers.

## A Suitable Environment for Millennials

Millennials are the next generation to take over the many working positions occupied by baby boomers. The good news is that the fast-paced environment is what millennials like. Agility at work will therefore favor millennials. Accordingly, creating an agile environment guarantees that workers feel motivated to work toward meeting business goals.

## Delivering the Right Product

Above anything else, a huge benefit of using the agile method is that the right product is delivered to consumers. Since a product is carefully reviewed daily in each sprint meeting, any defects are easily identified early. Also, regular checking ensures that the product's requirements are met. If anything is not right, this can quickly be changed at any stage of the development process. The end product is close to perfection as the customer is provided with a product that has all the features it is expected to have.

## An Exciting Environment to Work

An agile environment is an environment that promotes active involvement, cooperation, and collaboration among team members. This is an experience that excites many as they get to share tasks. Also, through such collaboration, the team helps one other overcome their weaknesses. Therefore, it is not just the organization that gets to benefit from the agile method but also the employees interacting with it. This leaves workers motivated every time they work on a project. Undeniably, such a positive attitude amongst workers transforms into increased productivity at work.

## Focus on Business Value

One of the main core values of the agile method is that it places a high value on people and interactions over processes and tools. Consequently, the agile method sees to it that stakeholders are more engaged in the development process. This assists in guaranteeing that the team understands the mission and vision of the organization. The team will focus more on the most important tasks during the product development process. They put a strong emphasis on their cooperation and collaboration, which leads to a high-quality product being introduced to the market at the right time and within the budget range.

## Transparency

The agile method is all about transparency. Everything linked to the project is always discussed openly with interested parties and the development team. Since customers are also involved in the process, this helps to prioritize features and deal with bugs. Nonetheless, it is important for developers to inform customers that they are using demo products and not real products. Clearing the air prevents confusion and leads to reliable feedback data from customers.

## Customized Team Structures

The notion of self-management creates a working environment where teams get to make decisions on their own. An agile workplace creates opportunities for workers to customize their job duties. This means that they can choose to work by following rules that suit them. Customization of team structures could take any direction. A group can organize itself based on work styles. Another team could organize itself according to their respective skills. Such customization creates a friendly workplace where individuals are highly motivated to work.

## Improved Project Predictability

Using the Agile Project Management method also aids a team to forecast how the project will progress. Improved predictability can be gained by making sure that sprint lengths are always the same. Additionally, task allocation should not be changed throughout the development process. With these practices in place, it makes it easy to predict the progress or the outcome of a project.

## Higher Team Morale

Individuals who enjoy what they are doing are motivated to work without being pushed. Working around a self-managing team paves the way for creativity and innovation. The exciting thing is that the respective groups will focus on sustainability. Consequently, this prevents team members from getting stressed over work-related issues. Don't forget that a supportive environment will also have a positive impact on how people work.

## User-Focused

Projects, while they may start out this way, are not always focused on the end-user – the one that will benefit and utilize what is being produced. In any company, you have a multitude of political agendas at play that could throw a project off course and change the focus to something other than the original intent, of improving the experience or providing a solution for the customer. With Agile, everything is done with the user in mind. The user and their satisfactory experience are one of the guideposts that the Agile project team uses to measure their success.

## Improved Project Control

With the amount of collaboration and steps to an agile project, project control is improved greatly by allowing all members to be involved. The number of steps involved also allows for higher up managers to exercise more control over every step of the project.

## More Project Visibility

Daily sprint reviews, scrum meetings, and other types of meetings allow everyone in a project to know what is going on at any given time. The amount of information flowing from team to manager and how often it's flowing plays a big role in performance visibility. By increasing this flow of information through Agile Management, all members of a team are able to know exactly where the project is and what is going on, even if one piece of information is not a part of their specific step; they have the ability to see the entire picture. Being able to see the "big picture" is also a great way to boost teamwork and team morale.

## Reduced Risk

One of the last benefits is that there is reduced risk with projects managed in this way. This type of management allows you to be able to see what is working and not working on a small scale so that when it comes to finishing and testing software, you do not suddenly find a large scale problem.

## The Speed-to-Market Advantage & Higher Revenue

Agile projects are also more beneficial over traditional methods due to Agile's support for "perpetual beta" releases. And with the early realization of product benefits comes the incremental deliverables. This means that a product can generate revenue during the initial stages.

# Chapter 3:
# Understanding the Agile Lifecycle

The scope of the Agile lifecycle can vary from company to company or project to project. When the entire business works towards the development, this can later be turned into effective feedback for the company.

The development of solutions is complicated, yet it has to be broken into procedural steps which show the construction cycle. The main result is at the end when the project is successful and it no longer needs to be modified or changed.

### CONCEPT PHASE

This is one of the toughest phases, where you have to do the pre-planning regarding the sprint which you are about to launch. There is a target at the beginning of every project which you must achieve and is done by building the overall concept of the solution. Here there are the critically important things which you need to determine in this phase to provide guidance for work further in the project:

## DEFINE THE BUSINESS

When defining a business, it is necessary to have the market concern and the bigger picture of the business strategy in your head. You have to consider what new functions will improve your business in the market to enhance the presence of your organization. This is essentially the exploration part which needs to be short and brief without any elaborations. You do not have to invest so much time on the project within the conceptualization but just write down the points will help you get to the business potential. You can follow a good strategy with the identification of the scope and goals with the potential stakeholders as well.

## STRATEGY FOR THE PROJECT

A well-built strategy always helps you to reach the endpoint, with minimal changes needed to improve it or to make it look better. There may be many issues which come out as you draw out the strategy in more detail and you will have to answer several questions on your own, such as who will be leading the team? How will the subject of project matter to the organization? What will be the iterations? The geography? Location? Development? And many more questions to be answered.

## FEASIBILITY

You need to prepare a feasibility report for the conceptual phase where you see the suitability of the project and whether it can be established in the market in the future or not. This aims to identify whether your investment will be fruitful or not so that you do not end up wasting the costs and time of your business and the team. Every project requires effort, you should get the basic ones together to kickstart it and then you need to add in more hardware and equipment as needed for each sprint or iteration to move further.

## ESTIMATING PROJECT

When you have gathered all the information and started the project, estimate the project lifecycle and target again to make sure that you are staying streamlined and on-track. After the architecture, design, and environment building, you then review the estimation of the Agile project which can then evolve over the entire period to project completion.

## COLLABORATION

When you have good affiliation with the stakeholders and developers, it helps you to communicate with them and get their reviews and feedback to improve upon throughout the cycle. You have more chances of improvement between iterations when you have a close collaboration.

## IMPLEMENTING FUNCTIONS

There is a chance of change in the requirements of the customers if they wish to make improvements in the product during the cycle. There could be some new discovery that they would like to add to their project. Preparing the team members for this challenge is important at the initial stages of the cycle so that it does not take time for them to accept that they have to work with the demands of the stakeholders, rather than a given plan which they can stick to across all work to complete the project.

## DESIGNING AND ANALYZING

You must think overall their requirements and see if there is anything else needed, according to your own expertise by sketching out the design to your own satisfaction. Often, sketched diagrams are used to display the design and then changes can be made on to this chart easily, adding the requirements for the later stages as they change in between. The test-driven designs are also initiated in this phase of designing to see the development of each iterative for testing and producing the code for the fulfillment of the test. The complex requirements of any issues with the designs can be thought out and there can be further changes if required in the future.

## ENSURE THE QUALITY

As the project goes along, it is important to keep on monitoring whether the project is in line with the customer's requirements or not. There are guiding codes which can help the agents to learn about the quality of the project and if you have done a similar project before then you will know the quality concerns and issues. You have to ensure that the best design is being created by the team members and ensure that there is no lack in quality and functionality.

## WORKING SOLUTIONS

You have to keep on providing solutions for the problems which may arise throughout the project. Ensure that the regular delivery of work is being achieved through the development cycle, the collaboration within the team is optimized, and that they are focused on the product. There may be solutions which can be sorted out by the team. These solutions need to be tested before they get implemented by the team members. Testing the solutions makes it easier when you are demonstrating the product to the stakeholders to ensure they are satisfied.

## TESTING

When you test the product at each iteration, it enhances your own learning as well to confirm your confidence in the testing process of a certain solution for the product before it goes into the market, so the next time a sprint comes in you are ready to go immediately into it. The specifications that are given to you need to be confirmed within the software that you have made in each iteration at the ideal rate of testing and the developers need to follow the full requirements for testing it with the professional users. You cannot establish the product in the market without testing it because then you risk of losing the trust of the stakeholders. This would be a failure after investing so much in cost and time of the project.

# Chapter 4: The Difference Between Agile Project Management and Traditional Project Management

Here are some of the major differences between the two project management styles:

- Traditional project management is more rigid and directional, whereas Agile is more flexible and adaptable to change.
- Easy communication is welcomed in Agile, whereas traditional does much of this ahead of time and planning is done among the leads or product owners only.
- Management tells the workers what to do in the traditional management model, while workers are given more autonomy to do their best work in the Agile management style.
- Agile management is more fluid than traditional management.

- Agile management welcomes change, whereas traditional management resists change.
- Agile management is involved with the customers throughout the process, whereas traditional management does not connect with the customers until the project ends.
- Teamwork is enhanced in Agile management but not in traditional management.
- Traditional management focuses on serious processes whereas Agile methods are less formal and so can be modified rapidly as things proceed.
- Traditional management favors the "anticipation mode" whereas agile management favors the "adaptation mode".
- Daily meetings are held in agile management for open communication amongst all parties but meetings are less frequent and more splintered in the traditional management model.
- Agile management breaks things into sections with short spans and small practices whereas traditional believes in long processes with details.
- Agile management is unplanned and analyzes processes on a continuous basis.
- Agile management has a mindset or philosophy that values focused thinking, vision, an incremental framework, customer value, and easy to understand processes.
- Agile management is more of a pragmatic and test-driven approach than traditional management.
- Agile management receives feedback throughout the cycle with the intention of ensuring the final result fits the client's needs and expectations, where the traditional model presents a finished solution only.
- In traditional methods, you do not usually care what other employees are doing; rather, you are focused on doing the best for yourself and the overall math can add up elsewhere. On the contrary, in Agile Project Management, you work as an integrated team of members from entirely different departments, and you

all have a common short term goal at any particular stage of the project.
- In traditional models you see the results after a long duration that may even be several calendar months. You see results very fast in Agile Project Management, in as little as between a week and four weeks.
- In traditional models, feedback is often given confidentially behind closed doors, via mail, or even through anonymous written communication. But in Agile Project Management, there is open communication where each member openly expresses ideas, concerns and any other sentiments related to the project.

# Chapter 5:
# Agile Methodologies

Agile Management has been around for years, if not decades. The idea that projects should be completed in a timely manner by achieving milestones is not a new phenomenon. The methodologies for this type of management have been advancing over the last few decades and have grown to include several different methodologies, each providing a different framework for the inner workings of a project. Having a deeper understanding of each available methodology will give you a better understanding of this management style and how you can use it with your own team on their projects.

## AGILE SCRUM

Scrum is a simple way to provide a lightweight framework for a project using specific guidelines. They are an incremental part of the project and help to make serious decisions that will affect the overall end goal. By having the product owner involved, errors are reduced and flaws or unwanted parts of the project can be dropped without detrimental harm being done to later steps. Scrum allows for small or large projects and teams to be organized easily and deliver a project within a quick framework of time. Therefore, the fast iterations make this methodology the best for teams working on a project where customers and stakeholders expect an early release of the working product. This kind of participation helps the team make any necessary changes that may be pointed out by the stakeholders or product owners.

## KANBAN

This Agile methodology is focused on manufacturing. At its core, Kanban may be considered as an extensive to-do list. Not different to Scrum, the requirements of the Kanban methodology are monitored based on their current stage during the process.

Kanban can be a simple transition if you have the right team. To make sure that the transition is smooth, various people in the company including the stakeholders, testers, business analysts, and developers need to meet on a regular basis to discuss the project. When your business is shifting to Kanban, you must remember that this methodology is going to provide you with the fastest means of productivity for the code, but there are still some risks of the code going out with some errors.

Kanban is not time-sensitive, but it is dependent on priority. This means that anytime a developer wants to jump into the next task, he or she can do that very fast. This approach has a few meetings to help with the planning. It is not like Scrum. Kanban has a simple transition for the ideal teams. To ensure that the transition to Kanban is efficient and smooth - developers, business analysts, stakeholders, and testers have to meet regularly and discuss. While shifting to Kanban, one should remember that this type of methodology provides you with the fastest means of productivity in your code. However, chances are that the code might have some errors.

Kanban is the best for small teams or those teams that don't build features that should be released to the public. Besides that, it is a top-notch methodology used in different types of product or teams whose major goal is to remove bugs in a system.

## Extreme Programming (XP)

Kent Beck is considered as the creator of XP. It is a popular and controversial Agile methodology. It focuses on the provision of high-quality software in a short period. It operates on customer participation, rapid feedback, subsequent planning, and testing. This methodology has been popular yet controversial since its introduction. XP allows for teams to deliver high quality work on a consistent and quick basis. It provides a framework for teams to help them work quickly and efficiently while still maintaining a very specific quality of work. With XP, software should be delivered within 1-3 weeks and involves constant testing, reviewing, and planning. This is great for smaller teams as collaboration and tight teamwork is needed to keep quality and speed up at the same time. Although this can work for larger teams and projects, they are more difficult to manage this way.

### Crystal

This is one of the more adaptable methods of agile management. There are several different forms of crystal management but each focuses on size of the team and project priorities. The team and how it works toward milestones is adjusted for each project to create a unique framework to work within. Those who use the various Crystal methods often take on many different types of projects over a short period of time. This method allows for teams to easily adapt from one project to another one that is completely unique.

There are a few metrics that come with the idea of Crystal. These metrics are going to include things like simplicity, teamwork, and communication. Like with some of the other methodologies of Agile, Crystal embraces early and regular delivery of a working product. It can also promote things like eliminating bureaucracy, user participation, and adaptability. This is by far the most lightweight and easy-going approach. Crystal consists of a collection of Agile methodologies, some of which include Crystal orange, Crystal yellow, Crystal clear, and many more.

A few metrics of Crystal include communication, teamwork, and simplicity. Like other Agile methodologies, Crystal embraces early and regular delivery of a working product. In addition, it promotes adaptability, user participation, and elimination of bureaucracy.

## The Dynamic Systems Development Methodology (DSDM)

The Dynamic Systems Development Methodology has processes that are refined over time to improve them. The requirements, known as iterations, are defined and delivered within a short period of time and all of the tasks that are noted as important are done.

DSDM champions fitness in the business as the major focus in the delivery and acceptance of a given system.

In this methodology, requirements are listed early in the project and processes are refined to improve them. Requirements, often called iterations, are defined and delivered within a short time. All important tasks must be done in a DSDM project. In addition, not every requirement is highly prioritized.

## Feature-Driven Development

Also known as FDD this method of development is meant to produce deliverables that are functional within a two-week period. It focuses on small teams and intense work with larger milestones and stages. FDD requires teams to meet often with the product owner or client and describes short phases that are done extremely quickly and put together in a limited time frame for delivery.

These are the current methodologies of software development. They each continue to grow and change with the years and evolve as the knowledge of development and software also grows. Picking the correct development method for your project and team is very important. If not picked correctly, you may have very serious unintended consequences. Take a look at the project details and your team size to determine which of these development methods within Agile Management are best for you and your team.

# Chapter 6: The Authenticity of Agile Management

The hallmarks of Agile Project Management are the driving forces behind having a team of people that are agile and can successfully put into practice this technique for management.

## FIXED LENGTH ITERATIONS

The methodologies of Agile Management are structured around iterations (also known as milestones) that are a fixed length of time and are made up of features that must be completed. Iterations should last anywhere from 2 to 4 weeks and the result of each iteration should be software that is ready to be tested, is currently working, and is ready for release to the client. An iteration should be a constant stream of tasks being put together to create features that are made into top-quality software. Iterations help a Scrum Team feel that every single hour and day counts toward the final project goal.

## Tested Software

Agile teams never deliver software that is less than the best. Any bit of software that leaves an agile team's office should work to the best of their ability and should have been tested. Software should never be released if it has not been tested first. In fact, it should have been tested through every phase of development. Consistent testing allows a team to know that their software works and creates confidence, focus, and engaged team members; from managers to programmers and everyone in between.

## Value-Driven

Projects an Agile team takes on should always be value-driven. If it will not provide value for the client, it is not a feature that should be included in a program. Not only should the product be of value but it should also be delivered on a consistent basis. An iteration should never occur where the quality of value deliverables is not realized by a client. Even if an adjustment has to be made, valuable deliverables should always be leaving a team on a consistent basis.

## Adaptive Planning

That plan is not the end all be all, and as circumstances change, so should the plan. An outdated plan is never good especially in software development. Teams should be receiving planning updates on a consistent basis so they can delegate properly and release the correct features for each iteration.

## Multi-Level Planning

Planning should never take place simply for what is happening at the current time. It should take place on two levels: what we are doing now and what we will be doing in the future. However, you should also be planning for the next iteration as you go. You should be thinking ahead for what features will be top priority next. The short term may be important but you should never plan only for what is in the short term. Your next iteration will sneak up on you quickly and you should be ready or at least have some ideas that you can bounce around. Agile Management projects are quick, and advanced planning is necessary to meet rigid deadlines.

## Relative Estimation

Estimations can help keep a team on track and show which features may need to be broken down into further tasks. For example, the average feature should take 1 day to complete and can be completed in anywhere from 4 hours to 2 days. If you estimate that a feature will take longer than 2 days, it may need to be broken down into smaller more manageable tasks.

## Continuous Testing

Defects, errors, and glitches can be readily avoided at every stage with testing. Many traditional waterfall management projects have a "test and fix" phase. This is where before release, a team must go through and test their program and fix any glitches or errors. However, Agile Management allows for testing to happen at every stage of development so that errors are caught in a timely fashion instead of at the very end of a project. This speeds up the testing process and can be more efficient than the "test and fix" method that is so popular in the software world.

## Emergent Feature Discovery

With Agile Management all planning is done relatively quickly. The goal is to find what features add value and then begin work as fast as possible.

## Continuous Improvement

An agile team will consistently work to improve themselves and the quality of their work. Continuous improvement also is good for improving the process by which programs are created. Factories constantly replace their machines and practices for better one, why can't businesses do the same? Why can't they refine their practices so they produce top quality software and meet rigid deadlines?

# Chapter 7:
# Common Misconceptions About Agile Project Management

**THE AGILE TECHNIQUE IS A ONE-STOP ANSWER TO ALL YOUR BUSINESS PROJECT WOES**

The agile technique works wonders when it comes to reducing the wasted time, of course. However, this technique cannot solve the impossible for you. It cannot offer solutions to major faults in your production process that are unrelated tto it. What this means is that though the Agile technique focuses on the right things, you are only going to fail at what you are working on if you have other fundamental issues during the project. Agile Project Management technique simply encourages collaboration and shortens the lines of communication.

## AGILE PROJECT MANAGEMENT IS 'QUICK AND DIRTY.'

When Agile solutions were initially applied to projects, they were short-term. This gave people the impression that the technique is short, fast, and straight to the point in a way that cuts corners without following due process. Now, the Agile technique has gone beyond short-term projects and encompasses longer projects which require rapid growth as well as quality and control. The Agile technique requires a high level of professionalism. This means that the technique helps project teams deliver the right solutions at the right time.

## THE AGILE TECHNIQUE IS ONLY USEFUL FOR SIMPLE, SMALL PROJECTS

Many a project manager has been slow in adopting the agile technique in handling projects because of the belief that the technique is only meant for small, simple projects. This is untrue. When working on complex projects, corporate strength is a necessity. The Agile technique has a proven record of delivering on such jobs. Hence, the technique should no longer be viewed as not useful for larger, more complex projects.

## WHEN YOU USE THE AGILE TECHNIQUE, YOU DO NOT NEED DOCUMENTATION

Due to the fact that you do not have to fully know all the requirements for a project before undertaking it, there is the misconception that with the Agile technique, documentation is not needed. Though the agile technique prioritizes working solutions over detailed documentation, this does not mean that the agile technique completely does not require documentation. Teams using the Agile technique often have a range of roles which ensure that collaboration and conversations replace the extensive upfront paperwork required in traditional project management teams.

Documentation is necessary as a support for the solution that the Agile technique has provided. It shows how the solution was arrived at, especially since the technique shortens the time used and it is easy to assume that corners were cut and that the solution is substandard because of the less time used.

## PROJECT MANAGERS ARE NOT NEEDED WHEN USING THE TECHNIQUE

Since most approaches while using the Agile technique do projects which have no defined starting points, midpoints and endpoints, having project managers is important because these managers are often responsible for quality and control and for handling interruptions which arise in the course of the project in order to give other team members the freedom to focus on getting the job done.

## IT IS EITHER YOU ARE COMPLETELY AGILE, OR NOT

A spectrum exists, and on this spectrum, completely traditional techniques are on one end while completely Agile techniques are on the other end. What this means is that you can use some elements of traditional techniques while using some elements of Agile Project Management at the same time.

## DISCIPLINE IS NOT A PART OF AGILE ENVIRONMENTS

The true nature of Agile environments proves that this misconception is entirely untrue. While there is a great deal of flexibility allowed in Agile environments, Agile environments are still tasked with providing a predictable solution from the development efforts.

## The Agile technique is anti-governance

There is the belief that governance and agile projects do not go hand in hand. In reality, this is untrue. While the Agile technique uses different data items and routines compared to more traditional techniques, it makes room for some sort of governance and the use of policies especially in industries that strongly require governance like the pharmaceutical industry.

## Scrum and Agile are the same thing

While Scrum is a development approach or method that fits very well with Agile Project Management, it on its own does not automatically mean Agile. The Agile technique is a lot greater than just Scrum.

# Chapter 8:
# Agile Project Management in Practice

An Agile coach, who may use a push-based Agile coaching technique, can directly impart knowledge to team members. By using a strategic system, he can get a team to work straightforwardly with Agile. And once he does, the entire team can benefit not only from his teachings, but from his examples, too. And if you think a push-based Agile coaching technique won't be beneficial, you can choose to hire an Agile coach who teaches pull-based Agile coaching techniques via consistent and encouraging feedback instead.

### USE TESTABLE REQUIREMENTS DOCUMENTATION

This is the better strategy of focusing on functionality. While doing so can eventually eliminate problems, proposing a solution at the wrong time, such as early on, can defeat the purpose of problem-solving.

Thus, instead of introducing solutions, you should focus on testable requirements. As a guide, answer three important W questions:

Who – Who is the product owner?
What – What does the product owner want?
Why – Why is the product owner pursuing advancements?

### ASK FOR THE OPINIONS OF DEVELOPERS & TESTERS

Other than using testable requirements documentation, you should leverage the expertise of developers and testers. Don't ignore that fact that any discussion of requirements is most productive when accomplished in a form of workshops – with the presence of teachers and experienced individuals. Here are a few important reasons why:

- Identifying testable requirements will be easier
- Prioritizing testable requirements will be easier
- The complementary skills of teams will be given priority
- The ideas of team members will be addressed properly
- The opinions of team members will be addressed properly

## TURN TO PROTOTYPES

Once the testable requirements are set, next up is clarifying the requirements for the customization of a user interface. And you can do this by using prototypes – in the form of mock-ups and sketches.

Especially when communication becomes challenging, prototypes will help make discussions go smoothly. Remember, if the required documentation is quite complicated, making it easily understandable is necessary. It may be challenging, but providing an explanation is mandatory.

## USE PROJECT MANAGEMENT TOOLS

Another way that Agile teams can improve their operations is by using project management tools. Not only can these support their modern approach of working, these tools can also accommodate traditional project management.

In the event that not all teams in an organization are working in an Agile style but rather chooses traditional project management, their participation should still be valued. By using these tools that can run the projects of both traditional and modern project management, the organization will benefit greatly.

# Chapter 9:
# How to Create a Product Vision

A product vision provides focus and direction for the project team. It solves problems about delivering a product of value that will satisfy customers. A well-communicated and well-made product vision is the glue that connects the business model, user stories, the product roadmap, the product backlog, and product development.

The initial product vision usually comes from a standard template that is available online. However, it usually is so long that people do not read it anymore. A product vision must be visual, concise, and simple so that anyone can understand it.

The project team must have a vision statement. Team members must choose the words in the statement wisely. They must be straightforward and not generic. The vision statement must be long-term but not overly restrictive and it must trigger the stakeholders to act.

## STEPS TO CREATE AN AGILE PRODUCT VISION

First, the product owner creates a product vision statement because he is someone who knows the product, requirements, and goals well. The vision statement will serve as a guide to the project team.

To develop the vision statement, the product owner must first determine the product objectives. He must know the important product goals, the customer, the needs, the competition, and the basic difference of the product from its competitors.

Next, he must draft the Agile vision statement. This statement must convey the product's longevity, maintenance requirements, and quality. For the statement to be compelling, he can use present tense in writing it, even if the product does not exist yet. By using present tense, the developer can easily see customers using the product. The vision statement includes conditions that must be present before the product is complete. The product owner must avoid generalizations and technological specifications.

Next, the product owner must validate and revise the vision statement. He must review it based on a quality checklist. He must show it to the stakeholders to help him determine if the vision statement truly exemplifies the product. He must also show it to the other team members so that they understand the kind of product that they must complete.

Then, the product owner finalizes the vision statement based on the inputs of the stakeholders and team members. He can place a copy of the vision statement on the wall so that the team can easily see it daily.

## TIPS FOR CREATING A PRODUCT VISION

It is great to have an idea for a new product. However, there must also be a vision statement to guide the team members to make the project successful. This vision statement will serve as the guiding light for product managers, marketing, support, development, and sales personnel.

The product vision is the reason why the company will create the product. It offers a continued purpose and acts as the product's compass. It also motivates team members and facilitates efficient collaboration.

The product owner must choose the best product vision. He must search for answers as to why the company must develop the product and why the team must care about it. He must determine the positive effects of the product as well as its future direction.

The vision statement must be concise in order to capture the company's intention in developing the product. It must also describe the changes the customers must experience by using the product. The product vision must not be in conflict with the company vision.

The product owner must state clearly the difference between the product and the product vision. He must not confuse the two. The product vision is the reason why the company will develop the product. On the other hand, the product is the overarching goal of the product vision.

The product owner can conduct a collaborative visioning workshop to help him formulate the product vision. He can invite important people to help him. The workshop can discuss the product idea and the attendees' motivation for making the product successful. After the workshop, the product owner can compare the various visions and combine the goals into one effective product vision.

The product vision must inspire everyone. It must connect and motivate people to work for the product's success. Usually, a product vision that provides benefits for other people can be a lasting inspiration and motivation.

The product vision must be brief. It must convey the reason why there is a need to create a product. Readers must find it easy to understand and communicate the product vision. Other reports can tackle the product details. Readers must be able to memorize and recite the product vision because of its clarity and simplicity.

The product vision must act as a guide for product decisions. It must enable team members to focus on product development. It serves as a filter for change requests and new ideas, and helps the team move closer to the product goals.

# Chapter 10:
# Roadmap to Agile Fluency

Agile fluency is a model that helps the project understands its own goals and its relevance to certain requirements and context. It does not assume that teams have to progress from the first level up to the last level. The model's important aspect is to identify the fluency level that applies to the team. Some teams can go backwards if it makes sense for them to do so.

Fluency, in the context of this model, means that the project team does things automatically. It is about understanding the fluency level and working towards fulfilling the project's requirements.

The agile fluency model has four levels, from 1-star to 4-star fluency. The first level is about transparency. The company and project team must share information. They both understand their responsibilities to be of value to each other.

The team and the company search for ways to improve practices as well as internal and external relationships to meet their goals. The basic metric for this level is for everyone to find if the team delivers value and if they see progress in the company.

The second level highlights practices like Continuous Integration and Continuous Delivery. The project team delivers products of high quality on demand. It focuses on product development processes to support its goals.

Level 3 focuses on investing in development by improving technology. The team strives to be fully functional and decides on product delivery within the team. The focus of management is to remove any roadblock to the team's progress.

The last level completes the business involvement in the delivery process. It needs a culture different from most established companies. The important measure of progress is the work of project teams that drive an organization's success.

## How to Create the Product Roadmap?

The product roadmap may be simple. It can be post-it notes on a white board which allows for additional notes and the re-arranging of notes during the scheduled update.

### Identify the product requirements

Initially, the team may create a product roadmap with large requirements that may include themes or features. Themes are features and requirements in logical groups with the highest levels. On the other hand, features are high-level parts of the product. They describe the capabilities to the customer upon completion of the feature.

### Arrange the product features

After identifying the features, the project team can group the requirements according to themes. They may need to conduct a stakeholder meeting to do this. Grouping can be by business requirement, technical similarity, or usage flow.

## Estimate and order the product features

To order requirements, the project team must have a score to represent the effort and value for every requirement. It must understand dependencies. For example, an application that needs a username and password can require the customer to create a username before he can create a password.

## Relative priority = value / effort

For example, a requirement has 55 as effort and 89 as value. Its relative priority is 1.62.

After knowing each requirement's relative priority, the project team can prioritize them. It must consider the relative priority and the requirement's prerequisites. In addition, it must consider the features with similar requirements so that it can group them together for a solid product release.

# Chapter 11:
# How to Create an Agile Team

A team leader organizes his team around features or products. He must create a team that understands business capabilities and aligns these capabilities with organizational and technical architecture.

## TEAM STRUCTURES

### Product Owner

As the name suggests, this is the individual with expertise on the product and its requirements. The product owner works hand-in-hand with the development team to make sure that product requirements are considered at every stage of its development. A product owner could be identified as a customer representative.

### Scrum Master

The scrum master works closely with the development team. This individual works to offer support to the development team by making sure that the agile process remains consistent throughout the process. Scrum masters are most effective when they have the power to push for changes without necessarily seeking permission.

### Agile Mentor

The mentor knows all the strategies and rules for allowing feedback to come in freely. The mentors are not responsible for looking after the progress of the project, but only making sure that the plan is progressing. He or she cannot direct and has no formal authority over team members but can convey the approaches and techniques of Agile Project Management.

### The Team Members

Agile Project Management works with the team members who collaborate with each other and know how to coordinate the processes to get the work done efficiently. Each of them is an expert in their field, and knows what they have to do and how to get it done on time. In software development, there are developers, testers, writers, engineers, programmers and other important roles. All these roles must coordinate and work with each other to provide coherence and support to follow the goals of the project and complete it on time. The team is made up of diverse workers having various skills allowing each of them to handle a variety of different aspects at the same time, while working towards a common project goal.

### Stakeholders

The end customers are stakeholders as they will depend on the product and use it. They are not responsible for the product but are affected by the outcome of the project. This group can include people from different areas of expertise or other companies. In Agile Project Management, the support for customers and the project team is essential for continuous improvement which brings greater results.

## BUILDING A KICKASS TEAM

Teamwork is important if a team wants to deliver a great product. An Agile team shares the adventure of creation with its engaged team members. However, there is no formula for success. There are Agile teams that choose Kanban while others opt for Scrum. Other teams use distributed development while others choose colocation. There are teams that need specialists while others have what they need within the team.

An Agile team needs shared skill sets and continuous mentoring. Team members must learn and mentor each other. The shared skills sets enable the team to perform heterogeneous work. Each member becomes better equipped and more valuable to the team. Furthermore, everyone has equal load.

An Agile team is flexible, focused, small, autonomous, talented, stable, established, and cooperative. Each dedicated member works toward a common goal. He is open to do anything that will make the team achieve its objective. An Agile team charts its own destiny. It does not rely heavily on outside support because its team members have the necessary skillsets.

A small Agile team has few specialists and its overhead is small. Usually, the optimal team size is between only 5 and 12 individuals. Even if it is small, an Agile team has talented members. It is a high-performance team with each member able to manage his weaknesses. Every individual has the opportunity to master his skills.

An established Agile team has significant value because it provides long lasting benefits to the company. It is easier to assign projects to an established team because it had already gone through trials so each member works effectively with each other already. An Agile team is also stable and cooperative. All members work together to reduce bottlenecks and delays.

## The Importance of Stability in an Agile Team

A stable team is important, even if the project is short. It is not advisable to assemble an Agile team just for one project then disband it to form another one for another project. Team members need to bond as a team before they can work harmoniously together.

A stable team is most efficient and effective in working together. All team members understand the natural process of going through stages. They know that it takes time for them to get to know each other. They are confident that they will soon learn to work together in order to optimize not only their working relationships but their skills as well.

A stable, Agile team also learns to optimize processes over time. Team members perform retrospectives regularly so they continuously improve by minimizing, if not eliminating, issues that recur from time to time. They also develop their own speed in completing projects.

An Agile team has members with sufficient skills to get the project done. It does not rely on other teams or experts. It consists of generalizing specialists, who are individuals that can contribute directly to the team. It may include professionals who specialize in one area. Because of these generalizing specialists, it is easier to achieve stability.

## Common Mistakes of New Agile Teams

A new Agile team may have many fears that may result in bad practices and decisions. To counter fear, it must instill trust among all its members. Each member must know that the company trusts him to make right decisions and commitments.

- The team may communicate poorly because the members do not talk to each other on a regular basis.
- The agile team may have poor team structure when it must be stable and contain the necessary skills. The team leader must be able to choose his skilled team members and keep them from one project to another.
- The team may not be good in estimating scope and size of work. To remedy this, the team leader can have at most three inception sprints so that he will know the team's initial velocity.
- The new agile team may not be able to observe good planning habits. The team leader must stress the importance of continuous planning that happens in all process levels. This means that it commits at most 20% of its time in planning for success.
- The team is not able to deliver a defect-free product faster. The product owner must accept completed product only after passing rigorous testing. He must ensure that the product tester completes his task in every sprint.
- The Agile team might ignore customer feedback. In Agile philosophy, customers are very important. They help companies create better products and services. The project team can review the customer feedback during planning. It is good practice to include a customer service representative in the team to provide consumer trends and data.
- The new team is not empowered. The team leader can engage his members to participate in the whole process by asking and valuing their insights. He must ensure that everybody is part of the decision-making process.
- The team leader does not hold demo or retrospective meetings. Every meeting is necessary to complete the iterations. The standup meetings every day must include a retrospective. The team leader must initiate a demo meeting at the end of each sprint so every stakeholder can give his insights.
- The new Agile team does not have a plan for resistance. When implementing new strategies, people can resist them. Thus, the team leader must prepare for it by

keeping communication lines open. The company must be clear of its support for an Agile philosophy. It must help provide an environment of trust.

# Chapter 12:
# How to Lead an Agile Team

Today, organizations have to adapt to a turbulent business, technological, and economic environment. However, focusing on the delivery is not the only focus of Agile projects. Therefore, with the challenges of scaling the Agile delivery mechanism, it is also important to scale the whole organization up. This means that the company has to upgrade its leaders' adaptability to change.

## THE MINDSET OF AN AGILE LEADER

An agile leader knows that there has been a change in management thinking from Predict-and-Plan to Sense-and-Respond, and as a result, he has to equip himself in order to deal with turbulence, unpredictability, and complexity of businesses.

The Predict-and-Plan mindset embodies a set of practices and competencies that adopt only a few forward-thinking aspects. In fact, its reflexive assumptions still guide management functions like finance and human resource. The Predict-and-Plan mindset is the core framework of an effective organization.

On the other hand, the Sense-and-Respond mindset believes that nobody can predict the future so people should welcome even the most unexpected changes. It is not possible to anticipate relevant events ahead of time. Furthermore, it is not easy to observe the cause-and-effect relationship because of time, locality, or complexity.

## UPGRADING MANAGEMENT AND LEADERSHIP

The manager creates and executes plans. He gives tasks to his subordinates. Occasionally, he creates an organizational structure to realize the company's goals. His focus is on deliverables, milestones, and meeting the deadlines. The manager also coordinates with other functional units. Managing for results uses the Predict-and-Plan mindset. It focuses on telling and directing.

The agile leader does not limit his self to just one management methodology. He expands his capabilities in order to overcome any organizational barrier he may face. He relies not only on his own wisdom but on the wisdom of his team members as well.

Managers and leaders use various conceptual frameworks and tools like a balanced scorecard, work breakdown structure, SWOT, strategic diamond, and a results dashboard. These tools help individuals do their tasks and think about how they manage.

## SHARE THE BIG PICTURE WITH THEM

Teams can perform better when they have a clear understanding of how each task assigned to each member of the team contributes to the larger picture for the project and your management team in general. To do this, you need to carefully analyze every part of the project and everything task each member has to handle. When you are done with this analysis, you should compare your findings with the goals and vision of the project and clearly define how they fit in and how they contribute to the actualization of these goals.

## MAINTAINING A CONSTANT TEAM COMPOSITION

In project management, it is common for teams to be formed by putting people who are available to work towards a project together. What this means is that when another project arises, a new team will need to be formed. This is problematic because it will require going through the team bonding process over and over again. It requires having to learn and understand the way everyone's individual skills come together to create a good agile team.

## KEEP THE TEAM ADEQUATELY ENGAGED

Not having enough work to do or being less engaged is a huge demotivator for any team. Once you are done building your team and its structure has been finalized, it is important that they get regular tasks and jobs to keep them busy and to help them hone their skills. Instead of allowing your team members to go in search of jobs to do, provide a regular flow of prioritized jobs for them. This way, you are keeping them sharp enough not to feel pressured or rusty when it is time to engage in a project sprint.

## Full Transparency

One of the best things about an Agile environment is that no one is kept in the dark. Keep in mind that individuals gain quick access to the project's progress through the task boards. Therefore, if anything needs changing, each member of the team can have a say on what needs to be altered. Such transparency in an agile environment instills trust. Team members are more motivated since the organization trusts them enough to share everything relating to the project.

## Continuous Improvement

Another trait of an Agile environment is that it creates a way for continuous improvement throughout the project development process. When using agile, the main focus is not delivering a complete product after a particular period. Rather, the focus is placed on continuously improving a working product throughout its different developmental phases. Through continuous improvement, issues relating to the product can be identified and rectified. Also, the team improves products based on customer demands.

## Transforming to an Agile Mindset & Culture

The introduction of new technologies has transformed the way things work in most organizations. These technologies have pushed people to work in volatile environments where they have to adapt to changes fast. This mostly applies to the IT sector as systems can easily be considered obsolete quite quickly. To ensure that organizations keep up, teams have to be agile and flexible to adapt to fast changes occurring around them. This begins by transforming into an Agile mindset.

How do you create an Agile mindset amongst your team members?

## Embrace Flexibility

A key feature of the Agile method is that people should be flexible. For instance, when using a particular strategy to develop a product, the team members should be flexible to switch strategies at any step of the development process.

## Smaller Sized Teams Are Often The Best

Most times in Agile Project Management, the term "the smaller, the better" holds a lot of truth. The ideal team size for should be a team consisting of five to seven people unless it is entirely necessary that you have a large team for the project at hand. Having a smaller team makes collaboration and communication easier and faster.

## Set Meaningful Metrics For Your Team

Many times, the metrics we identify for our teams are either too many or too few. There are also times when we knowingly or unknowingly enforce metrics that are not suited for the goals we seek to achieve. Beyond placing emphasis on measuring the metrics from inception, you should also put in effort in measuring and boosting the overall performance of your group.

## Recognize And Compliment Team Effort

In a high performing team, every member of the team typically plays their own part in the best way possible. This means that high performing teams often consist of high performing individuals. You should promote and nurture this culture of putting in maximum effort to get the job done by measuring the performance of the team and rewarding them when they perform well. This way, they would be more motivated to keep performing well or to even put in more work. You can set up incentives which focus on team performance over individual performance.

## LAY DOWN SOLID ENGINEERING PRACTICES

For software development teams, it is important that you establish a sequence of continuous integration and deployment while working on a project. You can make use of automated tests, automated code reviews, automated deployments, and automated builds. These are helpful for early detection of problems and for boosting the confidence of the team.

## CREATE TIME TO HAVE FUN AND ENGAGE IN INNOVATION

Sometimes, projects are so challenging that they cause you not to be motivated enough to give your best. Teams which dedicate twenty to thirty percent of their time to have fun and to innovation often end up performing better. Beyond keeping them motivated and maintaining the high moral, it ensures that team members feel refreshed enough to contribute to more innovations related to projects.

## HAVE REGULAR MEETINGS

Almost every method involved in Agile Project Management encourages having daily meetings. The Scrum method refers to these meetings as daily standups. These 15 minutes meetings which require that everyone gets together are very important for building a functional Agile environment because it provides an opportunity for the kind of communication that fosters productivity to occur. It also provides an opportunity for the team members to talk about their needs and to share their progress while on the project.

# Chapter 13:
# Tools for Greater Team Effectiveness in Agile Project Management

## THE TEAM

Your team is your single greatest asset and tool for effective Agile Project Management. Because of this, you want to ensure that your team is running in the best way possible.

## TEAM MISSION STATEMENT

Just like the greatest companies have their mission statement, the best teams have their own mission statement. This is something that will allow the team to reference and serve as a guide for how the team functions. The mission statement doesn't need to be long, but it does need to embody what the team is about and what their overall goals are. Make sure to take some time to really think through what your team's mission is and also make sure that everyone on the team agrees with this mission statement. One way to solidify their agreement is to have each individual sign the mission statement and receive a copy of the signed document.

## KEEP MEETINGS AND INTERACTIONS BRIEF

Throughout the course of your project, you will have many meetings on various topics. Another way to keep your team efficient is to ensure that meetings that are set up are only long enough to accomplish the goal of the meeting. Try to keep your meetings short and finish your topics in 20 minutes.

## QUICK CONFLICT RESOLUTION AGREEMENT

One thing to consider as part of your mission statement is to add an agreement for a quick conflict resolution. As you've probably experienced throughout your life, conflicts will happen, however, if dealt with quickly, the conflict does not have to cause delay or derailment in your project. One of the things to consider for this type of agreement is to set up a time limit for any disagreement and after that time another member of the team is brought in to help resolve the conflict

## CELEBRATE SUCCESS

As you bond as a team and start to get better, you will start to achieve success. One thing that is often missing in many companies is taking the time to celebrate successes. If you are reading this book, you are probably motivated by personal achievement as your reward. However, I encourage you to take the time to celebrate your success as a team. This does several things. One of these is it allows your team to bond at a deeper level. When you're able to get your team out of the office and into an environment where they can be a little freer to speak their mind, deeper relationships are built, and this translates into greater trust in the work environment.

## Understanding Yourself

If you're going to be effective with any type of soft skills or be in a leadership role, you will need to first understand yourself. Knowing what your strengths and your weaknesses are is critical to your success.

## Communication Skills

While working on an Agile project, the majority of your interaction will come face-to-face with your team on a daily basis. In addition, as the scrum master, your role is to remove anything that is blocking the progress of your team. This may mean that you have to go to leadership or other individuals and be able to negotiate on their behalf. Your ability to communicate in the written word and be clear about your intentions will go a long way to making you a good Agile project manager.

You must go far beyond written and verbal forms of communication and be skilled in nonverbal communication.

## Confidence

One of the key components of leadership is confidence. Having confidence is as much a state of mind as it is a skill. Like any skill, confidence can be learned and developed. Going back to body language, one of the things you can do to increase your confidence has to do with the way to sit and stand.

You will need to show confidence. Your posture will need to show that you are in control or at least that you have things under control. One thing you need to remember is that most of the teammembers have no desire to be in a position of leadership and if you are in a leadership position, then you must belong there.

## DELEGATION

Delegation is as much an art as it is a skill. If you are going to accomplish the most you possibly can you must learn to delegate to those you know you can trust effectively. By doing this, the amount you can accomplish will be far greater than what you can do on your own. One of the keys to delegation is another soft skill, and that is to have patience.

## PATIENCE

You should have the patience to allow others to take things away from you and help them if they fall. For those of you that are real go-getters, and if you're reading this you probably are, giving up work to someone else is very difficult. After all, if you want something done right then you know you need to do it yourself. However, learning the skill of patience will help you in all areas of your career and personal life. Specifically, this will help you to be a more effective and influential project manager.

## ADAPTABILITY AND CREATIVITY

If you're going to succeed in any aspect of your career, you will need to be able to adapt to your environment and be flexible. Being too rigid, especially in an Agile environment, will not work. You will ensure your failure if you are not able to be flexible in your actions and thinking. The entire premise behind the Agile methodology is adaptability. So, for you as the project manager or the scrum master, you need to make sure that you adapt to the environment, the team, and the needs of the project.

## Mentorship

As a project manager you will be in a position of authority and leadership. Because of that, you will have people coming to you with questions and advice. The other thing that you'll find is that people are thirsty for knowledge and looking for somebody that can help them get ahead. Through your interaction, if they sense that you may be that person, they may start asking you questions and come to you for mentorship.

# Chapter 14: Managing Risk in Agile Project Management

When working with projects, managers and product owners often understand that there are risks. Anything can happen when developing a product to be introduced to the market. Customers could either accept or reject the products, or the product being introduced could succeed or fail.

The notion of risk-taking implies that there are possibilities that failure could occur in the process. It is for this reason that the term risk-taking is used. Risks, therefore, are influential factors which would hurt the outcome of a project. Risk occurs through uncertainty. Project managers strive their best to deliver a quality product in spite of the many uncertainties which they face. Risk analysis allows a team working on a project to understand the likely uncertainties they could face.

Risk management is the plan that the team formulates to mitigate effects that could pose a risk to the success of a project. Things can easily get out of your control when handling projects and it doesn't matter if you are working on a small or a big project; sometimes things go wrong. It is vital to ensure that there is a plan to minimize the possible impact when unpredictable events occur. What follows is a look into how managing risk in an agile environment should take place.

Risk has an effect on a team's chosen path and is uncertain and may occur in the future. A realized risk becomes an issue. Usually, an Agile Project Manager ensures that all his team members share the risk responsibility. In Agile projects, everyone knows that there are uncertainties and complexities.

Risks can influence a project outcome. The project team conducts risk analysis to understand uncertainties that can affect its project. It creates a risk management plan to mitigate, preempt, or contain the effects of risk. It is important for any agile team to understand that it has to minimize the impact of risks even in small projects.

## IDENTIFY THE RISKS

The first step is to identify the dimensions of risk. There are two aspects in which risk could take. It could either be helpful or harmful or internal or external. There could be a SWOT analysis which could help in comprehending how risks affect the project. For example, if the risk is helpful, this could be regarded as a strength or an opportunity. On the other hand, if the risk is harmful, then it could be a major weakness or a threat.

## CLASSIFY RISKS

The project team must categorize all risks, according to impact level, likelihood of impact, and affected project area. It can use risk classifications in order to organize, summarize, and report risks to stakeholders. There are risks that can affect different classes. Thus, the project team must show them in the summary.

The classification should be done based on the areas that are affected. Grouping should be done according to the likelihood of the risk. Likewise, the level of impact will also be an important consideration when classifying the risks which have been identified.

## QUANTIFY RISKS

To quantify risks, the project team can use probability and impact. The Subject Matter Expert performs risk assessment and the project manager does not assess risks because he is not an expert. Furthermore, he can experience political pressure in producing risk reports that do not reflect the correct results.

Quantifying risks can be done using impact and probability. The impact of risk will measure the effect that it has on a project. Here, the impact could range from minimal to extreme. Minimal impact means that there is little influence that a particular risk could have on the project.

## CREATE A PLAN

The project team creates a plan on how to reduce or mitigate the identified risks to ensure that the project is successful. It creates an action plan for the different risks it identified. For example, it can notify management of critical risks that need urgent action. It also tracks these risks on a daily basis. On the other hand, risk that has little or no effect on the project can undergo quarterly review since there is no required action for the time being.

The team can keep a risk register, which is just a simple spreadsheet of the risks assessed during every sprint. This method is particularly useful in tracking risks as the team acts on them.

To this point, you have identified and classified potential risks which could occur when handling any project in the organization. So, what should be done about these risks? Risk planning comes into play. You need to come up with a simple approach to use to deal with these risks. The plan should identify the actions which will be used to effectively manage risks. For instance, when dealing with risks with minimal impact on the project, ideal actions would be to review the risks quarterly. Also, it should be specified that no explicit actions are required since the risks pose no harm.

On the other hand, critical risks require urgent attention. Your plan should also explicitly point out that a responsible executive should be informed about it. A critical risk must be tracked daily to ensure that its effects are reduced considerably. Depending on how risks have been classified, your plan should clearly state the necessary action to be taken. In an Agile environment, the risk plan should be accessible by all members working on a project. This helps in making sure that the team knows what actions should be taken contingent on the level of risk being faced.

As part of ensuring that risks are continuously managed, it is important to have a risk register. This is a register where records of the risks and their mitigation strategies are jotted down. The importance of this register is that it shows how a particular risk has changed since it was identified. If the risk was critical, the management strategies which have been used should make sure that the risk moves to the minimal category. This way, everyone is assured that risks have been effectively handled.

## Act

Essentially, you implement what has been stated in the risk mitigation strategies. However, the process is not as easy as it sounds. Often, people are accustomed to putting off things to a later date. Doing this renders the risk management useless. Risks should be dealt with as soon as they are identified.

Remember, working in an agile environment means that you need to act swiftly.

## Repeat

The process of managing risks in an agile environment means that you have to repeat the process over and over again to make sure that your project succeeds. It is important to note that the risk plan being used should be reviewed regularly to guarantee that ideal measures are used to mitigate potential risks.

Managing risks will always be a part of any project. Bearing in mind that numerous uncertainties could come up, it is essential to have a risk management strategy. The steps outlined here should help you in initiating a practical plan to manage risks. Note that a risk management strategy that works for another organization will not necessarily work for you. Different companies face different risks, whether they are developing similar products or not.

# Chapter 15: Common Challenges Faced When Using the Agile Method

### YOU FIND THAT SCRUM IS A GREAT INTERFERENCE TO THE REAL WORK

In order to be as efficient as possible, a Scrum Master the rest of the team needs to have the right experience necessary to handle all of the team projects. This will help you deal with issues including delays and more. An experience of six months can be enough to handle a lot of the issues that come up, however, the longer the team can work in Agile, the better they will get at dealing with any and all problems that may arise. Experience will provide value and purpose when it comes to Agile development.

## Developers who are used to autonomous working may find that Scrum can slow them down and not be necessary

There is no doubt that at times, the Scrum framework is going to create a bit of overhead compared to some of the other processes that don't have a formal methodology attached to them. This is because Scrum is a tool that is used in order to control the Agile projects. It is going to help create some useful insights in the management of the project status.

## Refusal to Accept Change

One of the main challenges facing organizations trying to implement the Agile method of project management is their unwillingness to accept change. People find it difficult to change the culture to which they have been accustomed and project managers find it a huge challenge to enforce an Agile framework. To ensure that the agile method is successfully adopted, it is necessary for the organization to understand the importance of embracing new ideas. It is essential to note that once senior executives acknowledge the value of change, they will lead by example to push for a successful implementation of the Agile method.

## Distributed Team

Implementing the Agile method also becomes a challenge when the team working on a project is not located in the same place. The success of the project is affected by geographic boundaries. People in different time zones sometimes have a hard time working together. Hence, collaboration is difficult to achieve. Ineffective communication influenced by the distributed team members will lead to dwindling productivity.

## Changing Team Membership

The progress which had been initially achieved could all fade away if the team membership keeps changing. It takes time for the team to recover the time lost when team members change. If this keeps occurring, it means that the team is unstable. This also affects the team's morale as they feel frustrated when they must repeat tasks.

## Absence of Skilled Product Owners

To some extent, some team members think that the transparency that the agile method promotes prevents them from fully controlling how things are done. What they forget is that the agile method does not require stakeholders to keep pushing people around. Instead, self-organizing teams are there to ensure that tasks are handled with minimal supervision. Consequently, the absence of skilled product owners makes it challenging to fully adopt the agile method.

## Tactical Issues

Using the Agile Project Management method demands that users are provided with the necessary quality and risk management tools. These tools aid in promoting efficiency at work. If these tools are not provided by the organization, it is difficult to achieve the level of agility that the organization expects.

## Unfamiliarity with Techniques

The adoption of the agile method means that different departments must be trained on how to implement the strategies in their routine activities and how to use these tools. The process could take a lot of time, which often discourages organizations from adopting the management method in the first place.

## Management is not onboard

If you aren't able to get management and everyone else onboard with the ideas of this methodology, then it is not going to work. You must make this a collaborative endeavor and if you find one group who is not supporting the methodology, especially if that group is management, then you will have a lot of trouble implementing Agile development.

## Slow adoption of the Agile technique

The Agile technique does not work in the same way in each and every organization, business, or company. Something that worked fine for another business does not need to fit into the way your organization works.

## Remote teams

Remote teams are a significant part of the cutting edge software development industry. Organizations contract individuals from various parts of the world since they can work with capable individuals from different areas. In addition, remote workforce enables them to effectively cover the solicitations of their customers on a worldwide scale due to the fact that these remote teams are in various time zones

## Managing enormous projects

One key part of Agile Project Management that often proves to be a huge genuine test for project managers, development teams, and everyone involved is the handling of large scale projects because of the many things that need to be factored into such projects. Irrespective of how experienced the agile project manager is, huge projects can be tasking,

## BEGINNING WITHOUT ALIGNMENT

Many Agile participants believe that the process allows you to "skip" the requirements gathering section. Since the requirements are going to change anyway, why bother collecting them? In fact, there will be a portion of the team who will say that they know some things that will have to be built, so they might as well get started on them now.

## FORGETTING TO LAUNCH

The Agile framework is a very test-and-learn type methodology. Put something that you think is pretty good in front of your customer, and let them use it. If they don't like it, find out why, and adapt. Once you've adapted, put it front of them again. If they do like it, also find out why, and build more stuff like that. The concept is pretty simple, and amazingly powerful at times.

## MISUNDERSTANDING THE IMPORTANCE OF THE PRODUCT OWNER

Many of the team members will have been on projects where they feel as if the business owner or project sponsor, client or customer, "ruined" the project. So, when they hear that Agile allows them to self-organize and manage themselves, they are likely to misunderstand the point. It's not that the project members manage themselves in isolation, nor is it that there is a single person directing everyone.

## LOSING THE VISION

Learning where the value lies is one of the keys to getting your product out in the market as soon as possible so that it can be corrected if necessary. When a project begins, everyone understands the goals of the project, roughly what needs to get done, and how this aligns with whatever strategy you are trying to implement. But over time the well-understood goals and vision start to erode and become less and less understood.

# Chapter 16: Understanding Agile Programming Practices

By being agile, you as a manager promise to understand the work that your development team puts in and to listen to their ideas and concerns about certain aspects of a project.

## TEST-FIRST

Just as you must practice planning and collaboration your programmers practice test-first programming in the Agile Management environment. Testing allows for programmers to check for bugs and other errors that may not be easily seen just looking over a product. It is the programmer's job to ensure that a program is up and running correctly before it is delivered to a client.

## CONTINUOUS INTEGRATION

Classic teams may work for days or weeks on a project and not realize how many bugs or glitches they are creating. This is why an agile team will integrate the system on a consistent basis. However, it is important to provide planning for

Continuous Integration during every iteration of a project. This type of integration creates a robust code and also encourages discussion and collaboration between a customer and a programmer. It allows for a team to make changes before iteration deadlines and helps to keep all parties happy.

## The Art of Simple

A simple design is going to make the client happy and will be much higher quality than a program delivered quickly and jam packed full of unneeded features simply thrown together. Your programmers know what they are doing, trust them.

## Pair Programming

Pair programming boasts of keeping quality of code up while boosting long term productivity. Without years of programming experience, it is almost impossible to understand even in the simplest sense what "pairing" is. It involves coding together more than one task but helping them to remain as two separate tasks that can still come together as a feature. It is a confusing form of programming that has been highly controversial in the past few years; some saying that it does not have the benefits it claims to.

## Common Code Base

This is a codebase that is shared by most programmers on one floor and works for those who are practicing test-first programming. Having a common codebase helps with flexibility. If for some reason one programmer cannot do a specific task or cannot be at work, a common codebase allows another programmer to jump on those tasks. No one needs to be retrained and the project is not slowed down.

## Coding Standards

Programmers should always adhere to one set of common standards. This helps to eliminate errors and flaws in the coding process. It also allows for the work of each team member to be judged in a similar fashion. By using standards, it is also possible for code to be changed easily if need be.

## Open Work Space

An open work space has shown to boost team morale in almost any environment and helps coworkers become friends and create lasting relationships that make office work less demanding and stressful. Teams that like each other, respect each other, and can trust one another have higher productivity than those who do not have these qualities.

# Chapter 17:
# Examples of Agile Project Management Software

## MONDAY

Monday is formerly called DaPulse. It mainly focuses on social communication and sharing of internal information. Monday has prioritized top choices in Agile Project Management. Collaboration is achieved by a board outlining who is working on what within a specific time. Then teams can move on to comment on other teammate's work or add required files. There is a mobile or desktop application that facilitates real-time notification. Monday is great software to use for basic and enterprise plans.

## WRIKE

It is SaaS project management and collaboration software. Wrike is designed based on a minimalist user interface. It has a project management feature that allows one to monitor dates, project dependencies, and manage assignments and resources. It features an interactive Gantt chart, sortable table and workload view that one can customize to store project data. The collaboration features of Wrike help in conversations, decision making, and asset creation by the team members. These comprise Wrike's Live co-editor, tools to attach documents, track changes, and discussion threads. Wrike has an "inbox" feature and browser notification to remind users of updates from their dashboards about pending tasks. It is available both in IOS apps and native Android.

## ASANA

This is web-based software designed to enhance collaboration. It mainly allows users to control projects and online tasks without using an email. Asana supports team sharing, organization, planning, and monitoring progress of each member in a simple style.

## TAIGA

This is an open source Agile Project Management platform designed for smaller teams of project managers, developers, and designers. It facilitates project collaboration, time tracking, and task management. Taiga features a customizable Agile functionality like Kanban boards and backlogs. This software supports Web-based deployments that are flexible with a lot of operating systems. The system can be accessed as a free self-hosted model where projects are public. There is also a paid plan where projects are private.

## Planbox

This supports members with different business functions to collaborate, plan, and create Agile projects. It has a Scrum methodology that features iterations, Scrum roles, backlog, sprints, and story points. Planbox has a four-level platform that includes tasks, projects, initiatives, and items. This supports drag and drop prioritization, to-do lists, messaging, bug tracking, and reporting among other functions.

## Smartsheet

This is another SaaS-based application that supports collaboration and work management. Smartsheet has an interface similar to that of a spreadsheet to track projects, manage calendars, monitor progress, and manage other works. Every row in the Smartsheet might have files attached to it, discussion board linked to it as well as emails stored. While information is updated, another Smartsheet which monitor the same task is updated automatically.

## Trello

It is web-based project management software and a well-known brand. With a free account anyone has an opportunity to use the majority of the functions, while a premium account offers more complex features.

# Chapter 18: Techniques of Agile Software Development

Agile is an excellent methodology to use to build a product or software. It is a flexible approach that empowers individuals who want to achieve success in software development and product development. Below are important techniques that make Agile approaches succeed.

## NONSTOP INTEGRATION

This technique consists of team members working on a product and then combine their smaller development with the rest of the team. Each integration is evaluated to determine whether there is a problem with the integration process. If a problem is found, appropriate action is taken to fix the problem.

With this technique, you are going to have a group of team members that will work on the software or the product. The members are going to then combine the smaller developments that they work on with the rest of the team. The team members can work on the problem on their own or in smaller groups, and then they will come together and see which iteration or solution is the best. This is like a form of brainstorming where each person can bring in their ideas, and it ensures that many ideas are present as possible in this process.

Each integration is going to be evaluated in the hopes of determining whether there is actually any problem with the integration process. If there is a problem found during the integration, the team will take the right actions to make sure that the problem gets fixed in a timely manner.

## TEST-DRIVEN DEVELOPMENT

The next option if you are looking for a technique is the test-driven development technique. This is a coding process that will come with multiple repetitions of a short development cycle. The first thing that one of the developers or the team will do is to create an automated test case which will measure any of the new functions that we have made. Then, there will be a short code produced to pass a defined test before the new code is refactored to accept some new standards.

## PAIR PROGRAMMING

If you are looking at this technique, there will be some teamwork present. With this one, there are going to be two programmers who will work at one station. The first developer is a programmer while the other developer the driver. The second one reviews every line of code that is entered. This ensures that the code works and everything is put in place and provides immediate feedback so the work is done properly without issues.

## Domain-Driven Design

The next technique is domain-driven design. The idea behind this technique is as follows:

- Align complex design on a given model.
- Put the project's primary focus on the domain logic.
- Start a creative collaboration process between domain experts and a technical team in order to reduce the conceptual heart of the problem.

A domain driven technique is not as much of a methodology. It is more of a collection of practices which help determine the design and speed up software projects that deal with complex domains.

## Code Refactoring

This is a process of modifying the software system without affecting the external features. The most important thing is that the changes improve the internal structure of the software system. The most important thing that you have to remember is that the changes you make will need to improve the internal structure of the software system.

## Design Patterns

In software engineering, a reusable solution is an important aspect of the design process. A design pattern is not complete until it is translated into a code. It is a procedure of how one can solve a given problem that can be used in many different situations. Patterns are a formal practice that a programmer can execute in the application. Object-oriented patterns show relationships and interactions between objects and classes. They do so without describing the object classes and applications used.

As you can see, there are a lot of different techniques that you are able to use when it comes to using the Agile method. Each of them can be effective depending on the product that you want to develop and the way that your business is set up.

# Chapter 19: How to Implement Agile Project Management Effectively

STEP-BY-STEP GUIDE IMPLEMENTATION

## Have A Strategy Meeting to Set Your Vision

At the start of a new project using the Agile technique, you should define the need or vision your project is delivering on. While you may not have all the details because many of these details will arise in the course of the project, you should be able to at least pinpoint the need of the client or the vision of the client. Basically, setting the vision is providing an answer to why you are embarking on the project. This will serve as the foundation for building your project and you will repeatedly refer to it throughout the course of the project. One way to do this is through a strategy meeting.

During this stage, you need to take some time to find out the people who are most likely to purchase and use the product. You can do some research and talk to various customers to figure out who they are, what they like, what they do for work, how they spend their free time, and more. The more that you are able to learn about this prospective customer, the better you will be when making your vision.

The vision setting strategy meeting for your project should happen before you embark on any project. It is then followed by other periodic meetings. This initial strategy meeting helps you explore the validity of your project.

## Build The Roadmap

Once you are done setting your vision for the project and the strategy for the project has been validated, the next step is to translate the vision for the project into a workable roadmap. You will be identifying and placing priority on putting together a rough estimate of the amount of effort and time that would be invested in each level of the project to get a functional product.

A roadmap visually shows the direction of the project. The best roadmap for a project using the agile method is a goal-oriented roadmap. This type of roadmap is also known as a theme-based project roadmap. These types of roadmaps concentrate on the goals, objectives, and outcomes that the client hopes to achieve.

## Start Working On Your Release Plan

Now that you have set your vision, drawn up a strategy, and put together a visual guide for your project, it is time for you to start setting tentative timelines for your project.

There will be many releases within the Agile management cycle so the segment that is released first must be prioritized. There are about three to five sprints in a cycle typically, but the plan must be established first.

A release plan is extra important because it serves as a rallying point for everyone involved in the project. Showcasing your release plan to the members of your team helps them get motivated enough to engage properly with the project. Having a release plan supplies the extra oomph needed to get the job done. While creating your release plan, you should be realistic about how long it will take for a release to be ready.

## Plan Your Sprints

Now is the time to move from focusing on the macro view of the project and concentrate on the micro view of the project. In this phase, you focus on planning the sprints. Sprints refer to short development cycles in which specific goals are achieved, and specific tasks are carried out. Usually, a sprint lasts between one week to four weeks. The product starts by determining each of these iterations and the planning of the sprint takes place before it starts. The scrum team makes sure to cover all the necessary measures to achieve the desired result before it starts with the iterations.

## Ensure That Your Team Stays On Track Through Daily Standups

Throughout each sprint, you need to create opportunities to ensure that there are no stumbling blocks creeping up without you noticing and that you and your team are firmly on the path to achieving your goals on time. Daily meetings help the team to learn about new things and information which one may otherwise miss out on or forget. It updates the team with what has been done and what is still outstanding on a daily basis. It should be no more than 15 minutes every day, before the scheduled work for that day starts.

## Review Time

It is important to check and verify that all the requirements from your initial plan were met and that the functionalities of the product or software meet the client's initial needs. The product owner or customer has the right to reject and accept certain functionalities.

If you find that in the course of the sprint something went wrong, do not hesitate to ask why this happened — understanding why will be helpful for making adjustments to the next sprint so your team can get the job done. The agile technique requires continuous learning and iterations on the processes as well as the product of the project.

The spring reviews should happen when each sprint ends. Reviewing the sprint should take place when each sprint ends. This process should take between an hour or two hours.

### **Figure Out What Is Next**

For you to effectively apply the agile methodology in managing your project, you should be clear on what is next after each step. The next step is usually determined while you are doing your sprint retrospective or review. During your sprint retrospective, you should decide on what to focus on next.

Immediately after a sprint has ended and the features from that sprint have been exhibited, the next step is to decide on the work that gets done next. Reflect on the things you learned during the previous sprint, which could change the initial vision or the initial timeline for the project.

# KEYS TO SUCCESSFUL IMPLEMENTATION OF AGILE

## Start with the right project

If you work with these methodologies on some projects, you may find that it doesn't provide you with the positive results that you want. Often, one may lose control of members of the team that may want to head back to the methods they used in the past. On the other hand, you may find that presenting a narrow scope or a highly dynamic scope can make these methodologies in Agile more effective.

## Define the role of the team

When you are working with an Agile project, there needs to be a lot of organization and discipline among the team. This can be hard to get to work for you. Realizing the importance of this kind of team can be valuable, and making sure that the team is cohesive and shares the same vision and similar goals can be the best way to succeed.

### Approximation of efforts is very important

If you find that a given task isn't done or finished in the sprint it was chosen for, there is most likely a mistake in the estimate and this is something that needs to be corrected. The task must be subdivided into manageable sections and then the level of commitment from each member of the team should be checked. A flexible level of management is going to make sure that each reflects on the tasks which offer the largest value.

### Handle your expectations

You may find that when you are implanting Agile, the first round is not going to work as well as you may hope. And if expectations were high, this can make your team feel uncomfortable with some of the features that come with this method. If this happens with your implementation, it is not something to be worried about. You will find that progress is going to show itself and then when that happens, the results you get can be very positive.

### Choose the right tools

As you work to implement Agile, you will want to be careful. There are many companies who are going to fall into the trap of working on free tools. These tools seem really cool and fun to use, but if they don't have any connection with your own organization and they aren't going to help you actually work on one of your own projects, then they aren't worth your time. Agile methodologies are never going to be implemented by a team that uses tools that are unprofessional.

### Pick out the right product owner

Implementing an Agile project can sometimes be a challenge when the business is first getting started. But, if you are able to get past some of the beginning troubles that occur and actually see the product do well, you will find that the Agile method can make things easier and that most people in the company will soon be onboard with the results and the method in no time.

## Learn and manage the limitations

Agile methodologies come with certain limitations that must be considered. These include scope, deadline, cost, and issues related to quality. It is okay to negotiate on the scope but maintain limitations related to the deadline, cost, and quality. These methods dictate that a given task should not go past a specific effort. Additionally, a time-box should be created to help make use of the sprints.

## Control tension

There are certain organizations that look at Agile approaches as a rapid way of moving things. However, for these methods to last tension in the team has to be controlled. If you can create a team that is motivated, self-managed, results-focused, and efficient, one can be sure to be successful with Agile methodology. In addition, every team must develop the right attitude towards productivity to realize a positive change.

## Stick to the methodology

Agile methodologies come with a few standards, rules, and products. Therefore, it's best to adhere to the method correctly. It is always a good thing not to change anything so that you can provide room for experience. If there is anything odd, be patient and give it another chance.

## Quality

Quality refers to improving the speed of delivery and controlling the estimates. It is vital that products are delivered right on time when you use Agile methodologies. One thing that must be ensured is that the products delivered must work. The products have to fulfill what it was meant to do. For this reason, no one should try to abandon quality in the process of product development until the end is attained.

## **Optimize Visibility**

This is a key element when it comes to the success of a methodology. Implementation of these methods never happens publicly in some of the organizations. However, it is recommended that this type of implementation should be made open so that both the public and the whole of the organization can see everything that is being done.

## **Remain calm and Automate**

A product owner has the role to manage many people alongside their expectations. This is a lot of work that needs more effort and time. There are times when you may feel extremely tired. During such occasions, it is advised that you take a break. You can even ask others to assist you. Another way that you can remain effective is to automate communication. The most important thing is to learn to ask for support from a higher management when you don't feel ready to make decisions.

# Chapter 20: Monitoring the Progress of an Agile Project

The company assumes the risk if the product does not meet the customer's quality standards. Thus, even in Agile projects, there must be metrics to measure delivered value. Monitoring a project is not enough to manage risks. Even if everyone sticks to the original plan, it is still possible that change in market assumptions or conditions can cause the product to fail. The sprints protect every stakeholder from risks.

Progress monitoring relies on value approximations because the true worth will only be realizable upon project completion. Thus, it is important to compute such approximations correctly. Agile strategies focus on delivering a working product. Therefore, the value approximations relate more to the work outputs than the process used.

Agile projects use direct customer feedback, story points, and defects in the development process as the usual metrics. By following a fixed schedule, the project establishes a pace so monitoring focuses on the delivery of finished features and the remaining work.

## IMPORTANT AGILE METRICS

### Velocity

Velocity is the amount of work done within a period by a project team. It uses accomplished story points per iteration. It takes into consideration seasonal trends and local conditions. Thus, velocity is unique to a team. The project team establishes its own velocity and incorporates the associated velocity stability and trends across different conditions and over time.

Some people may think that velocity is a measure of productivity. The project team uses velocity to measure the progress of its project. It is a local measure so it is a mistake to consider velocity as a productivity metric.

### Defect Handling

The project team can discover and correct defects by testing and fixing defects within the iterations, and conducting testing by a group of testers working with it. Some agile teams test the product within iteration so that they can deliver a potentially shippable product after iteration. Some teams use integration or test stories during testing. There are also agile project teams that use a flat level of effort in each sprint to know the kind of work that can resolve defects from the previous iterations.

It is important for the agile team to monitor the defect backlog because it can make corrective actions immediately rather than wait for more defects before fixing them.

## Handling Spikes

A spike is an activity in a sprint for team members to gain knowledge. It may include short tasks to resolve an issue or elaborate a product feature requirement. It is a time-bound activity after securing a release plan.

A spike becomes part of the progress monitoring to address issues. The project team must have the discipline to examine spikes in order to gain knowledge of how it is performing. If it conducts numerous spikes, it may slow down the development progress. If it does not include spikes, it undermines the ability of the members to improve the product.

## Velocity Lag

Once they become at ease with each other, team members show an increase in the team's velocity. They show their real performance after a temporary velocity lag where they acclimatize with their working conditions. Therefore, as they resolve issues, they tend to increase their velocity also.

## Coefficient of Variation

The coefficient of variation allows the team to gain insight into its velocity stability, which indicates its steady state of performance.

## Flow Analysis

The cumulative flow diagram is a tool to monitor performance effectively from different perspectives. It focuses on work items that transition from one state to another and allows users to evaluate items to identify potential bottlenecks and roadblocks in the process.

## The Task Board

The task board is an agile management tool used with the sprint backlog so the project team will know the items within the sprint. You can use sticky notes on a white board and users can easily move a user story from one phase to another.

# Chapter 21: Tools for Quality Control in Agile Project Management

Managing projects is not an easy job. For that reason, there are several agile tools which help in dealing with the challenges of management. A fundamental step in any management process is to ensure that product quality requirements are met. Therefore, as part of making sure that the Agile method is implemented successfully, it is imperative to make use of quality control tools. There are several quality control tools which can be used, and some are discussed in this chapter.

Meeting quality demands when developing any product is always a major project constraint. To ensure that the quality of a product is up to par, there are three quality management processes to follow that include planning, performing quality assurance, and quality control. Depending on the process, there are varying tools to use. However, some tools can be used interchangeably.

When selecting the right Agile tools, it is vital to have criteria to help make the right choice. This is why there are several tools out there. Picking just one is not the best way to find the best quality control tool. Features you should consider are task management, integrations, team collaboration, agile metrics, reporting, and analytics.

### CLARIZEN

Undeniably, when working with certain projects, there are activities or processes that are repeatable. The idea of going all over these activities at each phase of product development is a waste of time. An automation tool is helpful in this case. Clarizen serves the purpose as it is an automation software solution. A business with several related activities can use this software to transform how they do business. The automation of services will speed up processes and lead to efficiency.

### TRELLO

Another agile tool that comes highly recommended is Trello. If you are new to the world of Agile Project Management, then this is the right tool for you. Trello is regarded as one of the easiest project management tools available. The best part about this tool is that you get to see it in action without paying a dime. With its simplicity, there are specific features that are not available in the free version of the tool. Nonetheless, for the best functionality, one has to pay for the full version.

### GITSCRUM

GitScrum is a project management tool that will help any project manager succeed in using Agile. This tool stands out from others due to some unique features it offers. For instance, it has a time-tracking tool which aids in logging hours. Additionally, it has bug tracking feature which also allows the user to pull bug reports and check their statuses. Useful Scrum features found in the product include a project calendar, checklists, changelog, customizable workflows, sprint planning, and reporting tools such as burndown charts. With this tool, the project team can upload and share files and communicate via discussion forums, as well as remaining constantly updated through email notifications.

## JIRA

When searching for the best Agile Project Management tools, you will likely find Jira since it is widely used. Initially, Jira was used for checking bugs and tracking issues. However, as time passed, it was designed to become a fully developed, agile tool. With this tool, task management, reporting, and team collaboration become relatively easy.

One of the main pros of using Jira is that it offers flexibility when dealing with unique workflows. As such, the user can customize the workflow and process to suit their project. Equally, it offers the advantage of integrations. Users can take advantage of the seven day trial period to gauge whether Jira works for them.

## TAIGA

Taiga is an open source project management tool that is simple and easy to use. More importantly, it is powerful. Its functionality is focused on Kanban and Scrum and it can easily create backlogs with sprints, user stories, and epics. Taiga allows social management, which helps teams when they need to assist each other. Additionally, there are other team collaboration and task management components for users. Nonetheless, its weakness is in its integrations and reporting aspects.

## PIVOTAL TRACKER

Project development following the Kanban style is best managed using Pivotal Tracker. This tool is appropriate for task management. With well laid-out workspaces, multiple projects can easily be managed. The workspaces are also arranged in a way that a user easily identifies their priorities. There are also great analytic tools which aid in better understanding the project's health. Reporting using this tool provides a quick snapshot of how the project is performing. Besides these amazing features, the tool also takes integrations seriously. As such, you will find helpful integrations such as Slack, Zendeck, and GitHub. Smaller teams of less than three people can use this tool for free. However, larger teams will have to pay for the features that Pivotal Tracker offers.

### NOSTROMO

Individuals working on digital projects will benefit from the all-in-one Nostromo. Ideal features, including time administration, task management, reporting, analytics, and to-do lists. Since it is a new project management tool on the market, there are few integrations provided.

### HANSOFT

Hansoft is an ideal choice for many due to its adaptability. Organizations which tend to scale quickly should use this Agile Project Management tool. There are also an array of learning tools provided with the package that include courses and webinars.

In terms of backlog management, Hansoft exceeds expectations. Users can easily group items based on themes, sprints, and epics. Also, items can be prioritized before assigning them to a particular sprint. The prioritized view of items helps users effectively work on the most pressing issues first.

Similarly, there are intuitive dashboards to provide all the team members with the insights they need throughout the project development process. This ensures that better and improved decisions relating to the project are made.

## Blossom

Distributed teams can take advantage of the Blossom project management tool. Its customizable workflow shows the status of the project. Blossom facilitates the easy addition of comments, files, to-do lists, and more. The easy-to-use interface is uncomplicated and allows the team to see activities on the project.

Likewise, there are performance analytic tools which help to gauge how a project is performing right from its inception to delivery of the final product. Blossom is also good with integrations.

## Ravetree

Ravetree is yet another good project management tool. Unlike other tools, Ravetree is not limited to use by software teams. Any Agile organization can utilize the unique features that include resource planning, time tracking, expense tracking, CRM, and digital asset management. Ravetree has a highly intuitive interface, which makes it easy for the team members to find the information they need.

This list is just a summary of some of the best Agile Project Management tools available. There are varying features which make these tools stand out from each other. Therefore, it is important for you to go over the features and determine which one is the best Agile tool for you. Don't overlook the significance of the trial periods provided, they can be a great way of testing the product without actually paying for it.

# Chapter 22:
# Key Metrics to Measure Agile Success

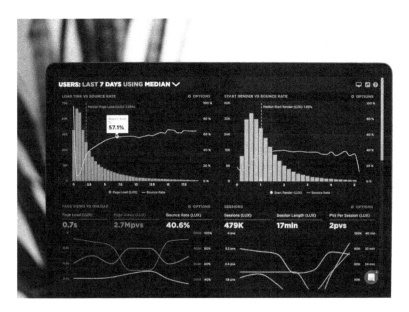

After successfully implementing your Agile method, you will want to find out whether it succeeded or not. How will you know whether the Agile system made a difference? The chances are that you are thinking about the product quality since the Agile method promotes the idea of focusing on the product and not the process. Well, you should understand that there is more to success than just delivering a quality product. This section will help you understand the key metrics to help you in gauging the level of success of your Agile system.

### BEFORE GAUGING THE SUCCESS OF AGILE, THERE ARE SEVERAL QUESTIONS YOU NEED TO ASK YOURSELF.

### Does the organization have an Agile culture?

The success of your organization will be determined by its Agile maturity. All the departments in your organization should portray some level of maturity since the Agile system developed. How processes are handled will also tell a lot about how the Agile culture has transformed your team. For instance, if you notice that sprint meetings are conducted daily, then it will mean that your team has transformed. Since you are aware of the agile values, the actions of your team should be in line with these values.

### Is the organization credible?

Additionally, you should also strive to find out whether your team is delivering the product that was promised to the customer. This is a straightforward process as you only need to confirm whether the requirements of the end product have been met. An agile system that helps the team meet customer demands can be identified as a good system. With time, your company will gain the credibility it seeks since it will be producing top quality products.

### Does the organization meet its commitments?

It is also crucial for the project manager to consider whether the organization meets its commitments by using the Agile technique. Its commitments here relate to the product features and meeting project deadlines. Equally, the company should be delivering the product in time just as the clients were promised. The velocity of a team will have a huge influence with regards to the group meeting its obligations. The collective efforts of the entire team should complete an array of tasks within a specified period.

### Does the organization produce quality products?

Getting answers to this question will reveal the performance level of the company. If the team produces quality products, then it implies they are performing well. On the contrary, defective products mean that something is not right with the Agile system being used.

# Essential Metrics That Will Aid You in Measuring the Success of Your Agile System.

## On-Time Delivery

One key metric which will help you measure the success of your agile initiative is on-time delivery of the product. By meeting the expectations of customers, you can gauge the level of success. A product that hits the market at the right time gains a competitive edge over rivals in the market and people will want to use products that get to the market first.

If the product meets its requirements, there is a good chance that they will stick to that product in the long run. Measuring the success of an Agile initiative through on-time delivery is done through the burn-up charts. These are tools which help project managers to track the progress of a project. These charts provide the development team with the information they need to predict the completion dates. The charts also help them to ensure the process is on schedule.

## Product Quality

A product that satisfies the needs of the customers performs well in the market. It means that the project was carried out successfully. Also, a project is successful since the revenue gained from the sale of the product meets the organization's goals. So, in many ways, the product quality tells a lot about how the organization performed.

## Customer Satisfaction

The success of your Agile system can also be gauged through customer satisfaction. Here, you will have to consider the sales figures. If the product is selling in the market, this is a clear sign that you performed well. Your efforts in delivering a good product will pay off. You could also consider the number of calls you get concerning the product. If many calls are asking for details, then it means that your project performed well.

Simply put, customers will be happy with what you delivered, and therefore your returns on investment will be high.

## Business Value

The overall business value gained through the use of the Agile method is also used to measure how good your Agile system is. It is important to remind you that this is what the Agile Manifesto promotes. The business value is highly regarded above anything else. The value of the business increases when contract requirements are met or a product is delivered at the right time.

## Product Scope

You can also measure the success of your Agile initiative by looking at the product scope. At the beginning of the development process, you set goals regarding the features and requirements that you need to put into a particular product. At the end of the process, meeting these goals is truly rewarding. As such, knowing that the product delivered to the market has all the requirements the product owner expected, is a sign that the project is a success. It is a clear indication that the agile method worked.

## Project Visibility

The level of success of your agile method can also be defined by its visibility. The best Agile system is one where everything is open for the entire team to see. Knowing that all members with interest in the project are aware of its progress is a way of determining its success. It wouldn't be successful if things were not laid out in the open.

## Process Improvement

It is also possible to measure how your agile system is performing through process improvement. One of the main reasons why the agile method leads to an overall enhancement in product quality is the notion of continuous improvement. The frequent changes made after every sprint will, in the end, determine the quality of the product. If there is a steady improvement of the product at every stage, it means that the end product features what the customer expects. So, your agile method should constantly make things better in the project development process.

## Satisfaction Surveys

The highest priority of any agile program is to meet the needs of the customer. One way of finding out whether this goal is being achieved is through satisfaction surveys. Customers can use demo products to help in knowing whether their demands are being met. Also, satisfaction surveys can be filled by team members. In this case, members answer questions relating to their experience working with the organization. Such team surveys identify existing loopholes in the product development group.

## Defects

Defects will always be a part of any project. Regardless of how skilled the development team is, there will be errors in the product development process. Any good team should work to make sure that they minimize flaws. The idea of tracking mistakes also assists in measuring the performance of the agile program. The team working on creating a new product will know how well they are doing to prevent defects in the development process.

Project managers want to know how their agile initiatives perform. Therefore, it is imperative for them to consider the metrics pointed out in this section. It would be difficult to determine the direction you are heading without knowing whether or not you are succeeding in the first place. Project managers need to look at their product quality. Are they delivering the best quality product in the market? If yes, is this product getting to consumers at the right time? Beyond that, they should also look at customer satisfaction. Are customers satisfied with the product? Such metrics give project managers deeper insight into their performance levels. More importantly, they should seek to improve continuously as this is the best way to counter competition in the market.

## HOW TO TRACK THE PROJECT?

Tracking the project is necessary for transparency and the measurement of value added to the product. If there is no monitoring, then it can result in negative circumstances for the company that is executing the project. Here are some of the ways to track progress in Agile Project Management:

### Vision Statement

A vision statement needs to be created regarding the product and how it will benefit the company. It is a quick summary of the product along with matching it to organizational strategies and how it can improve profitability. It should include an outline of the main goal for the company and how agile management procedures will be implemented to achieve this.

### Roadmap

Again, a roadmap of the product and project needs to be reviewed once a week to see if everything is on track and on time. It needs to connect with the vision and goal of the company giving the timeframe for each stage as well.

### Backlog

It is the list of the products, features, and requirements which have been defined on a prior basis and where these are still outstanding. It needs to be updated every day following a review of what work has been done on the day and what is still left to be completed, indicating whether the project is on track to be completed by the deadline or not.

### Release plan

A complete timetable of scheduled releases of software at the different stages of the project as it is developed. This should be reviewed on a weekly basis to the team on track and identify major milestones achieved in the project lifecycle.

### Increments

Keeping track of user responses when each stage or increment of the project is completed and if the customers have preferred it or not. Receiving feedback after each increment is necessary to generate improvements in the next sprint release.

Using each of these processes in the tracking of a project will ensure value is constantly being added to the product and it is staying on target. It is something that should be done on a daily basis. These ways will help in ensuring the focus on the project's goals will be kept and prevents team members getting lost in between releases. Where all the team can track progress so knowing exactly what still must be done and what has already been achieved throughout the entire project will generate confidence in the leader. This also allows everyone to know their job and that they are doing it the right way which will surely make the result more successful.

# Chapter 23:
# Closing and Evaluating Project Success

## CLOSING A PROJECT

Projects have a definite ending. In this phase, you'll focus on submitting the deliverables to your clients and terminating all the pending activities. This phase ought to be simple but unfortunately, it can be challenging at times. For example, if a project achieved notable successes, some people won't want the project to end. They will try to bank on the project's successes by expanding its scope.

This phase has two major parts: Close Project and Close Procurement.

### Close Project Stage

The "Close Project" stage produces the final product and result/service transition. This stage requires you to capture all the artifacts of the project (e.g. list of risks and stakeholders). In addition, you'll have to document the project's termination or completion.

Ask your team members to discuss the issues they faced. Their stories will educate others regarding the issues that might occur in the future and the proper responses. Thus, simply talking about past problems can help in boosting a team's chances of success.

## Close Procurements Stage

In this stage, you will review the procurement contract and communicate with your seller/s. You also need to record the procurement-related lessons and artifacts of the project. The information you'll obtain here will help you in finding good suppliers for your future assignments. If you conduct this stage properly, you can greatly minimize the risks you will face in supplier selection. Here are the major tasks that you should complete:

- Review all the procurement contracts for the project
- Update the organization
- Ask suppliers to confirm the end of the contracts through written notices

## THINGS TO REMEMBER

At the end of a project, you have to close the procurements and the project itself. Release organizational resources as soon as you can so that they can be utilized by other teams. Closing a project lets you appreciate everything you've learned and share the data with other people. This way, the entire organization can benefit from the project you just completed.

Important Note: These stages are mandatory. You have to do them even if the project was cancelled.

The list given below shows you some tips for closing projects:

- Make the end of a project official by scheduling a meeting for it. Most project managers include this meeting in their Gantt charts.
- Ask stakeholders to attend the meeting.
- During the meeting, share the things you've learned from the project. Encourage your team members to do the same. Openness and honesty are crucial here.

## EVALUATING PROJECT SUCCESS

For many project managers, evaluation is a learning process that can benefit many people - from team members to the most remote stakeholders. Project evaluation is a practical and theoretical process. It feeds useful data back into existing activities and projects. In addition, it is a process that gauges the efficiency, effectiveness, and relevance of the activities you'll do in a project. In this part of the book, you'll learn how to evaluate completed projects accurately.

An evaluator can take different roles. He can be a coach, facilitator, mentor, consultant, etc. These roles are important in almost all types of projects, so an evaluator should know how to play them. To get you started, however, here are the typical responsibilities of an evaluator:

- Establish policies and references for the evaluation process
- Create a plan for the project evaluation
- Set the scope and limitations of the process
- Work with project managers in determining the goals of the evaluation
- Determining the criteria of evaluation
- Secure the objectivity of the evaluation

### Evaluation Teams

Evaluation teams assume one of these setups:

- Internal and external evaluators working together
- A main evaluator with a supporting team

- A main evaluator with a third-party consultant and a supporting team
- A third-party consultant with an in-house supporting team

# Chapter 24:
# How Agile Can Easily Fail

It is also crucial for you to learn a thing or two about how you can fail when using the Agile approach. There is no Agile technique where the goal is a failure. However, poor planning by an informed team can easily lead to defeat. You might be using the best Agile method, but it will not work if you do not use the right approach. The following lines will discuss how things can go wrong with the Agile strategy. This information will provide you with the insight you need to avoid common pitfalls, which could hinder your organization from succeeding.

## PLANNING CHAOTICALLY

A common myth surrounding the use of the Agile method is that planning is not important. This is not true. Having an agile system in place doesn't mean that planning is not important. Planning is the best way to execute your strategy. Fortunately, there is a tool to help your team plan effectively align their actions to the business goals. This tool is called the Agile Release Train, and it can help a company to plan projects even twelve months in advance.

## TESTING LATE

Some software developers think that testing at a later stage is the better approach because it can consume less time – compared to testing early which can end up with a re-testing. But since the purpose of testing is to determine a product's weaknesses, the amount of time consumed should not be a concern.

## DOCUMENT MORE

Another mistake is spending a lot of time for the documentation of an Agile project. Some managers and developers assume that if they detail a project closely, and spend plenty of time studying it, other team members can learn well from their approach. Well, they're wrong. As the Agile framework encourages, documentation should be minimized. It emphasizes that good, effective communication is more important than documentation.

## RELYING ON THE ELEMENT OF SURPRISE

Giving a surprise to the team members is also a mistake. While it is built around the idea of flexibility, Agile is not meant for overwhelming team members with new priorities, new budgets, new assignments, and new roles. Rather, it is meant for team members who prefer to work in a stable environment.

## Relying on Unskilled Project Leaders

Some software developers are also hindered by their own project leaders. Turning to new project leaders can be a big mistake especially if the project leaders are unskilled in Agile or they are struggling with the transition to Agile.

Since they hold the responsibility of setting a good example for their teams, project leaders should be skilled in Agile and be able to express confidence in an Agile mindset. That way, the team members won't be doubtful when following their lead.

While there are teams that are authorized to make decisions without supervision from upper management, these teams will still need support – lots of it -- from project leaders. So, if their leaders are incapable of supporting them, these teams are less likely to succeed with Agile.

## Forming an Unstable Team

If you work with a team of individuals who understand each other, then you will have the upper hand. On the contrary, if your team is made up of strangers, it will be daunting for you to achieve the success you are looking to achieve.

Teams should be optimized to aid in reducing dependencies. An ideal group must be comprised of individuals who understand their job specifications and they should not wait for the project manager to guide them constantly. The best agile teams are made up of generalists. These are experts who will not depend on other specialty groups to complete their tasks.

## Communicating Infrequently

Agile teams with poor communication will fail quickly. The flow of communication in an agile environment should be continual. Regular interaction should be maintained with stakeholders who have an interest in the end product. It is quite likely that there will be certain terminologies that will be used in the workplace and a good team should have a uniform vocabulary concerning the product.

## Poor Testing of Products

Having regular tests guarantees that quality is maintained when developing products. Poor testing is the fast road to failure. It is crucial for developers to accurately test products to make sure that they are up to standards. Regular tests aid in guaranteeing that the team finds it comfortable to adjust to changes.

## Disregarding Customer Feedback

Customer feedback is what will bring about changes in the Agile system. Failure to heed to consumer evaluation only leads to frustration. Your team will be disappointed that in spite of their efforts, they did not succeed. Customer comments should be highly regarded as they warrant that product requirements are fully met. Absence of customer feedback makes it a daunting task to know how to prioritize. Ultimately, the development team might end up disregarding what is most important in the eyes of the customer.

# Chapter 25:
# How to Apply the Agile Project Management Method Effectively

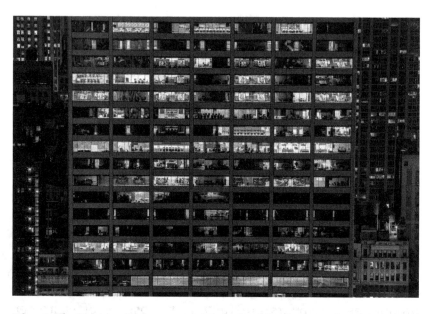

The Agile Project Management method is designed to boost the chances of successful projects. In this case, the agility of your team ensures that the team is productive over an extended period. From the information discussed in the previous chapter, there are many benefits associated with the Agile management method. On the surface, these benefits appear easy to attain. However, it is worth noting that not every project will benefit from using the Agile Project Management method.

To ensure that you effectively apply agile to your project management, it is imperative to understand whether the method is right for you. Adopting the agile method means that your company will depart from how it used to work. Agility will demand a fast-paced way of doing things. Accordingly, it is vital for your organization to determine whether or not it is up for the challenge.

To find out, you need to answer the following questions:

## ARE YOU WILLING TO INITIATE PROJECTS WITHOUT KNOWING THEIR OUTCOME?

By adopting the Agile Project Management method, you will have to act fast. The method fosters the idea of moving quickly and constantly conducting tests during the product development process. This is not easy. It is stressful if not managed effectively. So, are you ready to take on the challenge?

Before adopting the agile method, reflect on whether you are prepared to put your product out there for testing before it's completed. It is essential to be prepared to test your cake before it is fully baked.

## HOW RISK-CAUTIOUS ARE YOU?

Adopting the Agile method of project development implies that you will be taking on more risks as compared to the traditional way of doing things. While using this method, you must embrace the idea of learning from your mistakes as you strive to deliver a product that meets customers' requirements. Having said this, take a step back to evaluate whether you can handle risks. If you are going to take the Agile route, you must be ready to deal with unknown issues or risks which could arise during product development.

## DO YOU HAVE AN AGILE TEAM?

Determine whether your team is agile enough to handle the project's demands. Remember one of the principles of the Agile method is that it pushes for a more collaborative environment. As such, your team should be ready to work together toward a common goal. The team members should set their differences aside and work harmoniously. Undeniably, if your team is not agile enough, then the Agile Project Management method will not be as effective as it could be.

# Chapter 26:
# The Need for Agile Project Management in Today's Market

An easy way to understand Agile Project Management is that it is much more self-organized and the rapid pace which is achieved through shorter iterations proves much more effective for longer-term projects as well. There are certain managers who have suggested that the Agile project process does not need management but most experts believe that some supervision, guidance, and motivation are required for good agile project development.

Most drivers for the processes are advocated where the vision is communicated within the meetings and other inputs provided by the customers. Maybe there is the need for some planning but if the team all have lists of tasks and procedures assigned to them, they will know what they have to do without having any major obstacles created, which directly link to the main goal of the company. The plan needs to be affiliated with the project goals so that everyone can connect with it while working on their tasks. When the vision is shared with all the team every day, it works as a guide for them to get done with the work efficiently, knowing that they must stay on track and if that is not the case then get off the track somewhere in between. This is why it is important that the vision is mentioned in daily meetings that are held by the leads for 15 minutes every day.

The vision may also come from other stakeholders such as the customers which you can implement and allow more chances of improvement while working with each other. Rather than having a detailed comprehensive written purpose, you can simply have it written in a form that everyone can relate to. Even if the team wants to add their own visions which can drive them to work effectively, they should have the autonomy to do so under an Agile Project Management system. Great results can be generated when you have collaborations and when there are frequent discussions regarding the project and are more likely if you stay away from a command and control plan which does not work anymore. The layout of the project needs to be defined for everyone so that there is a mutual understanding of the emergence and the adaption of the entire project, which is going to be run by all the members and gains mutual consent, so all the team members can work on the same vision. The main nurturing of the project begins when everyone in the company understands how important the project is and how it can benefit all of them, achieved through dedication and hard work.

It is obvious that no project comes along without some obstacles which is why you need to be prepared for any challenges which you may face while completing the project. There will be some obstacles which can be irrelevant and you can ignore these so they do not waste time, whereas there will be some crucial ones which you have to sort out so that they do not disrupt the plan more in the future. It is dependent upon the leader and his experience to know how it can affect the goal while working on the project and what needs to be done to make the path easier. Participating in Agile Project Management is a huge success in itself because it is really hard to retain and manage all aspects with the calmness that is required by the lead.

A good team can quickly manage to decide on the features and divide them amongst those with the right expertise for each of the iterations, again whilst keeping to the deadlines. There have to be tasks done by the end of each day to make sure that everyone is on track, doing something which they have to report to the agile agent to show progress. This will keep everyone focused, knowing that the project will be done on time, making any corrections if needed at the testing phase before delivering it to the stakeholders.

In some companies there can be at least one dysfunctional area which can hurt the programming or the standard of the software. There are projects which work instantly with full commitment from everyone, but those projects are not all likely over the longer term. A leader's responsibility is to ensure that all projects can work in the long run, as he is the motivator for the team. It is not just about getting the work done within a few weeks by taking on smaller projects.

The productivity of the team depends upon the possible solution which the manager provides along with making sure that the work is completed by the delivery dates for the software submission. A project manager should know all the ins and outs of the product along with discovering what is needed and researching for information if they are doubtful of something or are lacking the knowledge.

The ideas for projects could be different, diversity, resources, too many deadlines, work pressure and a lot of other factors can create a space for politics to rise easily. When the manager has Agile mechanisms in place then the politics can be minimized even if they cannot be eliminated completely. Regular communication where the goals are made clear to all provides less chance of having some kind of politics and if it still exists then this may be due to the personality mix.

## Turning Your Organization Agile

Now that we know more about the Agile method and why it is a great choice to go with, it is time to learn how to turn your own organization into an Agile one. Usually, with organizations that have been able to fully implement these Agile practices, it is the role of the manager to make sure that all the members are committed to their abilities and duties to get the best results. Once every team member is dedicated to the tasks they are given, greater value will be delivered to the customer on time. In addition, in an Agile organization the manager should have complete confidence in the action taken by those who are in direct contact with the customer, while also trusting their team to take the right steps to get things done.

When you start to implement the Agile system into your business, you will find that it is not a top-down or even a bottom-up approach. The focus on this is to change up the management to determine what should be done and then provide instructions to the employees about how to do that work. The managers are also going to oversee whether the employee is able to complete all of the work on-time and based on the instructions that have been outlined.

The model is also going to assume that the employee is meant to follow instructions while trusting that the manager knows what they are doing without asking questions. The main goal of this model is to generate money for a firm. Basically, the manager is the boss and everyone else just follows along. When the company is set up this way, it is hard to implement the practices of Agile. To successfully implement the Agile system into your company, you must make sure that you change up the management system to have a team atmosphere, rather than a boss and follower atmosphere.

### Why partial fixes aren't the best solutions

There have been times when an organization finds some tension between the management and the ideas that come with Agile when they try to adopt it. To help reduce some of this tension, you need to make sure that the team leader is someone who understands the Agile method. This can be done by creating a new job description for the project supervisor. However, this approach is only to provide a temporary solution and there are a few reasons why you need to change up to something more permanent.

With some big organizations, there are various ranks for the managers. Redefining the job description means that the top hierarchy and the Agile team only see a reduction of friction on a single layer. It is hard for this friction to stop if some of the top managers in the company still embrace the traditional leadership roles and they don't want to give up their roles.

Another reason that there is some friction is because the top managers in a big firm have just one purpose, and that is to generate money for the company and its shareholders. This approach is known as maximizing the shareholders' value, and it is not part of the Agile method. Remember that with Agile, you want to deliver value to the customer and not money just to the shareholders. Because of this, unless you are able to find a permanent solution, it is going to be difficult to change up some of the management roles and implement the Agile method into the organization.

Finally, there are times when the top managers just aren't interested in implementing Agile, or they see it as a waste of time. It is impossible for the company to accept Agile without actually discussing the goal of the organization and working together to turn it into reality. The top managers are going to use the command and the control approach in order to address the creation of large profits and to make sure that the price of the stocks goes up. If you are able to solve the tension that occurs between the top management and an Agile team, it will be easier to implement it in your business.

Now, there are a few things that you can do with your business to make sure that you can easily implement Agile into it and to get the best results possible.

To make the shift into the Agile method, there are five fixes that you should concentrate on including:

Rather than aiming to just make money for the company, your main focus and goal should be to satisfy the customer. If you are able to do this, then you will bring in more money.

Instead of having those who perform the tasks for the company report to the bosses, the work needs to be done within the self-organizing team. In addition, the management shouldn't have to spend their time verifying that the work gets done. Instead, the management should aim to facilitate and help those who are responsible for completing the task.

Aim to allow the work to be carried out using the Agile principles as a basis, instead of the work being coordinated by plans, reports, rules, and other things that stifle creativity and just take up time.

Instead of being preoccupied with a defined predictability and efficiency, the major values of the company that uses Agile should be transparency and continuous improvement. You should aim to eliminate the one way, top-down command system that is in your business and change it over to a horizontal conversation instead.

## **Changing the culture**

When you choose to apply the five fixes above in order to help implement the method of Agile in your business, the end result is that the corporate culture in your business will have a new image. This isn't always easy to do and often it is the hardest part of trying to implement Agile. It requires agreement, a lot of changes, and some understanding of the system to get it to work.

Overall, you will find that the best strategy to use here to deliver success is to start with the tools of leadership. Some of these tools will include the tools of power, a vision about the future, and having a control system. It may be hard to change this and to make the culture friendlier to this process, but it can do wonders when it comes to implementing Agile.

# Chapter 27:
# Tips and Tricks to Make Your Agile Project Management System Efficient

## USING TIME MANAGEMENT TECHNIQUES

To help you plan your day, make use of Agile tools to assist you in keeping track of what needs to be done. Agile tools will conveniently schedule pending tasks which need to be completed by you and your team.

## POINT OUT THE PROJECT REQUIREMENTS

The success of a project is determined by the outcome. This implies that the end product after completion of the project defines whether the project was a success or not. In line with this, the project's success is evaluated by considering whether the product features all the requirements that consumers expect. Therefore, for a project to succeed, pointing out the project requirements is necessary.

## Hiring a Qualified Project Manager

The Agile Project Management system will not function optimally without a qualified project manager. This person who has sufficient experience will understand what needs to be done for a particular project to succeed. Equally, a credible manager will know how to allocate tasks to different individuals based on their qualifications. More importantly, they will find a way to make sure that the process is not only productive but also fun at the same time.

## Providing Frequent Updates and Demos

When the project is underway, there needs to be constant updates about the product's functionality and deadlines. If there are any issues with the product, this information should also reach the client. Effective communication confirms that the project is progressing smoothly with minimal hitches.

## Regular Communication with Your Team

There are many benefits to making sure that regular communication is delivered to your team. Undeniably, communicating more often prevents misunderstandings from occurring. If there are any unclear requirements that the team fails to understand, this can also be ironed out through regular communication.

## Set the goals and requirements

Engage with the product owner so you both can converse and put together the goal and requirements for the project in general and for each sprint of the project. Having goals and requirements helps you have a direction, and this helps you and your team focus better on your project.

## DEFINE IMPORTANT MILESTONES

Do not just stop at pointing out the requirements; you need to know how to measure progress and eventual success. Defining your milestones will help you be able to judge whether you are actually growing or not.

## MAINTAINING REGULAR COMMUNICATION

The nature of agile projects is that they thrive off regular communication. In Agile Project Management, people need to communicate on a daily basis to ensure that they are still on track when it comes to getting the job done and delivering on the job. If you do not maintain regular communication between development team members, the product owners, and even stakeholders, you will probably end up putting out a product that falls short of the requirements.

## PROVIDING FREQUENT UPDATES AND DEMOS

Though this is closely related to communication, it is more of an offshoot of communication and is a reason why communication should be prioritized. The Agile technique makes room for reviews to be done after every sprint and the purpose of these reviews is to improve on the product. Since the Agile techniques involve bit by bit development and repeated steps even after the first workable prototype is released, you and your team need to constantly put out updates and demos.

## Anticipating setbacks

It is true that everyone would rather their projects happen without any setbacks and that the products are delivered without any issues. The problem with not anticipating setbacks is that you are setting yourself up for failure since you are not on the lookout for things that could go wrong.

## Prioritize accountability

Agile project teams are typically made up of self-motivated people who do not have to be micromanaged. Team members are allowed to bring their own unique approaches to the job. The problem with this is that sometimes when people have nobody to be accountable to, they tend to slack off on the job. Incorporate an accountability system in your team. You can use the daily scrum meetings as opportunities to foster accountability since reviews and feedback are always received during these meetings.

## Place value over-activity

It is indeed true that your team needs to put out deliverables within a certain time. It is also true that the agile technique requires almost constant activity from one sprint to the other. Focusing on activity instead of value can have you engaging in things that are just wasteful and hold no real relevance in the grand plan of the project. However, focusing on adding value ensures that you stay in touch with the core requirements for the project.

## Try not to add unnecessary elements or be wasteful when handling projects

Too much information or data, unnecessary and nonfunctional features or traits are instances of being wasteful with elements that ought not to be added to the project. A few ways to minimize such wastefulness and to know your customer and the project by extension are by organizing iterative meetings between the customers and the developers, reviews to recognize prerequisites and issues to be fixed, and spending budgets that are separated by deliverables.

## CONCENTRATE ON THE PRODUCT'S BEST RESULT

Another tip for a more successful project management approach is to concentrate on the product's best result. This advice should work well with the advice that you should focus on current goals. While needs and demands can change midcourse, you should still keep your eye on the end goal and encourage team members to do the same.

## AIM FOR EXCELLENCE

Aiming for excellence is also another tip from top project managers. Don't simply settle for mediocre results. If you already have a product, don't hesitate to think of ways to make a better version of it. Just remember that your definition of "excellence" should be in line with every team member's definition, as well as the client's.

## ALWAYS WELCOME CHANGE

Top project managers recommend that change should always be welcomed by all the team members. Embracing change can be challenging, yes, but a hack that can make it less challenging is to embrace change as a team.

## ALWAYS APPLY THE LESSONS LEARNED

In the event that major problems have impacted a project, project managers suggest that a brilliant strategy is to continue working – instead of getting demotivated by unfavorable situations. Everyone in the team should adopt a resilient mindset, and let failures shape them to work towards a much better product.

## YOU SHOULD REGARD CUSTOMER EXPECTATIONS

A customer isn't just the client of a product or service we offer or the supporter of a project. We ought to also consider the customer as integral parts of our inner team and the outside endorsing elements.

## TRY NOT TO SIT AROUND DURING MEETINGS

Meetings that are organized with numerous invitees and with an interminable plan are a part of the traditional and non-agile culture. A team using Agile Project Management prioritized short and straight to the point meetings over lengthy meetings which end up not going the way they were planned. Coordination meetings should just be made to encourage continuous project delivery, while collaboration meetings should just cover technical issues.

## REMEMBER RISK PROJECT MANAGEMENT

Carrying out a risk evaluation, analysis, and examination before beginning a project is being proactive by working to minimize future issues, which will enable you to have an increasingly coordinated and productive project.

It is true that risks cannot be entirely eliminated. Be that as it may, we can generally mitigate them through great planning, distinguishing proof, subjective investigation, quantitative examination, reaction planning, checking, and controlling.

## Stay Away From Long Composed Writings, Rather Use Figures

To compose long messages expressing the status of your project is wasteful. Rather, you should utilize realistic strategies that will attract more attention: hues, pictures, images, tables, models, and so forth. For senior management to think about deviations in a project, it is critical to impart the exceptions, rather than the similitudes.

If you could create a visual representation of the exceptional cases, it would be extremely helpful so as to recognize needs and be proactive while destroying the issues influencing the project.

## Oversee Reserves and Turns, Keeping Away From Long Queues.

We have to take a stab at working with a system of reservations and turns rather than a first-in, first-out model which overlooks prioritizes. For some projects, it would be better if a procedure of electronic documents is implemented rather than a physical, sequential process.

To streamline the organization's procedures and processes does not mean that you have to relinquish control and have less of it.

## Remember the Basic Resources

While getting ready for future projects to be managed, it isn't sufficient to work with the critical path strategy. This conventional methodology ought to likewise mull over incessant issues faced during projects, for example, risks related to resource accessibility and risks related to the utilization of new advancements and technology. It is usually more imperative to think about what the basic resources related to the project are than to know whether an action you are taking is part of the critical path.

## HOLD PROJECT PRIORITIZATION SACRED

To deal with different assignments with no arrangement doesn't compare to applying the Agile technique to handling projects. Rather, to plan projects with devoted teams based on delivering on priorities leads to an increase in the value of the organization.

To satisfy this tip, give priority projects the sacredness they deserve. Do a breakdown of projects based on where they rank on the priority scale and the ability of you and your team to handle the project and to deliver a workable product within the expected time.

## DEFINING CRITICAL MILESTONES

The success of a project is largely dependent on the main phases which need serious attention. As the project manager, you must make sure that these phases are identified as the project continues. The team members must understand that certain phases are more important than others. To guarantee that the stages are successful, it is vital for the project manager to evaluate after each stage ends. Before proceeding to the next stage, the project manager should confirm that the project requirements have been fully met. Ultimately, when all the milestones are put together, there is a high probability that the project will succeed. Defining critical milestones acts as indicators that the team is doing its best to meet the project's goals.

## ANTICIPATING PROJECT SETBACKS

In spite of your well-laid-out plan, you should always expect that something can go wrong. It doesn't matter whether you hired the best project manager in town or not. Anything can happen to your project. Note that preventing a crisis from happening keeps your project on track. Moreover, your team will be confident that the project is progressing just as expected. So, it is vital for any project manager to anticipate setbacks and learn how to deal with them effectively.

## Project Evaluation

Another tip which guarantees your agile project thrives is through evaluation. Every project you handle should be considered a learning tool. A good manager takes the time to review how the project performed. All the components of the project should be evaluated to determine whether some areas could be improved in the next projects. By learning from past performance, a project manager can find ideal ways of improving in the future.

## Transition Support

Implementing the agile method in your organization will not be an easy task. There is a lot that needs to be done to embrace the agile culture. This calls for good coaching, which will ensure that people understand the benefits that can be achieved by adopting the agile method. Coaching should be there to provide support when mistakes are made. Truly, you shouldn't expect your team to be perfect right after introducing the agile method. Give them time to adjust.

Support should also be provided in the form of mentoring in specific roles. Some members of the team might be faster in understanding the method better than others. This doesn't mean that you should allow others to drag behind. As the project manager, work to empower each person and ensure that they are in line with other members. This is what brings about stability in your development team. Ultimately, you will increase the likelihood of a successful project.

## Total Openness and Transparency

Once you implement the Agile method in your organization, nothing needs hiding. You cannot mask how people are doing things and you cannot hide the progress of the project. The poor quality of your product cannot hide since you will be testing it with the consumers. There is nothing hidden in an Agile environment. This is how your optimal agile environment should look. The agile tools you use should help you in maximizing on the quality of output. Total openness and transparency guarantee that you solve existing challenges, which might be evident in the project development process.

## Early Feedback

An agile system will also succeed if the team works to find a way of putting the product being developed in front of the consumers. As the product develops, consumers should test its demo product. They should know how it is functioning. This way, the team gets early feedback and can make changes where necessary. Getting early feedback warrants that the team can easily adapt to changes.

## Value over Activity

The notion of working in an agile environment might be confusing to many. Yes, agility requires that rapid changes should be adopted in any process. However, to succeed in your agile system, your team needs to embrace value over activity. Their focus should not just be to get things done. Rather, a higher emphasis should be on creating value. To ensure that this point sinks in, your team should go over the core values outlined in the Agile Manifesto.

## SHARED ACCOUNTABILITY

Your agile system will blossom if you develop a culture where no one gets blamed for their part. The team working on a project should value the importance of shared accountability. All team members should be accountable for the outcome of the project. This means that if anything goes wrong, the entire team is at fault. This way, individuals understand the importance of collaborating for a common goal. Working together is what leads to increased productivity. Thus, this is what should be advocated for by the project manager.

# Conclusion

A huge demand for Agile Project Management rose in the marketplace a few years back when it emerged. There was an urgency to adopt it as soon as possible for those organizations which used it as a test and were successful at achieving their projects more effectively than their competitors. As technology advances, there are changes that are meant to come into the processes and the entire organization has to go through these changes which some people may resist. Changing processes in an organization can make some people leave their job, but if they wish to accept the challenges there is nothing that a person cannot learn.

The techniques and methods that are included in this book will help you go through a project with Agile management even if you are trying it for the first time. All of the more successful companies in the market are currently following Agile Project Management, depending upon their own genres which they excel in.

If organizations do not adopt changes then it can be hard for them to survive, due to the customer demands which change every day. An organization must modify itself to meet these demands as the market has become customer driven and it is necessary that the client is satisfied with your service. Meeting a customer's needs is a critical factor for success in a competitive market. If you are not offering something which the client needs, then there will be some other similar company which will be doing so and the client will shift to them to get the services they want and need.

The next step is to figure out how to implement this methodology in your own business. We discussed many of the benefits of using the Agile method and even some of the challenges that you may face along the way. The first thing that you will need to concentrate on is looking at management and making sure they are onboard and ready to work with this system. Once you have everyone in agreement and ready to use it, it becomes infinitely easier to implement this methodology in your business as well.

On the surface Agile Project Management may seem confusing. It may seem as if it demands that you throw out all of your old management skills and adopt new ones. But, once you dig deeper you learn that that is not what Agile Management is about. By embracing Agile Management, you make a declaration of care and commitment to not only your employees but to your clients as well. By adopting Agile practices, you tell a client that the value and quality of their work matter. You show them that their input matters and that what they want ultimately trumps what a team may want to do. Employees in an agile team will see that you are taking their ideas into consideration and tasks and instructions will no longer be "passed down the grapevine." Instead, team members will be a part of small teams that delegate tasks delivered directly from the client. They will learn to trust their team members and they will form a bond that allows them to work diligently, efficiently, and quickly; providing high quality work in a fraction of the time a waterfall management system would.

Agile Management is the management style of the future. Although it does not work for every company, many that put it into practice are successful. With this guide, you know have all that you need to implement it at your business and with your team.

# KANBAN

*The Ultimate Guide to Kanban Lean Methodology for Agile Software Development to learn how to manage your team and improve your efficiency and quality at work.*

By Adam Ross

# Table of Contents

Introduction .................................................................... 161
Chapter 1: Overview of Kanban and In-Depth Details ....... 163
Chapter 2: Types of Kanban Systems ..................................... 172
Chapter 3: Benefits of Kanban ................................................ 175
Chapter 4: The Current Status of Kanban ............................. 181
Chapter 5: The Two-Bin Kanban System ............................... 184
Chapter 6: What Is the Kanban Board? ................................. 187
Chapter 7: What is Personal Kanban and Why You Should Use It .................................................................... 195
Chapter 8: How to Implement A Kanban System Effectively 199
Chapter 9: Project Management and Kanban ....................... 206
Chapter 10: Applying Kanban to Lean Manufacturing ....... 210
Chapter 11: How Can Kanban Help in Forecasting ............. 216
Chapter 12: How to Use Kanban to Improve the Full Value Chain ....................................................................... 221
Chapter 13: How to Apply the Principles of Kanban with Software Development .......................................................... 225
Chapter 14: Introducing Kanban to Your Company ........... 232
Chapter 15: How Kanban Will Change You ......................... 239
Chapter 16: Kanban Challenges .............................................. 243
Chapter 17: Problem-Solving with Kanban .......................... 246
Chapter 18: How to Use Kanban for Continuous Process Improvement? ......................................................................... 251
Chapter 19: Applying A Kanban Process to Workflow in Your Company ....................................................................... 255
Chapter 20: Top Mistakes Made by New Teams .................. 258
Chapter 21: Kanban for Kids at School and Home .............. 262

Chapter 22: The Difference Between Kanban and PAR ........266
Chapter 23: Bringing Kanban into Real Life ..........................271
Chapter 24: Kanban Maturity Model .......................................277
Conclusion..................................................................................293

# Introduction

In this guidebook, we look at the Kanban system and how you implement it into your system. We will look at Kanban and how it is used today, how you can use the different processes, especially with Lean Manufacturing, and how to apply some of the principles of Kanban to the idea of software development.

We can then move over to how Kanban can reduce the risks that you are taking when working on a new software program, how to easily add Kanban to your workflow to save you some time and waste, and how to apply Kanban and implement the digital boards to help with production. There are so many different parts that come with the Kanban system, and they all work to make your business more efficient and better.

This book is your guide to learning the ins and outs of Kanban and how you can implement it successfully into your business. Kanban's simplicity is the major factor in how your team can work together efficiently and produce effective projects in less time and for less money. You may have heard rumors that Kanban is "dead," but what you need to learn is how the world has evolved and implemented Kanban and other methodologies to improve their workplaces and workflows.

Not all industries and organizations are suited to the Kanban system!

When you are ready to learn more about how Kanban works and how you can bring it into any kind of business to save time and money while reducing waste, make sure to check out this guidebook to help you get started.

# Chapter 1: Overview of Kanban and In-Depth Details

## WHAT IS KANBAN?

Kanban is a process control method, which was originally used in the production industry by companies that wanted to better manage their stock and enable production that was just in time.

These days, Kanban is applied to pretty much every industry under the sun but the very first company that used it was Toyota. To date, Kanban is the main project management method for the Japanese car manufacturer.

The entire Kanban process is organized based on a visual board. The board is split between process stages, and each stage has cards with tasks stuck to it. These cards will move through the process stage board as each project is completed.

Kanban believes in transparency almost as much as it believes in waste reduction, and that is precisely why a Kanban board will always be visible to everyone in the room so that all of the team members know exactly what a project manager or other team member is working on. This should not be perceived as a way by which the project manager can micromanage everyone; it is just a way for the entire team to help with the entire process by spotting any kind of flaws and pointing them out for the better of the team as a whole.

Waste elimination is the primary concept behind Kanban, second only to the concept of transparency. The Kanban board, as it was described in the first book of this series, and as it will be briefly reviewed here as well, is all about transparency and providing everyone with the chance to know what everyone else is doing and where the product development process is at any moment.

The main guiding principle behind Kanban is to do as much as you can in as little time as you can. This might seem lazy at first but those who have already applied Kanban to their companies have learned that focusing on the essential steps can improve productivity.

Furthermore, your Kanban reviews should also include a chat with your team members to help you find out what processes work and what processes don't work. Kanban ensures that you can minimize shortages, control inventory, and accomplish higher turns in inventory.

Many different companies have found that the Kanban system can be effective at helping them to reach their goals but this is not always the case. There are five general situations where using the Kanban method is not the best when it comes to delivering materials and these will include:

- The operator responsible in the line for using all materials to make the finished product, has to then turn around during the process to reach the materials.
- Sometimes when you just glance at two or more materials, they will look the same, even though they are different. Getting these materials mixed up in the manufacturing process can sometimes cause some big errors. If this is the case, there needs to be some measures in place to prevent it.
- The rate for completing the product is too short. When there is a lower amount of time to do the work, there is a greater percentage of time that will be required for selecting the part. This is true even if the products are well distinguished from each other and when they are nearby.
- Material usage ends up not being that consistent. When your business is offering a ton of different products but each one of those products has a low volume of demand, then the bins are going to stay full. These materials that aren't used are going to take up space and can cost you a lot of money.
- Your materials need to be traceable. Kanban is not going to allow you to mix up the loose materials into another bin to use in another lot. You must make sure that a record is kept of the lot you use, and then you must document all of the materials that aren't used.

When you are working on a product, you don't need to have just one Kanban Set. To make sure that there is a minimization to material handling and the number of movements that the operators need to work with, and this can open up more space on the production line. The materials that come in at this point are going to have a limited amount of handling because the Kanban Set is placed where it makes the most sense.

## WHAT MAKES KANBAN SO DIFFERENT

Kanban is different in its very nature, in the way it originated (at Toyota), in the way it has spread across multiple industries, and in the way it has been combined with other project management methods.

The main features that set Kanban apart from everything else include the following:

- The product is delivered on an as-needed basis, and there is no set period in which a feature must be completed (like you will find in Scrum, for example). While timely execution and due dates are present in Kanban, they take a different dimension than those in Scrum, for example, and they are determined by actual needs, rather than set deadlines.
- In Kanban, team members start working on a new task only when they have already delivered the one before it.
- Most modifications and changes are made mid-stream in Kanban, which allows for continuous improvement before the project is completed.
- Kanban projects are split in "Cycle Times," which are defined as the total amount of time needed to complete a chunk of a project (e.g. a full feature of the software, for example). The production efficiency is measured through the velocity of each sprint. Every sprint's success is heavily reliant on the previous sprint's success.
- Kanban is best applied to projects that have a wider range of priorities that might change a lot over time (unlike Scrum, which, although Agile too, is best for teams where the priorities don't change as often).
- this is but a brief overview of the features that make Kanban a distinctive project management approach. The features make it a great ally in so many different contexts and situations, so many industries, and so many types of projects.
- This brief overview has mostly compared Kanban with Scrum not because it is the only other Agile project

management method Kanban can be compared to but because it is one of those that frequently comes into the discussion when a project manager decides which methodology is best for their particular team.

Many other things set Kanban apart. Most of them have already been discussed, and some will be (re)approached throughout this book as well, to help you understand in-depth why Kanban is such a great project management method.

## KANBAN RULES

If you want to implement Kanban correctly, you must follow some rules. It is only when you follow these rules that an organization will reach its maximum output.

If every member of the team is not involved in the process, you should avoid using physical or information product. This means that you should take the customers and external suppliers into account. You can never be a top manufacturer if you do not have the top suppliers.

- You must ensure that the suppliers always deliver quality products. You should never accept any defective products, and you should refrain from providing wrong information or the defective product to the customers.
- If you want to implement Kanban, you must ensure that you have the necessary equipment. You should, therefore, apply the Kanban principles in areas where there is total productive management or TPM.
- You should always try to apply the Kanban principles on numbers and products where there are monthly requirements. You should always include processes that require a short setup and have a steady lead-time.
- Both internal and external suppliers should possess or be given some assistance to develop processes or programs that will help to reduce the time it takes to complete some tasks. You can unleash the potential of the Kanban system fully when you can influence the

lead-time and manufacturing capacity through setup times.
- You should remember that customers are the end-users of the product, and therefore, a supplier must deliver the products or materials directly to the customer. If there is some certification pending for some suppliers and further inspection is required, you should train the customers well to perform that inspection. Alternatively, you should replace an uncertified supplier with a certified supplier.
- A Kanban system is never permanent, which means that you can experiment with it. You must always be prepared to make some alterations or adjustments to reduce the workflow or maximize the workflow.

## How to Use the Processes of Kanban?

There are three main parts that come with Kanban. The three elements that come with the Kanban system will include the board, the list, and the card. Essentially, when you use the board you will notice that it contains a list, which is supposed to help create the workflow for the team based on the various cards that are given. Each of these parts of the Kanban system are defined below:

- The board: This is the first part of our Kanban system. This is what holds onto the workflow so that the team can just come and look it over when ready. In the other processes of project management this can be known as the project or the workspace.
- The list: This can also be known as a lane because it is going to contain a series of aligned cards inside of it, usually related to the same part of the production line. It is going to have the title of the column on the board for easy sorting as well. This is often known as the to-do list or the task list with other systems of project management.
- The card: The card is found under a list title on the board. This will be any product that the team needs to create

or any kind of task that they need to get done. These are items that need to get done and can be considered the to-do items or tasks.

You will find that working with a Kanban board can be very versatile, and the way that you apply it to your business is going to be different for every company.

## THE CORE PROPERTIES OF KANBAN

### Workflow Visualization.

To create a good, efficient Kanban board, you must first understand what you should be doing to make sure an item goes from a request (demand) to completion (delivery). Once you understand this, you can create the correct Kanban board and then make adjustments based on your particular situation.

### Limiting the Work in Progress.

This has been discussed before but it is one of the core properties of Kanban, so we will include it here as well. As you may very well know it by this point, limiting the WIP is a very important part of every Kanban process, so you and your team members should try to only work on one item at a time before you move to the next one and pull it into the Work in Progress column.

### Flow Management.

As it was also discussed in this book, Kanban relies a lot on continuous improvement. However, changing things in the workflow just for the sake of change is not an efficient way of tackling the issues. First, you must have a good knowledge of what needs to be changed. This will eventually create a positive change, one that truly affects the team in the best way there is.

### Be Very Clear About Process Policies.

Although Kanban is quite easy to combine with other project management methods and introducing it to your team may feel like a slow change, the truth is that you still need to be very clear about the policies connected to your upgraded process. This will make it easy for the team members to understand why this new method is applied and how it will function from hereon.

### Collaborate to Improve.

You and your team make for a "whole," you are parts of the same process and you should work in collaboration, not only when it comes to assigning tasks but also when it comes to continually improving the process.

## KANBAN BEST PRACTICES

Aside from the basic principles and core properties of Kanban, you should also keep in mind a handful of best practices that will help you successfully embrace Kanban as part of your project management approach.

Here are the **don'ts** of using Kanban in project management:

- Do not overcomplicate the Kanban board. While it is a great idea to adjust the basic Kanban board to your needs and your specific purposes, it is also important to make sure you don't make it look too complicated.
- Do not make your Kanban board too simple either. Indeed, Kanban advocates for simplicity and minimalism but a Kanban board that is too simple can create a lot of confusion as well.
- Don't forget to include the feedback loops too. Feedback is very important in every process, so you should make sure to include it in your Kanban board. Feedback loops can help you perfect the Kanban board by adding or removing columns and tasks, by minimizing the WIP

even more, or by simply adjusting definitions of what a stage of the Kanban board means.

Decide if you want to use a digital board or a physical one. Although it might seem old-school, a physical board can frequently be more beneficial because it will encourage team members to look at it. However, if you have workers that are remotely located, a digital board can work as well.

Start with the simple three-column board we have described earlier in this book. You can adjust later.

Set a clear limit for the WIP and make it clear to your team that you don't want them to exceed that limit.

Allow team members to pull the items they want to work on but do prioritize those that need to be done sooner. Create a process for task prioritization and planning. Explain it to your team members very clearly so that they are fully familiar with it and understand why some tasks are more important than others, as well as why planning happens with a certain cadence.

Kanban can change everything in your company—not by taking it by storm and revolutionizing the processes your teams are already used to but by providing everyone with a method they can use to level up to the maximum efficiency and quality of work. Not only will Kanban improve the way you make your deliverables (more timely, better quality, etc.) but it will also improve the way your team feels at work. By not overwhelming them with too many tasks, your team will be able to flourish in a stress-free environment that promotes growth, leadership, and collaboration.

# Chapter 2:
# Types of Kanban Systems

Many organizations have started to use Kanban systems to improve their productivity. The different types of Kanban systems are listed out in this chapter.

## PRODUCTION KANBAN

This system is made of an exhaustive list of tasks that must be completed to ensure that a product is delivered on time. This system brings in information on different materials and parts that are required along with the information from Withdrawal systems. This system allows the team to start with the production of the product and also explain the services or products that must be produced.

## Withdrawal Kanban

This system is also known as a conveyance or move cards. If any component needs to be transferred from the production Kanban to another type, this system is used for signaling. The cards are connected to different tasks that must be taken to a workplace when they should be completed. Once the tasks are complete, the cards are returned.

## Emergency Kanban

This type of system is used to replace any defective parts or to signal to the entire team that the quantity of a product or service required to be manufactured has either increased or decreased in number. Organizations often use emergency Kanban systems when a particular part of a system has stopped functioning the way it is supposed to or when there are any changes made to the process.

## Through Kanban

Kanban systems comprise both production and withdrawal Kanban systems. These systems are used in situations where both the workstations associated with the two Kanban systems are adjacent to each other.

## Express Kanban

This system is one that comes into the picture when there is a shortage of parts within the system. These systems send signals to the teams to increase the number of parts that are required to complete the process in hand. This system aims to ensure that the manufacturing process or production process is not slowed down. These systems are often called signal Kanban systems since they are used to trigger any shortage or purchase.

## Supplier Kanban

A supplier is an organization or individual from whom another organization sources material to make its products. This system moves directly towards the supplier and is often entered as a representation of the manufacturer.

# Chapter 3:
# Benefits of Kanban

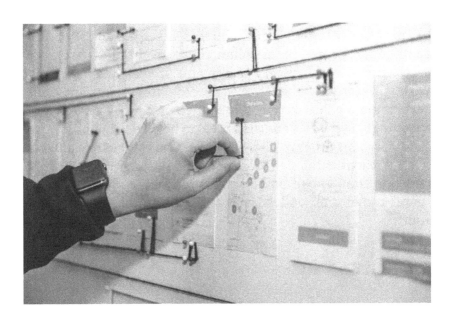

## IMPROVES VISIBILITY

A lot of work that is done in an organization is often under the parapet, and it is essential to make that work visible to the leads of the organization and its customers. This is a core attribute of Kanban. Kanban boards can be used as radiators of information to view the progress of a process and any impediments or bottlenecks in the process at a glance.

## REDUCES CONTEXT-SWITCHING

Kanban prevents teams from overburdening their members using personal WIP limits. Any member can only start another task when that member completes the task that they have committed to deliver. This list of Kanban works on the following principle – 'Stop starting, start finishing.' This system has helped many teams focus and successfully deliver downstream activities.

## IMPROVES COLLABORATION

In most organizations, departments are isolated from one another. There are times when there are battles that exist between software delivery teams and product management. Through Kanban, the teams become integrated into the development value system. Kanban is a pull-based system that encourages synergies and also breaks the walls down between different departments and specializations, which results in cross-departmental collaboration. The transition of work items on the Kanban boards offers teams the opportunity to share knowledge, collaborate and communicate with one another.

## SIMPLICITY

Kanban is getting to be a popular valuable tool. It's extremely great for software jobs of particular kinds. But, there's a threat of false motives behind Kanban adoption.

## USER STORIES DIVERSITY

It's extremely simple to say you cannot split user reports, so iterations must be left-handed. A simple solution isn't the very best one. There's something important behind that you cannot divide tales. Most probably you do not understand how to split tales right. It's fairly difficult at the start and needs creativity.

## BALANCE

Limiting WIP throughout a procedure has multiple advantages. This produces flow in the work's standpoint and retains demand and supply in equilibrium from the group or employee's standpoint. With only a little additional elegance we can readily find equilibrium between different sorts of operational labor and involving operational and advancement work.

Kanban's aid in evolving resilient systems that could provide predictability for many different work item types with a variety of performance expectations (timescales may range from days or hours to months or even longer) is a killer feature.

## COLLABORATION

Building on the arrangement, esteem and client focus, collaboration generates the anticipation that we'll look beyond our own group's bounds in addressing impediments to stream.

The entire version of the practice talks of working methodically in a manner that enhances understanding through monitoring, model-building, experimentation, and dimension.

Learning and alignment have powerful relationships with comprehension. I fully recognize that a solid case could be made for every one of them but I have gone with the one I believe best reflects Kanban's origins in system thinking.

## REDUCES WASTEFUL ACTIVITIES

The Kanban board reinforces some WIP limits that make the system a pull-based system, which allows an organization or team to maintain a reliable number of high-quality ideas that can be delivered within the right timeline. This also helps to eliminate any work that is considered wasteful thereby reducing the number of queues needed to be developed.

## INTRODUCES TRUE SUSTAINABILITY

Kanban processes help multiple teams manage work at a humane, sustainable and smooth pace. This reduces stress, frustration, and lack of commitment thereby increasing employee turnover. WIP limits help to control the pace of a process dynamically thereby fostering creativity.

The teams will never commit to a process initially and break that promise down the road. Teams will be allowed to address and innovate issues in different ways to create solutions that have fewer quality issues.

## IMPROVES QUALITY

For most professionals, the initial quality is an integral part of the successful delivery. Defects can always impact the team's throughput and also help the team tackle any quality issues right from the start, which helps to boost productivity. Many activities such as collaborative analysis and user documentation contribute to high-quality software.

The policies in Kanban software strengthen professional standards that are agreed across different boards including project managers, software items, product managers, business stakeholders, and customers. The software explicitly defines these policies at every stage of the process.

## IMPROVES MORALE

The Kanban software allows many traditional and agile teams to move from pressure and command and control strategies. Every member of the team must build their schedule around the workflow that is organized by the system and not by their managers. Every member of the team is required to deliver work at a rapid, sustainable and steady pace, which helps to create beneficial stress called eustress thereby allowing members to visualize the fruit of their labor. Since Kanban manages the work of every member of a team, the members are less likely to be stressed, and they always get on with their work and unfold their talents and creativity.

## INSTILLS KAIZEN CULTURE

The Kaizen board provides the managers and team members with queues that are controlled and require shorter buffers. A pull-based system helps to expose any bottlenecks, process inefficiencies, impediments, issues with delivery, miscommunication, agency issues, synergies and lack of clarity.

## LIMITING THE WIP (WORK IN PROGRESS)

If you want people to be able to focus on one task at a time, it is of the utmost importance that you limit their Work in Progress. This means that team members should not have too many tasks they are working on at the moment. Ideally, they should only have **one** task to handle. Once that one is done, they can pick up the next, finish that, and then pick up a new one.

Aside from limiting the Work in Progress, Kanban will also help you promote the Minimum Marketable Features. In other words, when you break all the work into small chunks, you get to work on them individually, and each of these tasks is a Minimum Marketable Feature. Each of these MMFs will move independently through the workflow, rather than relying on other tasks to be done.

## INTRODUCES PREDICTABILITY

Kanban was thought to be an information radiator in the past. Through the queues and lists found on the board, Kanban helps a manager predict most issues based on actual or historical data. This reduces the risk of any guesstimate made by a project manager. When improvements are introduced based on actual data, the lead and delivery times improve over time.

There are many benefits to using a Kanban system. An organization will be able to save money and also increase efficiency through the Kanban system. However, there are a few things to keep in mind before setting up the system.

To ensure that the system works best for the team you should understand the strengths and weaknesses of every member in the team and also assess the time taken by each member to complete a specific task. A manager must use that information to build a system and divide the processes between the members of the team.

# Chapter 4:
# The Current Status of Kanban

Kanban development is rumored to be from processes employed in American supermarkets in the mid-1900s. These stores would replenish products in smaller quantities based on their sales. In the 1950s, executives from Toyota came to visit the United States and took notice of the streamlined process in the supermarkets. Today, a lot of the Kanban process is attributed to Toyota's adaptation of this "supermarket" method.

In the 1990s, almost every business and industry was implementing Kanban lean methodology for delivering materials to their manufacturing line. For companies like

Toyota, those that have a manufacturing system with an operator repeating their actions continuously, this was an ideal situation. For other industries, like machine shops or aerospace, this was more of a challenge. These organizations like aerospace and machine shops ended up employing other material delivery systems, like a pick-list or kitting system. Pick-list is a list of materials needed for an order that the operator should gather for production. Kitting is when a manufacturer groups different but connected items into a bin to be assembled into a product.

There are five general situations when a Kanban method may not be the best for delivering materials:

- The operator, or the person on the manufacturing line using the materials to make the product, has to turn around to reach the materials or even walk to get what they need to complete their job. These additional activities create even more waste in the process.
- The rate for product completion is too short. This is called the "takt" time. When there is a limited amount of time, a greater percentage of the time is required for part selection. This is true even if you have the products well distinguished and nearby.
- Material usage is not consistent. When you offer a wide variety of products but each product has a low volume, your bins will stay full. The unused materials are then taking up space and costing you money.
- Materials must be traceable. Kanban does not allow you to mix loose materials into another bin for another lot. You need to keep a record of the lot used and document the materials not used.
- If the traditional Kanban process is not right for all situations, what other choices are there? As mentioned earlier, Kitting and Pick-list are ideas. Kitting; however, is a "bad" word in the Lean community, so instead, think of it as a "Kanban Set." This methodology involves a selection of materials related to the sequence of building a specific product. An AGV or cart would bring the set to the manufacturing line. Because the set would

not be delivered until is it signaled, usually by the return of an empty set or tray, it is considered a "pull" system.

A "pull" system means materials and products are delivered when an order is placed. This type of method is beneficial because it reduces the need for storing inventory. Lower inventory levels and reduced costs are the secondary benefits. The opposite of a "pull" system, is a "push" model. The "push" system is a forecast for inventory needs. The company then manufactures to meet the forecast and then pushes, or sells, it to their customers. The problem with this model is forecasts are typically wrong and results in many leftover products.

A product does not need to have just one "Kanban Set." To minimize material handling and movement, the materials could be chosen in smaller amounts. This process also minimizes the number of materials on the side of the line, which opens up more space on the production line. Materials coming in can have limited handling because the "Kanban Set" is placed in a logical location.

As an alternative to having materials on the line at each workstation, the "pick to light" process can be more efficient for the manufacturer. "Pick to light" is a system designed for fulfilling orders or manufacturing products. Normally the operator scans a barcode that is adhered to a tote or carton. These bins are a temporary holding place for materials. The scan reveals the location for materials so the operator can retrieve the necessary items. When the correct quantity of items is selected the operator presses a button to indicate the activity was completed. The operator continues to refill bins as indicated by this system until all materials are gathered for the manufacturing process.

What people have realized since the 1990s is that Kanban is still relevant, in the right situations. In other scenarios, like the ones mentioned earlier, quality, use of space, and labor inefficiency can result from trying to force a Kanban process where it does not belong. Instead, these situations should consider a "Kanban Set!"

# Chapter 5:
# The Two-Bin Kanban System

Making use of a Kanban system to handle your inventory of manufacturing parts could be a fantastic means to enhance lean production initiatives, and the two-bin technique is just one of the most typical variants of this supply chain administration approach. A strong Kanban approach can decrease stock-outs as well as manufacturing downtime, Also, to boost preparations and also general procedures. The two-bin Kanban system relies upon aesthetic hints to increase the sharp when inventory of specific components like bolts and also course C elements are running reduced so you could get replenishment to prevent manufacturing hold-ups.

## EXACTLY HOW DOES IT FUNCTION?

Manufacturing facility employees have two containers of inventory where they could draw for builds, overcoming one and afterward the various others. The amount in the containers is identified by the preparation to restore and also the uniformity of use. A vacant bin is a trigger to reorder. This consistent procedure is developed to lessen any type of stock-out, which can influence manufacturing, as replenishment is generally taken care of.

While the principle behind this inventory monitoring method is rather simple, there is a great deal of technological subtlety that enters making the system job. Mark Rosenthal, a commercial designer and also writer of the blog site The Lean Thinker, believes that for a two-bin system to operate efficiently, the time it takes to utilize all the components in a container requires to surpass the order and also distribution timetable. Or else, you risk of utilizing all the components in the 2nd bin before replenishment for the very first also shows up.

## WILL THIS CAUSE EXCESS INVENTORY?

As you're making your method via the 2nd bin, the suggestion is the initial will certainly be replenished as well as on-line before you get to completion of your existing inventory. As long as the organizing has been taken care of you will certainly have extra inventory compared to you requiring for a construct, however, you likewise will not have to fret concerning running out. With a two-bin system, you're not likely to have as big of excess, because you're normally operating in smaller sized amounts.

## WHAT VARIABLES ENTER INTO KANBAN PREPARATION?

To guarantee your two-bin system is reliable, you will certainly take into consideration a couple of various elements of inventory and also manufacturing. Oracle detailed a typically made use of computation to figure out the most effective arrangement for the system to work, based upon making use of one Kanban card each bin. The formula considers the variety of Kanban cards (C), the dimension of the Kanban (S), the preparations to renew the inventory (L) and also the day-to-day need for the component (D). The dimension of the Kanban amounts to the number of components you would certainly buy to renew it. If a bin holds 100 components, the Kanban dimension would be 100. The formula Oracle provided to develop a functioning two-bin system is about that when you increase the variety of Kanban cards, minus one, with the dimension of the Kanban, it ought to equate to the preparation increased by the day-to-day need for the component, or (C-1) **S** = **L** D.

# Chapter 6:
# What Is the Kanban Board?

The Kanban board allows teams to visualize the work and the workflow. Teams can use this board to optimize the workflow. If you want to use a physical Kanban board, you can use a whiteboard and sticky notes. These notes will communicate the progress, issues, and status of every task. You can also use online Kanban boards but these are only a refinement of the physical Kanban board.

## CHOOSING A KANBAN BOARD FOR YOUR TEAM

Some teams always want to use a physical Kanban board. This board is either drawn on a wall or a whiteboard, and the team can use sticky notes and Kanban cards to view the workflow. This is something that will work with every team that is located in the want building. This is because every member of the team can interact with the Kanban board and does not have to rely on their colleagues or the management to give them an update. Some teams prefer to use low-tech applications and therefore choose to use the Kanban board. The metrics can always be measured through some manual calculations.

Physical boards are a great way to start with Kanban for teams that are located in the same area or building. That being said, Kanban works best for teams whose work does not intersect.

Teams that are distributed will need to use a virtual Kanban board. The same goes for small teams that trade work between each other and for enterprise organizations that want to expand. A virtual Kanban system will provide the following:

- Real-time accessibility for stakeholders and remote workers
- Additional collaboration features
- A detailed trail that allows stakeholders and remote workers to view the history of a card
- Ability to integrate with different systems to remove duplicate data
- Sophisticated metrics and reporting that will take less time to generate when compared to physical Kanban boards

An enterprise team should always look at virtual Kanban if they want to improve security features and enhance scalability for any pilot project. You never have to switch tools when you need to expand. This will help to improve productivity and reduce the cost that the team will incur.

Regardless of whether your team chooses to use a physical or virtual Kanban board, the board by itself will make your work transparent. This will help you define the status of the project or work at a glance and will also help to optimize the workflow to improve efficiency.

## THE FEATURES OF YOUR KANBAN BOARD

Several different features are found when you are looking at a Kanban board. These function in the same way for the most part, no matter how you choose to implement them. Some features will apply better to the physical version, some do better with the app, and some will work with each one. Let's take a look at these different parts and how they can work together to make the Kanban board as efficient as possible.

## The lists and the boards are filled up with cards that can move.

No matter how you decide to set up your Kanban board, you must make sure that you can move the cards around as easily as possible. The cards are going to be moved around often when you are using this model, as you move them from one side of the board as they get completed. The existing cards that start on the board are going to move more than any of the new ones that you decide to create.

## People are invited to the Kanban board

As with what you will find in other systems for project management, you can invite anyone that you want to this board to help you to make the board work. This means that you can add in the teammates, clients, and collaborators. An invitation can be extended through the app for access to the entire board or only for an individual card. Some apps will only allow you to invite the app members to the board but then there are others that will allow you to enter anyone that you would like into this by entering their name and an email address into the system.

## The back of the card can include notes or any communication that is related to it

Typically, on the backside of your cards, there will be some room for you to add the information that is needed. You will be able to upload any files that are needed, add in a discussion forum, and write out a description for the card where you need it. You can even tag someone in the description or in a comment to make it easier for them to find it.

## Cards will sometimes have checklists and tasks attached to them

Each of the cards that you will work with needs to have a checklist attached to it so that others on the team know what they need to get done with each task. When you are working on a virtual board, the cards need to contain one or more task lists or checklist to ensure that your card is as functional and efficient as possible.

## Limits to the work in progress for that time

For someone new to the Kanban board, taking the time to create an epic task list can be an exciting but sometimes overwhelming process for them to work on. This is why some Kanban boards will provide the team with a way to limit the tasks that can be created in each list and will offer you limits on the work in progress or the WIP's. This restriction can be applied to as much or as little of the board as you would like. When you know the workload that the team can handle regularly, you can set the limits that work best for the team. For example, if your marketing team can produce about three pitches each week, then you would want to make sure there is a limit for Press Pitches don't get above three cards.

## You can label or tag the cards

When you take the time to add a tag or a label to the cards, this means that you can clarify certain details with the card, especially when some of the details can't be determined just by its location on the list. Your administrator, or the app, is going to determine if this is known as tagging or labeling but this will be the same in the Kanban system.

## You can assign some due dates to the cards

It is best if you add in some due dates to these cards to ensure that things get done and to make sure that no one is going to get off-topic or run into trouble. When there isn't one of these due dates on the card it will probably not get done. Deadlines can be a pain but they are essential to getting the task done.

### View a calendar with the cards.

Another benefit that comes to the Kanban cards, especially if you are using the electronic app, is that it is going to offer all the people on your team a seamless calendar view that is related to the board. When you are using this in the app, you can go back and forth between the cards and the calendar view with just a few clicks.

## HOW TO IMPLEMENT THE DIGITAL BOARDS OF KANBAN FOR PRODUCTION?

When you are working on your Kanban board, remember that simplicity is important. When you are looking at some of the digital boards that are out there, many come with a ton of different features and cool things for you to try out. And while these can be beneficial in some processes, there are also times when they are just going to take up too much of your time, or they will end up distracting you. In some cases, these features are just going to make things so complicated that it ensures the Kanban board is too difficult to work with.

You do not want to end up overcomplicating the board at all. This is supposed to be a method that adds in some more simplicity to your business and how the various processes of production are done. If you place too much information on the board, this is just going to make it too complicated and can slow down the process. Your team members will run into issues knowing what parts of the board to pay attention to, bottlenecks will occur, and more.

You need to be able to strike a good balance between simplicity and making sure that all the right parts are on the board. You need to find a way to get in the information that is needed so everyone knows where they are in the project or what they need to work on but not so complicated that they are constantly confused and don't know what they need to get started on.

## How can I set up a digital Kanban board?

While each program is going to be a little bit different, you will find that it is pretty much the same when it comes to setting up a Kanban board for your needs. Some of the steps that you will need to follow to set up your successful Kanban board digitally include:

- Determine which of the software systems for Kanban that you would like to use for the digital board. There are a few different options available, so do a little bit of research online and see which one is going to suit your needs the best.
- Begin with the basic setup of your board. You may need more columns and lists later on but keep it simple here. Have three lists that are titled to do, doing, and done, and then add on as you need later.
- Figure out how many WIP's that you can take on at a time, and then limit the rest. You will have to know how your team works to come up with this one effectively. If you take on too many tasks for your team at the same time, you will end up crushing them and can make everyone fall behind.
- Allow your team to feel empowered to choose the items they want to work on. They can then choose what items work the best for them based on their abilities. This is part of the foundations of the pull system, and it is one of the biggest benefits that come with many of the agile methodologies, so it works well with Kanban.
- Organize the planning and prioritizing of steps. You can use demand to prioritize each item and then from this, you can select items to help you get the work done in the right order.

After you have gone through and done the initial setup of the digital board, you can then put it to work. During this time, take the time to observe the needs of the company and then make the necessary adjustments to the board. Consider looking online sometimes so that you can get some new ideas on how other companies are making adjustments to the board and see if any of these ideas can make you more efficient.

## TIPS YOU CAN USE TO DEVELOP YOUR KANBAN DIGITAL BOARD

### The good list

To determine if your list is going to be a good one with your digital Kanban board, you need to be able to check off a few items. If you are missing one of the items in this, then you need to go through and make a visit with your planning process again to ensure that you are using the right board for your product and your team. When you are working with a digital Kanban board, you want to make sure that this board can check off all of the items below:

- Did you choose to use a physical format or a digital format, based on the workflow for your company and the things that your team needs?
- Do you have the minimum number of columns? Many companies can get away with just using the three that we talked about earlier. But some companies may find that they do need to add in some extra columns.
- Do all of your tickets apply to the present workflow while also embodying the complete process at the same time?
- Are all of the tickets that you are working on considered high level? This means that you took the time to represent the whole story and the major tasks that need to be done to complete the projects, rather than writing down every little task that needs to be done.
- Did you make sure that the items placed in the backlog have a direct link back to the ticket so that you can pull this information up as you need?
- Did you name the tickets with the right label so you know what they are all about?

- Did you take the time to provide clear conditions for the definition of to-do and the definition of done?
- Did you take the time to balance out your workflow? You can do this by handling any of the showstoppers and bottlenecks, limiting the WIP and more.
- Did you reject items that didn't end up meeting the standard that you had placed? If you don't meet the standard, then this can refer to the items of poor quality or overly large products or outputs that do not fulfill the definition of done.
- Did you assign a team member to a task that is placed on the doing list? If you don't have enough time or enough team members for this item, then it needs to head on back to the to-do column.
- Do you have a system in place that will make it easier to figure out if the items that have been moved to the done columns are items that are done?

This is often going to depend on your business and what all needs to happen to get the project all the way done. You may add in some testing to the process to ensure that the product is ready to set up to do well with the customer. You don't want to add in too many columns here because this can make the whole system a mess. But adding in three or four, and maybe a few more will ensure that you can handle each of the parts of the system and that everyone on the team knows where in the process they are for each task.

# Chapter 7:
# What is Personal Kanban and Why You Should Use It

For anyone looking to use Kanban in their personal life, there are great methods that can work for you on a personal basis. You might think that Kanban is great for some businesses but you wonder if Kanban could help in the flow of your real life, far away from the workplace.

Notwithstanding, on the off chance that we can expand your points of view a tad, you will see how utilizing personal Kanban can be valuable for individuals who are simply searching for a superior method to deal with their general life like organizing chores and errands around the house.

With the correct structure, you can make and deal with your special individual Kanban plan. Kanban is an extremely helpful asset when hoping to improve the utilization of your time. Planning can help you make the most of your day.

Kanban isn't just an extremely successful tool to use in your life; it very well may be depended upon as a strong method for completing things like managing the house or manning a garden or your DIY projects.

Life can sometimes be surprisingly complex and this is the reason knowing how to oversee and assemble a plan for personal Kanban can be so imperative: it'll help guarantee that won't overcome yourself with every one of the things going ahead in the meantime. It will help you organize your life in a way that works for you.

So on the off chance that you took every one of your assignments, kept in touch with them, and partitioned them between to-do, doing and done, wouldn't it be much less demanding to monitor what is it you assumed as a liability, what can you at present do an interpretation of, and do all the while, and prevent yourself from beginning a 10 tasks but only finishing a couple.

In our life, we manage due dates for charges, installments, a wide range of exercises with decided time allotments to be done, so you have to ensure you are dependable on time.

On the off chance that you include things like managing a wellness administration of eating regimen and standard working out, taking youngsters to after-school exercises and so forth and even simply dealing with your home can wind up overpowering without the assistance of a savvy, straightforward and viable individual Kanban procedure!

Personal Kanban is a weekly structure that you follow for yourself and afterward take after to the letter (or as much to the letter as you can), guaranteeing that you'll always remember an undertaking or you invest the majority of your energy endeavoring to juggle such a significant number of various things while it makes you feel lost!

With the correct sort of arranging you can without much of a stretch expel the greater part of the standard anxieties and strains in your endeavors to deal with the present current life, helping you enhance timekeeping and efficiency.

With the correct prep and the correct learning, you can utilize your essential individual Kanban procedure for pretty much anything. Dissimilar to other individual instruments that you can attempt to use to help efficiency, however, you will find that an individual Kanban can be utilized as an individual method to enhance your life. Attempting to chop down the time it takes to complete the shopping with the goal that you can get your youngest kid to their soccer practice? At that point, you ought to consider utilizing individual Kanban as an approach to enable you to deal with your schedule.

## FOR WHAT REASONS SHOULD I UTILIZE PERSONAL KANBAN?

The principle motivation to attempt and utilize Personal Kanban, however, is because it encourages you to imagine and prepare. Pick the most ideal approach to meet your requirements, either a physical Kanban board or an online instrument. If you begin arranging and sorting out yourself, isolating work undertakings, home errands and individual assignments you will find that it turns out to be substantially simpler to begin doing (and completing) those assignments when they are altogether classified and separated regarding achievement, profitability, and planning.

You might figure exactly how difficult it very well may be to set up this for yourself and perhaps with the assistance of a little visual guide you can make it less demanding on yourself when you need to attempt and hold things within proper limits and guarantee that you are in good shape pushing ahead.

Another great thing about using Kanban personally is that it will allow you to measure your work in advance. This great for anyone that likes to stay organized. An immensely preferred standpoint of utilizing an individual Kanban as quickly remarked above is that it will enable you to confine the measure of work you disregard or desert as a work in advance. With the assistance of an individual errand administration device, it before long turns out to be considerably less demanding to set up an arrangement that enables you to continue enhancing specifically.

# Chapter 8:
# How to Implement A Kanban System Effectively

Below are rules, guidelines, and considerations necessary for a successful Kanban system implementation. Before you begin the process of implementation, consider the following.

A Kanban process can be:

- A device to communicate from the operation last conducted to the usage point. Or, from the supplier to the customer.
- P.O.'s provided to your suppliers.
- Orders for work to your areas of manufacture.
- A tool for visual communication.
- A method for reducing paperwork.

A Kanban system should not be used for:

- Batch or lot or single-item production. Something you only create a few times a year should not be managed with a Kanban process.
- Stock designed or used for safety purposes.
- Inventory held by a supplier. For example, consignment or dropshipping is not appropriate for a Kanban system. This situation is not considered a "win-win" lean situation.
- A tool to plan long-term. Traditional management methodologies are best for situations like introducing new products, changes to a customer's usage, and changes in engineering.

To start, within your company, select one area to implement a Kanban system. Begin implementation with less than eight items in this area. Alert your business regarding the implementation and answer questions they raise about how the methodology works. Once the initial implementation is successful and smooth in the one area of your organization, consider adding more areas or items to the process.

## TRYING OUT KANBAN

If you are interested in implementing the Kanban process in your business but want to test it out first, below are some ideas on how to start small before applying it to your whole company or department:

- Use a Kanban board for your to-do list
- Customize a calendar for editorial content
- Create a space to house ideas and content for projects
- Share a plan of action with teammates or clients
- Follow a sales funnel
- Develop a tracking system for applicants to streamline your hiring process

## Guidelines for Successful Implementation

Before implementing a Kanban process:

- A reduction is arranged. If this is ignored then the typical process, a "batch production," continues because the sizes of orders are still large.
- Production and requirements are uniform or level. Kanban can work for complex situations but when it is early in the implementation phase it is best to begin with more uniform requirements.
- Suppliers outside your organization need to be certified. The history of the supplier's outside quality is the reason for not requiring the inspection of their deliveries. This way "on hold" or "rejected" deliveries do not prevent the workflow.
- Choose a bright color for any Kanban related container, cart, or tote and paint them all. Vibrant green is a good choice if you are stuck on what to choose. This allows all members of your organization to recognize a Kanban tool, especially during the implementation phase.

## The Rules for Implementing a Kanban Process in Your Organization

Your customers, suppliers, stakeholders, and entire organization need to be involved in your implementation. Do not even try to launch a Kanban process without their knowledge. Anyone that adds value to the chain of production needs to be included. After all, these are the people that support and report your company as a revolutionary. They must be a part of the revolution, too.

The source is the origination point for quality. Customers should never receive a defective product or poor information. Immediate correction is required. Otherwise, you risk losing your customer's pipeline.

Support equipment must be reliable. Choose an area to implement a Kanban system where there is TPM or Total Productive Maintenance.

Lead times and setup should be short. Requirements for delivery should occur evenly every month. This means a Kanban system should be focused on parts and products that are consistent. Reduce setup and efforts to minimize the lead-time for raw materials for items that differ each month according to the requirements of the customer.

Programs to reduce setup at the supplier level, whether external or internal, should be developed. If they do not have their program in place, you should assist them with one. Lead times and the capacity to manufacture should not be influenced by the time required to set up. That is the only time when a Kanban process should be implemented.

Customers should receive the supplier's materials directly. Non-certified suppliers, or those that still require inspection upon delivery, require the usage point to do the inspection. If this is not possible, then a certified supplier should replace the option in use.

Trial and error are necessary to find how it will work best for your company. This is because nothing is fixed. When there are changes to the level of sales or containers or cards are reduced because activities are continuously improved, you need to be ready to make changes to your system. This is especially important during the implementation stage of the Kanban system.

## STEPS TO SUCCESSFULLY IMPLEMENT KANBAN

You can successfully implement Kanban in many business processes. All you need to do is follow the steps given in this section:

## Set Up the Kanban Board

The Kanban tool is used to visualize the work and the workflow. This will allow the team to optimize the flow of work. If you use a physical Kanban board, you can communicate any issues, progress, and the status of tasks using sticky notes.

## Visualize the Work

The first thing you need to do is break the workflow down right from the initial point until the job is complete. You can break the workflow into simple steps. For every step, draw a column on the board. Now, obtain some sticky notes and note down all the necessary tasks in separate sticky notes. You can use different-colored notes for different tasks. Place these stickers on the whiteboard, and shift the tasks from the left of the board to the right until you chart the workflow.

## Put a Limit on WIP

When teams juggle with many tasks at once, they will make some errors that will affect the quality of work. Kanban is a system that revolves around maintaining the workflow and eliminating the waste. To do this, you should impose some limits on every column where some work is being done. When you put in WIP limits, you will ensure that your team members will work toward completing their work on time while eliminating different types of waste.

## Pull Production Instead of Pushing

There will be some friction among team members. This is especially true when one member works better than another and can generate more work when compared to other members. If you want to solve this, you should ensure that you use the pull system. In this system, the team will only work at a time when it is ready to work. You can implement the pull system by adding some limited buffer between the various teams involved in the process.

## Improve through Adaptation and Monitoring

You should always use a cumulative flow chart since that is the best way to measure performance when you implement Kanban. You should always mark the tasks that are in every column or at any part of the workflow. This will ensure that every team member is aware of how the work is flowing. The team can also gather insights into how it has performed by showing past performance. This will also help the team predict future results.

## WHAT TO CONSIDER BEFORE YOU IMPLEMENT KANBAN

As mentioned earlier, a Kanban system is a lean information tool, which helps to control the workflow. If you want to implement Kanban in your business, you should consider the following things:

- A Kanban system will use some visual communication tools that will help teams maintain transparency.
- Suppliers will consider any signals as purchase orders.
- A Kanban system can also be thought of as a work order that will help to improve the manufacturing process.
- Kanban systems are crucial since they eliminate all paperwork!
- You should avoid using Kanban in the following instances:
- If your firm only has a batch or single productions, you should avoid using Kanban.
- A system where any supplier is expected to carry some inventory along with any other carrying costs. For example, any inventory scheme that also includes consignments should not use Kanban since that is now a win-win situation.
- Safety stock.
- Any tools for long-range planning.
- The prerequisites for the implementation of Kanban are uniform production and setup reduction. You cannot

bring the size of orders down if you do not have setup reduction in place.
- You should always try to paint any reusable containers including totes and carts. You should try to use fresh and visible colors. When you do this, you can make the Kanban initiative visible to every member of the organization when you launch Kanban. Your team also has the opportunity to identify when a container or signal is not in order.
- When you implement Kanban, you should certify all the external suppliers. The objective is to avoid having to inspect the deliveries of those suppliers who are certified. This is because you are aware of the quality of their products.
- You should always make use of Kanban supermarkets. These markets are an intermediate storage space. This market is between the suppliers and the customers who purchase from those suppliers and is at a customer level.

# Chapter 9:
# Project Management and Kanban

Most organizations that have used Kanban as a tool for project management will associate project management with visual management.

Nobody in the organization, including the project manager, will have an idea of what is going on in a process if he or she does not have a visual representation of the process available. Therefore, project management is a way of organizing the steps that need to be fulfilled before the goal of the project is reached.

## How does Kanban help

- With Kanban, work can be assigned and shared between team members. Each of the members is expected to manage their workload based on their priorities and preferences.

- Every member's assignments can be looked at easily and a sketch can be made to understand the problems that the member may face while working on the process.
- If there is a visual record of the processes, it becomes easier to understand if new employees are needed to share the workload. It also becomes easier to understand if a member needs to be guided.
- Individual and team efficiencies can be identified and measured using the metrics on the Kanban board. It is best to use digital systems since they do the calculations for you reducing the amount of work that would need to be put in.
- Every member of the team gains insights into what process the organization follows and also makes the role of every member easy to understand.

## COMMON MISTAKES MADE BY PROJECT MANAGERS

Project managers often make the mistake of micro-managing people. They take the feeling of empowerment and control from their employees leading to a lack of responsibility. People may also feel that they are not required to work on the processes to achieve the final goal.

Every team should ensure that it is self-organized. The members of the team should plan their work based on their final goal. They should not look at a step-by-step path. If a project manager micro-manages his team, he is wasting his time and his team's time.

## WHAT DO YOU GAIN BY USING ONLINE PROJECT MANAGEMENT TOOLS?

If a project manager uses online tools, he will be able to identify which member is busy or free and also assess the status of every process or task. These tools will save time since they provide the manager with an idea of how the work is shared, reviewed or commented.

It is best to use online tools like Kanban since the manager will cut down on the time spent on meetings and communication. Many companies turn to online project management since they work in large teams that are distributed across different locations.

## WHY IS KANBAN SO EFFECTIVE?

The simplicity of the tool is what makes it so effective. Teams and managers can list any tasks in the backlog on the to-do section of the board and choose tasks that need to be focused on right now. They will not have to worry about missing out on some tasks because of the workload.

There is also a sense of satisfaction and achievement when a card is moved from the to-do list to the done list on the board. This is a simple way to visualize the tasks that are complete and the tasks that are still in progress.

## WHAT MAKES KANBAN VERSATILE

Kanban tools can be used in multiple departments and different ways since it is a simple tool. There are very few processes where Kanban won't be applicable. Most organizations work with processes that can be envisioned, making a hectic day easier and seem more organized.

The manager and the members of the team can plan their work and also understand if everything is under control using the

Kanban board. If the manager is stressed, all he or she needs to do is look at the board and calm down.

## HOW DOES VISUAL THINKING HELP IN PLANNING?

It is believed that most people think visually even if they are not intending to. Visual thinking helps to bring order and to build a structure to constantly interrupted and disorganized thought processes.

This is true since most businesses, regardless of the size, appreciate the value that visual management and planning bring to the organization. This is proven when one looks at smaller teams. When smaller teams within an organization begin to perform effectively, the organization will look for more teams to use visual project management. As the knowledge of Kanban spreads through the market, more people wish to incorporate the tool in their business.

If any team is looking to increase productivity, take a look at the following points below:

- Avoid multitasking since it is more of a hindrance. Although, there are some occasions where you will need to multitask.
- Always take breaks since you will feel better and will be able to work more effectively.
- Always finish the most difficult tasks first. It is best to have a day that gets easier by the hour.
- Switch your phone off or switch it to silent when you are working.
- Do not call for too many meetings.

# Chapter 10: Applying Kanban to Lean Manufacturing

Lean manufacturing and the Kanban process are often considered a natural pair. When a manufacturer wants to remove or reduce waste in their process, they use a methodical approach, which classifies them as "Lean." Because Kanban is a method for systematically replacing materials when needed, it is obvious why the two work well together.

Any time that a company wants to work on removing some of the waste that is in their processes, they are often going to use what is known as a methodical approach, which means that they are now going to be classified as Lean. Because Kanban is also a method that allows you to systematically replace any materials on the line as needed, it is obvious why the two can often go together.

## THE FUNCTION OF INVENTORY MANAGEMENT IN A KANBAN ENVIRONMENT

There is a balance that the Kanban system looks to achieve between having the least amount of inventory possible and functioning at full capacity. This simple concept introduced by a supermarkets restocking process led to the introduction of Toyota's 6 principles of an efficient system:

1. The downstream remove materials in the exact amounts outlined by a Kanban system. "Downstream" can refer to customers, line operators, or anyone coming into contact with supplies or materials.
2. The upstream delivers materials in the exact amount and succession outlined by a Kanban system. "Upstream" can refer to the supplier, manager, or materials handler.
3. Movement or production does not happen without a Kanban task.
4. Every moment and every material should be part of a Kanban list or card.
5. The proceeding downstream should never receive incorrect or defective materials from their direct upstream.
6. The quantity of Kanban processes being used prudently lowers the levels of inventory while also improving the identification of problems in the current process.

Also, the inventory being utilized is aligned with the need for that inventory. "Pulling" is often the term applied to this concept. A signal is sent when a certain material is exhausted. This signal tells the supplier it is time to send more products and consequently an order is tracked in the cycle for replenishment. This simple method also tracks the frequency of necessary restocking. Cards or bins are used to signal the need for refilling specific products.

In Lean manufacturing, bins are a popular method for tracking. A bin process provides a visual indication to start the process of restocking. An operator or employee is given two bins to work from. They are to pull materials from the first bin until it is exhausted, and then they move to the second bin. When the employee moves to the second bin, the first empty bin sends a signal to the line manager to reorder materials. In an efficient system, the employee will be replenished with materials before the second bin is depleted. To decide how many materials should be placed in a bin, first determine how long it will take the supplier to deliver materials and then how long it takes for your operator to deplete one bin.

## THE BENEFITS OF USING KANBAN AND LEAN TOGETHER

There are a lot of great benefits that can happen when you use Kanban, and when you use Lean. But when you combine these, the benefits are going to expand out even more.

They can work to lower the levels and the costs of inventory. The amount of workspace that is available will increase when there isn't as much inventory cluttering up the area. And when you only keep the amount of inventory around that you need, it can help to save money. The business will not have to waste money purchasing materials that they won't use.

The need in these systems is going to be determined by how much customer demand is sent out. When the products and the materials are exhausted, you get a better idea about which products are selling the best. If the product rarely needs to have its parts restocked, then this means the customer demand for that product is low, and you may need to spend more time working with other products.

Production is to deliver, rather than a store. The line is going to just receive the material items that it needs the most. This means that you can get more storage space freed up, which then makes room for assembly.

The progress reports on how things are going will reach the managers organically. If your company is using Kanban to help monitor how the process is going, you will then be able to get the analytics that you need to see how the whole process is going.

These systems can decrease how much archaic inventory is there. When your company has a lot of excess inventory around, it is going to cost a lot of extra consideration and work for the manufacturer.

Overproduction won't occur with these systems. When you use the pulling system that is found in Kanban and in Lean, then you will find that the materials are only going to be brought out when they are needed. Necessity is going to be determined based on the customer demands for a product. This results in no excess around, which can make you more efficient and saves money.

## PROS AND CONS OF KANBAN IN LEAN MANUFACTURING

For lean manufacturing, using a logical process for inventory monitoring and customer demand fulfillment makes rational business sense. That is why the Kanban system makes so much sense for this type of application. Despite it being a sound pairing, some considerations must be addressed before a concrete process can be implemented. Recognizing the several pros and possible cons for Kanban lean manufacturing allows your business to implement a Kanban process effectively.

### Pros of using a Kanban Inventory Management Process in Lean Manufacturing

- **It lowers the costs and levels of inventory.** Work space is increased when there is less inventory cluttering the area. Also, providing the minimum quantity of inventory saves money. The business does not purchase materials that will not be used.

- **Need is determined by the demands of the customer.** When materials and products are exhausted, you can identify best-selling products. If a product hardly ever needs new parts restocked, you can assume it has a low demand by your customer.

- **Production is to deliver, not to store**. The line only gets the materials necessary to deliver what is needed. The saved storage space now opens more room on the line for assembly. Also, fewer mistakes are made in grabbing incorrect products because they are being stored on the floor and not a storeroom.

- **Progress reports reach managers organically**. If your company is using Kanban software or apps to monitor the process, many provide analytics to illustrate the volume of products being constructed and the time frame required for completion.

- **Decreases archaic inventory**. Excess inventory causes a lot of extra work and consideration for a manufacturer. In addition to finding storage space for it, the company must determine how long to hold on to it, and what to do when it comes time to get rid of it.

- **Overproduction rarely occurs.** Pulling only happens when materials are needed. Necessity is determined by the demands of the customer. This process means that all the products are selling, and no excess is created.

## Cons of using Kanban's Inventory Manufacturing Process in Lean Manufacturing

Before jumping headfirst into a Kanban inventory management system, you need to do a few things that take time and consideration. First, you must observe the number of materials already being used. This will tell you the number of stock needed for reordering. This observation can take a large amount of time, depending on your products. This means bins and material levels in the bins will fluctuate as you respond to the patterns and needs. This observational period can slow down production. Production can also be delayed if you do not factor delivery time properly for restocking bins. Consider a bin filled with seven materials. The line takes about 14 days to deplete the bin. This means the supplier will need to deliver more stock between 10 to 12 days. Otherwise, your production will lag. It is common to have these types of delays or fluctuations during the initial observation and implementation period.

# Chapter 11: How Can Kanban Help in Forecasting

It is surprising how organizations still apply practices of shamans and clairvoyants to predict the future. They believe that they can use big data to understand the behavior of the customers and the market. But the truth is that organizations trust their development teams to give them the right estimates. Instead, an organization can use Kanban boards to obtain estimates based on actual data and statistics.

## HOW TO CREATE KANBAN PREDICTIONS?

One of the greatest features of Kanban is that it allows you to not just estimate deliverables but predict them. There is a difference in nuance between the two terms: The first is more relaxed and approximate, while the latter allows you to get closer to the actual reality of the fact, enabling you to plan more accurately and stick to your plan with ease.

Planning and predictions are crucial regardless of what project management method you may choose to embrace. The reason they are so crucial is that sooner or later you **will** have to inform others, such as upper management and team members, on where the production process is and where it goes. Predicting this ahead of time will help you, your managers, and your team spot any kind of workflow and efficiency mistakes and fix them before it's too late and delivering the product must be delayed.

Furthermore, no matter what type of company you work in and no matter what industry, you will most likely have to synchronize with other teams as well. Planning and predicting your workflow and your deliverables correctly will help the other teams you collaborate with to plan and predict their workflow so that you all work together harmoniously and efficiently.

To be able to plan everything properly, you must start with a correct estimation of how much time is needed for each of the tasks. You can figure out this number by comparing it with other similar tasks on other projects, by asking each team member how much they honestly think it will take for something to be done, and by putting all of the information together.

Furthermore, it is also important to make sure you schedule your planning correctly as well. Too much planning might be a waste of time and resources, while not enough planning can lead to issues—including your company's inability to deliver a product according to the client's needs.

It is easy to estimate the time an individual may take to complete a task since there is some data to back the estimate. It is a very different thing to estimate the time it will take a system to move a task from the initial point to the delivery point.

If someone asks, "When do you think it will be done by?" they mean to ask you "When do you think the product will be in the production state?"

No member in the organization has a clue and they often guess or lie about the time. There are instances when an organization has both lied and guessed. It is dangerous to make an estimate, and sometimes a waste of time since the estimate is being calculated using the wrong data. The organization must take time to investigate data before making a claim. However, they do not have the time or resources to do so.

You should remember that predictability does not increase when one makes a prediction. The capability of any system is not affected by an estimate made on how long it will take for a team to complete a task. You should remember that predictability is a property of the system. If an organization fails to realize that, it will never be able to predict the behavior of the system.

The Kanban software does not make a promise or commit to a delivery date based on uncertain factors. Kanban offers a commitment to each class of service and allows the organization to commit to regular delivery, transparency, continuous improvement of quality and lead-time.

## Develop your Kanban system

The first step would be to design a proper and structured Kanban system. You must understand the demand, delivery, boundaries of the system, different categories of work, policies, classes of service and other attributes. If an organization wants to create a predictable system, it must identify the start and final point of a process. It is within these boundaries where you can make your estimates.

## Adopt the principles and practices

The organization must adopt the four principles and six practices of the Kanban tool. These allow the delivery systems to become predictable over time.

## Understand Variability

Predictability can be improved using Kanban tools by reducing any variability within the system. Lead Time Histograms, Lead Time Scatterplots, and Cumulative Flow Diagrams are the best way to understand how the system is performing and detect the areas that need to be improved.

Variability is considered to be a necessary evil and is required if an organization wishes to innovate processes but not to the point that the process is fully unpredictable.

You should allow for some level of variability in the initial stages of the process but not in the development stage of the process.

## FORECASTING

Depending on how an organization uses Kanban, it will be able to forecast some work items three to four weeks after implementing Kanban. If the implementation is effective, the organization can also forecast some full projects. Let us take a look at how this can be done.

### Forecasting of Single Features

Most companies tend to push processes into development lines under the assumption that these processes will be done eventually. They do not understand the capability of the members in the development team. These companies forget that the system becomes slower when the pipeline is clogged with many development tasks leading to undue stress and many errors.

Unless some data is collected using a predictable system, the organization cannot end this vicious cycle. Customers and stakeholders will continue to ask for estimates when they realize that the organization has stopped delivering on time. Development teams will continue to lie and the tasks are pushed between departments in the hope that at least something will eventually get done. This creates a slower and unpredictable system which makes the business or operations team push more work into the pipeline.

## **Forecasting of Multiple Features**

Troy Magennis, on his website www.focusedobjective.com, has developed many tools that will help an organization monitor and predict the development of software and other products. His website contains many resources that can be used for free.

# Chapter 12:
# How to Use Kanban to Improve the Full Value Chain

Kanban systems are perfect for organizations, teams, and teams within teams since it is a collaborative method. It is for this reason that the boards can work for any department in a business and the business as a whole.

## HUMAN RESOURCES AND ONBOARDING

The internal processes, especially HR processes benefit from the use of Kanban boards since they can organize every task at hand. An example of such a process could be the hiring process.

There are times when a single board cannot handle the number of applicants. In such instances, Kanban project management software can be used. The software will not only keep track of the board and the cards on the board but it will also keep track of individual applicants.

HR must deal with many internal processes such as onboarding. Since these processes have workflows, they can be dealt with quickly using a Kanban board. For instance, a visual aid can be made to track any new acquisition and see if they have been trained. Kanban boards work well with the short-term projects that the HR and Learning and Development Teams must work on throughout the year.

### Purchasing

Businesses that rely on incoming shipments can use Kanban cards and boards to keep track of the products that are coming and going out. They can also keep track of when the products are coming in. A Kanban board contains cards that allow every individual in the department to know the status of individual shipments.

A Kanban board offers the department members a quick overview of what is happening with the shipment, which reduces the need to check the files every day to know the progress.

This increases productivity and also allows every individual in the team to know when they can expect the delivery of the product. For shipments that have already reached the premises, the board can identify where the products are being unloaded and how they are going to be distributed.

### Development Department

Any business with a product development department will benefit from the use of Kanban systems because of its collaborative nature. A Kanban system allows for a project to be completed quickly and efficiently. Regardless of whether it is a project, web development or software team, a Kanban board can help facilitate the processes since the team will be able to visualize how the process will progress right from the beginning to the end. The system can be used for multiple reasons but at the heart of the Kanban system, it is a project management tool. It is essential to remember that Kanban was started in Toyota to facilitate the manufacturing process. The development, production, manufacturing, assembly and supply departments of the company used this system.

## SALES

As a tracking and visualization tool, Kanban boards help the sales department keep track of the progress made. The department needs to track every aspect of the sale, right from the lead to the end of the deal. Apart from this, the board can help the department keep track of any post-sale activity including feedback and issues.

Since all the information is available as an image, it becomes more comfortable for the department to improve the process for future sales. This will help businesses work on the sales methods and also help the team understand what works for their department and how they can capitalize on that.

A Kanban board helps members on the sales team to identify the leads that have moved to the next stage of the process. These leads can be color-coded depending on their movement across the board. This gives the team more information about how leads can be converted into potential customers.

## MARKETING

A Kanban board can do a lot for a marketing department and marketing in general. Every marketing strategy comprises many methods and it does get difficult to keep track of the different methods. These are some important things that the marketing department must do and they must work together. The Kanban board helps to organize the different efforts that the marketing team must make into a more cohesive list of tasks.

## Customer Support

Kanban systems and boards can help the customer support team deal with customer queries or complaints quickly. The team must deal with customers and respond to them as quickly as they can and assist them. Customers may want to send in queries, feedback or complaints at any given time.

If the department uses Kanban systems, any request via email or phone can be turned into a card and that card can be placed at the top of the board. When the team sees the card, the card must be moved to the next stage immediately.

This will ensure that things keep moving along and everybody in the team is aware of how a request from the customer is being handled.

## Helpdesk and IT

Support tickets often overwhelm and flood any help desk. A Kanban board can organize those tickets in order of priority and move them along the board. If a Kanban software is used, the tickets can be ordered based on the priority using color codes. Individuals in the team who are adept at handling such requests can pick the cards.

This process also allows the help desk to identify more significant issues and see what can be done to curb such issues. If many people have the same problem, the department can identify what can be done better to improve performance and reduce errors. The Kanban system can also be used to identify a problem.

# Chapter 13:
# How to Apply the Principles of Kanban with Software Development

Software development is an industry that has used a large variety of philosophies of project management for many years now but this is going to raise the question about why you would choose to work with the system of Kanban rather than some of the other methodologies, like SCRUM.

One of the amazing things that can be said about the Kanban system is that the pull system came from what was used in supermarkets at the time, and then was adapted to a car manufacturing company, and it can even be used to help out companies who work with software development to create products that are high-quality and can even reduce your risks. The biggest difference is that instead of pulling out materials from the bins, the Kanban agile project management system in software management is that it is going to improve your organizational output.

You will find that the throughput is going to be improved in the software system by:

- Reducing the work in progress or the WIP.
- Each of the phases of development will be observed in an unassuming manner.
- The organization will be able to improve their predictability through reports and metrics.
- There will be a minimal amount of impact with it, which is going to result because the steps for change are incremental, evolutionary, small, and continuous.
- Capacity to self-manage is going to be developed when you motivate and increase the opportunities that the teams have.
- The actual manage of the tasks and the knowledge of work processes is promoted through the team instead of just with the management.
- The risks and any of the issues that the team must face are going to be discussed rationally and objectively.

All of these are going to be accomplished by the actions that will occur naturally when you are following the process of Kanban.

## THE RULES TO REMEMBER WITH KANBAN

When you are ready to take the Kanban system and you want to implement it in with software development, there are going to just be three requirements that need to come into play and these include:

- The production needs to be visual. This means that the cards or the tasks need to be created so that the work can be divided. The cards can then be added to the board. Then the board is going to contain some lists that are presented in the individual columns. The cards that are located in a column will be there in order of priority.
- Each part of the production is going to try and minimize how much work in progress, or WIP, is there. This means that you will minimize the amount of work that

you are doing at the same time so that the team can focus on getting one task done, and can do so more efficiently.
- You will shorten the amount of time that you spend on the process. This will be able to do this by determining the amount of time that it takes to work on each part, and then working to reduce the time that it takes by eliminating waste.

## KANBAN VS. OTHER METHODOLOGIES

SCRUM is still a popular project management process used in software development today. For example:

- A Kanban system does not include time boxes like SCRUM requires.
- A Kanban system has fewer tasks, and they are larger than SCRUM tasks.
- A Kanban system does not assess the process often, if at all, as it does in a SCRUM environment.
- A Kanban system only considers the average completion time for a project instead of basing project time on the "speed of the team," like in a SCRUM setting.

For practitioners who are used to the SCRUM environment, thinking that a project is made up of the team's speed, increased dimension, and scrum meetings, may find the idea of removing them outrageous. Those activities are the primary methods for controlling development in a SCRUM system! The real problem with this concept is the illusion of control. Managers are constantly striving for this control but the reality is that they will never obtain it. A manager's supervision and influence only work if the team wants to work. If they collectively decide not to push for a project's completion, it does not matter what the manager does; the object will fail.

The Kanban system; however, focuses on tasks. This differs greatly from a SCRUM process. SCRUM practitioners want a successful sprint. Kanban practitioners want completed tasks. Tasks in a Kanban system are approached from start to finish, not bound to a sprint time frame. The completed work is presented, and the project is deployed based on when it is ready. Tasks do not have an estimated time for completion set by the team. The reason is that there is no need for this time estimate, and an estimate is often wrong, anyway.

## A SAMPLE OF THE KANBAN LISTS USED IN SOFTWARE DEVELOPMENT

There are going to be a few different lists or columns when you are working on a Kanban board specifically for the software development world. You can mix and match them or choose the ones that you would like to go with based on your project and its needs. Some of the examples of lists or columns that you may want to use with your Kanban board when working on software development will include:

- Goals. This one can be helpful but if you are limited on time and space, it is an option. You should place some of your major obstacles here. This is more to use as a regular reminder to the team of what they are trying to accomplish, rather than a list that you can act on.
- Story: Here you are going to place any of the tasks that are on deck. The card that is on the top of the list is the one that should have the highest priority to get done. The team will then take off the top card and work on it. When they are ready to do that, they will remove it over to the next column, they develop one so that they can get started.
- Elaborate and accept. There are a few other descriptions that can be used for this column before the team proceeds to move the card over to the done list. Each team and each workflow is going to vary from the others.
- Develop. Until you get done with one of the tasks in the lists, the card needs to make sure that it stays on the list for develop. It doesn't matter what item is on the card for you to complete. If the task is not done or more steps

- need to be completed on that card, then it needs to be kept on the develop list until that happens.
- Done. Once a card ends up on this list, it is going to show you and the rest of the team that the task has been fully completed. It is a good signal to the team that the task has been completed and that there isn't any further need to look back or do more work on that task.

This kind of layout means that any of the lists and the columns that you have can contain a high priority task. Each task on the board should be completed as soon as you can to get it to be as efficient as possible. Sometimes you will start with a column that is the most important and needs to be done first, then some tasks that can be done a bit later, and then those that you do need to get to but you can wait a bit until the other tasks are done. Then the cards would be easily moved around as you finish some, add more to the board, and so on.

## THE BENEFITS OF KANBAN TO A SOFTWARE DEVELOPMENT TEAM

There are many benefits that a software development team can get when they start to work with the Kanban system. To begin, if your team needs to complete a few tasks at a time, Kanban will help you to cut back on the time that was required for completing each of them. The actions that the team takes will only be the ones most necessary so that you won't have to be switch between frameworks and tracking various articles.

Planning is going to be needed here. Tasks that can be developed when the project begins, not before. Any of the problems or the showstoppers in the process are identified and the solutions are found together as a team so that the process will continue to move forward.

For example, if the task requires the assistance at some point from another department but the other department is already working on their series of tasks, the production of the project must come to a halt as you wait for the other department. This is not seen as an efficient way to deal with the process though. Kanban recognizes ahead of time that there is some need for teamwork, and if you had planned out this with the other department ahead of time, you could work the process out together and kept things moving, rather than having to wait.

## How Kanban Reduces Risk and Creates Improved Software

Amazingly, a pull system created by a supermarket and adapted to a car manufacturing company can help software development companies create quality products with reduced risk but it works. Throughput is improved in a software system by:

### The work is always visual

The board that you use in Kanban is going to be the tool that is used to show the different stages of work, starting at the micro-level. When you use this tool, you will be able to see the problems and the roadblocks ahead of time, because they become major problems that need to be dealt with. At the most basic level of this board, there are going to be three lists or columns.

### Changes are going to be incremental

The changes that are implemented in this system are going to be there to ensure that constant improvement is always met. But to make sure that this happens, the changes need to be smaller. If you try to force your whole team to make some big changes along the way, this can often spell disaster. It leads to too many things changing at once, a lot of big issues coming up, and an unhappy team.

## WIP is Limited

Using up your time multitasking is something to be avoided in an agile environment. Taking on several tasks at one time opens the developer up to making more errors, each deliverable takes more time, and the cycle for delivery takes longer. The limits placed on the WIP mean nothing and can be added until something is removed and the limit is chosen compared to the capabilities and capacity of the team. When each phase can take on more work it is pulled from another place, not pushed on top of existing expectations.

## Flow Enhancement

Organizations that adopt a Kanban system find that the time and effort put into the adoption phase is worth it. The challenges of trying a new agile system like this reap several benefits, including reducing risk and improving the outcome. This is feasible thanks to virtual boards and integrated Kanban software. These systems provide easily viewable WIP and strategy to provide tracking systems for project status and individual tasks. These tools are designed to make a Kanban system easier for your team.

# Chapter 14: Introducing Kanban to Your Company

If your company works on a traditional project management model at the moment, it is quite likely that introducing Kanban to everyone will be more or less of a challenge.

Kanban is very different from anything traditional, and this is primarily because it encourages a lack of hierarchy and similar traditional structures. While you may not want to overthrow the well-established hierarchies of your company, it is still quite important to acknowledge that, at some point, titles will not mean much when it comes to Kanban.

In this project management methodology, everyone helps everyone. There should be a certain level of competency that pushes a workmate to help you with your task but aside from that, it won't matter that he is the team leader and you are the junior developer that just landed.

Introducing Kanban to your company may be met with dismay, too, as some might feel that this is a way to micromanage them. Some may simply believe Kanban is nothing but a gimmick. And others may believe it is completely useless.

There will be people excited to try something new, sure but they are not necessarily the ones you should prepare for. The ones you should prepare for are the ones who are keen on sticking to what they know—to the familiar, old routine.

## Changes You Must Implement in the Organizational Culture

Nothing drives Kanban's success forward better than good company culture. When your culture is in the right place, Kanban changes will flow naturally. They will be nothing but a basic consequence of the fact that you and your team's hearts and minds are in the right place.

Although company culture is frequently left to the bottom of the priority lists in many companies, the truth is that it can make all the difference in the world, particularly when it comes to implementing Kanban as your main project management method. Company culture is a key ingredient in everything connected to business performance and it can truly push everyone to be better, do better, and aim better.

Here are the main things you should understand connected to company culture when it comes to Kanban implementation.

## Understand that Company Culture Is an Inherently Agile Challenge

A lot of project managers see Agile as a mere set of rules to apply to make their teams more productive.

Beyond the rules, however, lies something far more complex, and which can carry a heavy weight when it comes to how successful Agile project management methods are within your company.

Culture is, many times, the actual root cause of failure when it comes to Agile adoption. It makes sense that moving from a very hierarchical-based structure, where everyone has very clear tasks that come from "above," to a structure that focuses on self-discipline, problem-solving, and agility is difficult for many team members. It can make them feel dazed and confused, it can make them feel micromanaged, and it can make them feel downright resistant to change.

If your company culture is not in the right place, you will lose the battle before you even start. It's enough to have **one** team member that doesn't like the idea of an Agile project management method. Soon enough, he will lobby against it during lunch hours and over breaks and the doubt will spread out among other team members just like the plague does.

The reason company culture is so important is because Agile project management goes beyond rules and regulations. It is, in many ways, a work philosophy, one that comes with its own set of values, beliefs, and ethics. One that will naturally influence the way you work and the way tasks are assigned and tackled.

Company culture lies at the very core of a business, acting as the engine that drives everyone forward. If your company culture relies a lot on hierarchy and if it's all about paychecks, numbers, and procedures, Kanban will feel like a 180-degree turn from everything you and your team know. It's not impossible but it will take some work.

## THE SCHNEIDER MODEL

The entire theory starts with Schneider's definition of a culture model—the collection of values a company (or any other group) adheres to. For some companies, this might be connected to innovation and cutting-edge technology, and this will naturally influence the way people in that company run their daily tasks, always focusing on pushing the boundaries of technology. For other companies, it might be about stability, a case in which the teams working in that company would focus on slow, steady evolution, for example.

According to Schneider, there are four types of cultures:

- Collaboration: all about teamwork
- Control: all about keeping everything under control
- Competence: all about winning the race against the competition
- Cultivation: all about growing and trying to achieve a specific purpose

Schneider also says that there are four directions a company can take when it comes to its culture: It can be people-oriented, company-oriented, reality-oriented, and possibility-oriented. The first two directions go in opposition to one another, and the same goes with the latter two directions. A company may be, for instance, 55% people-oriented and 45% company-oriented, **and** it can be 33% reality-oriented and 66% possibility-oriented.

To be able to implement Kanban properly, you should first look at your company culture and work with it, rather than trying to revolutionize everything. Fortunately, Kanban is balanced enough to allow you to do that.

Look at the key problems your company has and how they connect to problems connected to company culture. Look into whether or not your company culture is too extreme. Look into the possibility of creating bridges between teams and departments that might have a different approach to work.

Once that is done, you are ready to start introducing Kanban to your team, step-by-step. You should acknowledge the fact that completely changing the company culture of any company under the sun is difficult, and it takes far more than nice speeches. It doesn't happen overnight, and it only happens when the team is properly guided in the new direction by actions, rather than just words.

It's not impossible to achieve that, though! While it might take hard work, shifting your company culture to a more balanced one, ready to embrace Kanban at its full power, will surely bring you plenty of benefits!

## THE IMPORTANCE OF DATA COLLECTION

Data collection is extremely important in Kanban, precisely because it will help you make accurate assumptions on how much product you need to create to fit the market out there.

All Kanban projects should start with a step that is frequently referred to as "sizing the Kanban," or, in other words, gathering the necessary data to make sure your plan is on par with it.

The information you will need to properly size the Kanban includes the following:

- Changeover times
- Scrap levels
- Number of elements produced in the process
- Downtime

It might feel tempting to make the information look better but it is of the highest importance that you are honest with yourself. For instance, if your company has one hour of downtime every week, do not undermine this by reporting it as thirty minutes; it will only lead to a poor estimation of the future project plan and it will not help you, the team, or the company at a general level.

To make sure the data is accurate, do the following:

- Be very specific about the data you are collecting
- Asses it to make sure that it is coordinated with the experience your team had and the knowledge of the process

Sometimes, you might find that comparing the data against this last verification reveals that something is untrue. In this case, review the data again, review what the team says about it, and, if needed, collect new data until you are fully certain of the numbers in front of your eyes.

Keep in mind that a lot of data can be overwhelming but you mustn't simply allow yourself to feel drowned in so much information. Keep your cool, stay focused, and pay attention to the numbers and what they reveal.

Yes, data collection can be tedious, confusing, and downright annoying but it is a step you should never skip when it comes to Kanban project management. In many ways, this is the very foundation of the Kanban house you are trying to build, so make it a good, solid one.

## How to Create a Kanban Team?

Training your team to understand how Kanban works is essential regardless of the size of the team. Everyone involved in the Kanban operations should be properly trained to use this method so that everything goes as smoothly as possible from the very beginning.

While there may be many training materials already available, it is probably best that you learn how to create training materials to suit your particular situation, your team, and your company.

There are a few points your Kanban training should cover:

- The basics of how Kanban works: signals, how the material will move, the main rules, etc.
- The rules for making decisions (make sure to include examples of different conditions for scheduling and the decisions to make in those circumstances)
- The rules of asking for help and moments when you encounter a red signal
- Show a diagram of what the Kanban signal looks like and how it moves through the entire process
- Help the team understand how Kanban is a demand-based process more than anything

- Test all the Kanban basics and the rules you want to apply in a practice exercise that includes a Kanban board as well

When applying the training, be receptive to the reaction the team members have. Some of them might be confused but they might not say it. If you see any confused looks, be sure to re-elaborate your points, one by one, and repeatedly ask if anyone has questions.

When testing the Kanban, congratulate people for making the right decisions. If they don't make the right decisions, tell them the correct path to take and explain why this is important. Don't be critical—this is new for your team members and they have the right to feel confused if Kanban is completely new to them.

At this point, your main role as a project manager will be that of coaching and mentoring all of the people in your team. Be kind to them, explain and re-explain things. It's better to spot confusion and doubt now and address them, rather than wait for the actual production process to begin. By that point, the problem will most likely be much larger, and you will have to address it while managing the production process as well.

All in all, Kanban is not difficult to understand. Once you and your team have a good understanding of the basics, everything else will flow naturally. However, always be open to questions and always be open to suggestions that might improve the process.

Much of the success of a Kanban team relies on creating an efficient Kanban board. There is no set recipe for this, and this is why you must understand Kanban very well so that you can create a board that makes sense for everyone and helps the entire process be more efficient.

# Chapter 15:
# How Kanban Will Change You

Like many other project management methodologies, Kanban was created to help make processes more efficient. These include the changes you should plan for, as well as the changes you should expect to appear as a natural consequence of everything you will implement.

## HOW YOUR ORGANIZATIONAL CULTURE WILL SHIFT

Kanban is more than just a way to organize tasks it is a way of thinking. Kanban is the kind of project management methodology you can apply after hours as well; you can take it home and use it to make your life better, to grow your skills, and to improve anything you want in your life.

Bringing Kanban to your company will help you gain more structure, reduce waste, deliver more quality, and do it on time, every time. While there might be changes you have to bring to your organization to make Kanban work at its maximum efficiency for you, you should note that there will be changes that will ensue naturally from applying this method as well.

All of these changes will eventually affect not just the way you and your team work but the way you all think as a culture as well. Moreover, all of these changes are tightly knit into the very essence of Kanban itself: the principles that drive it and the practices that define it.

The changes brought by Kanban will follow naturally once you implement certain methodologies and practices.

To be more specific, the following changes can be considered to be both perpetrators and direct causes of implementing Kanban:

- You will see a lot more transparency in your company.
- People will be more balanced in their approach to work.
- Teams will collaborate better.
- Everyone will be more customer-oriented.
- The flow of the projects will be smoother.
- Team members will embrace leadership in the true sense of the word.
- Team members will understand each other, respect each other, and agree with each other better.

## How Your Productivity Will Change

Agile project management is all about productivity. Sure, the approaches to achieving great productivity may be different in the different Agile project management methodologies but in the end, they all aim for better products, delivered on time, and within the budget. Kanban is a very visual project management methodology, and this propels it to the top of the list of interest for many industries.

Aside from the flexibility of Agile project management methods, Kanban itself helps productivity in several ways:

- It is very visual, and thus, it helps everyone stay focused on the tasks at hand. The tasks will always be there, under your nose, showing you exactly where you are and where the rest of the team is.
- It helps you avoid false multitasking. Nobody can multitask, not even computers When you are "multitasking," all you are doing is starting a lot of tasks and not finishing any of them in due time.
- It will help you build a company culture based on cooperation and understanding. Instead of working in your cubicle, isolated from the entire project, each team member with his own little slice of "land" to "cultivate," you will be included in something bigger, you will collaborate with the other team members, and you will be able to avoid making mistakes that would set anyone back.
- It will help you create just enough. Although it may seem that a software product that offers more features is more desirable, the truth is that most of the time, customers might not be willing to pay for all those extras.
- Kanban will provide you with the ingredients that were missing from your team until now, with the values and principles that will drive you forward, and with the practices that make for healthy, productive, and efficient teams.

## How Your Company Will Mature

Incorporating Kanban in your company can have a truly transformative effect on your company. Not only will it change how you organize your projects but it will also change the very way in which you see business, withdrawing from a push approach and embracing a healthier, more cost-and time-friendly pull approach.

Although all of this means that you will work in a closed circle from the framework and estimations you make, it also means that you can make better calculations and deliver a better product in a timelier manner.

The more qualitative software programs you can deliver, the more likely it is that your company will flourish: Customers will be happier, teams will be happier, upper management will be happier.

# Chapter 16:
# Kanban Challenges

## FAILED RETROSPECTIVE MEETINGS

A well-known pitfall is not being able to take action. Without actionable content, a Retrospective Meeting is merely a sort of casual chat that you might have over a glass of beer. You meet, talk about your issues, and return to precisely the same track the next moment. Rule #1 is to accumulate and compose a record of Action Items you will attempt to complete during the following sprint or another time box.

## JUMP INTO ACTION THINGS IMPLEMENTATION.

You might even attempt them and then abandon too fast. Virtually all new rules set you off the comfortable zone. It requires some time to understand them, use them as you like them (or dislike) but it ought to be a professional opinion, not simply a gut feeling.

If you anticipate, you will replace neglected retrospective meetings using a pleasant and easy "stop the line" principle. You are going to fail, as it's even tougher than scheduled routine retrospectives and requires a higher degree of self-discipline.

## WE CANNOT FORM STABLE JOB TEAMS

If you're having issues intending sprints with a shared pool of programmers, attempt to repair the origin of the issue first – change to cross-functional teams and remove multi-tasking. , Kanban seems easy. Nonetheless, it supplies nothing interesting alone. To guarantee a successful Kanban adoption, then you will need to apply Lean basics. This new buzzword may seem like a silver bullet but it isn't. Hard work, subject, the goal of perfection and continuous improvements – all that's needed to employ some other agile methodology.

## COMMUNICATION FAILURE

Project communicating begins from the moment that the project has been conceived and ends in the present time the job ends and is composed of job preparation, sharing of data between stakeholders – essentially the entire communication system. Communication's significance increases once the job begins. That is because communication describes what will be the responsibilities of every team member and also what the job timeline looks like.

## KANBAN AND MANAGEMENT ISSUES

Help them understand that their goals, your goals, and your team's goals are all fully aligned. The reason you want to implement Kanban is that it provides you and your team with the opportunity to work better, faster, and more efficiently. It allows you to reduce waste and align with the company's financial goals.

## Kanban and Escalation Issues

The best way to deal with problems that might appear along the way is to teach the team when to escalate the issue to their superior (their project manager, you, in this case). Once a pink sticky note/digital note has been added to a task that cannot move further, your team member should use a ticketing system to notify you of the problem. If the problem is one that you can solve (e.g. ambiguous requirements), resolve the ticket as soon as possible. If the problem is one you cannot resolve, escalate this further to the accredited departments or the superiors in charge of those specific types of tasks.

## Kanban and Reporting Issues

Any kind of issue your team members stumble upon should be a priority issue, precisely because it needs to be taken out of the way as soon as possible.

Do keep in mind that a simple mark on the visual board is helpful but issues have to be reported some other way as well. The reason this happens is that, even if an issue is small, solving it and documenting it should pass through a system that allows you to use that issue (and its solution) for further planning.

# Chapter 17:
# Problem-Solving with Kanban

Beyond Kanban boards, this project management method is all about problem-solving and finding the right solutions for your team's problems.

Most of the time, cause-effect diagrams are used in the Kanban world to resolve any kind of issues that might arise. Most of the time as well, people coming from outside of Kanban are scared by these diagrams but the truth is that, once you learn the basics, these diagrams will speak to you in terms of stimulating your problem growth.

### HOW TO RUN A CAUSE AND EFFECT ANALYSIS?

Most of the time, cause-effect analyses are made based on a basic pattern which starts with the identification of the cause.

In manufacturing, these causes have been referred to as the 6 M's:

- Method – is the training good enough, is the policy good enough, are the regulations good enough, or are any of these creating unnecessary steps that diminish the productivity of the worker?
- Machines – do you have any kind of maintenance issues with the machine's tools?
- Materials – is there any kind of problem with supplying raw materials for your process?
- Measurements - is there any kind of error in the calculation that has made people report false readings?
- Mother Nature – is there any kind of environment-related issue that might arise?
- Manpower – do you have enough people to run a particular production process?

Depending on the company and the process, some project managers might want to add two other dimensions to the causes of failure in the production process: management (issues connected to actual management) and maintenance (issues that must be solved by technical people in the team or another department) In the service industry, the main causes of any problem are re-worked in a way that will allow you to understand why certain things are happening the way they are.

The 6M's in the manufacturing industry are re-shaped into the 4S's of the service industry:

- Surroundings - is the establishment project projecting the right image?
- Suppliers - are your services delivered correctly? Is there an issue with dropped phone calls or bad food delivery, for example? If you have a restaurant, can your server handle potential traffic spikes?
- Systems - are your policies and procedures correctly set in place to cover all scenarios?
- Skill - are all of the team members properly trained?

Last but not least, in the marketing industry, the cause-effect diagrams are based on the 7P's:

- Product - the quality, the image, the availability, the support, the warranties, the customer service connected to your product
- People - the people customers interact with when buying your product: sales, customer service, delivery, etc.
- Process and procedure - the way you handle problems if they arise, the way you escalate them, the way you train your staff to handle them
- Promotion - the way you advertise your product, the sales, PR, direct marketing, social media marketing, branding involved in the promotion process
- Price - how your product is priced compared to that of the competition
- Physical evidence/packaging - how your product is presented to the customers
- Place/plant - how your product is distributed (is it cost-effective? is it efficient?)

All these causes are meant to provide you with a good starting point in determining flaws in your process. Although the reasons behind something going wrong may go beyond all of the causes described above, it can still be said that most of the time, the cause will lie either with one of the aforementioned points or with a combination of them.

## HOW TO USE CAUSE-EFFECT DIAGRAMS FOR PROBLEM-SOLVING?

It can be said that cause-effect diagrams are simple ways of running a root-cause analysis. The fishbone diagrams, as described before, are meant to help you understand (and solve) a wide range of problems in your company, from the more technical ones to the more organizational ones.

# How To use the Diagrams to Achieve the Problem-Solving

## It's Not About the Symptoms

In medicine, many diseases are still treated symptomatically, and one of the most prevalent ones in this category is none other than the common flu. While doctors were not able to find an actual cure for flu, they can treat the symptoms of the disease until they are completely gone but they do not have the power to completely eradicate the flu virus itself.

The main issue with simply fixing the symptoms is that they frequently appear in one place, while the root cause is in a completely different one. For instance, you might notice that someone on your team is slower and doesn't deliver in time but the problem might not be with them but with the process that leads up to them.

## Apply other countermeasures

It is extremely important for you to acknowledge that whatever countermeasures you may choose to implement; they should be seen as experiments rather than direct solutions. In the end, this is a very important part of the entire Kanban project management approach and Lean thinking: knowing that you should always try new solutions and focus on continuous improvement no matter how many times you "fail."

## Kaizen: The Heart of the Problem-Solving

In short, Kaizen is a composite word made from "change" and "good" in Japanese. It could be roughly translated as "a change for the better." The concept of Kaizen itself was not born together with Kanban but they came to complement each other to perfection.

Kaizen refers to continuous improvement—the flow of the development and productivity under any kind of circumstance. This flow is a continuous "dance" between the small teams and the higher ranks of the company, all of which come together to create a change for the better.

# Chapter 18:
# How to Use Kanban for Continuous Process Improvement?

Kanban systems provide organizations with a stable foundation to achieve continuous improvement since the nature of the system requires that every process and task is transparent and explicit. It also ensures that people take ownership of their work. When the team members view the workplace as a flowing organism instead of a machine, it will become easier for them to visualize the errors and address them as soon as possible. When the work moves as expected through the system, the process of continuous improvement will begin.

## USING KANBAN TO REDUCE WASTE

Kanban is a method that is highly effective when it comes to reducing waste in a process. This helps to decrease the idle time and also allow the teams to focus on continuous delivery. This helps to minimize or eliminate waste in every process because of the following reasons:

- The projects are managed using a pull system. If a task is pulled by a customer's demands, it will reduce the possibility of overproduction, thereby helping the team control the inventory.
- When you limit the work in progress, it will allow teams to focus on a maximum of three tasks at a time. This will help them produce high-quality work and increase engagement.
- It is easy to reduce the wait time since any contingent steps or tasks are visualized on the board, and these can be addressed before delays occur.
- Managers can visualize the process and the workflow on the Kanban board and allocate any tasks that are in the backlog lane to resources that are idle when compared to other resources.
- Automating the workflow by evaluating repetitive tasks and looking for opportunities that will allow you to automate or eliminate those tasks.
- You should always ensure that you align the team to improve the process to help you gain some insight into the resources that are going to waste. It is always a good idea to empower and educate your team members to help them identify waste in the process and eliminate that waste if they can. This will also help to engage your team members and improve communication between teams.

## USING KANBAN TO IMPROVE EFFICIENCY

The use of Kanban boards will increase efficiency since they communicate visually and not textually. This ensures that real-time data and information are always available and can be accessed immediately by all stakeholders.

Kanban boards will visually communicate what the status of the projects and tasks are. This will help to reduce the time that teams spend on creating, delivering, and requesting status reports.

The board will help you visualize any roadblocks or delays in the process, which will allow you to adapt and maintain the flow of the process.

Kanban boards will reflect the changing priorities and needs. They also help to spread the information, thereby reducing the time that the teams will spend on communicating about any changes in scope.

The boards will help you speed up approvals and also identify the points that need to be improved upon to ensure that processes run smoothly.

Have regular meetings with the whole team that will help every member stay connected and aligned toward the goal. It will also ensure that there are no gaps in communication and will give the team a chance to solve any problems they may be facing.

You should ensure that every individual in the team devotes some of their time to learn about new software, innovative techniques, and the best practices to use. This will ensure that every individual has sharp skills. You should always pursue learning opportunities and encourage your peers to do the same.

## CONTINUOUS PROCESS IMPROVEMENT WITH KANBAN

Regardless of whether you analyze the metrics weekly or monthly, you must ensure that you measure the workflow if you want to track any changes over time. You should also note the changes or process improvements that are made during that time to measure the results.

When you use Kanban, it becomes easier to capture the metrics and compare instead of having to rely on emails, to-do lists, or calendars. If you want to improve your processes, you should implement Kanban since that helps you see how the workflow had evolved. This system will work at any level of complexity and scale while helping you improve your outcomes and communication. It is also flexible enough to adapt to your needs.

It is hard to build a process that is efficient and waste-free. The Kanban system was designed for ongoing and continuous improvement and refinement. In today's workplace, where there are social, economic, and technological changes, the process you develop today will not be the right process tomorrow. You should always adopt an approach where you continuously improve the process by reducing waste, measuring outcomes, and promoting efficiency.

# Chapter 19:
# Applying A Kanban Process to Workflow in Your Company

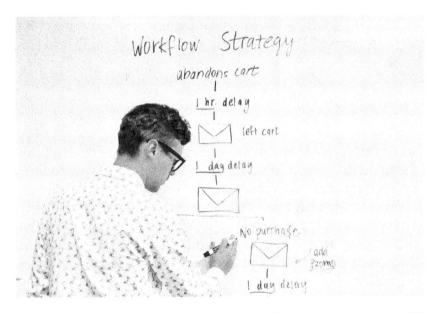

When you are working with the Kanban process, you will notice that a lot of the companies who want to work with this system are not going to provide physical products to their customers. But Kanban can still be used to help improve these businesses and help them to see a lot of changes in the amount of quality and efficiency that they could provide to their customers.

Knowledge work, just like what happens with your company's workflow, can follow the four steps of the Kanban process effectively, even if you are not selling a physical product. Some of the ways that this can happen are discussed in this chapter.

## You Can Visualize the Workflow

Just like we did with software development and manufacturing, the work and the workflow can both be visualized using the Kanban system. This process is helpful because it allows the members of the team and the stakeholders to see the process of any tasks that need to be done. The results, as well as the communication, are then going to be improved thanks to some transparency that is built into the process.

## The Flow is Going to Be a Focus

The beginning of the end of the project should be free to flow when you do place a limit on the WIP, and it is going to be a visual workflow. The formation of backlogs can sometimes be prevented when the team can identify, early on, the problems and then find ways to resolve them. These interruptions can be prevented, or at least kept to a minimum, if you can catch them, which means that you will avoid a major breakdown in the production of your product or your service.

## An Improvement That Has to Happen All the Time.

Improvement opportunities can be identified in the Kanban system due to the continuous analysis and monitoring that are required. Things like the quality, the pace of production, and the flow tracked throughout the entire process and more can be used and measured to see how effective the team is being. Being able to look up and visualize the workflow for the company can be a valuable instrument that any business can take advantage of to make it more efficient and to save money.

## How can I get Kanban to fit into my workflow?

When it comes to implementing the Kanban board into your business, there are a few benefits and a few things to consider. These include:

### You can use a simple board to tell a complex story

The first thing that you are going to see when you go into a company using the Kanban process is a gigantic board. This board can be a sleek online board with a lot of cards and lists that are interactive, or it could be a regular board that has colorful post-its scattered around. Regardless of the method that is used, it is going to be there, and it is going to do some wonders for helping that company do so much better with waste reducing and efficiency.

### The board is simple so there won't be a learning curve

The idea of using a board to organize all of the work that needs to be done is a pretty simple thing to keep track of. You will find that none of your team members will need to go through a lot of extensive training to learn how to use the board. And since all of the stages of the project can be divided up easily, and the board is decorated with all of the tasks that are needed in each specific category, it is going to be easy to look at the board and know what needs to happen, and what has already happened, without needing any training.

### You can quickly account for any priorities that change.

When your customer specifies what they want when the project management system, they may assume that these requirements are going to be frozen, and nothing can be changed up at all until the final product is delivered to the customer. But in reality, this is not the case at all.

# Chapter 20:
# Top Mistakes Made by New Teams

Some reasons why mistakes are made when implementing Kanban and lean processes within the organization are:

**FEAR**

People encounter fear in many forms, and it is a powerful emotion. Fear makes people drive bad decisions and practices that will frustrate a new team. You should counter fear by creating an environment that fosters trust in every employee at all levels. You should let the team know that the organization and the team trust that they will make the right decisions and work toward the goal of the organization. You should take the time to learn, grow, and make the right choices as a group. You should never expect them to take any orders from the management.

## Poor Communication

Trouble will arise when members of the team do not communicate regularly with each other. The best way to identify any issues or blockers is not through documentation but face-to-face communication. You should always work in a dedicated team area to ensure that the team members can all work together and are always within the other's reach. If you work with teams across the world, you can use instant messenger software or use video conferencing. You can use dashboard panels, discussions, and notifications to improve team communication.

## Poor Team Structure

A stable team will always have time to grow with each other. You must ensure that the teams always stick together, and you use the same teams for different projects. You should remember that a team member would always learn across his or her roles. They can always challenge each other once they are familiar with everybody's skills. These teams will know how to improve their efficiency and productivity and will be able to provide better products to their stakeholders and customers.

## Poor Estimation Habits

It is difficult to estimate the scope and size of new work, especially if you have a new team. You should hang in there and stay confident that estimation will always become easier over time. You must let the management know that the new team will need at least two or three cycles to understand and calculate their efficiency. You should never accept project deadlines until you know how quickly your team can complete tasks.

## Poor Planning Habits

You should schedule a daily standup meeting, iteration planning, release planning, and backlog-refinement meetings. You should always develop a return schedule for this meeting so team members can plan and set some time aside for these meetings. You should build a planning cadence, which will allow the teams to look at more than one iteration.

## Poor Testing

Lean and agile processes are not about delivering the product faster. The objective is to deliver a quality product faster. The team manager should never accept work until it has been completed, tested, and meets the acceptance criteria. You can combat any protesting habits for emphasizing automatic testing. You should test every product or task until it passes the criteria.

## Ignoring Customer Feedback

You must remember that customers are the most important stakeholders. You should allow them to help your organization build the vision for any task including its functionality. You can review the most popular request when you define the backlog during your planning. You must always include a customer support agent as a part of your team to obtain the feedback and provide that to the team. You should check with the feedback loop every time a task is completed, and assess if it meets the customer's requirements.

## The Team Isn't Empowered

You can empower the team by allowing them to make decisions that will impact commitment. The business or the management should never tell the team what to do but you need to provide data on what tasks are most important.

## No Demo or Retrospective Meetings

Always have release retrospective meetings with every member of the team. During these meetings, talk about what processes worked, what problems were encountered, and what the team should do to prevent such issues in the next cycle.

## No Plan for Resistance

It is tough to make changes, and many team members will resist switching to an agile or lean process. You should always be prepared for this scenario when you start communicating with the management. The management and organization should always make it very clear that they support the success of the team over individual performances. You should eliminate all personal metrics since you will only win and lose as a group. This will help to combat any cultural problems that may arise. This will also help to foster an environment of trust.

# Chapter 21:
# Kanban for Kids at School and Home

Kanban for Kids is a concept derived from Personal Kanban that specifically focuses on children. It can help your child stay organized and be productive during school or at home. When studying, it can be helpful to use a Kanban board to stay on track.

Here are some tips to get started:

- Select your Kanban board. Determine whether your board will certainly be on the internet or physical and also establish your board.
- Document every little thing you do. On paper, brainstorm every little thing you're most likely to need to obtain performed in the direct future. Do not attempt to fit everything on your Kanban board. You simply desire a system for catching all the crucial points you have to obtain done.
- Determine the number of things you'll carry your Kanban board each time. With institution, social life, as

well as perhaps your work, you have a lot of time to dedicate to an institution job. Making a note of every little thing you can do at the institution is also frustrating. Concentrate on a couple of points at once as well as you'll discover it less complicated to obtain encouragement. In the meantime, choose the number of things you want to carry your board each time. If you begin to discuss that number, you'll recognize its time to complete a couple of points so you could obtain them off the board.

- Pick your Kanban board headings. Choose the number of columns you desire as well as exactly what each column will certainly be called. The most basic Kanban board will certainly have 3 columns: points to do, points I'm dealing with, and also points I have finished.
- Choose exactly what things go where on your Kanban board. Check out your lengthy checklist of every little thing you have to do. What products require your time today? Those points most likely ought to take place on your board currently, so go on. Include due dates if any one of your jobs has due dates or due days.
- Begin on relocating products from right to left. As quickly as you have obtained your board your objective ought to be to relocate points from left to right (completely to "Done!"). It's time to take a look at your "Exactly what I'm working with currently" column and also dive in!

## CONTINUING TRACK AS A PUPIL

The Kanban approach functions well with various other company systems. Along with your Kanban board or your online Kanban arrangement, you might desire:

- A big wall surface schedule. A schedule that shows several months at once allows you to write down upcoming examinations, tasks, jobs as well as various other vital days. When you look to your Kanban board to include jobs, you could utilize your wall surface

schedule to discover just what you have to concentrate on following.
- A day-to-day organizer or little notepad. A little notepad or coordinator could select you for courses as well as spending on supper. If you unexpectedly remember you have to be servicing a task or you all of a sudden obtain a motivating concept, you could write it down so you could include it to your Kanban board at some point.
- An area made for the job. A neat world is with the pens, paper as well as tools you require makes it less complicated to in fact relocate college tasks via your Kanban pipe. Pick a silent room for your work desk and also see to it you obtain lots of light. Border your work desk with a couple of points to lighten up the room up, and also do not forget to hang your Kanban board where you could quickly see it.

## EXTRA TIPS FOR MAXIMIZING KANBAN

There are a couple of institution hacks making your Kanban system a lot more reliable:

- Maintain a variety of products on your Kanban workable. If you have a lot of, you cannot picture exactly what you have to do, and also the system isn't as reliable.
- Usage color and also pictures. Kanban is implied to be aesthetic. You could utilize various colors for your various classes or you could utilize various colors for various kinds of tasks (for instance, yellow for projects and also pink for reading assignments). Pick what helps you!
- Utilize your system to discover productivity issues as well as various other concerns. If you're utilizing the Kanban system, however, you're still not obtaining points done or are still neglecting points, it's time to take a more detailed look at exactly what's taking place. Do you have way too many things on your board? Are you simply attempting to do way too much? Are you

simply placing points off, also when you understand just what you need to do? Kanban allows you to identify just what's incorrect so you could deal with any kind of issues.

- Since you recognize the best ways to utilize Kanban, you now know the best ways to track whatever you should do to obtain great grades. Kanban can not only keep you on track. It likewise aids you to handle your time and also lower stress and anxiety. Anxiety about school is a big problem for a lot of kids. A simple system like Kanban can make all the difference.

# Chapter 22:
# The Difference Between Kanban and PAR

PAR systems are still the most common method for healthcare companies to manage medications and supplies. Hospitals are the systems that use it the most. PAR requires each item to have a level set for it. When it drops below "par", it needs to be restocked. The concept is simple; however, to determine "par," inventory conducted manually and counting in a cycle is required. The supply chain is burdened by the added manpower and cost these actions require because the activity does not add value to the system.

Unfortunately, another common practice is to guess at the inventory levels of an item, not physically count each item. This saves time; however, it is inaccurate and can cause waste. It can increase costs and inventory levels. Understanding the opportunity for error, it should come as no surprise why leading manufacturing companies do not utilize this method, despite similar goals: always have on hand a consistent amount of inventory.

The Kanban process, on the other hand, reduces non-value adding activity, like physically counting inventory, because of its visual nature. Each bin has a set number. When it is empty, it is restocked with that number. While it is waiting to be restocked, another bin is being pulled from. Because of the clear advantages of the Kanban system over the PAR methodology, many healthcare systems are beginning to change their processes to a Kanban system. Professionals involved in inventory management for hospitals and healthcare environments have reported positive results thanks to the extra time they now have to focus on valuable activities due to less time spent in the storeroom and ridding of the need for a daily inventory count.

## WHY KANBAN METHOD SHOULD REPLACE PAR

There are seven reasons that a Kanban process is a preferential methodology for inventory control over the PAR system.

The practice of properly managing inventory is promoted through a Kanban system, not through PAR. Eyeballing the bins to determine if an item is below par is not a good practice but physically counting each item would require intense amounts of labor and is virtually impossible, especially in larger systems. Keeping the storeroom orderly and "clean" can be maintained easily with a Kanban process, while it cannot be with PAR.

The discipline required to restock inventory is easy to maintain with a Kanban system. A set number for each item is marked on the bin label, making it very simple for the handler to know exactly how much should be restocked for that item. It is easy and accurate each time. This means Kanban methodology can prevent shortages much better than the PAR system.

Inventory is lean. Does it sound attractive to you to have 50% less inventory on hand and still meet your customer's needs consistently? It should! Imagine all the cost, time, and space savings you will experience! 50% is the average inventory reduction PAR users had experienced when they switched to a Kanban practice without compromising their inventory targets.

Improvement and management are easier to achieve with the Kanban process. The amount of time between depletion and restocking can be tracked. This information can then be used to set the quantity in each bin appropriately. Also, this information can be adjusted easily if the supplier's shipping times change or demand is different. PAR makes this management and improvement hard because it restocks items every day, in undetermined quantities.

Fixed quantities for replenishment are possible with Kanban processes. PAR requires the daily counting, costing your team a lot of time. Instead, their efforts can be focused elsewhere because a Kanban system provides a fixed amount needed to be ordered and visually signaled by the empty bin. It is a much simpler process.

Trips to resupply are reduced with a Kanban process. Bins are refilled when it is needed, not daily, as it is with the PAR system. This means your trips to restock a bin is greatly reduced. Some Kanban practitioners have estimated their trips to restock have been cut down by as much as 50%.

Since bins are not refilled every day, counting does not need to happen every day, as it is required with the PAR system. Kanban methods keep the process as simple as possible: when the bin is empty, reorder the fixed number for that item. While you wait for it to be restocked you pull from the second bin for the product. You continue to pull from that second bin even if the first bin stock arrives before it is empty.

When the second bin is empty, you move the first bin forward and pull from it while the second bin is being restocked. The cycle continues on a loop, refining and improving over time. Not spending all that time counting while using the PAR system will save your company hundreds, maybe even thousands, of man-hours each year! Imagine the improved efficiency and cost-savings.

Inventory management for all healthcare and hospital systems should use a Kanban system over a PAR system. Any industry that must regulate inventory should consider utilizing a Kanban system over the "eyeball the stock" approach of PAR. The industry and your organization can expect enormous financial savings thanks to the reduction in inventory, a minimal shortage, and improved productivity.

## HOW TO EASILY CHANGE FROM A PAR TO A KANBAN SYSTEM

Because of the obvious advantages of a Kanban process over a PAR system, you may be wondering how it is best to change processes and also avoid errors and frustration. As with anything new, it is best to roll it out simply and clearly after you get the buy-in from all the people involved, including your suppliers! Thankfully, there are technological solutions out there that you can consider to help make the transition easier for your company.

### Space saver

On the shelf, in front of the two bins containing materials, there is an RFID tag. When an inventory manager recognizes the front bin is empty, they scan the RFID tag and move the empty bin behind the second, full bin. When the tag is scanned, it alerts the person or department in charge of ordering what needs to be refilled. The reason RFID tags were chosen is that they tend to be more accurate and use less time than a barcode that is printed on a Kanban card or the box. Also, RFID tags and the reader cost extra money.

### PAR Excellence

To minimize the manpower required even further, PAR Excellence looks to remove not just counting but also scanning barcodes or RFID tags. Instead of tags, scales are placed under the bins. A weight is associated with a full and empty bin. When the bin reaches the empty weight, it signals the person or department in charge of ordering the need to restock that particular item. As with the other solution presented above, this system adds the initial cost of installing scales in your stockroom, and each scale needs to be calibrated for the inventory item and set up on a specific network. Then you need to monitor and maintain a lot of associated data

## Logi-D

Similar to Spacesaver, this solution offers an RFID tag to reorder the item that is depleted. Instead of scanning the tag and returning the tag to the shelf, like Spacesaver, Logi-D has a board located on a stockroom wall, which collects the tags of all the items that are being restocked. When the tag is removed from the shelf the empty tag space is colored red, signaling quickly to your inventory manager that the tag is on the wall for reorder.

Technology is cool and exciting but it is an added cost to consider. Do not jump on any technology bandwagon because it is new and looks fancy. Choose a system if you think you need it because you see the value it can add to your organization. If it helps, choose a solution. If it does not, keep it simple with a card or a bin.

# Chapter 23:
# Bringing Kanban into Real Life

Kanban is extremely popular for a very, very good reason: it is versatile enough to work in multiple industries, for companies of all sizes, and even in combination with existing project management methods that are anything but Agile.

## KANBAN ACROSS INDUSTRIES AND SITUATIONS

When it comes to how Kanban has adapted to multiple industries and types of businesses, it's not just a theoretical assumption that pushes more and more people to adopt this project management approach. On the contrary: there are countless examples of how Kanban has worked and continues to work for companies with very different verticals.

## THE ORIGINAL KANBAN: TOYOTA

The history between Toyota and Kanban runs very deep but to date, Kanban is the primary project management approach used by car manufacturing companies in Japan. That says something about its efficiency, as well as about the adaptability of Kanban. Times may have changed but Kanban was able to adapt to the new world and work its miracles in the 21st century as well. Even more, the end of the 20th century and the beginning of the 21st century not only maintained Kanban's popularity but increased it as well, as more and more companies adopted it—if not entirely, then at least bits and pieces of it that prove to be useful across multiple verticals around the world.

## KANBAN AND THE HEALTHCARE INDUSTRY: SEATTLE CHILDREN'S HOSPITAL

Take Seattle Children's Hospital, for example. The hospital was in dire need to fix their short supply on important items, such as surgical dressings, catheters, clamps, and specialized tubing. Since these items are crucial for the care of patients, nurses had to constantly ensure they have a full stock on each of these items, so that they can properly tend to their patients. However, when they stocked on these items, they didn't follow a clear procedure or standardized inventory method. Instead, the aforementioned items were more or less randomly stashed around the hospital, making access to them difficult because it took more time than needed to find them. Consequently, medical staff found themselves in a situation where they were spending too much time searching for basic items, rather than taking care of the patients and helping them heal. Kanban allowed the Seattle Children's Hospital to save storage room, to save money by only ordering the supplies they need.

## KANBAN AND THE ELECTRONICS INDUSTRY: MILWAUKEE ELECTRONICS

Milwaukee Electronics is another example of Kanban's success. As a company manufacturing parts for consumer, medical, industrial, and aerospace electronics, Milwaukee Electronics started an assembly service called Screaming Circuits back at the beginning of the 2000s. This assembly service developed prototypes and produced small-volume items based on quotes and orders customers placed via the company website.

To ensure the entire system worked and that they could deliver what the customers ordered, the company used a Kanban approach for contract customers. , they stocked for the number of items equivalent with two weeks of orders, and then they backed up the entire system with a Kanban board that ensured the replenishment time was always two weeks. This way, they ensured a constant inventory based on actual demand, avoiding waste, and making sure that they are always stocked with the products the customers needed.

## KANBAN AND OTHER MANUFACTURING BUSINESSES: DYNISCO

Dynisco is another manufacturing business that embraced Kanban and succeeded as a result. The company makes mercury-free pressure sensors but at some point, they noticed they had a constant excess inventory.

To boost efficiency by using the existing resources, the business implemented a design for their manufacturing and assembly processes. They were able to simplify the product designs, to standardize the production costs, and, overall, improve the way the suppliers were managed.

Even with all the standardization, the company still had problems with lead times, as well as with the quality of their deliverables. This is where Kanban saved them, by providing them with an inventory system that created a smooth flow of materials. Moreover, the same inventory system improved the communication between the company and the client by boosting the latter's response times.

## KANBAN IN IT: SPOTIFY

Spotify representatives have pointed out that scalability was an issue in their company, in the sense that the operations team was not able to coordinate with the constant growth of the business.

Implementing a Kanban system proved to be life-saving for them. They took a very basic Kanban board and its rules and applied them to their tasks. Their Kanban board included three columns (To Do, Doing, Done) and three horizontal lanes (standard, intangible stories, expedite swimlane). Furthermore, they limited the To Do stage, which helped them make sure the intangible tasks were fully completed as a priority. Everything they did in this direction helped Spotify's operations team become more efficient from multiple points of view: They achieved shorter lead times, they managed to get more internal tasks done, and they managed to promote inter-departmental collaboration as well.

## KANBAN AND GOVERNMENTS

Perhaps unsurprisingly for you at this point, where you already know all the benefits of Kanban, this project management method has been successfully applied to government projects as well.

Governmental institutions and departments are notorious for a series of stereotypical issues, all of which can be successfully addressed by a Kanban system. More specifically:

- Governmental institutions are known to be very slow when it comes to taking action. This is largely due to a high level of bureaucracy (which can at least be

partially explained, given the importance of the actions taken by a government).
- Governmental institution teams are also known to be frequently de-motivated. However, as it was shown in this book, Kanban can help breathe a new air of motivation in your team, precisely because they will see more tasks moving through the process.
- Lack of communication between the various departments of a governmental institution is also an issue that has been reported quite frequently. However, in Kanban, the very concept of having a board that helps everyone visualize all the tasks at hand encourages teams to communicate among themselves.

## KANBAN, AGILE, AND LARGE PROJECTS

The first tests rolled out in 2009 on approximately ten police officers, and they were scaled up to thirty people in 2010. By the end of 2010, more than sixty people were testing the project, showing that the system implemented by the Swedish government was based on aggressive scaling and a quick release of every cycle.

Not only did Agile project management allow the Swedish police to aggressively scale their tests but it also allowed them to have "moments of truth" every time they were releasing a new iteration of the system. Consequently, they were able to spot mistakes, errors, and bugs from infancy and fix them as soon as possible, rather than fixing them at the end, when it would have taken more time and effort to handle this kind of problem.

## KANBAN, MEET THE WORLD: HOW TO KANBAN WITH A GLOBAL TEAM

Kanban teams can work remotely. It may not be ideal but situations ask for it, and you should adapt. In the end, Kanban's adaptability is one of the characteristics that has pushed it so far in time, in space, and across different industries, so it only makes sense that Kanban adapted to a remote workforce as well.

One of the easiest ways to make sure your teams are Kanban regardless of where they might be located geographically is by providing everyone access to a digital Kanban board. This can be easily created with a multitude of tools, some of which are free. Trello is a good example of one tool but if you are searching for something a bit more advanced, you should look into Asana.

## Applying Kanban to Personal Development

Aside from the organizational application of the Kanban project management method, it is also worth mentioning that there are ways to implement Kanban in your life for personal development as well. Kanban can be perceived as a personal development methodology. You might not be able to adopt all of its concepts but the basic ones can be very easily adapted to your development journey, helping you be better, do more, deliver higher quality, and reduce general waste when it comes to your work and your life too.

# Chapter 24:
# Kanban Maturity Model

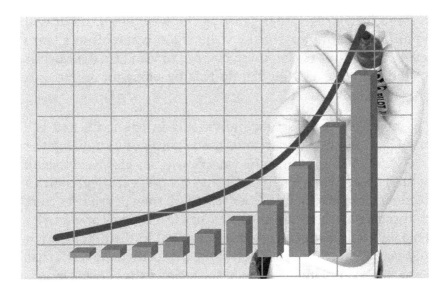

The Kanban Maturity Model collects, collates, and summarizes the many years of experience of applying Kanban principles and processes across many organizations and industries. This model is useful for organizations that want to develop an agile business. This model will give you a framework that will help you scale Kanban and evolve the process to help you achieve agility and robustness. This will ensure that your company survives any social, economic, and technological changes.

This transition will help you overcome some resistance, and when you implement the tool correctly, you can facilitate the transition between the different levels with ease. You must follow the core practices to ensure that your team achieves the objectives of every maturity level. An organization that is at a lower level will often resist these practices unless they prepare themselves in advance.

Without further ado, let us look at the model and see how you can apply different Kanban tools to improve efficiency.

## Maturity Level 0—Oblivious

If your team does not know that it needs some structure when it comes to the numerous processes that you perform, it is at the maturity level 0. Many organizations do not follow a systematic approach to organizing the way they work. It will be difficult to implement the various Kanban tools at a team level. It is for this reason that you need to visualize the work at an individual level. You can do this by using an online or a physical Kanban board.

The objective here is that individuals in the team and the organization must understand the benefits of visualizing the tasks that are invisible in the workflow. They also need to look at some ways to limit the working progress if they want to become more productive. Your team will then be ready to start the process of transition and move to the next level of maturity. This will only happen if every individual in the organization and team will realize that you should prioritize the tasks that need to be completed next from the tasks in the backlog lane.

Teams need to realize that it is always good to use work-in-progress limits to reduce lead times and also avoid multitasking when it comes to delivering tasks. If every team member is here, you can then move to the next level.

## Maturity Level 1—Team Focused

At this level of maturity, the team members have developed the habit of using Kanban on an individual level. Once individuals realize the advantages of using simple workflow visualization at an individual level, they can transmit the benefits of using Kanban to a team level.

### Visualization

At level 1, this is related to taking the Kanban from a personal level to a team level. This is associated with the following practices:

- Visualize the work for many individuals by using an aggregated Kanban board.
- Visualize how the team works together using an emergent workflow board.

## Transition

When the team members initiate the transition, they should ensure that they move the work from an individual board to the team Kanban board. It is easy to differentiate between the work and tasks during the first few weeks. This is because you can differentiate the work by using swim lanes, where each lane can be assigned to one individual.

## Limiting Work in Progress

At the first level of maturity, it is extremely easy for the team to apply work-in-progress limits. If you remember, at the beginning of this level, every team member has his or her own swimlane on the Kanban board.

## Transition

Every team member has a swimlane dedicated to him or her. Therefore, you will need to create a work-in-progress limit for every individual member. For this, you will need to observe the number of tasks each member can complete in three days or less, and this will be his or her work-in-progress limit.

## Core Practices

When you switch to a team Kanban board from an individual Kanban board, you need to set a team work-in-progress limit. It is always a good thing to back every decision you make using numbers. It is for this reason that it becomes easier to use an online Kanban board. Online Kanban tools will collect historical data about the team's workflow, which will help you determine the work-in-progress limit.

## Maturity Level 2—Customer-Driven

Your team has realized that the use of Kanban will help to bring transparency to the workflow and boost the collaboration between the team members. The next step is to understand that workflow. In simple words, the team will begin to understand how it will need to do things. When the team reaches this stage, it means that the team will begin to understand the need to define the workplace and how the tasks will get done.

### Visualization

The teams have only been using the Kanban board to visualize the workflow. In this state, the teams will begin to understand the value of these practices.

### Transition

If you move from the first level to the second level, you should go through the following steps:

- Visualize the tasks using the means of the work-in-progress limits on a delivery Kanban board.
- Visualize the tasks using board rows and card colors.
- Visualize the blocked tasks.
- Visualize the development of the options using a discovery Kanban board.
- Visualize the workload for individual team members on the discovery Kanban board. You can do this by using the work-in-progress limits for every individual member using an avatar.
- Visualize the initial policies.

An online Kanban tool will always give teams the freedom to apply any changes or adjustments to the team's workflow. When you keep this in mind, you can restructure the board easily and apply any of the principles to the workflow.

## Core Practices

Since you are at the core of this level of maturity, you have a solid base that we help you build the workflow. To do this, you should follow the steps given below:

- Visualize the unordered or concurrent activities using checkboxes.
- Visualize your activities that are performed concurrently by specialist teams using partial lanes.
- Visualize the activities that follow a sequence that does not depend on any other tasks using vertical spaces or rows.
- Visualize any rework and other defects in the process.
- You should use a combination of the emergent workflow delivery system and CONWIP to ensure that no team member is overburdened. This is the basis of a pull system.
- Visualize the workflow using enhanced delivery and discovery Kanban boards.
- Visualize the progress using a portfolio Kanban board.

There are times when numerous team members will work on single items. In such cases, you should apply checkboxes or subtasks. You can move a task to the next column only when every checkbox is marked as done. You can also use different lanes to differentiate between tasks that need to be performed in parallel. In this step, you can split the tasks into different lanes depending on the skills that they require.

## Limiting WIP

When it comes to moving from one level of maturity to the next, you learned how you should place a work-in-progress limit on an individual level before you assign a limit at the team level. You will need to achieve the customer-driven state of the implementation of Kanban. For this, you will need to achieve the steps mentioned below. The first of these steps is for the transitioning period, while the other is associated with the core principles and practices of Kanban.

- Establish the work-in-progress limits for activities.
- Establish the CONWIP limits on an emergent workflow.

When you place a work-in-progress limit on an activity, you can ensure that you manage the team capacity. You should also keep in mind the different types of work items that you need to look at. You must always place a maximum limit to the tasks that your team will need to complete, and also decide on the number of tasks that can be in the "In Progress" state.

You will then need to place a constant limit on the amount of work that is in progress. This is known as CONWIP and is an advanced way of ensuring that the workflow is stable. It does this by ensuring that the same number of items are always being processed or worked on at all times. If this limit is higher than the capacity, every team member will need to multitask. If the limit is lower, you will have some idle team members.

## Managing Flow

At this level of maturity, you will apply the concept heavily. There are four practices that you will need to follow or implement if you want to manage the workflow. These will need to become a part of the work life.

- Define the different types of work based on customer requests.
- Map the flow of upstream and downstream requests.
- Manage the issues with blocking.
- Manage the defects and other types of rework.

## Transition

In this maturity level, there is only one step that you need to complete that is of great importance. You must define the type of work based on the customers' requests. When you define the work types, you must visualize them on the Kanban board.

### Core Practices

It is at this level of maturity that the concept of upstream Kanban will come into the picture. This type of Kanban is related to the parts of the process that you must complete before you commit to delivering an assignment. This state will reflect all the steps through which the requests or ideas will need to go through before you commit to the delivery of the product. For instance, these are synthesis, opportunities, and analyses and ready to commit. If you advance further into this level of maturity, you should start managing the blocking issues and also discuss with the team to develop some solutions to overcome any common blockers.

## MATURITY LEVEL 3—FIT-FOR-PURPOSE

You should know the definitions of process, policies, workflow, and decision frameworks when you move to level 3. You must sit down with your team and agree upon those decisions, and also ask them to give you their feedback. You should also help them to understand the definitions to achieve good results. It is at this level that the main focus should always be on improving the implementation of Kanban and the six core practices.

### Visualizing Workflow

When you have achieved level 2, you will begin to transition from a customer-driven process to a fit-for-purpose process. In this level, the practices that are related to visualization move upstream.

### Transition

In this level, you will need to complete the action items listed below:

- You should visualize the "ready to commit" status. This is also called the "ready to pull" status.

- Visualize the criteria that are associated with the "ready to pull" criteria. This is also known as the "definition of ready" or "entry criteria."
- Visualize the workflow and the teamwork items using the aggregated Kanban board.
- Visualize the project work items on the two-tiered Kanban board.
- Visualize the peer-to-peer and parent-to-child dependencies.
- Use the parking lot to understand the work that depends on other tasks or requires some assistance from another service.

When you want to initiate this transition, you must always set up new columns on the Kanban board, which are dedicated only to those items that you are ready to commit. In this step, you will need to distinguish between the items that are requested and those items that you are ready to pull into the progress column. You should ensure that you prioritize your work correctly before you progress.

The next thing you must do is ensure that the team will stick to the order of the tasks and does not pull the items that are not in the upstream column but have been requested. The best thing to do would be to make it very clear about what must happen with the items in a specific column. It is always a good idea to use names like "Next," "Ready to Start," "Ready to Pull," "Ready to Commit," or anything similar.

## Core Practices

When you have successfully implemented everything that has been explained so far concerning the visualization of work, you are just about to reach the next level of maturity. You can tell the organization that you have managed to visualize the workflow.

There are a few core practices that you must adopt to ensure that you stay at this level:

- Always visualize the upstream options using a discovery or upstream Kanban board.
- You should visualize the discarded options by using an upstream or discovery Kanban board through a bin.
- Visualize the signals that indicate replenishment.
- Visualize the pull signals.
- Visualize the criteria for pull signals.
- Visualize the available capacity.
- Visualize the aging of a work item or task.
- Visualize the SLA or target date.
- Visualize value demand versus failure demand.
- Visualize any work that has been aborted.
- Visualize the class of service by using board rows, ticket decorators, or ticket colors.
- Use the earned value portfolio on the board to visualize the progress on any project.

When you continue upstream, you must ensure that you improve the Kanban board so you can get a good view of the available options that your team can work on. To do this, you should break the "Requested" section on the board into smaller segments and add a few tasks or steps between the initiation of the task on the board and the commitment step.

### Limiting Work in Progress

Like in the previous levels, when you advance toward implementing a fit-for-purpose Kanban method, you must enhance the practices that have already been established to limit the work in progress. Once you achieve a customer-driven level of work-in-progress limit, you can shift to the maturity level 3 without having to go through a transition.

You will need to follow these practices to identify the work-in-progress limits in this level of maturity:

- Use a minimum limit, also known as an order point, for upstream replenishment.
- Use a maximum limit that will help you define capacity.

- Always use different work-in-progress limits for the different states.

You will first need to calculate the minimum limit that you want to maintain for upstream replenishment for every task. The goal should be to ensure that the stream of ideas to complete the work or task is constant. The minimum work-in-progress limit will let you know that you will need to replenish the pool of ideas once your team reaches the limit.

## Managing Flow

The levels 0–2 will help you lay a foundation to manage a complex workflow. When you move toward the third level of maturity, there is a lot that you will need to do.

## Transition

There are seven practices that you will need to stick to if you want to transition to this level. Most of these practices are small tweaks that you need to make to the style of management. This section will only mention these practices but we will look at how these practices are related to the Kanban boards.

You must implement these seven practices in the order mentioned below:

- You should organize the process of discovering new information.
- You should allow team members to defer commitment at the last moment.
- You must use some cumulative flow diagrams to monitor the queues.
- Use the little law.
- You must eliminate the buffers slowly.
- You should always report the flow efficiency to help the team understand the advantages of reducing the buffers. This should also help them eliminate any sources of delay.

- You should always close any upstream criteria that meet the criteria of abandonment.

You must implement all the practices listed above if you want to move to the third level of maturity. When you know how to organize the team around some services and have also deferred commitment, you should manage the workflow and maintain its stability.

## Core Practices

When you are done with the process of transition, there is a lot of work that you will need to do to manage the workflow.

You will need to:

- Develop the triage discipline.
- Manage all types of dependencies.
- Analyze any items that have been abandoned and report why they were abandoned.
- Use classes of service to aid in selection.
- Forecast the delivery of the completed items.
- Apply the real options thinking to improve quality.

All the items in this checklist are important; however, you should place special attention to learning how to manage dependencies. If you fail to do this, you move back to level 2. Any type of dependency will increase risk, and you should visualize these dependencies and manage them effectively to meet a customer's expectations.

## Making Policies Explicit

In the previous level of maturity, you defined the process policies but when you move toward the fit-for-purpose implementation of Kanban, you will need to tackle a new checklist before you meet the policies.

## Transition

To transition to this level, you will need to:

- establish the purpose of the metrics explicitly,
- establish the policies that talk about the acceptance of initial requests,
- define the policies that define the work abandonment, and
- establish the commitment point for replenishing inventory.

We do not have to dwell too much on why you should establish some metrics that you want to monitor. All you need to say is that you can use these metrics to differentiate between vanity and true performance metrics. When you establish the policies for initial request acceptance, you can reduce the lead-time of the tasks. This will also provide enough time to define the assignment before you commit to it. When you have decided what you want to do and what the policies are, you should drop them under the column they apply to on the Kanban board.

## Core Practices

When you have transitioned from level 2 to level 3, you must do the following to ensure that you stay at this level:

- Establish the pull criteria.
- Establish the commitment point for delivery.
- Establish the criteria for customer acceptance for every task or a class of items.
- Define the class of service.

You should ensure that you define the pull criteria in advance since they will help you start tasks that you know you can process. These will vary for different services, and you should take some time to establish them. One way to visualize these criteria is to list a criterion for any subtask on the card. These criteria should be written based on the task that is being worked on.

When you establish the commitment point for delivery, you will move onto level 4 maturity. The easiest way to do this is to dedicate one column on the Kanban board before you deliver the value or product to the market. This can be marked in the "Done" or the "In Progress" stages. You should then establish the customer acceptance criteria and define the classes of service.

## MATURITY LEVEL 4—RISK HEDGED

This level of maturity is characterized by data-driven decisions and risk-hedged processes. This is characterized more by the use of Kanban cadences and the use of the fit-for-purpose framework. It does not specifically focus on the design of the Kanban boards. There is still some progress that the teams will need to make when it comes to the visualization of the workflow and managing that workflow. When you move from the third level to the fourth level of maturity, the model will focus more on how it can evolve the process and management practices.

### Visualizing Workflow

Unlike the previous levels, organizational maturity is not driven by practices that are related to the visualization of workflow alone. The core practices and the transition are fewer when compared to the previous levels, yet they are more significant when compared to the other levels.

### Transition

If you want to make the transition from the third level to the fourth level, you should start with the following:

- Visualize the local cycle time.
- Use ticket decorators to indicate different types of risks.
- Visualize the various risk classes and categorize them into different swimlanes.
- Visualize the merge and split workflows.

The local cycle time is the amount of time any task spends on a specific activity or a sequence of activities. In simple words, this is the amount of time that a card will spend at every stage of the process. If you want to measure the local cycle time, you must indicate the time you want to spend on each task at every stage of the process. Some teams will stick to the physical implementation at this level and mark every card with the number of days it has spent in a specific column. Since this is not a feature that is commonly developed in an online Kanban board, the teams that prefer this method will leave a small note in the card indicating when the card moved from one state to the next.

## Core Practices

If you have stuck to every word that has been covered about visualization in this chapter, you have reached level 4. In this stage, you have three objectives that you must adhere to if you want to ascend further concerning visualization.

- Visualize the work-in-progress limits on dependencies.
- Visualize the waiting time in dependencies.
- Visualize the SLA that exceeds dependencies.

At the core of this level, you must always ensure that you have the dependencies under control. You must put a cap on the maximum work-in-progress limit in the column. You have to also visualize this limit at the top of the stage.

## Manage Flow

This is one concept that is addressed in level 4 of the Kanban practice. There are twelve steps that you will need to take if you want to progress from a fit-for-purpose implementation of Kanban to a risk-hedged implementation concerning the flow management.

## Transition

There are five steps that the team must go through if you wish to advance flow management.

- Collect the detailed analysis of flow efficiency and report it to the respective team leads.
- Always use a buffer to smoothen the flow.
- Use the two-phase delivery commitment.
- Analyze the dependencies.
- Establish irrefutable vs. refutable demand.

In level 3, you learned how you should measure the flow efficiency. If you use Kanban software, it is easy to make the transition from measuring the data to collecting and reporting it. This will help you mature sooner. You will need to pay attention to the buffers in the process and also use those buffers to smoothen your workflow. You should always place the buffer column if you expect or anticipate a bottleneck.

## Core Practices

You have to ensure that you abide by the following points if you want to achieve the fourth level of maturity.

- Always identify the class data set that you want to use as a reference.
- You should use Monte Carlo simulations, reference classes, and other tools to forecast.
- Identify a way to allocate the capacity across every lane.
- Allocate the capacity based on the color of the card.
- Ensure that you use forecasting appropriately.
- Assess if the forecasting models are robust.
- Always use statistical methods to make decisions.

We will first talk about the second point in the above list. Monte Carlo simulations are the most reliable way to predict the performance of a process since it relies only on past data. Using these predictions, you can always forecast the throughput and cycle time based on many simulations that use past performance as data.

## Maturity Levels 5 and 6—Market Leader/Anti-Fragile

If your team and organization have reached this state, you should be proud since you can now work toward achieving the last levels of KMM. These levels are focused only on building a robust process that will sustain the organization. When it comes to visualization, you must visualize floating workers and fixed teams. These floating workers are shared resources that are used across aggregated services.

In these levels, you cannot do anything concerning the work-in-progress limits, so you should be confident that the team has mastered these limits at this level of maturity.

The only thing you need to do is utilize all the fixed services teams and ensure that there is a flexible work pool. You must also align the team with the goal and strategy.

# Conclusion

You just read all about Kanban! Now is the time for action. Now is the time to prepare your Kanban board and visual system to make your life easier and your team happier. Now is the time to lower costs and increase production using a simple and effective method.

While you are planning, get the buy-in from your team, company, stakeholders, and even your customers. Sell them on the benefits of adopting a Kanban system and stay close to the process, refining as needed, so it is the most efficient system for your business. Remember, the goal of this is to assist your team members in working alongside one another efficiently while also benefiting your company. Keeping your eye on this goal during each decision you make will help with all the changes and challenges.

Now you can determine the unique needs of your organization and create a way to make this basic system work for you. The more you use boards, lists, and cards; the better your team will get at running an effective Kanban project and process. As they continue to feel empowered and successful, imagine the positive atmosphere and engaged work environment you will have! Success will come to you in a variety of forms thanks to implementing this methodology in your company.

Kanban is great because any team or individual can get started right away but there are so many things to learn and understand about Kanban. You can delve further into any of the topics and even take a course to become certified in the various aspects of Kanban. Remember that Kanban is intuitive. Its goal is to fit into your already existing teams, not the other way around. When you treat Kanban this way, you will reap a lot of positive rewards.

Kanban can also help you and your family both at home and at work or school. It is great because even a very small child can understand its basic properties making it something that anyone can use.

It is now up to you as to how you will apply Kanban in your own life so that you and your business can achieve your goals.

# LEAN ANALYTICS

*The Definitive Guide to learn how to use Data to Track, Optimize and Build a Better and Faster Business For your Startup*

**By Adam Ross**

# Table of Contents

Introduction .................................................................... 303

Chapter 1: Introduction to Lean Analytics ........................... 305

Chapter 2: Getting Started With Lean Analytics .................. 311

Chapter 3: Lean Analytic Progress Stages ........................... 315

Chapter 4: Lean Analytics Cycles ......................................... 319

Chapter 5: Simple Analytical Test to Use ............................. 326

Chapter 6: The Metrics That Matter for Your Business ....... 332

Chapter 7: Identifying Good Metrics ................................... 339

Chapter 8: Key Metrics and Your Targets ............................ 345

Chapter 9: Implementing Lean Analytics in your Company. 348

Chapter 10: Understanding Lean Manufacturing Tools and How to Make the Most Out of Them ............................ 354

Chapter 11: Lean Deployment .............................................. 357

Chapter 12: Data-Driven Approaches .................................. 360

Chapter 13: The Impact of Key Performance Indicator(KPI) and Team Meetings ............................................................. 370

Chapter 14: How to Automatize a Company using Analytics 375

Chapter 15: The Importance of Lean Thinking for Entrepreneurs ...................................................................... 380

Chapter 16: How Do You Engage Lean Management in Your Office? ........................................................................ 388

Chapter 17: How to Utilize Analytical Information in the Business Service Management Sector ................................. 394

Chapter 18: Common Mistakes to Avoid While Using Lean in Your Office ............................................................. 402

Chapter 19: How to Perform Workforce Analytics Using Lean ......................................................................... 406

Chapter 20: Using Lean for the Public Sector ........................ 412

Chapter 21: Tips to Make Lean Analytics More Successful for You ................................................................................. 418

Conclusion ................................................................................. 426

# Introduction

The Lean Support system is a great way to ensure that your business is as efficient as possible by eliminating the amount of waste that is present. Thus, you'll determine where the waste is present, and this will help you to pick the right metrics to implement.

This book will discuss Lean Analytics and how its processes can help you reduce waste and find the best strategy to improve your business. It is just one step in the Lean Support System but it is an extremely critical step. This guidebook will provide you with the information that you need to get started so that you can become an expert in Lean Analytics in no time.

The Lean Analytics section helps with data collection and analysis so that you can make the most of your production process, your tools, and workforce. You can also bring more cohesiveness to your relationship with success through the use of Lean Analytics. Most management processes need constant supervision and overhauling but the Lean Analytic method handles the corrections on its own. You can make short-term and long-term plans for business growth with the knowledge of the cost reductions and enhancement in the workplace productivity made possible by Lean Analytics.

Lean Analytics is an arm of the Lean Startup model. The Lean Startup has three stages to its product development cycle: Build, Measure and Learn. This methodology stresses on efficiency in the smallest possible time. This is the key to an effective product development cycle.

In this E-book, we will discuss some important aspects of Lean Analytics and how to deploy it. We will go into the intricacies of Lean in the workplace, how to implement it in management and service management. This book is not limited only to entrepreneurs or businesses; we will discuss how to use Lean in the public sector too.

When you are done with this book and have reached the last page, you will be equipped with all that is needed to employ Lean Analytics in your business

For those who want to start a business. I recommend running Lean. It doesn't matter if you're a layman who wants to turn his life around and be the boss or if you're a business graduate. Running Lean is the best way to start a business today.

Lean Analytics focuses on understanding how data can be used to efficiently and effectively build, launch, and grow a business. You will learn how not only to collect data but understand exactly what this data means for your business idea and how to use it so you can make quick adjustments and improvements to keep your business moving forward.

# Chapter 1:
# Introduction to Lean Analytics

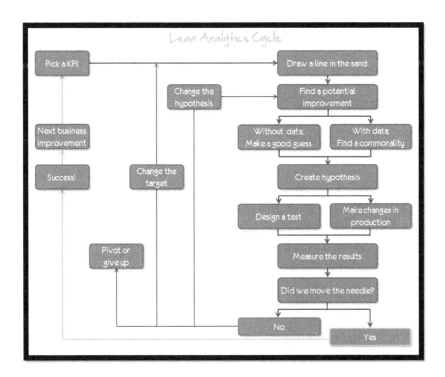

## WHAT IS LEAN ANALYTICS?

Lean Analytics teaches new entrepreneurs how to be more data-informed and data-driven, how to recognize the stage they are at within their startup, and how to purposefully choose a data metric relevant to the stage they are in. While data collection is a part of nearly every business, it is often not used to correctly identify the best path for a business to take to avoid risk and increase growth.

Lean Analytics isn't a static approach as it was before. Every business has its unique needs and it changes, depending on the state it is in. This means that you need to change your One Metric That Matters from time to time. You need to reevaluate your company's performance and goal to know the proper metric to use next time.

To start with Lean Analytics, you should have great knowledge of the industry you're in. You should also know the current state of your business. Is it on its way to success? Is it failing? Or everything is doing fine with no signs of sudden success or failure?

The next step is to set a goal. It can be better sales or it can be company expansion. Once the goal is set, you will need to determine your One Metric That Matters. If your goal is better sales, your One Metric That Matters is the number of sales your company will make.

It's important to focus on one goal and metric at a time. Choose the metric based on where your business is at. This is referred to as the One Metric That Matters (OMTM). As you transition from one stage to the next with your business, your OMTM should also change.

The Lean analytic structure is quite easy but can become overwhelming if you veer off the main focus. Because it is so data-intensive, this data can cause you to shift focus too quickly. Always remind yourself of what your business is and what stage it is at. These two factors assist you in choosing the right metrics and goals as you progress.

## THE FUNDAMENTALS OF LEAN ANALYTICS

Lean, Lean Startup, and Lean Analytics all have different methods, cycles, and stages. While they rely on different approaches, they do have a few fundamentals in common. The three fundamental issues that should guide businesses are the purpose, process, and people.

- **Purpose:** Focuses on the problem you will solve for the customer.

- **Process:** Assesses the value streams to ensure it is valuable, capable, and available as well as adequate and flexible. A value stream is similar to a map that tracks all the business actions taken that in some way, create a product or value for the customer. These should help link each step of the process with the flow, pull, and leveling.

- **People:** Who will be responsible for evaluating the purpose and process? How can engagement be increased and encouraged among those involved in each value stream?

The ultimate goals and focus of implementing the Lean startup method and Lean Analytics are to minimize waste, continuously improve upon the business idea, and always have the big picture in mind.

The Lean startup runs off a simple cycle of collecting and measuring data to help improve on the key fundamentals. Lean Analytics is the process of not just gathering data but also knowing when and how to analyze that data to understand where your business is and where your business is headed.

Lean Analytics takes a more scientific approach to develop a product or business idea where you first address the problem that needs to be solved, then go about trying to find a solution and ultimately create experiments that will allow you to test and measure the results.

## Waste and the Lean system

The goal of the Lean process is to eliminate waste completely. Waste, according to the Lean startup method, is anything that doesn't lead to validated learning. Instead of keeping all things separated for the development and growth of a business, things are instead able to flow together in a more unified way. This results in reducing the need for space, time, and effort, which, in return, lowers the cost.

Minimizing waste in this manner increases the response time when new customer needs or desires are discovered. More emphasis can be placed on the quality and variety of products or services offered.

## STARTUPS AND LEAN ANALYTICS

Lean Analytics restrains a business from losing its focus on its goal. Startups benefit from it. It helps them overcome the initial pitfalls of starting a business. That pitfall is the fervor to do all things at once and recover investments made.

Lean Analytics pushes startups away from going through premature scaling or growth. Instead of expanding, it pushes a business to establish a solid foundation. Businesses using Lean Analytics become solutions specialists and it gives the company a direction and a very narrow one at that.

As mentioned before, Lean Analytics uses a single metric to measure progress. This approach has been developed from a business methodology called Lean Startup.

Lean Startup is a business methodology that promotes running a business as Lean as it can. Steve Blank and Eric Reis helped popularize it.

The methodology encourages an entrepreneur to start a business with minimal resources. This includes minimizing employees, products, and services. Regular and large-scale businesses use a Swiss knife to operate. A Lean startup only uses a sharp and flexible single knife.

As the business operates, it improves and adds elements to the business when needed. Progression means the business obtains essential tools to help the single knife.

## CHANGE SIGNIFICANT TO LEAN

The focus shifted from the responsibility of the engineer committed to his machine, to the broad perspective of the movement of the product concerning the entire process. They incorporated simple things like the use of the correct machine size for the volume of production needed and adding changes to the working of the machine to handle the small changes needed in the part number to maintain the output volume.

By sifting through these principles further, Womack and Jones reduced the number of principles to five.

- **Value**. Only the customer's need gives us value. You get value according to the timeline for production and delivery. The price point defines another sign of value. Did you meet any quality specifications? These define the value in the product and service we provide. You have the most demand in the market when you are the only manufacturer that can provide the value the customer seeks.

- **Value stream.** After we have defined the value in full, we sum it up to get the value stream. This accounts for the entire raw material we take and the entirety of the products we make and relates it to the processes.

- **Flow**. When we bring the processes to one page, we can find and get rid of those that do not add value to the product. This number-crunching becomes possible due to the bird's eye view we have on the processes, material, products, and services.

- **Pull**. In any normal ERP type of production, one makes the products as per the forecast of the demand and the need of the schedule. In the Pull system, there is no production until the customer orders the product. To achieve this productivity rate, you need very small productivity cycles including those of the design and the delivery of the product. It has an inbuilt information cycle that keeps the downstream informed of its activities on that day.

- **Perfection.** To achieve product perfection, total quality management undergoes continuous and systematic overhauling. This key attitude symbolizes the unyielding pursuit of perfection through the removal of unneeded processes and methods. By optimizing the technologies used, and realigning the focus of the management, each product and service reaches or passes through its perfect value in the demand curve.

# Chapter 2:
# Getting Started with Lean Analytics

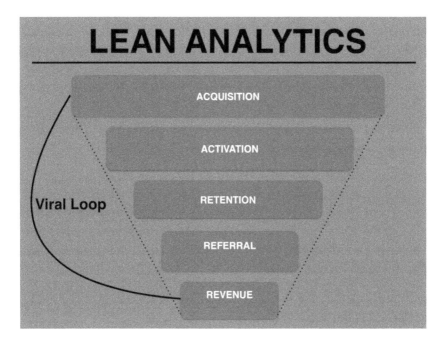

Having the right tools to assist you can be of great help. Lean Canvas is a tool that helps you organize your business idea from beginning to end and helps you identify key metrics to test through each stage.

The Lean Canvas approach allows you to identify key factors from the beginning to the end of your project development or business ideas. This can be done in a few simple steps:

### THE PROBLEM

The problem is the whole reason you are beginning your business. There is a problem that the customer needs to have resolved. By now, you already know what the problem is but do you also know three existing solutions for that same problem?

List your problem first, and below that, list the three existing solutions you know your customer already uses.

## THE SOLUTION

After the problem, you will list the solution you have come up with. For every problem that you write in the first step, you should have a relating solution in this step. You also want to write down the top three key feature or functions your solution offers that further help solve the problem

## THE KEY METRICS

As you just learned in this chapter, metrics are the most important factors in your business. In this step, you want to list the key metrics that are both relevant to where you are in your business and that you think you will need to keep track of to stay focused on the solution.

## THE CUSTOMER SEGMENTS

After all the research you have done, this should be an easy section to fill in. Here you want to identify your intended audience. You should be able to easily come up with three to five key customer characteristics of your early adopters. These individuals are the ones who are eagerly awaiting the launch of your product or service. You must understand what makes them so interested in what you have to offer.

## THE UNFAIR ADVANTAGE

You likely have a few things that put you ahead of your competitors. These unfair advantages that you possess shouldn't be easy to copy or acquire. They can include things like inside information or an in-depth understanding of the problem, being an expert in the industry, having a large supporting network or community, having the ultimate team, or having a highly respected reputation. These are things that you will want to use to your advantage through the process.

## The Channels

What are all the ways you can contact or reach customers? List all the social media sites, people, networks, and touchpoints. Touchpoints are where customers will most likely encounter your product or brand. There are three main time frames that you will want to break this up into:

- Before purchase
- During purchase
- After purchase

In each time frame, you want to list the top three channels of how you will contact or connect with your customers.

## The Unique Value Proposition

This statement answers the "how" and the "why" of your business model. This should be a clear statement that highlights how your business stands out and places value above any other alternative. You want to write your unique value proposition and look at it as a high-level concept as it will be the statement that helps show customers what they should expect from your business.

## Cost Structure

Here you will list all the costs you can think of that will occur when doing business. Look at each step you have completed so far and consider the cost that can be attached to each step. One of the main reasons startups fail is because they do not properly plan for how much it will cost for them to launch and start their business. Using Lean analysis can greatly reduce these costs but you still want to address all. Some cost can include:

- Customer acquisition
- Distribution
- Product development
- Services to launch
- Connecting with customers
- Branding
- Researching your market
- Marketing

## THE REVENUE STREAMS

What are your sources of income? How will this source of income continue to keep your business running?

Once you have completed all the steps, you will have a simplified business plan that will get you started and help you stay focused on your business idea.

# Chapter 3:
# Lean Analytic Progress Stages

| Lean Analytics Stages | "Gates" needed to move forward |
|---|---|
| Empathy | You've found a real, poorly-met need that a reachable market faces. |
| Stickiness | You've figured out how to solve the problem in a way they will adopt, keep using and pay for. |
| Virality | Your users and features fuel growth organically and artificially. |
| Revenue | You've found a sustainable, scalable business with the right margins in a healthy ecosystem. |
| Scale | |

There are five main stages that every startup must go through to stay focused on the end goal. These include:

## EMPATHY STAGE

Many startups never take off because they begin the process with the assumption that they already know what the customer wants. This way of thinking most often results in wasting time and money developing a product that there is no demand for.

In the empathy stage, the main focus is on finding the solution to the problem your customers have. This problem has to be a significant issue for them. If it is just a minor issue, most people may not be willing to pay for the solution. A problem that causes pain or serious inconvenience to the customer is one they would be willing to pay to have solved.

## STICKINESS STAGE

In the stickiness stage, you begin to build a solution to the problem. This is referred to as the Minimum Viable Product (MVP). You will begin to test the value of this product to see how many customers not only engage in the product but stick around and continue to use it. You are looking to see how much value you add to the customer. When you have provided enough value to the customer, you move onto the next stage.

### What is an MVP?

An MVP is the way you will test your solution. MVPs can be several things from landing pages to demo videos or even a small group of people doing everything manually before moving on to developing the technology behind their business idea.

The MVP needs to have only the most viable features. These are the features that you will be testing to validate your hypothesis. This is not a perfect product, and in many cases, it is something that you would be embarrassed about sharing simply because it is so incomplete. The MVP is for measuring and learning. It should help you better understand what the customer's problems are and if your product solves that problem, as well as how much those customers are willing to pay for it.

When you build an MVP, you can gain valuable customer feedback that allows you to improve and adjust to the product while it is still being developed. This can help you prove or disprove an assumption you may have.

### Types of MVP

#### Concierge MVP

A concierge MVP requires you to take on all the responsibility of operating your business idea. You act as the concierge for the customers. It may not sound effective but Zappos and Food on the Table successfully used this type of MVP to launch their business ideas. These MVPs are best for testing out a business idea.

### Wizard of OZ MVP

This MVP is meant to test user experience through a product simulation. The MVP looks as if it was the end product or service with all the functions operating but it is run by a human. While this is similar to the Concierge MVP, a Wizard of OZ MVP does not reveal that all operations are being performed by an actual person. This type of MVP can help test out specific solutions.

### Smoke Test MVP

The smoke MVP is one of the lowest cost MVPs you can create as it will cost the price of a landing page. You can give visitors the option of either signing up for a waiting list, scheduling demo tests, or preordering the product. This will give you a clear idea of whether or not you have a product people want or are interested in.

MVPs are designed to simply test out your idea or some specific features with a small group of your target audience. Remember that it needs to have just enough features that make it look credible so you can test and analyze your assumptions.

Once you have created and tested your MVP, you should have a clear understanding of whether or not you have the solution your customers are looking for. If you have several customers who enjoy your products or services and are using it regularly, then you pass the gate to the next stage.

## VIRALITY STAGE

Virality is when you begin to look at ways to attract more customers with minimal investment. During this phase, your main focus is on how to retain customers. This is also when you begin to consider your engine of growth method.

## Deciding on an engine of growth

Customers are the driving force behind a sustainable business. When you are focusing on customer retention, you also want to consider how you want your business to grow. Customers bring in more customers through word-of-mouth, as a natural occurrence from using your product, through paid advertisement, and from repeated use.

### REVENUE STAGE

During the revenue stage, you start to focus more on optimizing your cash flow. This is where many businesses try to prove themselves as a viable business entity.

Ask yourself: Do the economics around your company work in the long run? While you will probably have been charging a price for your product before this, this is the stage you work out all the numbers to ensure future growth. At this point, you can begin to look at the expected revenue from the customers and the cost of acquiring new customers.

### SCALE STAGE

In the scaling stage, you will focus on ways to further grow your business. There are several ways you can approach this stage and even more ways you can bring in more revenue. Ultimately, this is the stage where you decide what new markets you might want to enter into and how you can reach new customers across the world.

These five steps are the key to building a solid foundation for your business. If you don't take the time to go through each step properly, you run the risk of encountering problems that can quickly destroy all your efforts and dreams.

# Chapter 4:
# Lean Analytics Cycles

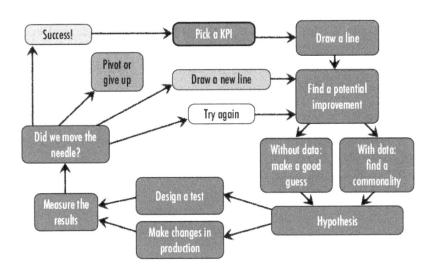

The Lean analytic cycle is similar to that of the scientific method. Through the cycle, you begin to piece together all the data, concepts, and information you have thus far and begin to execute the best way to approach each business problem. For each stage, you will begin a new cycle where you will identify the main problem, choose the one metric, and get to work.

The Lean Analytics Cycle is vital in helping you get started on this part of the Lean support methodology with your business. Four steps will come with this process, and following each one can be crucial in ensuring that this works for you.

The Lean Analytics Cycle will be incredibly helpful when you begin going through the entire process. Let's take a look at the steps that you need to fulfill to use the Lean Analytics Cycle.

## Form a Hypothesis

The hypothesis is when you create different ways to test out your KPIs. This can be by developing a marketing campaign to test features on a product or changing your pricing, just to name a few examples.

This is a stage where a level of creativity needs to come into play. The hypothesis gives you the answers that you need to move forward. You will need to look for inspiration, and you can find it in one of two ways. You can look for an answer for something like "If I perform ___, I believe ___ will happen, and ___ will be the outcome."

The first place you can look into is any data that you have available. Often, this data will provide you with the answer that you need. If you do not have data at all, you may need to do some studying to come up with an answer. You could use some of the strategies from your competitors, follow the practices that have worked well for others, do a survey, or study the market to see what the best option will be.

What you need to keep in mind here is that the hypothesis is there to help you to think like your audience. You want to keep asking questions until you understand what they are thinking, or learn to understand the behavior of your audience or customer.

You can often turn toward data collected to come up with the best way to improve your KPI. Look at what your customers have in common. Focus on the customers that are doing what you want. For example, if you are focusing on lowering your churn rate, or the yearly rate of how frequently customers stop subscribing to your services, then you want to understand why the customers that stay are staying. Where do they come from; what is their buying process? Get inside the head of your customers to form your hypothesis.

If you do not have data collected, then you can turn to several other sources to make the best-educated guess. Do this by:

- **Understanding your market.** Surveys, feedback, or just getting out there and talking to your audience can give you enough information to create your hypothesis.

- **Look at what your competitors are doing.** While you have your unique idea in mind, it doesn't hurt to rely on what is already being done to understand how it can be improved. Your competitors may be doing something well that you can implement but also improve upon; you won't know how to improve it if you don't test it out yourself first.

- **Get up to date on what the best practices are.** You can gain inspiration from reading up on the ways different companies are doing business. How are they using content marketing? How have they been able to grow quickly? Understanding the best practices in your industry and the business world can lead to a hypothesis that truly accelerates your growth.

You create your hypothesis by considering the action you will take and what the result of the action will be. The result should lead you to the desired outcome. It should be written out in this way:

- If I do (insert action), I believe (insert result) will happen, which will get me (desired outcome).

- This hypothesis should be placed in a location where you and your team can view it daily. Having it visually present will remind you what you are working towards.

## EXPERIMENT

Once you have your hypothesis set, you will begin to come up with a way to put it into action. This may require making changes to the production process to test the product out with half of your customers.

When choosing an experimental path, you need to be able to answer the who, what, and why about your target audience.

- **Who will your experiment be for?** You need to know what target audience you want to test your experiment out on or which target audience you are expecting to act in a certain way. You need to know if the audience you are trying to reach is the right one if you appeal to them and if their behavior can be changed.

- **What do you want this target audience to do?** You need to be clear about what you will ask this audience to do. You will want to determine if there is something that might get in the way of them completing what you expect them to and how many of them will do what you want them to.

- **Is what you are asking worthwhile to them?** You need to be sure your targets understand why they would want to do what you are asking them. What is their motivation for doing it, or what makes them do the same thing for a competitor but not you? Your target audience wants to know what is in it for them, and if what you offer is more appealing or convenient than what your competitor already offers.

The answers to these questions are derived from your customer development, which is how you can fully understand your customers.

After answering these questions, you should have a statement that looks like: WHO will do WHAT because WHY.

The who, what, and why should result in improving your KPI. If you have a solid hypothesis, then you will come up with a solid experiment to test this hypothesis. Once you have decided on the experiment, you move on to determining how you will measure the outcome. Before you can begin to measure, you need to have a starting baseline to compare to.

Types of experiments can include:

- Marketing campaigns
- Application redesign
- Change in pricing
- Location of shipping costs
- Testing out different platforms
- Wording or word usage
- Rest new features
- How your business appeals to customers.

## MEASURE YOUR OUTCOMES AND DECIDE

Was your experiment a success, or did you learn what did not work? If you had success with your experiment, then you can simply move on to determine the next metric to test and start experimenting again.

You can't just get started with an experiment and then walk away from it. You need to measure how well it goes to determine if it is truly working; if some changes are needed; or if you need to work from scratch. You can then decide on the next steps you need to take. Some of the things to look for when measuring the outcomes during this stage include:

- **Was the experiment a success?** If it is, then the metric is done. You can move on to finding the next metric to help your business.

- **Did the experiment fail?** Then it is time to revise the hypothesis. You should stop and take some time to figure out why the experiment failed so that you have a better chance at a good hypothesis the next time.

- **The experiment moved but was not close to the defined goal.** In this scenario, you will still need to define a brand new experiment. You can stay with the hypothesis if it still seems viable but you would need to change up the experiment.

If you did have much success, it doesn't mean you just give up. You now have several options as to how to move forward:

- If the experiment was of no success whatsoever, then consider first what you learned, then revisit your hypothesis. You may need to come up with a new target audience, a new action taken by the target audience, or a new motivating factor.

- If you had slight success with your experiment, again first look at what you learned, then make minor adjustments to your experiment and try it again. If you saw some success with your experiment, it might not be that your hypothesis is completely wrong; it might just mean you need to tweak a few things.

Through the experiment, you will be able to determine if the result moves you closer to your end target. If you are moved closer to the end target, then you can move forward to the next metric that matters. If, however, you notice you are moving farther away from the target, you need to evaluate your data and make a shift in your business, your model, or your market.

## DECIDE

After reviewing all the data and determining whether your experiment was a success or not, you now need to decide: Do you pivot or persevere?

Sometimes, you need to change your strategy to meet the overall vision you have for that product. This may require simply adjusting a part of your experiment and repeating the process. You may need to pivot in a new direction in one or more areas.

Pivot does not mean failure; it is a way of bringing to focus on what is working or is not working in the process. When you can catch what isn't working, you can make adjustments to experiment in a new direction.

You can also persevere. In this case, you don't need to pivot but move forward. When your experiment is a success, you can feel confident that you are on the right path to developing the right product.

# Chapter 5:
# Simple Analytical Test to Use

Another thing that you should concentrate on to do well with Lean Analytics is to have some familiarity with the tests that are used. These tests are helpful because they are used to help you examine any assumptions that you are trying to use here. These tools can also be used to help you identify customer feedback so you can respond to them properly. Let us take a look at some of the best analytical tests that you can use when working with Lean Analytics.

## SEGMENTATIONS

Segments are groups that have common characteristics. These can be certain individuals who purchase the same type of products or have similar shopping patterns. These groups can also relate to demographics. When performing segmentation tests, take into account all your users. This can be a major drawback when it comes to measuring your metrics.

This takes into account all your customers, whether they are valuable customers or those who just hang around. This results in data that may not be true for what is occurring. Keep in mind that those who were on board early will have had a much different user experience than those who came on later. Your systems may have improved, features may have changed, and focus may have shifted. Those who started with you may not have had the best experience, and these individuals can throw certain metrics off from what they are.

This process involves comparing a set of data from a demographic bucket. You can divide up the demographics in any manner that you choose such as gender, lifestyle, age, or where they live. You can use this information to find out where people are purchasing a particular product; if there are different buying behaviors between female and male customers; and if your target audience seems to be in a certain age group or not.

The reason that you want to build up a user segment is to make it easier for the data to be actionable. Analytics can teach you a ton about the people who purchase from you but there is often a lot of information there, and it can be hard to draw good conclusions from this information. After all, while this information from the past can be useful, it isn't the best to tell you how to improve either retention or conversion rate.

With segmentation, you don't want to only look at the data to learn some more about your users but you also want to come up with data that you can act upon. Segmentation can help you with this. You will be able to divide up the people in your customer base and learn how to advertise to them better than ever before.

Remember that not all customers are the same. There are some of your customers who may purchase something once, and they aren't regular customers. While it is still good to reach out to them, you want to learn who your regular audience is, what they respond to, and what keeps them coming back. This ensures that you keep them coming back and earn as much profit as possible.

So, how do you create a segment of your customers? There are many different options that you can use when creating a segmentation. But let's look at the process that you can use to create a segmentation for your Lean Analytics project. The steps you need to use include:

- **Define the purpose of your segmentation:** You should first figure out how you want to use your segmentation. Do you want to use it to get more customers? Do you want to use it to manage a portfolio for your current customers? Do you want to reduce waste, become more efficient, or something else? Defining your purpose can make it easier to know how you should segment out your customers.

- **Identify the variables that are the most critical:** These help influence the purpose of your segmentation. Make sure that you list them out in order of their importance, and you can use options like a Decision tree or Clustering to help. For example, if you want to do a segmentation of products to find out which ones are the most profitable, you would have parameters that are revenue and cost.

- Once you have your variables, you will need to **identify the threshold and granularity of creating these segments.** These should have about two to three levels with each variable identified. But sometimes you will need to adapt based on the complexity of the problem you are trying to solve.

- **Assign customers to each of the cells.** You can then see if there is a fair distribution for them. If you don't see this, you can look for the reasons why, or you can tweak the thresholds to make it work. You can perform these steps again until you get a fair distribution.

- **Include this new segmentation in the analysis** and then take some time to look it over at the segment level.

## COHORT ANALYSIS

Cohort analysis compares groups that are similar but over a longer period. Each group is referred to as a cohort. Using cohort analysis is ideal when you want to focus on per-customer metrics.

Comparing these groups with when they encountered your business can help you identify whether your metrics are improving. In many cases, users you may have had around since the very beginning phases of your business will often have a different experience from those who join later on, as much testing and adjusting should have been made to improve their overall experience. Those from the beginning may not result in high conversion rates but those who join later may have great conversion rates.

Each of these is significant because it helps you to figure out which customers are likely to come back and be full-fledged customers when in the future. Those that show up in the initial stages when the product is free are often not the customers you see when sales start. They may have just wanted to try it out and didn't have an investment in the product.

Those that are in the later two stages can be customers who are better for you to work with. They will be the most interested in the product because they invested some money to get it. You want to study these using the cohort analysis to figure out who your real customer base is and how they behave so that you can better market to them later on.

## A/B TESTING

A/B testing is one of the most common ways to compare attributes based on customer experience or preference. A/B testing can also help identify the most actionable metrics. An easy example that explains A/B testing is deciding on which color to use for your website. You choose two colors you are considering and ask users to decide which they like better.

Applying A/B testing is one of the easiest ways to gain more feedback on new features or functions. They should be a continuous part of your development process. You will measure data between three different groups: your control group, the group you test your first hypothesis on, and a second group you test your other hypothesis on. Then you track the actions of your customers. You want to see in what areas your hypothesis is improving. The hypothesis you choose should be the one that shows the greatest improvement among all actions taken by the customer

Multivariate testing is a type of A/B testing that can speed up the learning cycle when you have several features you want to test. This allows you to combine testing of different features instead of having to test them separately. You can see which features will better improve your key metric.

A/B testing is a process where you examine an attribute between two choices. This could be something like an image, slogan, or color so that you can figure out which option is the most effective choice.

Let's say that you had two products that you are comparing and you want to find out which ones customers liked the best. Did they choose one product over the other and why? Did they respond better to the choice that was in green or the one in blue?

For this test to work, you must assume that everything else will stay the same. So, it would have to be the same product but there is one variable that is different between them. You could put up a website, for example, and have a red background on one version and a yellow background on another. Then you could use A/B testing to figure out which one the customer responded to the best out of those choices. Also, you can work on multivariate analysis. This is pretty much the same thing but instead of going through and testing out one attribute, you will go through and compare several changes against another group of changes to see which is the most effective.

This one will require there to be a few changes in the second product compared to the first to be the most effective. There are several keys that you need to have in place when you are ready to do an A/B test. These include:

- The item that you are testing needs to be noticeable to the audience. If you make a minor change that no one notices, then your results are not that reliable.

- Know the reason that you are running this A/B test.

- Stick with testing just one variable at a time. If you go through and do multivariate testing, or test more than one thing at a time, you will run into trouble. You may not know for sure which variable is causing the changes you see.

- Your test needs to end up being statistically significant. This means that it must have a sample size that is big enough to test and know that the results are valid within a certain margin of error.

# Chapter 6:
# The Metrics That Matter for Your Business

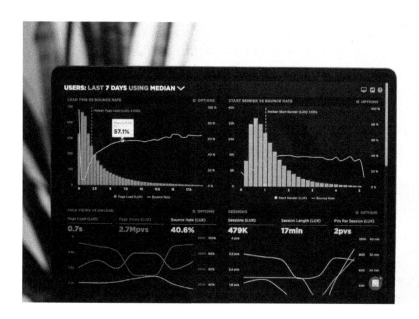

## WHAT ARE METRICS?

Metrics are calculative measures that are used to track and review the state of your business, and performance. It is how you determine whether or not your business is doing well. Different persons are involved in a business, so whatever the metric, they must address the workforce and the customers, the investors and the managers. Every aspect of a business has a specific performance metrics to it but generally, metrics are those quantifying measures with which you keep the status and performance of your business in check.

Lean helps your business grow and improve continuously, business metrics, on the other hand, helps you follow up on the growth and performance of your business. It helps determine how much or how well your business is doing with all the Lean principles and practices in having been put in place. Take for example, in marketing, marketers have a metric system to with which and through which they stay on the success of their marketing, the same thing applies to media advertisers and as well for politicians who do campaigns. Some questions will be asked, questions such as how many persons were we able to reach, and how many persons responded, and then how many persons gave a positive response? The idea is to know what the success and the failure is, having a target result in mind with which they will judge the performance result.

A metric is more like a guide; it helps your business track and achieves target results. In that case, there are certain checkpoints or tracking measures. Let us take an athlete for example; they know they train against various factors. They have to train enough to get to the point where they can now beat the time. Time is probably the athlete's highest target.

## NEED FOR METRICS

- It will help drive the strategy and direction of the organization: When metrics are put in place, the path to take towards the organization's destination will be known.
- Focus: it will help put the organization, employees, and everyone involved in check and keep them constantly focused, with their eyes on the ball. If there is a target to meet in a month, with the right metrics, the numbers will be rolled up so that progress can be tracked
- Decision – In cases where decisions on certain matters need to be made, metrics are the best resort to turn to. It will help give out in clear terms, the need to make or not to make a move at a point
- Performance – It enables an organization to do better. Metrics monitor activities going on, when this is viewed by the head of an organization, the level of progress made is known and the organization knows how much effort should be put in

- Change and evolve with the organization – As metrics are being monitored, the organization changes and evolves as more progress is made, there is also an evolving of metrics as the organization strives to get better
- Objective process – The goal of every organization is to make a profit and at the same time satisfy the customers, in a bid to satisfy customers, quality services must be rendered, processes have to be organized to suit the customer's needs.

## METRICS THAT YOU LOOK AT TO KNOW THAT LEAN IS AFFECTING THE HEALTH OF YOUR ORGANIZATION?

Success must be measurable; if not, you cannot tell whether this is a success or not. To know if you are successful, you would first have to have a defined perspective/vision. What did you want to achieve with this business you started? Where do you see this business in 50 years? All these are essential steps to know if one is along the path of success or not. With your vision in mind, you can quickly look at specific metrics to see if you are succeeding or not.

- The cost that it would take to retain a customer: as a business, you should have a strategy that you implement to maintain customers, and that strategy comes with a cost, that cost should be minimal as you engage in Lean methodologies; you should find more cost-effective ways to keep your customers.
- How viral is your product? The virality of your merchandise can be an excellent pointer to the health of your business. If you get more people to know you exist, you stand a better chance of getting engaged. Your viral reach can be measured by how many you have participated on Facebook, Instagram, and Twitter.
- Lead time: the lead time is the amount of time it takes for a product to go through a Lean process to completion. To be able to track your progress, you need

to know how fast your products are produced and how fast they get to the consumer.
- How easily is work distributed among the team? This question is fundamental. It answers the issue of the workflow. For a product to reach its final stage, it goes through many departments, and the rate at which this work gets executed is essential. Your company is healthy if your team members distribute well, have a strong team spirit, and deliver the task before or right on schedule.
- Increased number of open issues: it is only reasonable that mistakes would be made, and problems would arise but if these issues are becoming overwhelming, you must look into it before it ruins something. The state of work is essential for the quality of the product—it is garbage in, garbage out. What you invest in, would, in turn, affect you.
- Customer feedback: apart from internal evaluation, some external assessment is necessary as well. What your customer says about your product is the brand your product has in the mind of that customer.

## OVERVIEW OF OVER-PRODUCTION

The production cycle has inbuilt questions to start the next cycle. The first one is to please only the customer and stop when you reach the target. Have I achieved today's quota? If the answer is yes, then stop production. Until the customer places a new order, do not make anything.

This principle applies to all departments in the organization. The idea is to achieve the perfect value stream. Other than this, there is nothing you need to worry about. In Lean, we reduce the steps we use to help cut waste, while the Six Sigma principle checks for variation. The more variations there are in the process, the more chances there are for waste to accumulate. You need to follow only Lean principles of keeping the number of steps down.

## USE OF LEAN PRINCIPLE AT WORK

To separate technicality from working, workers must understand and use Lean principles. Often, some problems seem technical but involve real people. You begin to use Lean principle at the core, the place where the problem arises with only one man. Then, expand the core team to as many as you need, until the problem gets resolved.

It takes some time for the principles to go into operation because there is a learning curve involved. If you do not have the Lean thinking, then there will not be much progress. Also, the team must know if the circumstances are right. If they are not, they must identify the cause and size of the problem. It may be due to one or more of the following:

- Lack of commitment: The worker does not feel there is a need for Lean methods. He uses traditional principles but gets foxed when others seem to feel something is extraneous. Shift the focus and reexamine the problem.
- Performance not aligned with commitment: This is more serious because work is ongoing and the value is not reaching the expected level. We need a change in the attitude because the worker wants to get measured according to the performance parameter. He is not worried about the process parameter.
- Lack of training: The workers get deployed before they have got trained. So, they keep looking at the others when the work proceeds. Change the worker to another place and keep the work going. Wait until the person addresses the problem by confronting it.

We see that the Lean working method is not a toolbox we can pick from to achieve our ends. It is a total perspective that involves the entirety of the work process.

## CHOOSE TO OPERATE THE PULL

You have many aspects affecting how to operate the Pull. The Pull is important because there will be instances where the workflow gets interrupted. One of the ways to use it is to address the question or problem from two or more perspectives. Pull exists at the nodes or joints of the structure in the organization.

The workflow question is, "Have you finished this work?" The problem question is, "Where is the box of material I am supposed to deliver?" And the Pull question becomes, "Who is the driver delivering the box to the work spot?" You can change the Pull in many ways until you have got rid of the externality existing in the structure.

So, you see the work proceeding but there is a lag due to the lack of the box. The Lean principle tells you to cut the waste. Here you are wasting time. To cut this, you must address the issue by finding out who is bringing the box. The truck needed to deliver the box must undergo preparation. And then the box must get loaded onto the truck. But, since there is a problem, you shift the focus of the problem by diverting the loaders to a new place to do new work.

The problem is now resolved at two or three levels. One is the basic worker level where you give new work to the worker. The second is at the management level where you identify what caused the lack of the box. The third is at the deployment level where you keep alternatives ready to prevent any further occurrence of this event. Lean, thus, operates at many levels.

## MAKE COMPARISON OF THE STEPS

As the value stream progresses, the number of options keeps on adding up. Many businesses keep these options open in the hope that some good will come of it. But, it ends up as a waste of space and effort. So, it is wise to get rid of all but one working option. When you have more than one option, it will end up in confusion.

If you have to make a choice, list out the options. Then, compare the merits and demerits of each one. Try reducing the steps in each and see, which one gets done first. This will prove to be the best choice.

# Chapter 7:
# Identifying Good Metrics

Lean Analytics allows you to look at data collection as a tool that will help you be more aware of your business. The main component of this tool fully relies on the metrics. It helps because it can be easy to lose focus through the process of starting your business. You have several things to consider. There is constant information being thrown at you. It is no wonder so many entrepreneurs make the common mistake of focusing their attention on the right thing but at the wrong time. Understanding metrics will allow you to identify the ones that give you product the most value.

## A GOOD METRIC MUST BE

- Measurable to compare: Metrics are valued for measurement and comparison sake. Your metric data's use cannot be fully actualized if it cannot be compared. The information lies in the comparisons made. From

the comparison, you can ask and answer questions about just how well your company is faring.
- It should be expressed in ratio: We express metrics in ratio to other metrics. It is much better to state profit levels and also state them in ratio to profits at this same time a year or month ago than to just state profit levels.
- Easy to understand: Businessmen who make use of metrics are people who specialize in making money and not reading data. If a businessman with little to no prior knowledge of Analytics is to use metrics, it must be easy to understand.

## UNDERSTANDING THE DATA

You need first to establish what needs to be measured. To do this properly, you need to understand what your business goals are then you will be able to determine what it is that you need to measure to show how you are making progress.

Metrics must be comparable, understandable, and a ratio or rate:

- The ratio or rate metrics are best used when they are more specific. Relying on absolute numbers can keep you distracted instead of focusing on the vital numbers that will move you forward.
- When the metric is comparable, you can specify actions or details for a given amount of time and see how they have improved over that time.
- For your entire team to stay focused on the one metric that matters, they need to be able to understand it easily. If you spend all your time trying to explain what metric you are tracking, then you stop focusing on the tracking and start focusing on ensuring everyone understands.
- Most importantly, your metric that matters needs to encourage you to change your behavior, and everyone in the company needs to be aware of what metrics they should be focusing on. Just picking a metric without understanding how the result will affect the way you

progress forward means you did not choose the right metric.

## WHAT ARE THE FALSE METRICS?

False metrics are those that are wrong. These metrics are often tampered with so that the goal is achieved but in a way that isn't a viable solution. These metrics offer no real valuable information.

For example, if your metric is to increase the number of sales in your company, then this can be a valuable metric. But salespeople can offer bigger discounts for everyone. As a result, there would be an increase in sales but it would not be a realistic solution for properly increasing sales. Track sales to see if the increase can only benefit you if you have an end goal in mind as well.

## THE BIGGEST FALSE METRICS TO WATCH OUT FOR

As a business that is trying to cut out waste and ensure that you provide the best customer service and the best products possible, you must always ensure that you watch out for some of the false metrics that may come up. Many people who don't understand how data works will be taken in by these false metrics that, in reality, will mean wasted time and resources. Some of the most common false metrics for you to watch out for include:

- **The number of hits:** Just because you have a website that is attractive and contains many points of interest, doesn't necessarily mean that it will tell you what the users are interested in. You should not focus on the number of hits your website gets.
- **Page views:** This metric refers to how many pages are clicked on a site during a given time. This is slightly better than hits but you typically don't want to waste your time with this metric.

- **Number of visitors:** The biggest problem with this metric is that it is often too broad. Does this type of metric talk about one person who visited the same site a hundred times, or a hundred people who visited once? You most likely want to look at the second group of people because you've obtained more impressions. Otherwise, just looking at the number of visitors will not give you this information.

- **Number of unique visitors:** This is a metric that tells you how many people got to your website and saw the home page. This may sound good at first but it is not going to give you any valuable information. You may also want to find out things like how many visitors left right away when they saw the page or how many stayed and looked around.

- **Number of likes, followers, or friends**: This is a good example of a vanity metric that shows you false popularity. A better metric that you can go with is the level of influence that you have. What this means is how many people will do what you want them to do.

- **Email addresses:** Having a big list of email addresses is not a bad thing by itself. But just because you have this large list does not mean that everyone on it will open, read, and act on the messages that you send out.

- **The number of downloads:** This is a common metric that is used for downloadable products. While it can help with your rankings in the marketplace when you are in the app store, the download number is not going to tell you anything in-depth, and it won't give you any real value.

- **Time spent by customers on a page or website:** The only time that this is useful is for businesses that are tied directly to the behavior of the engaged time.

They may look good on the surface but in reality, they are just giving you information that could be pretty useless, and you will end up wasting a lot of time and money to follow them.

## WHY DO THE RIGHT METRICS MATTER?

By this point, you probably understand metrics and that they can make or break your success. Choosing the right metric cannot be stressed enough. It is one of the keys to ensuring your startup takes off. Here are some specifics as to why you need to choose the correct metric to measure.

### You state the most important question for your business.

Building a successful startup will require you to confront and answer hundreds of questions, oftentimes daily. The right metrics will help you narrow down all these questions so you can focus on the most important one that helps bring to focus what the biggest risks are for your business. When you choose the right metric, you will be able to measure and answer this question easily.

### Set clear goals and an end target.

You will hear the phrase "draw a line in the sand" often when using the Lean model. This line in the sand refers to the goal you are striving to reach. You may understand that the revenue your business is bringing in is too low for you to sustain your business, so you may state that your focus should be on increasing this revenue. But what do you need to increase it to? Setting clear goals and an end target goal will force you to get more specific about what you expect.

### Involves the whole company.

The metric should be the focus of everyone in the company. There is no such thing as being overly focused on the right metrics. When the whole company is made aware of where the focus needs to remain, the whole company works together to find the best and even the most innovative ways to reach the target.

### Builds your company culture.

Experimentation is an important aspect of building a solid company culture. Everyone can become involved in the Lean cycle in a way that encourages engagement and innovation. This can be implemented throughout your entire organization. Bringing the one metric that matters to the focus allows everyone to participate in the experimentation step to work toward a common goal.

# Chapter 8:
# Key Metrics and Your Targets

Have the best working stream by working upward from the fundamentals. This involves the integration of the organizational structure and deployment of the tools needed to work. The value stream management focuses on improving shared vision and helping workers achieve their goals.

## LEAN THINKING HELPS BUSINESS SYSTEMS TO GROW

Systems and processes remain based on principles. Here we use the 5S principles of Lean thinking to build our business model. The idea behind developing the business system is to plan and create a strategy. We also use it for the development and implementation of the business process. You meet customer expectations and add value to the brand.

For this, you have to measure, compare, and analyze the customer based parameters. The Lean thinking points out the areas to develop and those you can eradicate. When you create more space, you see the demand grow among the customers.

## USE POLICY DEPLOYMENT

The purpose of initiating a working policy or strategy is to expose the customer to the goals of the origination. It translates the vision and strategy into Key Performance Indicators by setting targets.

Continuous improvement remains the main target of the Lean accounting system with the Value Stream Process being central to everything. The effort is to increase the flow through suitable Lean strategies. Employees get motivated and empowered to use Lean thinking so there is change present throughout the organization.

Due to the improved flow, we find increased accountability and a quicker turnaround. This comes under the control of the Value Stream Team Management that takes into account the entire value streams and not any individual ones.

The calculation of costs encompasses three broad groups. One is the raw materials and input costs. The next includes the conversion and processing costs. And the last one covers the facility cost.

## CHANGE THE PAY TO REFLECT THE LEAN THINKING

The first thing to do is to improve the focus on things that add value. The process comes to nothing if it makes something that the customer does not want. But, there will always be some element of the process that does not add value to the system. Identify the people who add value and reward them. This will encourage them to work better. The process will become more efficient and the customer will have more satisfaction.

When you invest in Lean Analytics, you get profit whenever there is a redundancy in the process. You also get profit due to the increased efficiency of the people in the organization. To keep the output high, you must pay the people having higher efficiency.

## DEFINE PERFORMANCE MEASUREMENT WELL

To improve participation and for better deployment of tools related to Lean, the team must make sure that everyone understands what the performance-defining parameters are. For instance, if you want better employee attendance, tell the workers how they will get the bonus points if they are present ahead of time. When the employee knows what will reward him, he will keep looking for that. This is the basis of Lean thinking.

## MORE TRAINING FOR ALL EMPLOYEES

One way to increase employee participation is to keep changing the way you instruct them. They have a method of understanding things and once you hit the right method of speaking or instructing them, they will understand and work faster and better.

## MAKE USE OF PROPER TOOLS FOR THE JOB

The use of wrong tools or tools of the wrong size will decrease productivity. Make checks to ensure that at all places in the workflow the tools are of the needed size. You can improve work performance through the use of automated tools. This will reduce worker fatigue and also the time it takes to do the work.

# Chapter 9: Implementing Lean Analytics in your Company

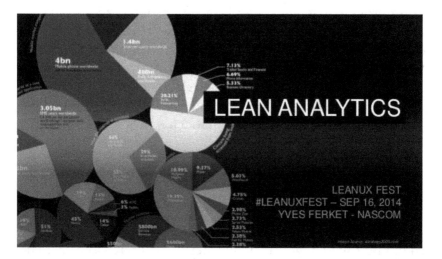

Before you implement Lean analytic, decide what type of business you run. What are the things that you know in and about your business? The answer to that question should be "a lot" as you need a large amount of knowledge. Lean Analytics works on knowledge of your business which you have and does not teach you about your business. You must then decide how progressed your business is? Businesses go through 5 stages: Empathy, Stickiness, Virality, Revenue, and Scale.

At each stage of this process, data is collected. However, using tools to analyze this data is what Lean Analytics is about. From the onset, you should ensure you have Lean data that has not been influenced in any way it should not be. The collected data are your business metrics. Business metrics are measurable data that businesses use to analyze the failure or success of various decisions taken. Metrics are either quantitative or qualitative. Qualitative metrics focus on value and quantitative on the amount.

As we now understand, Lean Analytics deals with building, analyzing, learning, and improving. It is analyzing, learning, and improving to become a continuous cycle. The last stage of the cycle, improving, is where depends on the implementation.

## IMPROVING FROM LEARNING

When you learn, you find out what needs to be improved. This is why you need to understand your business as we spoke about before. Lean Analytics acts as a builder. However, it needs a foundation which is your knowledge about your business. Once this is done, you can focus on metrics. You can combine metrics from your business with metrics from other related businesses. When this is done, you focus on a singular metric and decide where improvements need to be made.

## BE CREATIVE WITH POSSIBLE SOLUTIONS

Using the various Lean tools, you can get to the root cause of your problem and come up with solutions. Now it is time to think out of the box. Although you are to be creative, these solutions are not to come off the top of your head. Your solutions should be created after carrying out research. Now that you have a problem, find out why. If you know your business that well, you should know if it a common one or if it is a peculiar one. Carry our research on both larger and smaller-scale companies who perform the same functions as you. If you have suitable data, it will be easier to discover key factors causing the issues. Coming up with solutions is usually a team duty. Managers and business owners have found it benefitting to have their employees brainstorm along with them. However, ultimately you hold the veto power and your employees can only suggest.

## Implement Your Solutions on a Small Scale

Remember that your solution is still theoretical. It is not proven. A genuine as your data and analyzes may be, it may simply not just work. This is not the fault of the tools but rather the fault of the chosen solution. The great thing about this stage is, either way, you win. If your solution turns out suitable, you have a problem solved. If it does not, you have not only learned, you have also acquired more data. Have a clear view of what your solution is to achieve. After that is done, you can move on to implementing it on a smaller scale as it is still a test.

## Study the Outcomes

This is when you need to sit back and watch. You are to measure the outcome of the experiment. If your chosen, solution solves the problem, you have succeeded. You can now move on to the next metric and solve the next problem. If your solution did not perform as expected, it is back to the drawing board. Depending on the outcome, you may need to revise and edit your solution or throw it away.

## How to Effectively Implement Lean Analytics into Your Company

Many companies either plan or have already implemented, Lean over the past ten years. Many of those have been able to obtain some quantifiable results, which meant that they saw some big transformations in their business. Even more than this, though, is that some saw a lot of great effects and worked hard to keep this system going in their business, and others started on things that were too small or unimportant, and then their efforts ended up stalling or stopping.

The key reasons for failure when it comes to Lean include:

- There was a lack of commitment or a lack of understanding from the directors or the senior managers in the company.
- There wasn't a clear vision for the program before it was started.
- There were issues with politics. This could be something that occurs when more than one manager has an idea for a program and wants to prove that Lean is the wrong option.
- A lack of understanding of what the purpose is for using this program.
- A lack of commitment from the finance community
- The inability to capture any of the savings from the profits that do prove to be a success with Lean.
- The measures of performance are not able to align. This is the idea that I will continue to concentrate on what I am measured on, rather than what might be the most important to the program.
- A deployment that is half-hearted. This is when only part of the team, rather than all of them, work on the deployment process.
- A selection of the wrong people to be the Champions or the Black Belts.
- Selecting the wrong projects to concentrate on first.
- A loss of the Black Belts forms the company for some reason or another.
- A lack of training when it comes to the effective change of management for any Black Belts on the team.
- A lack of the right kind of coaching when it comes to the Black or Green Belts. There could also be problems with a lack of time for these two belts to finish their products.
- Projects that are not defined properly, or working on too many products at the same time. You need to have projects that are defined well, and always remember with Lean that less is more.
- Issues with communication when it comes to the program and the burning platform or the goals.

Now, there are a lot of neat things that you can do to make sure that Lean deployment does work. It takes some time and you may find that it is a bit of a challenge but over time, implementing Lean is one of the best things that you can do for your business.

The secrets that you need to know to make sure that your Lean deployment is 100 percent effective include:

- Make sure that everyone, from the top of the company down, is committed to the Lean methodology and that they all have a clear understanding of this method.
- Having a clear and burning platform as well as a good vision for what will happen in the future.
- Set up the organization for the deployment. Having a plan in place makes all of the difference when you are working on this part.
- Communicate the program and make sure that everyone knows their voice will be heard. Make sure that communication is possible on all levels.
- Training of the Change Agents. You should make sure that they are not only trained in the technical skills to pull this off but also in the right people skills so that they will be effective in their roles.

## **Why is it important to have a good change agent?**

For all of the programs and projects that you work on, you are expecting them to take some kind of effect on your business. Because of this, you must make sure that some change agents are around and can help to develop and then implement these projects into the business.

This means that the most important skills that you need to have in both the Black and Green belts are for them to be effective as these change agents. The skills and attributes that are needed to be a good change agent will be as follows:

- They should be able to start and finish the project without delays and without stopping or giving up.
- They need to have discipline and be a self-starter

- They should be able to work well with others on the team and they should be able to convince and encourage them to work on the product.
- They should be creative and have the ability to think outside the box and challenge the norm in many cases.
- They should have a level of drive and enthusiasm for the project they are doing.
- The skills of a good change agent
- They should be able to negotiate.
- They should have a good understanding of the change that comes with Lean and how to implement those changes.
- They should be good at listening to others and then asking questions.
- They need to be able to work well on a time, so making sure they can do team working and team building is essential.
- They should be able to work on project and time management, on themselves and in the team, to make sure that the work gets done.
- They should be able to mentor and coach the rest of the team.
- They should have the motivation, be able to sell, be analytical, and have the ability to deal with conflicts as they arise.
- They should be able to work with the different parts of the company and present on the process as needed.

If you can find someone like this to work on your process, you will find that it can make things much easier. They will be able to help with some of the teamwork that needs to happen, they will ensure that the process stays on task, and they can be a mentor and a coach to the process as well. If you do not have one of these individuals, it may be a better idea to postpone starting until you can find someone to make it more likely that your process will do well.

# Chapter 10: Understanding Lean Manufacturing Tools and How to Make the Most Out of Them

Before you work to get started with the idea of Lean and before you try to use Lean Analytics in your business, you need to make sure that you have the right tools to make the job easier. Without the right tools, it is a lot harder for you to make the Analytics work for your business.

One of the important tools and one of the best ones to use, in Lean Manufacturing is the 5S approach. This can work no matter what kind of business you are in and what you wish to do with the Lean system. This approach is a way of organizing and structuring your team and your process to make sure that all of the waste and the clutter are taken away. It also focuses on cleanliness and having a place for everything that you use in the process so you don't waste money and time trying to find the items that you need.

Now, there are 5 parts to this system and they include:

- Sorting things
- Shining daily maintenance of the system
- Setting things out in a particular order
- Standardization throughout the process and the whole process
- Sustainability

Cutting costs while also reducing waste can be something that will be applied using the simple techniques that we listed above. Not only is the work that your team does important to the process but making sure that the right organization and the right standardization in the process can be just as important as well.

Mistake proofing built-in safeguards will also be able to reduce the number of defects that you have. Trying to reach the goal of zero should be the central idea of this type of approach. Being able to highlight the problems that happen as they occur, not allowing mistakes to occur, and never allowing things like errors and oversights slip through the cracks is a big key.

Another thing that you will want to work with on Lean, and to ensure that you can find tools for, is making and retaining customers. Lean Manufacturing is a great option because it will offer you the right tools to do this consistently as easily and quickly, as well as practically, as possible.

To take the theory of this Lean process to the practical implementation and to see some results with it, you will need to have some planning, some patience, and some persistence. It also doesn't hurt to have discipline, be detail-oriented, and have lots of determination around this process. We refer to these as the THREE Ds and the THREE Ps to make it a bit easier to remember. The thing that you need to remember here is that you should make the most of your shareholder value, and you won't be able to go wrong. You need to achieve high levels of customer satisfaction and improvement rates, low costs while still providing a high-quality product, and you want to do this all quickly and efficiently. If you can do this, then it is easier for you to become competitive and make a profit.

Customers are more likely to work with a business or with a provider they see as predictable, stable, affordable, quick and reliable. This can be done with both a transactional and a manufacturing process. This means that the 80/20 rule will do well no matter what kind of Lean process you are working with including:

- Transactional
- Design processes
- Manufacturing of all kinds
- Logistics
- Supply chain acceleration and management

Lean can help you to learn how to work with your process to improve it in a way that gets rid of waste, which helps you to provide more value to the customer and makes it easier to stay productive in the market that you want. And the main way that this happens with Lean is by getting rid of the amount of waste that is there regularly.

# Chapter 11:
# Lean Deployment

Many times, when the Lean methodology is brought out, it is prescriptive. Because of this, it starts with introspection by the company of their current state of affairs, usually by a site visit from some professionals in Lean. Then, after that visit, there will be a bunch of tools, techniques, and things to do so that the company can fix some of the areas with the biggest waste and see results.

It will then seem like everything is trucking along well until someone comes along and asks for the return on investment. Once you try to start the Lean method, without deciding on its key purpose, it can be hard to manage or discontinue the process to get results. Because it is more prescriptive, several of the Lean techniques can become rituals in the corporate world, and often, they are continued just because the boss wants them to be there, not because they are doing any good.

Because of this, a company should restrict the Lean deployment to where it makes the most sense for your business.

The cultural spiel that most professionals with Lean sell doesn't help if your business isn't going to receive some value from it. What this means is if you use the Lean method at all, make sure you are doing it in an area where you are likely to see the results and where you benefit the most. Don't try to implement it throughout the whole company just because it sounds good on paper. And if you look at the numbers and how Lean works, and you don't see it providing you with a good enough return on investment, then it is best to pick another methodology and not waste time and money.

If you already know a bit about the 5S system, then you would agree that this method is a disciple of using common sense regularly to improve your business. But the problem comes when many organizations get this implemented, and then they stop. They may find, after doing the work or experimenting a bit, that the Lean method is not the right one for them. To help you decide where to implement Lean to get the best results and to ensure that you complete the setup stage, here are some simple steps to help you out:

- Get clarity on the organization. Take a look at the three to five-year strategies. These can help you figure out which areas will benefit the most when you implement Lean and are the ones that will help you achieve your mission and vision the best.

- Determine if every strategy can be executed by an action plan. Then find out if this matches up with the areas where the organization is lacking clarity from before.

- Carry out a deep analysis such as a root cause analysis. If your strategy, for example, is to increase how much an item can penetrate in a small and medium segment, then you would want to collect data on how the product is doing, how the company is doing with that, turn over, historical performance, demographic spread by industry type, and so on.

- See whether or not using the Lean system can enhance any of your key drivers. You could work with Lean to eliminate some of the waste in documents, to make the process easier, eliminate how long the customer has to wait and to shrink the delivery process.

In the process of doing all of this, you will naturally start to work with the 5S. Also, you will establish the need for lines that are dedicated, a multi-skill select staff, and single-piece flow.

Now, when we go through all of this, it could look like we are talking about a piece-meal approach but it isn't. It is more of a way to prioritize your roadmap for Lean so that the entire organization can benefit from it. When this cycle can be repeated through more than one quarter, and even through a few years, most of the company could then be covered by the Lean method.

There are so many benefits that come with implementing Lean into your business but you have to think through the deployment process and not just jump all in. There may be some parts of your business that wouldn't benefit from Lean, and trying to implement it there is just going to lead to a lot of wasted time and money. But if you can figure out where this deployment should happen first and put your effort towards there before moving on to other parts, you will see some amazing results with the Lean process.

# Chapter 12:
# Data-Driven Approaches

To understand the bottlenecks in a workflow environment, we gather all the data affecting the flow. We feed this into the computer and use advanced Lean Analytics to understand the nature of the problem and get the possible solutions. The use of data helps to uncover hidden facts that a manual inspection might overlook. This is the primary motivation behind using data-driven Analytics.

The second thing is the change and the amount of change that the system will take for best functioning. Changing the value of the parameter one way might improve the profitability of the business. But, it might prove detrimental to the other aspects affecting the flow. We use data analytics to understand the impact of the changes and how we can govern the individual aspects to suit the working of the business.

Improvement in the work must arise from the betterment of the individual. This is the basis of the Lean approach. It transforms the thinking to such an extent that the thoughts of money and gain will vanish before that of adherence to quality and addition of values. So, where does one draw the line? This is the vital question that the Lean expert faces when he tries to use the data-driven approach at the workplace.

## BUILDING THE FRAMEWORK FOR THE LEAN TRANSFORMATION

You have many readymade models to use to build your framework. These evolved over the years through continuous use and change and so they have a good degree of consistency and dependability built into them. You can build your framework by addressing the issues that you want to solve through the framework.

## ADDRESSING THE ISSUES

First, address the issue that you face. This might be getting established in the local market, finding a good place for the business, or choosing a good name. Create hypothetical solutions and apply Lean methods to drop the inefficient ones. Often, this is the starting point of the business and so you will need to address this and solve it completely.

## STRUCTURE OF THE EXISTING CULTURE

This remains based on the place where you are. If you are a local person, then you will not have any problems fitting in. The method of movement and distribution of goods depends on the practices of the place. If you are not familiar with these, then you will not find many customers here.

The process of implementation is simple. The user gathers the metrics to use with the site. Usually, the pattern of usage will change for each different user. You can add features to the website to improve usability or conversion. So, a framework gets made. User testing feedback will give an idea of how well the site works and what improvements you need.

We analyze the work detail information for one kind of user. Lean programming helps us choose the right parameters for the use of the system. The performance gets tested and if this has a positive response, the number of users gets increased. When the performance is satisfactory, the other users get included in the testing. The testing carries on until there is a uniformly positive response from the user.

## Your Journey to Become a Data-driven Person

For you to take full advantage of Lean Analytics, you should become a data-driven person. You should value the importance of every snippet of data you can gather. And give the utmost care when processing them logically.

Things that you should remember when approaching matters in a data-driven manner:

- Never ignore existing data, and never prioritize new data over old data.
- Squeeze out huge amounts of data as possible.
- Make data presentable and understandable
- Legally and ethically get data
- Data should back your every decision

A data-driven mindset can also help you:

- **Learn industry knowledge.** The industry has its methods, techniques, skills, and tactics that were developed to make things fruitful and easier for entrepreneurs. They didn't appear out of nowhere but were developed through the continuous work of gathering and processing data. If you can do the same, you'll have one that you can call yours.

- **See all the opportunities.** Have an eye out for every small thing happening in your business. It'll allow you to have greater insight and ideas on what to do next if a problem arises. You'll also see every opportunity that you can take advantage of.

- **Understand your competitors.** Things happen for a reason. If your competitors are having the upper hand or failing hard, you'll know the reason why using Analytics. It allows you to imitate best practices and avoid game losing actions.

- **Have a full grasp of Lean Analytics.** Lean Analytics is useless if you don't value data and think logically. And it isn't restricted to Analytics alone. A data-driven mindset can help you create logical and proper business decisions. This is true regardless if you have a Lean startup or not.

Remember that Lean Analytics seeks to remove any wasteful actions and decisions. It promotes valuable actions during the early stages of your company or startup. And with those benefits, it will effectively raise your chances of success.

## METRICS THAT MATTERS

### Customers

The first and crucial step is to get acquainted with your customers and extract data from them.

### Up Close and Personal

Build a connection with them, and data gathering will be easier. Do that, and they'll comfortably give you feedback and other information you need. Plus, they will appreciate the effort and time you give to them. This is highly effective on startups, and the ones that rely on foot traffic and walk-in customers will benefit from this strategy.

### Customer Service

Customer service representatives get the most interaction with customers and whoever is on phone duty will have the most interaction. You can get friendly and establish rapport on the phone like with the previous method. But unlike personal conversations, phone calls often end short.

### Customer Feedback Form

A customer feedback form will be impersonal, regardless of how you word it. It'll never be considered warm and friendly for customers. It's a cold way to gather feedback and it's often considered a bother. Also, customers who fill up feedback forms often have negative things to say. Consumers tend to not bother themselves with surveys. This is especially true if they're okay with the product or service they received.

### Observe Your Business Processes

Making your business Lean is like taking all the fat out of a cut of meat. But unlike meat, not all fat in your business can be seen easily by the naked eye. Because of that, you need to devote some of your time to observe the processes happening in your business.

### Check the Changes in Your Metric

After doing all the previous steps, check if there is some improvement in your metric. If there is, it means that you have done something right and the metric is spot on. If there isn't, the metric isn't a good indicator, and you should come up with another one.

### Oiling the System

Removing people and inefficiencies have one inevitable result: change. People hate change. In case you still have employees, be sure to reward them for their good work. Assure them that they are essential.

## Introduce Improvements

Once your business is working at its best state, it's time to introduce some improvements. This part of the process is entirely up to you. You can try to imitate some of the processes your competitors do. You can check out some books about businesses to learn more about how you can improve your operations.

## THE DATA FOR YOUR ANALYTICS

Analytics is a measure of progress toward one's goals. You need to learn your goals first before you can consider a metric. It's been iterated before but here are some extra things that you should learn.

The first and most important step in creating a good metric is to gather proper data. The data should pass certain qualities and requirements. Those qualities and requirements are:

### Comparable

A single point of data only gives little information. For example, selling three products today provides little and useful information. It can't help you measure your progress alone.

It gives you a starting point. Yet it needs another point of data for it to be useful in measuring your progress.

### Understandable

If you don't understand a data point, it becomes irrelevant. For example, if you live in the UK, you'll be much more familiar with kilometers rather than miles.

### Rate-able

A data point is convertible or translatable to numbers. It should be always in the form of a ratio or percentage. After all, you can always process raw data or numbers to ratio or percentage.

### Relevant

As mentioned before, the metric or data must be relevant. A relevant metric can make you think of improvements and changes. An irrelevant metric is something good to know.

## TYPES OF DATA

This is where it gets interesting. You should know that there are at least eight types of data. You can use those to create a business metric to measure your business' progress. Most Lean Analytics use the first two types for the one metric that matters.

But it should help you out if you know the eight data types to prevent you from improperly using them. Other types aside from qualitative and quantitative can help you create unique metrics. Those metrics might not help you measure progress but can help you in other things such as marketing, company management, and the likes.

### Qualitative

This includes customer interviews or anything that doesn't involve numbers. It can be in the form of gut feeling or personal feedback. This gives you insights. This allows you to think about how you can gather or collect data for the next type of metric.

Qualitative data is often converted to quantitative. For example, feedback can be converted into numbers: 5 for positive, 0 for negative. A product's success can be measured this way.

However, data in its qualitative form is useful in Lean Analytics. The comments from customers can help in the development cycle of your products.

### Quantitative

This is mostly numbers. It's the most used type of data that businesses use regardless if they're running Lean or not. The data you get from this type of metric allows you to know the data you need to gather.

Unlike qualitative, you can't easily revert quantitative data to qualitative. What you can do is to interpret it. Data can be reformed or skewed through interpretation.

### Vanity

It only makes you feel good. It does not help you create actionable plans that matter for your company. And it's often wrongly used as a metric to measure progress. It still serves as a good motivator and marketing material for businesses.

### Actionable

Actionable often comes internally from your organization. But it can be gathered from customer feedback, too. Actionable data and metrics can provide you with insights. These insights can directly affect and influence your business decisions.

### Exploratory

This is speculative data, one that's generated using currently available data on hand. This can involve predictions on how metrics will change over time. It can also show how the metrics can be influenced to achieve the result you want.

### Reports

Data gathered from reports can be actionable, vanity, exploratory, or lagging. It can be generated internally or you can source it from third parties. It is often acquired by businesses periodically, depending on how you set it.

## Lagging

People usually call lagging data as historical data. Not all data can be acquired instantly. Some of your business actions require some time to see results. These results can be interpreted as usable data.

## Leading

The biggest difference between leading and exploratory data is the time range it predicts. Exploratory data are often predictions set to the far future. Leading is predicted for data in the near future.

# ANALYZING DATA EFFECTIVELY - CAUSALITY AND CORRELATION

Data are often related or linked in one way or another. Two types of data relationships are causal and correlational.

Correlational: Two data points behave similarly because of another data point. For example, the number of umbrella sales goes up and the number of people getting flu goes up, too. You know that people buying umbrellas do not increase people getting sick. But you can say that it's the rainy season, which can cause umbrella sales go up and flu victims go up.

Causal: Two data points behave similarly because one of the two causes the other to change. The two data points can be considered independent or dependent. For example, it's rainy and it causes people to get sick. The independent data is rainy weather. And the dependent data is people getting sick. People getting sick does not cause rainy weather but rainy weather can cause people to get sick.

What does data relationships have to do with Lean Analytics?

Correlational data can help you predict events. For example, next month is the start of the rainy season. You can predict that the number of people buying umbrellas and getting sick will skyrocket.

Causal data can help you affect the future. If you sell umbrellas before the rainy season starts, you can help prevent people from getting sick.

# Chapter 13:
# The Impact of Key Performance Indicator(KPI) and Team Meetings

Growth comes from personal interaction with your team members at work. It does not matter whether you are the boss or the employee, if you are not communicating with your colleagues at the workplace, the office becomes a quagmire of confusion. You will not relish going there. So, you will not get much work done either.

Integrating KPIs into the workstream helps you keep up with the changes and make progress along with them. The KPI is a Key Performance Indicator. It is a measurable aspect of the work that tells you whether you remain headed in the right direction or you need to change. Choosing the right KPI is essential for correct performance estimation. These KPIs help to establish the operational and strategic goals of the company.

## ORGANIZE THE VALUE STREAM ACCORDING TO THE PRODUCT GROUPS

In the first part, you segregate the KPIs to improve the value flow. When you align the value stream, you set the protocol and ground rules along with it. Here you make a list of the attainable and relevant goals and set a time limit for it. The products remain arranged according to the usage at various points of the workflow.

You must find the KPI for each of the product groups and estimate the best way to enhance the value. The advantage of using the KPI is that you can automate processes that previously needed the use of spreadsheets.

You can optimize productivity and decrease the decision-making time needed by the use of KPI for that product in the value stream. Most of these indicators are standards specific to the industry where they find use. The KPI helps you measure the goals you make to reach your business aim. Here are some KPIs for different sectors:

- Marketing – Site traffic, time of visitor on site, newsletter subscribers, and so on.
- Sales – Margin, sales through existing customers, annual sales, and so on.
- Banking – Customer retention, asset quality, customer base, and so on.

Trace the path of each product and service from start to finish in the production cycle. As given above, check the KPI and find the ones that matter. It will help you to group the KPIs according to their nature.

- Qualitative
- Quantitative
- Directional
- Practical
- Actionable

Qualitative KPI reflects the level of attainment of the business aim. A positive value shows that you are achieving success. If you do not get this, you must work to develop the KPI toward the positive value. The Quantitative KPI remains represented as numbers. This gives a more accurate source of information.

Directional KPI will show which way you and your business go at present. This is mostly used in the initial stages where you set up the business and do not have any other clear indicators of the growth. Practical KPI is the one that shows your real-time position. This does not involve any calculations or predictions. And, the last is the actionable KPI that helps you make the changes you need for business development.

## IMPORTANCE OF TEAM MEETINGS

When you have the meetings, you have the team. The team that takes part in meetings knows what each of the others in the team does. They realize their responsibility and will chip in when it matters.

Make sure you have regular team meetings. The meetings must occur at least once a week and preferably once daily. The more interaction you have with the team, the stronger is the bond you develop and so you will contribute more value to the product. The team meetings help the team members ask others about strategy and clarify doubts. This helps build camaraderie and trust.

Use the team meetings as the fulcrum for your business activities. It may involve interaction with the supply or distribution chain members. Or, it may have the board members meeting to discuss the strategy of the day. Whatever it is, you are sure of one thing. It helps you know how the company stands and what your position is in the whole shebang. This system helps you establish the rhythm needed to promote your business well.

## SETTING UP A LEAN PROMOTION

The Lean technology uses the 5Ps to make the ideal Lean model. It deals with using focused energy to improve profit and efficiency. The first is Purpose. The aim for which they make the project is the Purpose. This may not always be money but could be one of the motives for the formation of the company. It may also have a philanthropic motivation.

The second P is the process that goes into the manufacture of the product or service. It details the internal working and the interface of interaction with its clients or customers. The way they operate determines its success and its profile on the market.

One of the most important P's is the People. It refers to the people who link with the product, the company, and the usage of its services. It shows the spectrum of people affected by the services or products.

The next P is the Platform. This is where they carry the product. It refers to the collection of tools and technologies that the company uses for its product. The platform may also mean the software or computer networks that the company uses to support its product. The last P refers to Performance. It shows how the company fulfills its obligation to its customers.

## MANAGE THE PERSONNEL AND GROWTH IN THE COMPANY

If you use Lean standards, you will know that when you recruit people, you must watch against over-staffing. This does not mean that you recruit a lesser number of people than needed. You do not recruit people until there is a need for it. Instead of hiring and firing people, use the right number of people from the start.

Use the proper metrics for monitoring and promoting growth in the company on a short and long-term basis. It means that you align the resources, working process, and policy in a way that shows the increase in the performance and profits of the company.

# Chapter 14:
# How to Automatize a Company using Analytics

Lean Analytics helps you track the metrics vital to the growth and profitability of your business. The first step involves identifying those that are good. So, what is a good metric? A good metric is one that satisfies the following criteria:

### YOU CAN UNDERSTAND A GOOD METRIC

This is important because unless people understand the metric and discuss it, they will not try to get involved. Only when people are involved in the change, the metric has a real impact on the growth of the company.

## It is Comparable

The users and people in your company can relate to the change of the metric over time. They remember the time when the metric was not growing so fast or when the growth slowed almost to a standstill. They discuss this aspect with the metric of a different company or competitor. It makes them involved in the growth process.

## Ratios and Rates are Good Metrics

The nature of ratios and rates make them good metrics. This is because they already relate to something and so you get the growth aspect straight by reading the number given. If you have this kind of metric, use them as they will help you develop the true picture of the company and its growth.

## Metrics are Adaptable

The changes you have in the business remain reflected by the metric. First, you must be able to read the metric. Then, you must be able to use the metric. An adaptable metric is more useful than one that is not.

## Find the Stage Your Business is In

You know what business you deal with and so you can arrive at the metrics involved in the process. To find the stage you are at, check the gating metrics.

Starting from the lowest one, you can pass onto the next gate by checking your present position. For instance, if you have found a need in the market that did not have enough suppliers, then you pass through the **Empathy** Gate.

In the second stage, you find the **MVP (Minimum Viable Product)** that satisfies the customers in the market now. The

MVP has only the bare minimum features but takes care of the need of the customers. This is the Stickiness stage and the early users will find your solution easy to use.

The third analytic stage is **Virality**. It means that you have the product with all the features that the customer looks for and they like it. You need to make your product more cost-efficient and attainable. Once you do this, you can pass on to the next stage. This stage is the Revenue stage where you get involved in the economics of the product.

Find means to optimize the **revenue**. The calculation involves determining how much money you expect from the customer and how much money you spend to get the customer. If the first amount is at least three times the second, you have good margins. This brings you to your last stage. This we call **Scale**.

The Scale is the stage where you grow your business. You can make plans to allow the business to grow. More than getting the metrics and working with it, you should make the wise choice of metrics at all times.

This means that you should work with one metric that matters to you most. This may be Churn. If the Churn is less than 3%, it means your business is stable and growing. But, if the Churn is more than 3%, then it means that your business is in trouble and that you have to take action.

## USE METRICS FOR YOUR AUTOMATION

Automation means letting the machines, here computers, do the work. This will involve three big steps other than the calculation and the setting up of metrics. They are as described below:

### Put a Global Strategy based on Lean into Place

To be a global player, the businessman must have access to the foreign markets. It is easy to build the market through the supply chain network or the sub-network if you invest enough money. This step is crucial and once this is in place, you have the means to merge your gains through Lean.

Every market has its risks and international exposure brings its share with it. Use Lean methods of testing and placing new footholds in the market. Eliminating wasteful methods and time-consuming processes will be the starting point in the process.

Many companies used low-risk and low-cost strategies for making market entry. One example of this is export. This proved fruitful for those companies that did not face much competition. Using the Lean strategy of labor reduction and cost optimization proved beneficial to the businessmen:

- Use of mobile app monetization
- Applicability of media sites
- Balance the inventory
- Create website content

You can hire local delivery services to take care of making deliveries in foreign lands. This is the first basis for expansion. The second is to establish an online presence that helps you become a household name. You need to use mobile-friendly content and ads. This will get you to most of the people in the world because they all use mobile phones.

## Completing the Transformation

Create an SEO friendly website that has links to heritage sites. Only this helps you establish your product on the internet. Facebook, Twitter, Tumblr, Instagram, WhatsApp, and others provide more exposure for your product. Provide the links for all these on your website. Conduct contests that give rewards to the users that link your website to the greatest number of sites. The publicity is cheap but effective.

## Get your customers and suppliers into the Lean chain

Integrating the supply chain and the delivery network through the market and finding the best point of entry and delivery for your product is the first step. Value stream management has lots of interest among Lean users because of the way it gives the best solution. To maintain market viability, you need to have a good delivery system.

# Chapter 15:
# The Importance of Lean Thinking for Entrepreneurs

Entrepreneurship is a strong word that has found its way into the business and enterprise environment. This word has fought, to receive the recognition it now has in the visions and missions of various business organizations. But unfortunately, when this term is used, it is usually to depict small-scale ownership management.

On a broader view, however, to understand the concept of entrepreneurship, the Lean Thinking framework can be employed. But before we consider how and the extent at which Lean Thinking affects entrepreneurship management; it is apposite to understand what Lean Thinking is all about.

When you are trying to improve the way that you are doing things, improving your processes and making your business more efficient, you should take a lesson from the method of Lean Thinking. You will find that there are a ton of lessons that anyone can learn when it comes to Lean Thinking, a method that is now practiced by most of the biggest organizations and companies throughout the world.

The reason that Lean Thinking has taken such a big prevalence in many of these companies is that it is effective. These companies know that if they can use the methods and the strategies that are found in this system, they will be able to increase your customer satisfaction, get rid of waste, and increase the number of profits you make in the process.

We will look at one of the parts of the Lean Thinking method that can be the most useful for entrepreneurs. We will look at the PDCA or the Plan, Do, Check, and Act plan. This technique can do some amazing things for improving the efficiency of your process but it is not a one-off review. It is meant to help you improve your performance, starting today and leading into the future.

## PDCA Method

### Plan

Define the problem or the issues that you would like to address with this process.

Understand the root cause of this issue. Why is this issue happening? What could be causing this? The 5 Why's can be used here. You ask yourself why at least five times to ensure you get all the way down to the actual root cause of the issue.

Develop the details of what you need to do to address the root cause.

You need to set up a list of priorities to ensure that you do the right things at the right times to get the process done.

## Do

Now, it is time to get to work. You need to implement the solution to the problem.

You might do a test, or some kind of pilot, first to make sure that the plan is successful to just go for it.

## Check

This is an important step to the process of PDCA. You will want to check on the results of the actions you did in the step before. Are you getting the results that you were expecting? If not, why weren't you getting the results that you want? What else are you able to do to make the results better? If you are online, you may spend some time using Google Analytics to measure the performance that you get.

## Act

Understand what you need to do to make things work the way that you want if they need to be done differently. Act on the findings that you have.

And then the cycle starts again. You will plan to go off what you learned before, do, check, and act. This is one of the techniques that can ensure that your business and its processes are continuously able to improve.

# ALL YOU NEED TO KNOW ABOUT LEAN THINKING

By now, you should know that Lean thinking involves waste thinking management. That is, thinking the right way and channeling your efforts into satisfying your customers by producing value-added products.

## More Than Just Cutting Cost

Lean is not reducing the cost of production. Rather, it is finding a balance between affordable products and the satisfaction to be derived from them. Even if you want to cut costs, at least make the benefits worth the money. In general, Lean involves making plans to create a product with values the customer will be interested in enjoying.

## Step-By-Step

You are expected to have a clue as to what you are making. A business plan must be launched first by a hypothesis. In this way, you can see similar products in the market, how they are distributed, and the rate at which they are consumed. Testing hypothesis gives you the understanding of your proposed product, whether it is a marketable product or otherwise. If there is, the product is then tagged as a Minimum Viable Product. In essence, Lean thinking involves starting with a hypothesis and not just launching the business immediately.

## Learn What People Want

Calling the workforce into a corner of your company would not solve the problem of what people want or how you can satisfy them. You need to learn by doing some research. All plans must be made upfront, so you must have the necessary information before production. Lean thinking helps you have real-time experience with the customers, and you can build the product in line with their taste and expectations.

## Get Ready to Run

You cannot always be in the same position. "No Growth" is terrible for business. Big enterprises, including startup businesses, are sure to have ups and downs at one point in time. There will be discouragement, break in production, and other hazards surround the business world. So, to thrive, get ready for the bad times.

## Find Your Network

When you have studied the market place, structured out your business plan, and have started making waves, find out others like you. Another best idea of Lean thinking is that it gives you the avenue of looking at what similar producers are doing wrong to help you improve your products.

## PRINCIPLES OF LEAN THINKING

### Find the Value

The first application of Lean involves identifying the values derived from the product. This involves taking a study of the use of the product by the customer, to know what kind of value or benefit is attached to the product. This way, you can prevent waste, set a reasonable target price, and ensure that the price is proportionate to the value attached.

### Check the Value Stream

This requires knowing the steps, procedures, and materials for the production of the product. To cut down cost and prevent waste, you must identify and remove those processes, resources, or other things attached to the production which do not add any value. You must ask these questions as regards checking the value stream; where and how fast can we get the materials? Where and how do week keep our tools?

### Make the Flow

When you have identified those things that do not add value and have discarded them, next is to create new steps. This principle directs that you must ensure that you create a value-filled production chain, maximizing efficiency, and avoiding waste. The principle of creating an effective flow ensures that the production processes fall in line with each other and that there is no delay.

### Establish Pull

When does the customer need the product? And how do we quickly respond to the order? These questions help you to make ready all necessary chains of production so that there is a fast response to the customer's request.

### Find Perfection

In conclusion, Lean helps you identify areas that need improvement. Those who follow these principles are somewhat called "perfectionists" because they look for nothing short of perfection. At every point in time, they evaluate every process to increase value.

## WHAT LEAN THINKING CAN DO FOR ENTREPRENEURS

Do not ask if there is there any assurance that Lean thinking will help businesses in this modern day. Instead, consider the fails you will encounter if you do not subscribe to a Lean methodology. It is not a get-things-done-quick model; it is a long term process that assures continuous improvement.

### Higher Level of Productivity

Applying Lean thinking helps you identify values, eliminate procedures that do not add values, and ensure efficiency.

### Fast and Smooth Operations

After you have eliminated the non-value adding processes, there will be more focus on ensuring the streamlined processes flow smoothly. There will be a quick response to the customer's order, and the production cycle will flow as expected.

## Quality Products

Because you regularly evaluate the production processes, you can identify and approach quality issues with ready problem-solving tools.

## Assured Customer Satisfaction

This is a major aim of Lean. To provide value to the customer and satisfy them. By adequately managing waste thinking and processes, you will be better equipped with functional tools to help meet the demand of the customer.

## Use of Resources

With Lean, you know when to produce and how to produce. This way, you prevent waste. When you consider the demand before you produce, you will only use as many resources as needed.

## Rework

Lean eliminates rework, which costs time, resources, and money. Having to deal with defects may cause you to lose the customer.

## Efficient Workforce and Work Environment

Because you have streamlined the processes to only value-adding ones, there is an active, skilled, and competent workforce. Also, the environment will be conducive, as there would not be unnecessary tools or processes running.

## Greater Level of Responsiveness

Your operations will be flexible, and you will be better able to respond to orders when the customer pulls. Like "Just in Time" manufacturing, Lean will help you get the product the customer needs and get it ready when it is required.

### Increases Everything Else

When you begin to enjoy the benefits of Lean in the above-listed ways, it also improves everything else and leads to more orders, more on-time productions, more sales, more deliveries, and more money. Lean is the best option if you want to grow your business because Lean prevents waste, provides value, and ensures continuous improvement.

# Chapter 16: How Do You Engage Lean Management in Your Office?

When an office decides that the way forward is through Lean Analytics, there is a lot to be done. Luckily, there is a lot of knowledge available on Lean Analytics when it comes to implementing it in the office. When it comes to implementing Lean, we can group most of the processes into analyzing and implementing. Yet a wide number of offices do not seem to succeed in implementation. This is because a lot of time is spent on making use of Lean tools rather than thoroughly understanding them. Eager to skip to the best parts, offices ignore the time that has to be put into making sure that the majority of the staff understand and subscribe to the Lean ideology.

Another reason why various businesses fail is due to Lean tools not being well-directed. The main objective of Lean is enabling a company to learn as much as possible as fast as possible which leads to profits. However, sometimes, offices attempt to implement Lean without explaining to their staff what the aim is and how to achieve that aim, they do not explain the entirety of Lean. For Lean to work and yield results, it is not simply a matter of implementing the tools into the business, it is a matter of implementing Lean into every single office in a business. In other words, it is all to ensure that each office absorbs and processes data about their work-area in large amounts and superb speeds. It is only when each member of your business is on board with the flow that it can be a reality.

With Lean management, no department in the office carries a much larger load. This is because every department that makes up a business has to change the way it runs. A single weak link in the Lean chain can negate the effort of others. Each office must know how Lean works and what it is to achieve. Lean Analytics is dependent on collective application and alignment. The offices must work together if the implementation of Lean will be a reality. Although Lean concerns every aspect of an office, it should be concentrated on the offices that directly affect the businesses' speed and ability to deliver. However, the ability of this to happen depends, once again, on collective effort. Delivering services is the last link on a long chain. Each office is a part of that chain. A delay from one point is usually a delay for everyone. With mass and speedy learning, these delays are obliterated.

In each office, the various delays in the rendering of services should be addressed. This includes understanding the problem, seeking out reasons for the delay and finding ways around them. Do customers have to wait for longer periods because they usually request ice in their drinks? Why? How can that be changed? Do customer complaints sit at the table for ages and cause disgruntlement before anything can be done about it? Why? How can that be changed? These are the types of questions that need to be asked and speedily too.

To keep it simple, you may be wondering how you can take the concepts of Lean and then apply it in the creative industries, in manufacturing, in a finance department, and in a law firm? This section offers some ideas on how you can do this.

## FLOW

One of the fundamental concepts that come with Lean is the idea of flow. It works with any setup where the intelligence needs to be applied to achieve an outcome. Even here, you will find that a partial adoption of these techniques can provide you with a substantial number of dividends.

You can start the process of flow by making a map of either the whole project flow or a daily workflow. The prime goal for the company here is to figure out where any roadblocks or delays are located and then concentrate on the biggest ones to figure out the best way to increase productivity. If you are doing this inside a factory, the constraints or bottlenecks need to be identified and then the output can be optimized by working on the production up to where the bottleneck is and try to fix it from there.

For this step, you need to focus on the constraints and the bottlenecks that can occur in your organization. Are you able to think about a few to get started? Think about the dependencies existing in any part of the process. You can then think about the scope and what you can do to reduce the dependencies that are there. Your goal needs to be finding ways to permanently elevate and then eliminate the bottlenecks that you see in the process.

## TAKT TIME

The next thing to take a look at is the takt time. In a factory, this type of time represents the heartbeat of the process; also, it is known as the pace of workload that your team can handle and that they need to handle to take care of the customers.

Here, you need to consider what your takt time should be or what your daily workflow should be for each product. And to figure out this number, you need to figure out what the critical quality outcomes that the end customer wants, how much of the product they want, and how much time and products it takes to create that product.

## Waste

One of the biggest things that you will try to work on when you implement the Lean system is to eliminate the amount of waste that you have in all of your processes. Many companies have a lot of waste that is present in their system, and this can lead to problems with unhappy customers, employees who aren't able to do their jobs as efficiently as possible, and they end up spending more money to get things done than they need. Being able to reduce the amount of waste that shows up in your system can make a big difference in how happy the customers are and how much profit you can earn.

The Lean system focuses on what is known as the seven forms of waste. It is your job during this process to learn these seven wastes and then look for them in your business. From there, you can go through and try to eliminate, or at least drastically reduce, the amount of waste that is occurring in your business. The seven forms of waste that a business can deal with and often they will deal with more than one include rework, conveyance, motion, overproduction, inventory, processing, and waiting time.

## Managing the Workload

Most of these professionals are entrusted by their employers to learn how to do this on the job. They are expected to maximize their productivity, and they are deprived of a typical modern office without any help of support for the workflow or secretarial help.

In short, when the application of these concepts and techniques of Lean has a wide scope, this can lead to some issues. You need to make sure that your company and all of the teams are able to manage the workload that you give them properly.

If you can use them properly, you will find that it will make some changes and revolutionize the daily workflow management in any office.

## Tips for Implementing Lean Management in Offices:

### Carry Your Staff Along

If your staff are not in agreement or are wary of Lean tools due to any reason, it will affect its implementation. Instead of simply giving orders and directives when it comes to Lean, explain the reason behind them as well as what you hope to gain. Having them behind you will support you in far more way than you imagined possible.

### Do not make changes to single departments

When making changes to departments in a single business or organization follow it up and watch how the change is received. Improper implementation of Lean can cause its problems. Make changes and study the reaction.

### Have Steady Departments and Well Defined Output-Standardize

It is quite impossible to derive structured information if there is no structure. It is quite impossible to implement structured processes if there is no structure. How well structured is your organization? Lack of structure in itself can be a reason for failures in some aspects. Order and structure cannot be done without. It will be hard to learn about each department if duties are not well outlined. Each department should have well outline duties to discern where delays often occur.

## Balance Quality and Quality

As a business, before aiming for 50 customers, you should aim for 30 happy customers. This issue is found more in companies providing one-of-a-type services or an innovation. A true business manager realizes that a long-term monopoly is hardly ever a possibility. If you have a new idea for an app, develop it, and then put it out for customers, in less than a month, similar apps will pop up.

## Work On Customer Service

Customer service is one department that has a lot to do. This is because they deal directly with your clients and customers. Your customer service should be efficient and trained. A customer-service staff should be trained to enable them to deal with the customers well. Some customers are nightmares however, except they go against our business's values, we still want their patronage.

## Think Outside the Box

Lean Analytics focuses on learning large information at a fast rate. With this information, decisions are made. Following conventional methods is not the only way there is. Brainstorm ideas. Have your staff present a solution alongside any problem they encounter. Deliberate on decisions slowly and make them only after careful research but once that is one, implement them as fast as possible.

# Chapter 17: How to Utilize Analytical Information in the Business Service Management Sector

Field service management is something that has a lot of support for analytical data. Data, which can come in as analytics in the form of charts, graphs, and dashboards. Performance indicators and key metrics are essential when it comes to business intelligence to help drive better service delivery and improved productivity.

The major difference between a progressing business and a regressing or stagnant one is the ability of the manager to observe, improvise, adapt, and improve. Thousands of businesses have realized this and have subsequently put in as much time as they put into improving their services into analyzing and studying feedback. The increased use of analysis has changed a lot in businesses. Businesses now use analysis to streamline operations which results in improved services and processes which ultimately results in increased profits.

## UNDERSTANDING BUSINESS INTELLIGENCE

Business intelligence refers to dealing with technologies and intricate strategies that are used to analyze data. It refers to strategies and applications that use business data to make better business decisions. This analysis helps business owners make better decisions that help grow their businesses in various ramifications.

Business intelligence (BI) is very wide. It involves data analytics, big data, and data mining. It also involves a wide array of processes that range from data collection to data sharing and even reporting. It is these processes that help with decision making. Luckily, Business intelligence has advanced and so businesses have been equipped with tools that allow them to carry out these processes themselves. Business intelligence deals with data mining, online analytical processing, querying, and reporting. The knowledge gained from these processes is then used to make decisions.

## SUPERVISOR DASHBOARDS ARE ESSENTIAL

The first thing that we need to look at is the supervisors. All of your supervisors and managers need to have a way to view all the data and information that is relevant to them and their projects each day. This makes it easier for them to track and monitor all of the progress and the performance that occurs with the jobs they are in charge of. With this data in place, the supervisors can make smarter decisions for the business, and this can help them improve their services and manage the work more effectively.

Supervisor dashboards: These can be useful because they enable the whole team to take a look at the projected and recent profitability sorted by resource and team. It can even go all the way down to talk about specific jobs. Supervisors are also able to monitor the different projects and the recent scheduling capacity to see if it is on track. They can also analyze any of the cost implications if the time isn't filled most effectively.

## LONG TERM SUPPORT

Another thing to look at here is how the data can be used in a way to support any kind of business decision, even those that have a long term effect on the business, and not just the ones that have a short term impact on the company. This could include things like a costs analysis to take a look at the performance of each section of the business, or an overall performance monitoring of the team to make sure everything is going as efficiently as possible.

The type of Analytics that is used here can include several jobs, the jobs that are on target at any given point, the jobs that are done each week or each month, the time scales, the customer satisfaction data, and so much more. All of this detail may seem a bit overwhelming in the beginning but it can support service management because it will provide you with some day to day analytical data that will drive these improvements through the long term.

## THE LEAN STRATEGY FOR BUSINESS

Every enterprise for the individual entrepreneur is very dear to them. They always think of ideas that they could use to develop the business more, to widen the product market that they have, to help them increase how many clients they have, and how to convert customers over to loyal ones. These are all great options to work with but it brings up the question of how this will happen.

These entrepreneurs are often going to spend a lot of time, both day and night as they can, to better their reach and how much exposure they can get to their potential customers. Yet, only a select few can see the success that they want when they do all of this work. This may seem bad and sad because you don't want to put in all of that work and have nothing good come out of it. However, we will now take a few minutes to look at the guidelines that you need to earn more about the Lean strategy and make it work for you.

## STRATEGY PLANNING

Business survival can also outnumber a person's maximum age limit. Business is just a mere activity and it can be handled by its founding member, and then, later on, heirs or other business people can take it over and continue to run the business, even when the founder is gone. But, one of the strongest things that should be evaluated with a business is the strategy that is being used, and the type and amount of planning.

While you are trying to figure out the strategy that you want to work with, the viability of your plan is then revealed. You want to make sure that the plan will solve your problem, that it is achievable, and that it still holds true with the business beliefs that you have. If these are all true, then the strategies that you outline in your plan will become workable. The strategy is so important because it lays out the instructions that would be implemented to attain the goal. Being the most integral part, it has to get the most attention out of this process.

## INNOVATION AND GLOBAL ENGINEERING

You will find that things like operations, sales, inventory, product life cycle management, and operations strategy can all fit in this. But before all of that can necessarily happen, innovation needs to be seen in the process as well.

You will find that your strategic plan gets the best direction and helps you to beat out the competition and do well if you can carry it out with the involvement of new or upcoming technology. This means that if something innovative can be added into the plan, then this to means that the company will be able to maximize their profits. You may want to work with options like an engineering outsourcing company to help you reach these developments and beat out the competition.

## TECHNOLOGY SOLUTION

Technology platform planning, tools standardization, and the engineering processes are the different parts that the last point dealt with. This particular category takes a look at the infrastructure, Analytics, and systems data of this process. Engineering outsourcing companies can come to a huge rescue under this section of the process as well.

## DIGITAL MARKETING AND E-COMMERCE

With many companies moving online to meet the needs of their customers, it makes sense that you want to make sure that the e-commerce site that you are working with, and your digital marketing, are working well and reaching the customers that you want to reach.

If your enterprise has its website or more, it already has more reputation than it would without this website. If you do not have a website up and running, one that is interactive, one that showcases your business, and one that your customers can go to when they want to look at your products, then this is the step where you need to make that happen.

## HR-INTERIM MANAGEMENT

Talent management and the recruitment that comes when your business needs new employees will fall under the division of human resources. There should be some procedures and policies that are in place to help management with these different tasks.

## IMPROVING THE PERFORMANCE

In the long run, financial growth is what will be calculated as a result of all the strategies that we talked about above. The revenue for the following quarter will be aimed at these strategies as well. If you would like to have it so that your business can reach some new peaks each financial year, then you must be dedicated to the Lean strategy for your business and implementing it into all of the different strategies that we talked about before.

## ARTIFICIAL VS. HUMAN INTELLIGENCE

The way people act and think is slowly being changed by artificial intelligence. Our minds are also taken up to the next level by artificial intelligence. Currently, many establishments are highly accurate that will depend on things like retina scans, fingerprints, and facial recognition to do different tasks such as opening doors and more.

While you shouldn't rely on artificial intelligence on its own, it can work along with human intelligence to see some amazing results with the Analytics that you use. Make sure that you take a look at some of the artificial intelligence tools that are available for your business and look at how they improve your business and your data analysis overall.

## UNDERSTANDING SERVICE MANAGEMENT:

Service management is often defined as a supply chain management that connects the customer and the company providing goods or services. Service management aims to keep inventory levels at a minimum thereby reducing high costs. Service management is focused on the customer. Through information technology, service management aims to give the customers what they want thereby strengthening the relationship. Service management does not focus on acquiring a new customer. Rather, it focuses on tightening the hold your business has over that customer. As it is often said, it is far easier to sell to an existing customer than to a new one.

## USING ANALYTIC DATA FOR BUSINESS INTELLIGENCE IN SERVICE MANAGEMENT

With Business Intelligence, you can discover to what extent your business is affected, if it is at all. When there are a particular number of staff on the ground, what are the profits? How do the customers react? What is the minimum number of staff needed to handle a particular number of customers to satisfy them without costing you too much in wages? Where is the balance? Do you fare better with multiple entry-level staff or with a fewer number of experienced ones? At different times with different numbers of staff on hand with different levels of experience, what were the profits like? What were the reviews like? Having the data on hand will give you the ability to answer such questions.

With analyzed data, a business can make decisions concerning inventory stocking. Less money will be wasted as we have a forecast of what performance is like. Teams that deal with service management will be able to predict what it is they need for a certain period. Business Intelligence can present information on how much time is taken to solve a problem. With such information, a manager can study the results to reduce the length of time taken in any possible way that optimizes time while giving the same great-or even better if need be-solutions.

## IMPROVEMENTS AND MORE IMPROVEMENTS

The aim of Business intelligence is not to give businesses a way of predicting happenings alone; that is secondary. It is mainly to give a clear view of where improvements need to be made. Having such data is invaluable; use it to make improvements and more improvements. Remember that such information is valuable; protect it. A rival company can flatten yours if such private data is leaked. Your Business Intelligence Analytic data is more than just reports. It shows your business's weaknesses and strengths. Be safe.

# Chapter 18: Common Mistakes to Avoid While Using Lean in Your Office

## NOT HAVING A BIG COMPELLING VISION

It is only logical to think that every and any business before starting up should have a big vision. A compelling big vision is what steers your cause as an entrepreneur or a startup. The company's vision is like a compass, keeping everyone faced in the right direction. Everyone knows what the company expects to see in the future to come and work collaboratively to see it happen. Your company's vision and type should also affect your Lean strategy.

## LACK OF READINESS AND UNPREPAREDNESS (NOT ASKING THE RIGHT QUESTIONS):

Starting up a business is a big decision and takes a lot. Before ever initiating a startup, there are a few questions entrepreneurs need to ask themselves;

The first question should be, "Can I do this thing I am hoping to do, well?" Here you need to assess your ability in comparison with what you are seemingly up against. The next question is, "Do I like what I am doing?" Now it is of the essence to know that startups are very tasking. They burn up so much time. The time that's supposed to be spent with friends, partner, children (as the case may be), even your hobbies. Something has to go in for something.

Then the final question; "will I make money doing it?". You need to give the market what they need, not what you think they need. Give them the value they can pay anything for in the most cost-efficient way possible.

These are questions an entrepreneur should ask himself before starting up a venture. Lean Analytics method or business models have no part to play in this. They do not answer the questions for you.

## HIRING INEXPERIENCED PROJECT MANAGERS/ TITLE AND JOB MONOPOLY

The Lean strategy is a very critical framework, thereby requiring a high level of experience and leadership skills. It is indisputable that it takes very ardent leadership skills, and not just that, a certain level of experience to get people driving towards an achievable or seemingly unachievable goal.

## FOCUSING MORE ON THE TOOLS THAN THE PEOPLE DEVELOPMENT

The Lean strategy is not a self-dependent or entirely digital strategy. What do I mean by this? The Lean approach, like many other strategies, requires humans for implementation. Other than that, it is just a beautiful plan, with prospects lying waste on a whiteboard or piece of paper. It does not make itself happen.

Another common mistake startups are prone to make shifting all the focus from everything else to just the tools outlined in this strategy. "Everything else" here encapsulates people's development and building. The Lean is a leadership philosophy rather than a methodology, and its success can be primarily attributed to the leadership style rather than the tools involved in the process.

## ADOPTING ANOTHER COMPANY'S LEAN PLAN AND EXPECTING IT TO WORK

This is another danger inherent in having inexperienced project managers and not developing your team as they ought to be developed. The Lean strategy has various levels of implementation. It specifies different stages and levels of company growth and pinpoints that of a necessity, a company should know what stage she currently is at every point in time and as the ladder progresses. Inexperienced project managers in a bid to shield their incompetence would quickly settle for the "Copy and paste" mechanism. This is how they think; "It worked for Company A; there is no cogent reason why it should not work for us too!" There are cogent reasons. It is never advisable to adopt another company's Lean plan for yours. Your Lean business model should consider the customers and their buying process too. You should ask yourself questions like; How customers buy your product, why they purchase from you, at which stage of your business they are in, and what the budget of your customer is before building your Lean business model. Your business model should work best for your customers. Startups should understand this and not be in a hurry to fly the kites above the cloud level.

## BEING OVERLY DATA-DRIVEN

This is one of the dangers that are inherent in using the Lean methods that startups usually fall prey to. It can be said that the Lean Analytics method is quite data-driven, if not entirely. Data is a potent tool that can be very addictive, causing us to analyze everything. But like humans, the truth remains that a bulk of what we do is mostly unconscious and intuitive, based on past experiences and occurrences. This is where experience would play a huge role. Just the same way we do not need to run tests and experiments to know what to eat every day, or when to brush our teeth or what to wear, human judgment should be placed in balance to Lean methods.

# Chapter 19: How to Perform Workforce Analytics Using Lean

Many companies spend a ton of time evaluating the performance of their investment. They will look at things like sales and marketing, capital equipment, research, and development. But one thing they never seem to analyze is human capital. And this is unfortunate because human capital is probably the greatest area of expense for any company.

## THE CONCEPT OF WORKFORCE ANALYSIS

There are numerous ways of describing workforce analysis in its simplest form workforce analysis; "the strategic planning of the workforce serves as a managerial reference framework to make decisions regarding staffing to have the right number of people with the right set of skills in positions and times adequate."

The concept of workforce analysis is not new, however, it is not a well-known concept in the world of small or medium-sized businesses since the management and management of their workforce is usually not very complex. However, this concept has been gaining importance among large corporations that have a global presence and have been forced to think and manage their human capital in a much more strategic way within an increasingly competitive market.

The concept of workforce planning can be understood from its simplest way, such as planning the number of employees and staff that are needed to carry out an operation of an organization appropriately, to the more complex approach that provides a strategic approach and global to not only ensure that you have the necessary staff but to know where to have it, when to have it, how to obtain it and how to evolve it in a way that represents a competitive advantage for a complex organization.

The concept, therefore, is a complex concept, which is not based solely on one dimension (quality, efficiency, effectiveness, cost, etc.) but on the combination of all these dimensions, so that they serve as a frame of reference to make the most convenient decisions according to market conditions, the mission of the company and the objectives and goals of each of its business units that collaborate in achieving the overall goal of the organization.

Based on the above, this concept should, therefore, be conceived as a tool of great value for any global company in achieving its strategy as a business, and not only as a responsibility of the human resources department but as a network of decisions between the operational, the tactical and the strategic.

## IMPORTANCE OF WORKFORCE ANALYTICS

This is an aspect that summarizes the importance of workforce planning. This process allows the organization to anticipate changes, creating a bridge between what you have in the present and the vision of what you want to have in the future, within the general vision and goals of the company.

An effective workforce planning process goes beyond a few discussions about what the organization will need in the future but that it consists of creating a blueprint of how it will be acquired, adopted and adapted to achieve the workforce that the company needs.

If the organization understands the structure, composition, skills, and abilities of its workforce, it can design an action plan to make the necessary adjustments that allow a difference between an average performance and be a leader in the market in which it operates.

## How to Organize, Structure, Analyze, and Then Optimize

When it comes to a workforce analysis, the most daunting part of the whole process is starting. Identifying all the relevant data is the first step needed. Usually, this is done by a common progression that involves organizing, structuring, analyzing, and optimizing.

Many companies find themselves with all of the different parts of finding and hiring, and then even training the employee in different parts of the business, and even on different platforms, that are isolated from each other. It isn't uncommon for them to run into a problem where the contact center data, training data, compensation data, hiring data, and employee data are all isolated from each other and on platforms that aren't compatible.

## Customer Analytics Parallels Workforce Analytics

The next thing that we need to take a look at is customer analysis. The need for a type of analysis that is more sophisticated will be triggered by any deviations seen from the previous trends or performance gaps that are found through the regular reporting of such metrics. Economic and statistical optimization and modeling advancements in the areas of financing, credit risk, and marketing are so great that you can easily adapt and apply them to modeling workforce issues.

It is very much important to consider an employee similar to your customers. You don't want to ignore your employees and treat them like they don't matter, or they will run off and find a company that does treat them well. Because of this idea, all of the Analytics that you can utilize for the customer life cycle can also be applied to help you understand more about the employee life cycle. This includes the various parts of reacquisition, post-attrition, retention, growth, and acquisition.

The parallels with your employees would be something like an engagement scoring model, an optimal compensation model, and a succession readiness score. Often, the scoring of the employee and the analytical models that you go with are more robust compared to the information that you get from the consumer because you can talk with the employees and get the raw data in-house.

## HOW TO CALCULATE THE BENEFITS OF YOUR CURRENT HR PROGRAM?

In identifying the key drivers, it is helpful that you analyze the information that you currently have. The workforce's most optimized strategy can be the result of acting upon these key drivers. To easily rank the training program's order, training courses should be evaluated based on the impact on the compliance benefits and productivity in the workforce. Taking the analysis a bit further could provide some insights into how many participants you would need to have in each training class, at a minimum, to break even. You can look at whether it is more effective to use web-based training or instructor-led training.

## How to Make Better Decisions with a Balance on Soft and Hard Data

The sensitivity around issues regarding employees can be emphasized by having a set of goals for this type of workforce's decision-making process. Looking at hard data cannot capture these. This is a valid concern. The good news is that a workforce analysis is not going to try to take away the softer issues that surround sentiments, motivations, and aspirations of the employees.

Rather, this analysis provides your HR, the individuals who deal with the employee issues that come up from every day, a more defined decision-making manner that can be supported by a set of data-driven tools. For example, a retention scoring model can help the company identify the employees who hold the highest risk of leaving the company, and it will also list out the top reasons that these individuals are considering leaving the company. HR can then make decisions based on this information and work to retain those employees who are most likely to leave.

There are times when similar low scores are achieved by two employees, and this could classify them as high risk based on those scores. But for one of them, the biggest issue is that there isn't a lot of growth potential in the company, and the second one may feel that the work and life balance in the company is low. Knowledge of these different factors can make the actions that HR takes for retention much easier to start with.

With that knowledge, your HR can work to implement retention strategies that are more actionable and targeted, and this means that they are more effective compared to the traditional methods. This can save your business millions of dollars compared to just using umbrella retention strategies. The workforce analysis is a good combination of objective and subjective points, which is why implementing it can be so successful.

## HOW TO TRANSFORM YOUR HUMAN CAPITAL INTO AN ADVANTAGE OVER THE COMPETITION

Finding strategies that have been grounded in strong workforce Analytics and are optimized for human capital show positive results in customer loyalty and bottom lines. Companies that can have the Analytics integrated into their workforce management and planning positively are the ones who can see the biggest return on investment overall.

Human capital can be one of your biggest costs, especially when your employees are leaving the business and you lose productivity and have to recruit and train new individuals to help your business grow. Being able to work with the workforce Analytics that we just discussed in this guidebook could make a big difference in the amount of money that you can save and how happy your employees are at the same time.

# Chapter 20: Using Lean for the Public Sector

When you are using Lean for the public sector and businesses, you will find that it can help you look at all of the activities that occur. You can then define what you think adds value to the public or the customer, while also eliminating all of the things that don't provide this value.

Following the system of Lean will help any kind of business, even if they are in the public sector, identify the defects that are within the process or even within the hierarchy, and then it will use a variety of strategies to combat these issues. In many cases, it is the use of analytics and statistics to try and identify and provide evidence-based on solutions.

Although many times Lean has been used more in a manufacturing environment, when it comes to businesses that are in the public sector, there can also be some benefits as well. The public sector may find that there is a huge influence when they use the Lean methodology because this management strategy is ideal when it comes to identifying and finding any defects in the running of all types of organizations, institutions, and even businesses. And then, it takes it a step further and helps to fix the defects while also listing ways to do the processes differently.

Any business can benefit from having some of that occur for them. The public sector is not immune to having some deficiencies in it and being able to avoid these can make a big difference in how well you can help your customers and clients. Let's take a look at some of the Lean manufacturing tools that can be used in the public sector to help you get the best results out of this program.

One of the biggest questions to answer is how to merge Lean into the training requirements of the public sector seeing they run on a different template than what Lean might offer. We could rather ask how a public sector run organization can merge the timeless principles present in Lean into their organization. Whether it is private or public sector; the customer/target audience/consumer is the prima donna, the primary focus of it all. That means there should be no room for too many mistakes with reaching your targeted customers.

The public sector unlike private is service-driven; it aims to serve the people more than getting remunerations. That's why it could seem out of place to think that Lean could be applied to the public sector just like it can be applied to the private sector. The public sector is run on taxes unlike the private that is revenue-driven. The public sector is designed to serve like government parastatal, schools and other public paraphernalia. Even the way employment occurs in the public sector is quite different from how it happens in the private sector. In the public sector, employment is designed so that government work can go on, and public offices could run. The police officers, teachers, fire-fighters, **etc.** are all types of public sector employment. The way staff gets paid is through taxes and internal or externally generated revenue—but majorly taxes.

Whether private or public sector, every customer wants to be satisfied with the services you render and we realized we can apply the Lean principle to running your public sector office. The issue of service becomes a bigger problem because the government is involved and the people want to get a benefit of their taxes.

Lean allows organizations to break down their processes into components and monitors each component analytically. This would Lean to the management of organization resources because the organization can see areas that they can improve on, improvise or cut out. If the work process is broken into fragments, it becomes easier to monitor than holistically. A holistic view is good when drawing out the plan and vision for the organization but when execution is concerned, it is the tiny fragments that matter. Lean methods view efficiency from the end user's perspective and what they define as value. Whatever process eradicates waste and delivers the value the end-user desires is the best process. From the spotting of the need to the choice of staff to handle the task to the resources available for the execution to the process of approval, the time take, the effect of the project on the community all can come under the lens of Lean and the best approach devised to conserve resources and have the best output.

Define measure, analyze, improve, and control the outcome of the project—these are simple steps that can be applied to ensure an organization functions at its optimum when delivering a product. Defining and measuring entails a careful perusal of the hitches that hinder the process of delivering the service and the extent of the damage. Analysis involve the careful examination of why things went wrong. Improvement involves the steps the organization would take to ensure that these problems do not resurface; it's an evolution of the system and its processes. Control finally involves setting up frameworks that allow the improved idea to work.

## SHOULD PUBLIC OFFICES INVEST IN LEAN TRAINING?

For every organism to thrive in its environment, the organism must learn and evolve. Any organization that refuses to learn, unlearn and relearn would soon be obsolete. Human wants are becoming more complex; our needs are getting more insatiable. We just are not satisfied with what is handed over to us. What about speed? The rate at which things react in the 21st century is alarming; it is needed for speed in real life now. Everything is moving on a fast lane. The need to constantly evolve to face these new needs is increasing and the best way to grow is to get acquiesced with this new world. You need to get trained; the whole organization needs an overhaul, if not you would be practicing processes that can't solve client needs.

If you found a way to improve your system and workflow process, why won't you latch on to it? The Lean methodology allows you to use timeless methods to solve company problems, conserve energy, conserve resources and save time.

With this training you can improve customer satisfaction: the customer is the reason why people do business. The citizen is the reason for the creation of the public office; the citizen is the focus of the public office. Every public office should take pride in the fact that projects are carried out to meet the needs of the citizen and the needs of the community. That's how every public office is evaluated.

Through this training, you would experience improved staff morale, and staff engagement; If your staff should understand you don't just care about what they give to you but what you can also give to them, they would be encouraged to see the organization not just as an organization but as themselves. You would inevitably impact staff engagement through training because they would be put in an environment that can allow them to express themselves and discover things about themselves that they might not have known. The Lean methodologies can be applied to personal lives; you would have allowed them to be better persons through the training process.

Increased revenue is a sure bet: a framework that can streamline your workflow process to tiny bits that can be monitored, which would invariably impact the quality of products that are delivered because the system is obvious and streamlined. It is imperative that for any organization to thrive, the organization should be able to curb wastes and overhead costs. Lean methodology endows you with the skill through a very effective framework. This framework would affect revenue. Let's streamline this to public office if the process can guarantee a reduction in lead time, increased productivity, lower costs, and improved staff engagement, the economy would be impacted; that means it would be easier to do business because the climate would be healthier. If public offices are effective, then the economy would be affected and there would be an increase in revenue.

Lean has easy to understand tools that any organization can master in no time. Every public office should apply these principles because of how effective it is.

## Lean Manufacturing Tools

These types of tools that are used in Lean manufacturing are used by a variety of companies, both in the manufacturing and the public sector fields, to help reach the objective of eliminating waste and making the process go as smooth as possible.

## Quality Function Deployment

This is often known as FD and it is an essential tool in Lean that you can use to identify what the end product will look like. It heavily relies on what the customers require because it understands that no matter how great the product is; it isn't going to bring you any revenue if the customer doesn't like it. You must talk to the customer, do some research, and figure out what they require from your products and your company.

These kinds of tools are able to track these results back to the original inputs that you use, and then they are controlled by the organization. This could include a lot of different parts like product design and even processes characterization.

## PROCESS FAILURE MODES AND EFFECTS ANALYSIS

The next thing that we look at is known as the process failure modes and effects analysis. This can also be known as FMEA. When we are working with this particular tool, it is the one that defines analytical techniques and can list out the potential sources and causes of any failures that are happening in your business, no matter where they are.

From this analysis, your process and the different problem areas that occur are given a weighted point score. This score will be based on the expected frequency of the issues, the chances that failure is detected, and the degree of the consequences or the amount of harm that it could do to your bottom line. This can make it easier for you to determine which parts of the process you need to focus on first.

## STATISTICAL PROCESS CONTROL

And finally, we will take a look at a process that is known as statistical process control. This is an important, as well as an effective, quality control tool that can be used in Lean manufacturing with some degrees of success. This is a tool that will require periodic measurement of the variables which is a result of the output of the system, and in the long run, when it is used properly, it can lower the costs that you take on.

# Chapter 21:
# Tips to Make Lean Analytics More Successful for You

Getting started with Lean Analytics is something that can take some time to get used to. It will provide you with great results and a winning strategy that is sure to get you ahead. Here are some great tips that you can follow to ensure that you are doing well with Lean Analytics and to ensure it is as successful as possible for you.

### SET THE FLOW PATH

Implementing the Lean Analytics envisages the use of change in the thinking at the workplace. When we use this, the clarity in the workplace remains enhanced. In most normal cases, this occurs by implementing the agent for change. This person remains responsible for all changes brought into force through Lean.

## USE THE SERVICES OF A LEAN CONSULTANT

Learning the Lean Path is essential. It is easy to govern the workers once the process has begun. But, only the people who are conversant with the method of Lean will know when to make the needed changes. The knowledge is needed for the parallel working types in Lean that control each other. All the decisions and management principles remain data-driven and systemized through actual use.

## USE A LEVER TO BEGIN THE TRANSFORMATION

When you face a troublesome situation, one must change. The Lean philosophy anticipates changes and makes provisions for each. By preparing for the change, you can overcome the negativity and create the positivity that will take the business to a profitable end. This situation applies to the client, the business owner, and the suppliers involved in transacting business.

## DO NOT AIM FOR GRAND SOLUTIONS

The idea is the avoidance of the key issues that precipitate the issue and look for solutions away from the hotspot. Many business problems solve themselves if you give them enough time. With this in mind, the Lean expert tries to figure out how to keep the mechanism of the business moving without overlapping in the key problem areas.

## Make a Map with the Implementation Timetable

The creation of the timetable helps to improve the flow value and the perspective. Each work function becomes more important or less important because they have to meet the time check. When the tasks fail to meet the time check, we check for alternative solutions that have a better possibility of meeting the timetable.

## Take the First Step Immediately

It is important for progress in any business to begin acting immediately. This means that one uses any one of the scientific approaches existing between theory and reality to come through with an action plan. In the most normal case, one uses the induction-deduction method. These are opposing methods of analysis and find applicability to any kind of work situation.

## Check for the Results Immediately

It is important to check the results fast and see the amount of progress one has made. Changes to the amount of working capital show in a clear way to all. But, the deeper metrics such as the Return on Equity and Vendor Expenses may not come to light as fast. Yet, these will impact the business in a big way.

## Use Progressive Results into Value Stream Building

The use of real-time targets will cut the amount of uncertainty and bring more cohesiveness into play. For practical values, one must use tests and questions. Then, one must study documents and information registers before using the suggested values. But, once you do this, you have a viable working system that you can depend on.

## Measure the Tests Properly

You are not going to get the right results if you are not properly measuring the tests. You need to have the right metric in place. Also, make sure that you never stop a running test too early, or you may miss out on some of the important results that you need.

## Use the Tools that you Need

Lean Analytics has a ton of tools that you can use to make it successful. Make sure that you are properly trained to handle each part and that you don't miss out on some important tools that can make this more successful.

## Know Where Your Business is Now

Make sure that you know the overall goals and vision of the business. This can help you to spot some of the problems that you need to fix and can make it easier to ensure that whatever changes you do decide to make go along with what your business is all about.

## Understand the Different Metrics

You should spend some time looking at the different metrics that are available for you to use on your project. Each one can be great but it does depend on the type of business that you are running and the project that you want to work with. You need to learn which metric is the right one for you.

## Focus on the Main Problem First

If you are like many businesses, there are probably many problems that you need to solve. But you don't have the time and resources to do all of them at the same time. When you get started with Lean Analytics, you must figure out what the main issue is, the one that will have the biggest impact on your profits, and work with that first. Once you have successfully implemented Lean Analytics and worked on the problem, then you can go back and see if any other problems need to be addressed.

## GET RID OF THE WASTE

Remember that the most important thing that you will do with the Lean system is to get rid of waste. And the data that you collect in the Lean Analytics stage is meant to help you to find the waste and learn how to get rid of it. Take a look at some of the most common types of waste that businesses may experience (and that we listed in an earlier chapter) to give you a good idea of where to start.

Lean Analytics can be a great way for you to get a strategy together that will help your business become more successful. If you follow these tips and some of the strategies that we talk about in this guidebook, you are sure to see some amazing results in no time.

## GET YOUR STAFF TRAINED

Your staff needs to know what the process is all about before you introduce it to the organization. Take out some months, and get them conversant with how Lean works sigma works.

## YOU WOULD NEED TO IMPROVE YOUR STRATEGY

The Lean methodology would be woven around your plans and nothing else. It means if you don't have a plan, you might as well just close down the organization because Lean methodology would not be effective. You should have a strategy that your entire team can look back to and work with so that implementing Lean would be easier and smoother—there would be a solid foundation to build the entire process on.

## TRY LABELING

Whether they are virtual tools/files or not, labeling or tagging them properly helps your team to easily navigate through to find what they need. It saves time and it makes work more efficient.

## SET SHORT-TERM GOALS

Short term goals come with motivation and energy. They also streamline the big, overall goal into small bits that can be worked on little by little until the ultimate goal is achieved and the company progresses. Goals without timeframes might at best be called wishes; time gives perspective to goals.

## LET YOUR RESULTS BE VISIBLE

Success is a motivator on its own. If you win a war right now, you would be motivated to win more. That's why games have levels so that you would not lose motivation at any point; the wins are designed to spur you to achieve more. You should have a culture of always showing results on your Lean board; let your people see that progress is being made with all the investment you are making; the sight of progress and success motivates people to act.

## COMMUNICATE

Communication is how the team is carried along; you need to carry your whole team along so that they can be effective. Each team needs to know what the other team is currently doing. This encourages team spirit and team commitment; they would look out for each other automatically because they know what is going on.

## Don't Be Rigid

Flexibility is the best way to lead because humans are complex and ever-changing. If change is a constant, flexibility must be your go-to guy. You cannot be rigid on the way the process is expressed; you have to be on the lookout for bottlenecks and how to free them to allow ease and a better flow of work.

## Don't Just Plan, Implement

If you just talk without carrying out, what good would the Lean process be? Actions are what deliver results, not just plans. Plans are there to guide your actions to that you can achieve a certain goal, so don't just say it, do it and see how effective your organization would be.

## Motivate Management

You are never going to see any sort of success when it comes to Lean if you aren't able to get the whole company on board. If there is some division within the management team, then there is always politics or some friction, and this can put a damper on the results that you can see with this process.

Before you start to implement the Lean methodology in your company, it is time to get as many people on board as possible. Having one or two people who aren't interested in the Lean methodology isn't that big of a deal. Once they start to see the benefits of this new system, they are more likely to jump on board and be all in. But if you have a big portion of management who is against this method, then it is time to work on them and see what you can do to change their minds.

## FULL-TIME LEAN

If you implement Lean, then you must make sure that your company becomes full time Lean. It isn't enough to just have it on occasionally. It is something that the whole team needs to be a part of to be successful. And even if you just start it out in one department and just on one project to see how it goes, make sure that the team members who are doing that aren't required to give their attention to other things. If the attention is split, then they won't be able to give the Lean process the attention and dedication that it needs to be successful.

# Conclusion

Lean Analytics provides the guidelines of how to properly analyze the data you gain from this feedback cycle when it is most vital to your business. This approach allows you to fully focus on the key activities that will push your business forward without wasting time or energy elsewhere. This clear focus is how you execute each step of production more efficiently. By taking the time to understand your target audience, making sure you know the business you want to build, and being honest about where you are in terms of your business lead, you will be able to give your attention to the one metric that will reach your target goals.

While Lean Analytics may give the impression that it is a complex system, it is quite easy to follow. The process can also be easily integrated into an existing business model that can result in completely changing the path of your business positively. By implementing the Lean Analytics idea into a startup or an established business, startups are more likely to succeed and find themselves on the positive 50% side while established businesses can adapt to changing industries and become leaders in those industries.

The beauty with Lean Analytics, and the Lean method in general, is that the end goal is not success or failure per project. Rather, the end goal is an iterative improvement per project. Whether a business model succeeds or fails is not much of a concern to the Lean entrepreneur. Rather, the importance is placed on what can be improved upon with each new project, product, or service.

Application of Lean Analytics helps you explore possibilities in every sphere and at all levels within an organization. You can use Lean in your workplace and if you have difficulty, use the services of a Lean expert. Lean improves workplace efficiency by changing your approach to problems and in the way you figure out the solution. It is growing due to its continued success and will remain one of the dominant technologies of the future.

# LEAN ENTERPRISE

*The ultimate Step-by-Step Guide to learn how to build a Lean Business with Six Sigma, Kanban, and 5S Methodologies to achieve success with your enterprise*

By Adam Ross

# Table of Contents

Introduction .................................................................... 433

Chapter 1: Introduction to Lean Enterprise .......................... 435

Chapter 2: Understanding Lean and Why it Matters to Your Enterprise ................................................................. 441

Chapter 3: How Lean Enterprises Are Built ......................... 449

Chapter 4: How to Identify the Value of Your Enterprise Using Lean ..................................................................... 457

Chapter 5: Creating a Lean System for Your Enterprise ..... 462

Chapter 6: Lean Concepts and Tools for Your Enterprise ... 466

Chapter 7: How to Foster Innovation and Develop New Ideas in your Enterprise with Lean ...................................... 469

Chapter 8: How to Set Lean Goals to Achieve Success in Your Enterprise ................................................................. 478

Chapter 9: Understanding the 5S System and How You Can Apply it in Your Enterprise ........................................... 483

Chapter 10: How to Carry Out the Production Process in Your Enterprise with Lean ................................................... 491

Chapter 11: Kanban and How It Fits into the Lean Enterprise 495

Chapter 12: How to Run a Lean Office? .............................. 501

Chapter 13: How Six Sigma Can Make Lean Enterprise Even More Effective ........................................................... 508

Chapter 14: How to Simplify Lean in Your Enterprise ........ 518

Chapter 15: How to Use Lean to Improve the Process of Large Programs in Your Enterprise .................................... 527

Chapter 16: Benefits of Introducing Lean in Your Enterprise 531

Conclusion ...................................................................... 537

# Introduction

Thank you for choosing my book. The following chapters will discuss everything that you need to know about the Lean system. Many businesses have heard about the Lean system and they want to implement it into their process to see all of the benefits. This guidebook will take some time to explore how to work with the Lean process and the different ways it can benefit your business.

Inside this guidebook, we will take a closer look at the Lean system. We will look at what Lean is all about, which industries can benefit from it, some of the tools that you should use to get the most out of Lean even how to make your value stream map so you know exactly which parts of the process you need to work to improve first.

When you are done with this guidebook, you will be able to determine if the Lean system is the right choice for you and you will know all of the steps that are needed to implement this system in your business and reduce waste in the process.

In the era of technology, most businesses are shifting towards automation and artificial intelligence. Machines can do many processes, however, only a few businesses are willing to accept that change.

Many processes in an organization or a team become redundant over time, after which they must be removed. This is when a company becomes a Lean business. Over the course of the book, you will learn about Lean businesses and their principles.

You will also gather information on how Lean businesses foster innovations and how those innovations are used to improve the business culture.

A Lean business ensures that its employees undergo a great learning and development program, which will help them hone their skills and capabilities. This book covers some tips that can be used for implementing Lean in your organization.

# Chapter 1:
# Introduction to Lean Enterprise

What sets apart the companies that have stood the test of time from those that failed to take-off? Well, aside from learning how to polish their branding, they continuously work on improving their human capital and management systems while changing accordingly with the times adjusting their strategies as they seem fit.

In contrast, brands that were never heard of again weren't able to plant a firm footing in the industry. It's mainly because each step in their workflow had issues that they weren't able to solve. It most likely didn't occur all at once, though. More often than not, a failed business' downfall started with a seemingly harmless misstep — until the rest of their system followed.

No matter how seemingly good a product or a service may be, it will only remain relevant to the market that it's supposed to serve if the whole work process is meticulously addressed. This is especially necessary during the beginning phases of building a business. The key is to lay down everything such that they will move in sync, so that when one part starts working, the rest will simply go with the right flow

The supposed workflow of any organization can be compared to a group of gears working in unison to move an entire machine. This is just an ultra-simplified version of how products and services — or more generally, outputs — are related to all the steps that come before it. So long as the gears are constantly well-oiled and nothing gets caught in them, the machine will move and operate as it should.

However, when faulty components start slowing down the movement of the smaller cogwheels, every part of the process becomes inefficient. Ultimately, the biggest cogwheel will be affected no output will be delivered according to the company's set standards — if any had been set at all.

This is why all parts of a process must be constantly assessed and measured. Otherwise, improvement will almost always be impossible moving towards the next goals will just remain a pipedream.

Thus, if you don't get your act together within the company, you're bound to offer people products that aren't serving any real purpose for them. This may also damage your relationships with investors and suppliers. All it takes is another careless mistake and your reputation will now be forever tainted.

Successful businesses will have none of that. They know exactly how to get things done by using the most effective processes that they have applied through the years. Otherwise, they wouldn't be able to keep their gears rolling at the speed they want to. The question is, are they going through their workflow in the most cost-efficient and most resourceful way possible?

# Lean Company, Lean Manufacturing Lean Enterprise

It's one thing to know how to get the job done. It's another thing to know how to get it done outstandingly. But it's a whole other level to know how to deliver high-quality outputs using the least amount of waste and resources. Given the complexity of planning and production, it's normal to wonder whether it's possible that simple waste elimination can lead to the best products and services.

This system attempts to operate on the idea that if each individual or group in the entire system can identify and eliminate the biggest waste in their tasks, then all of them — as a whole — will be able to produce more valuable outputs using far less expenses. Not only will this drive an organization to its golden age but it will also develop its employees' overall competence and confidence in themselves.

Lean thinking is the basis for all efficiency-driven mechanisms that are practiced in companies, manufacturing or productions even enterprises. But what does it mean when every aspect of an organization is "Lean"?

## How Lean Enterprises Are Built

### Step 1: Building a Lean Company

This is a company that follows Lean thinking methodologies when it comes to production. Each step of the process has been aligned with the rest of the workflow to give way to a smooth and continuous cycle. Goals are typically addressed by creating a team that is composed of experts from various departments (cross-functional team).

### Step 2: Employing Lean Manufacturing

Also called "Lean production", this involves a series of systematic methods for eliminating waste and hurdles within production processes. It carefully assesses the waste caused by uneven workloads, evens them out minimizes the chances of overburdening staff to improve output value and overall costs. A Lean company abides by several Lean manufacturing principles to enhance the workflow — beginning from the conceptualization phase, distribution even beyond.

## Step 3: Establishing a Lean Enterprise

This can be regarded as the ultimate product of all the offshoots of Lean thinking. The Lean enterprise is a grand collaboration among several companies — all of which are working to perfect a product or service that all of them will benefit from. The caveat, however, is that it can be tough for a Lean company to reach its full potential if it's working with companies that aren't following Lean methodologies.

## LEAN THINKING AND LEAN BEHAVIORS

For Lean thinking to make it to the enterprise level, it needs to be perfected on a personal level first. If individuals can make their tasks more efficient, these seemingly minute improvements are bound to translate to enterprise-wide successes.

However, members must also learn how to trade extreme individualism for team effort. It is inevitable that certain members or teams may have legitimate needs that are in conflict with other components of the system. A strong sense of cooperation then becomes necessary, which can only be achieved when all individuals agree to expand their roles in the name of a company or an enterprise's ultimate goal.

Members of cross-functional teams are usually trained to become more well-rounded. For example, full allegiance to their original function (e.g. marketing, financing, engineering, design, production) isn't encouraged in a Lean environment. Team-oriented thinking and behaviors are needed to ensure that no phase in the workflow will ever end up being stuck.

This is why it's necessary for members of cross-functional teams to accept, right from the beginning, that they will need to pursue an offshoot of their original career path to succeed as an employee of a Lean company. Instead of performing their original function, they now work together with other experts to establish new value-adding processes or best practices for the roles that people like them play in an organization.

When these roles are translated to the Lean enterprise, member companies will need to establish new behavioral standards that will help regulate behaviors and activities involved in the enterprise workflow. What's important is that companies focus on what they're good at to become a reliable member of the enterprise.

## LEAN AS THE KEY TO PRODUCTIVITY

For a Lean enterprise to succeed, member companies need to refine their existing models to become more adept at doing more tasks using less resources. The problem is, while companies work towards eliminating waste in their processes, this may cause stress in their employees, who fear that they might eventually be laid off from their jobs due to redundancy. Hence, companies need to explore and exhaust all of their options when it comes to job preservation as they work towards becoming Lean.

Becoming a Lean company may take years before you notice the fruits of all your efforts. , when you have more waste to eliminate, you also need more time to straighten out your workflow. This book will give you an overview of what you need to go through, plus the tools that can help you accomplish this huge task.

The Lean models of business may be the key to building a company — and eventually an enterprise — that will generate the workflow efficiency that you've always wanted. If you're looking for ways to improve how business is done within your company, gradually shifting to Lean thinking will not only help you increase your overall productivity but also provide your employees with their much-needed career growth.

# Chapter 2: Understanding Lean and Why it Matters to Your Enterprise

The core principle of Lean is to minimize waste and maximize customer value. In other words, Lean is to provide customers with products and services of greater value while using fewer resources.

Every Lean business understands what the customers want and focuses on improving fundamental processes to meet those demands.

The management will also need to look at how waste processes can be eliminated along the value stream. It will need to look at how processes can be optimized to reduce human time, human effort, space and capital, which help to reduce the cost incurred to finish the product or service.

Such companies can respond to the changing needs of their customers with high quality, high variety, speed and low cost.

Information management will also become more accurate and more straightforward.

As a whole, you can think about this process of Lean as a group of tools that are useful and can be called up to identify if there is any waste in the current system, either for the business overall or for an upcoming project. Lean is all about reducing waste. Some businesses will take a look at the Lean process because they want to fix the waste and issues within the whole business. They may see that they have too much time between processes, they see that there are a lot of customer complaints, or they run into other issues along the way. Other businesses may just want to work with just fixing and reducing the waste in just one process within them.

With Lean, there is more focus given to reducing costs, while also improving how the production goes any time that is possible. This can be accomplished by identifying the small steps that are needed and then considering the ways that they can be completed more effectively.

Lean is made up of a few principles that are all loosely connected thanks to the idea of reduction of costs and eliminating waste as much as possible. These would include load leveling, continuous improvement, production flow, visual control, automation, flexibility, waste minimization, building up good relationships with the suppliers, pull processing, reliable quality and more.

If these principles are used in the properly, it will result in a small increase in the amount of profitability. If it is used in the proper way and it is given the opportunity, this kind of process will strive to ensure that all necessary items get the space they need and at the right periods of time. Most importantly, it will work to make sure that the ideal number of items will move as needed so that your workflow remains stable while still allowing for any alterations that are needed without all the waste.

For it to work, you must have buy-in or an agreement from everyone in the company. No matter what level they are at or

Lean won't be effective for the short term or the long term. The Lean system in your business will only be as strong as the tools the support, that your company has for the process. If not everyone understands and is on board with the system, then this is when the Lean system can start to run into trouble.

The Lean method is one that many different businesses will try to implement into them. They want to be able to meet a bunch of different goals Lean can help them to get there. First, they want to make sure that they can provide a high-quality product to their customers. To retain these customers, reduce customer complaints other things that can waste time and resources to solve any problems.

Along with this, the company wants to figure out how to reduce any waste, reduce their costs earn more profits in the long run. Many times, the waste that the company can get rid of with the Lean process will result in the customer receiving more value as well. It may take some time you may need to work through the process of Lean for a while but when Lean is done properly; it can help your business out with all of those issues and can help it to grow more than ever before.

## Important Principles

While it was originally developed with a focus on production and manufacturing, Lean proved to be so effective that it has since been adapted for use in virtually every type of business. Before adopting the Lean process, businesses have only two primary tenants. The first one focuses on the importance of incremental improvement while the other one is the respect for people both external and internal.

### Incremental improvement

It is important to approach each challenge with the appropriate mindset which is one that supports the idea that every challenge leads to growth, which leads to positive progress. Finally, you will also want to ensure that you take the time to challenge your preconceptions regularly as you will never know when your business might end up operating on an assumption that is no longer true. This is ultimately the best way to find unexpected waste which will ensure that you start to improve internally not just in the short-term but in the long-term as well.

## **Respect for people**

Respecting the customers means going the extra mile when it comes to considering their problems and listening to what they have to say. When it comes to respecting your team, a strong internal culture that is dedicated to the idea of teamwork is a must. This should further express itself in an implied commitment to improving the team as a means of improving the company as a whole.

Before the digital age, businesses could determine their sales margin by starting with all the relevant costs, adding on a reasonable profit margin and calling it a day. Unfortunately, the prevalence of screens in today's society means that everyone is a bargain shopper, simply because it takes so little effort. This means that you are not only competing against other businesses in your city, county or state, you are now competing with businesses all around the world as well. As such, there are only a few options when it comes to squeaking by with any profit margin whatsoever. Companies can either add additional real or perceived value, or they can reduce the amount of waste they are paying for as much as possible.

Most businesses find that it is better to determine their margins by looking at what customers are likely willing to pay for specific goods or service and then working backward from there. Ideally, you will be able to reduce that price by five percent to ensure you are truly competitive in a cost-conscious world. While it might not seem like much, this extra five percent is extremely important as customers are constantly on the lookout for the next sale, regardless of how much is being saved. The mental benefits that come along with being five percent better than those around them will be more than enough for them to commit to your product or service over all the rest.

## WHY LEAN MATTERS TO YOUR ENTERPRISE

The basic idea is that, regardless of what type of business a business is in, it is still just a group of interconnected processes. These interconnected processes can be categorized such as primary processes and secondary processes. The primary processes are those that directly create value for the business. Meanwhile, secondary processes are necessary to ensure the primary processes run smoothly. Regardless of the type of process you look at, you will find that they are all made up of several steps that can be carried out in a way that ensures they work as effectively as possible and that they need to be viewed as a whole for an effective analysis to be completed.

When given the opportunity, the Lean process strives to ensure the required items get to the required space in the required period. More importantly, however, it also works to ensure the ideal number of items move as needed to achieve a stable workflow that can be altered as needed without creating excess waste.

This is most typically achieved via the tools listed above but still requires extreme buy-in at all levels of your organization if you ever hope for it to be effective in both the short and the long-term. Ultimately, the Lean system is only as strong as the tools your company is using to implement it these tools will only ever be effective in situations where its values are expressed and understood.

Companies are not only competing against the other similar companies in their area but also with those that are all around the world. Since customers can get online, they can compare and then pick out products to be sent to them for better prices, the competition for many smaller companies is steep. As a result, there are only a few options available for a company when it comes to squeaking by with any profit margin at all. Most companies need to either find a way to add perceived or real value to the product, or they can reduce how much waste is in the process to make and distribute that process then save money as well.

Many times, a business will find that it is better to figure out their margins by looking at what the customers are most likely to pay for the goods and services then work their way backward from there. Ideally, you would like to be able to reduce that first price by at least five percent to make you more competitive, while still providing good customer service. It may not be a huge amount but in a world where the customer is always looking for a discount, it can be a difference.

No matter what your business does or produces, you will find several principles of Lean you can implement. This can help you to improve how much value you can provide to your customers in the process, you can still show them that you appreciate the business that they send your way and that you respect them as individuals. This may seem like a lot of things to bring together but the Lean methodology makes it happen.

Often, you will be able to manage this simply by listening to your customers and figuring out their specific wants and needs. Value is often generated when you can add in something tangible, something that can either modify or improve the most common aspects of the service or the good being provided. The goal is that this improvement must be something that the customer will pay for, so when they get that benefit for free, they see it as a viable reason for your service to cost more in the beginning.

You will find that it is also important that the added value is as easy for the customer to claim as possible. Otherwise, they will feel like you have deceived them along the way. By making the added value something easy to see, easy to show off something of value can make a big difference.

The next thing we need to focus on is cost reduction. Every business wants to reduce costs as much as possible. This allows them to stay competitive in the market, helps them to provide a better price point for their products can help them make more money.

To help your company reduce the cost, you need to focus on reducing the amount of waste that you have. Here are the 7 waste you should focus on:

- Transportation waste: This will form when information, materials parts for a task aren't available because the processes for allocating these resources aren't working the way that they should.

- Waiting waste can be created when there is some part of the production chain has time periods where they aren't working on a task. This could happen because they don't have the right parts or they are waiting for another group to finish first.

- Overproduction waste can occur when the demand is exceeding the supply the business doesn't have a good plan in place to help deal with this. The Lean system is designed to make sure that this ends up at zero to help the supply and demand for a product to be in balance.

- Defective waste is another part to watch out for. This type of waste will appear when a part of your operating process starts to generate some issue that must be sorted out later on, often when the product is in the hands of the customer.

- Inventory waste may appear if the production chain ends up being idle in between runs. This can happen because that part of the chain doesn't have all of the physical materials that are needed to run all the time.

- Movement waste can occur when information, materials parts must be moved around to complete that part of the process.

- Additional processing waste can be generated if the work completed doesn't end up adding any kind of value for the company.

Sometimes there is an eight form of waste that needs to be considered. This is any waste that occurs because of underutilization of the team. This can occur anytime that a member of the team is placed into a position that doesn't let them use their full potential. It could also refer to any waste that occurs when members of your team are working on tasks that they have not been trained to do.

# Chapter 3:
# How Lean Enterprises Are Built

To understand how to build a Lean enterprise, it's important to learn how Lean businesses are built first. Lean thinking within a company is often considered the foundation of pursuing Lean practices, no matter what level you may be at. After all, it would be difficult to translate certain practices to bigger scales if you can't make it work at the lowest levels.

Lean thinking is known to enhance your workflow's speed and agility. Generally, it helps you become adaptable and competent enough to continue providing customer value in a world where people's needs are constantly changing.

## PRINCIPLES OF LEAN THINKING

Any business that is trying to get into the Lean mindset will need to integrate the following principles into their processes:

## Eliminating Waste

Waste found within the knowledge workflow are usually linked to the management and to the people doing the work not exactly on the production floor. Examples of waste involved in the knowledge work are:

- **Context Switching:** This occurs when people need to switch from one tool or platform to the other just to complete a single task. This may involve opening a ton of programs or apps all at once. It usually requires a certain process to accomplish so it's prone to confusion. In a way, it overlaps with multitasking since your attention is scattered across various tasks.

- **Poor Appropriation of Tools:** Sometimes, slow completion time can mainly be blamed on inappropriate tools. Oftentimes, when employees are forced to use a tool that certainly isn't the best for the job, the production flow doesn't move as quickly as it should.

- **Inefficiency of Information Systems:** This is related to the previous point. If the workflow relies heavily on information systems, yet company reports say that these systems aren't helping like they're supposed to, you can't expect that things will be accomplished as planned. It's even worse when user feedback isn't integrated into the design — either before the system was launched or after a system overhaul had been made.

- **Ineffective Communication Among Teams:** The phrase "communication is key" isn't emphasized in many contexts for nothing. The lack of open communication and transparency is often the cause of many delays during the production process.

- **Lack of Viable Market:** Any factor in your product that your customer wouldn't be willing to pay for is ultimately considered a waste in the whole workflow. What's the use of something if nobody wants it?

## CREATING KNOWLEDGE

For companies to become a truly Lean business, knowledge and learning must be integrated into the organization. When employees are constantly given the chance to learn the industry's best practices from experts, not only can they add more value to the work they do but they also learn how to be valuable in other ways. This is typically done by:

- Having retrospectives
- Cross-training employees
- Holding regular discussions about employees' work processes

When a company values knowledge creation, they will be able to perform their tasks with more value at a much faster rate. This is a way for them to constantly update their skills and competencies.

## INTEGRATING QUALITY

A company that envisions long-term growth needs to utilize systems that are as error-free as possible. Lean companies usually do this by automating tasks that are repetitive, mentally uninteresting prone to human error.

As a result, employees can pour their time and focus on skills that engage them mentally. This allows them to devote themselves fully to the pursuit of both personal and company growth.

## DELIVERING ON TIME

Lean thinking is primarily driven by the idea that focus is the root of all high-quality outputs. When your work environment isn't conducive enough to maintain an uncluttered mind, this slows your work down. Top-quality work is hard to produce when an employee is constantly distracted.

Lean systems always have steady workflows. This means that everything is delivered and accomplished on a consistent, predictable basis. A bad workflow, on the other hand, is always unpredictable because of unsustainable and unreliable work habits.

Lean teams are always refining their workflows to optimize value at every level. They do this by greatly limiting their WIPs (works in progress) and providing a good work environment so nothing gets stuck in the workload traffic. Multitasking is prohibited because it only prevents people from finishing tasks on time.

## Deferring Commitment

Careful planning is necessary to accomplish long-term goals. In Lean thinking, however, it is discouraged to plan for a product's release way out in advance. This prevents having stocks that may only end up being useless.

Instead, it recommends that you decide to pursue something at the last responsible moment — during the time when you've thoroughly considered all the factors that would help you come up with the best decision possible.

This goes back to the main goal of all Lean systems: eliminating waste.

Deferring commitment helps you decide more smartly by going over the data and reports that accurately reflect the current market situation. This prevents you from pursuing seemingly innovative projects that don't translate into an urgent or even viable market need in reality.

## Respecting People

The root of a Lean system's success all boils down to one basic thing: respect.

First, the concept of Lean was born out of a desire to respect the customer's needs and preferences. Second, Lean systems can thrive because their employees are well-respected by their superiors. They are provided with environments that encourage them to perform at their best.

On an individual level, respect generally entails maintaining kindness and courtesy to everyone that you're working with — whether it's your superiors, your colleagues, your employees, or your customers. Respect is also often shown through:

- Providing safe environments for idea sharing
- Encouraging employees to develop themselves in whatever way they wish
- Trusting employees' decision-making processes

Respect goes a long way in Lean systems because trust is required to maintain good workflow. After all, building good relationships is the key to creating a stable system that produces high-value outputs.

## OPTIMIZING THE WHOLE ORGANIZATION

All decisions in a Lean company must be made relative to the whole organization. For instance, decisions to optimize processes must not only involve one team — it must involve everybody else.

Naturally, an improvement in one component can already be enough to see significant differences in the workflow. However, to become truly Lean means to address all possible sources of waste.

Building a Lean enterprise all starts with creating a Lean business. The next step would be to find others who also share the same Lean ideas as you do. Maintaining collaborations among companies can already be difficult enough since each member will have their goals and agendas. However, if all of you can work towards operating under the same Lean system, then the overall work and production is a breeze.

## PRINCIPLES OF LEAN MANUFACTURING

Many businesses are beginning to switch to Lean thinking and Lean manufacturing to develop the kinds of products that have a good chance of penetrating the global market. Aside from consistently meeting customer demands, it also enables them to earn more profits and enhance product quality with less cost.

Lean thinking gave way to the five Lean manufacturing principles that have greatly improved the workflow of many successful companies today. These are often considered as key factors in improving overall efficiency in the workplace.

### **Defining Value**

The first step of Lean manufacturing begins with learning what exactly the customer values in a particular product or service. This will help a business determine how much a customer is willing to pay for what, which then allows them to set a reasonable target price. After which, the cost of manufacturing the product will then be defined.

To properly establish value in a Lean system, it is vital to learn about the market's recognized and latent needs.

While some customers may already know what they want exactly, others may not be aware that there might be a product or service out there that they want or need. Or perhaps, they know they need a particular something but cannot express what it's supposed to be.

That's where market research comes in. This is typically done through interviews, demographic assessment, web analytics, user testing, surveys, etc.

By defining what your customers want, you get to create something of great value — not just a product that seems innovative in theory. This also helps you understand your customers' purchasing power, as well as the way in which they want this product to be delivered to them.

## Determining and Planning the Value Stream

This is the product's journey from the raw materials stage all the way to the customer usage stage. The stream even includes the customer's eventual disposal of the product, which paves the way for considerable upgrades in the next release.

The latter should be completely eliminated, while the former should be continuously perfected so they don't get in the way of the value stream. Otherwise, they would only delay the rest of the process.

## Creating Flow

A river will always make its way to the ocean eventually, provided that nothing stops the water in its tracks. However, a significant amount of debris in one part of the river system may cause the water to be trapped and unable to follow its natural path.

This is exactly what waste does in a value stream. It interrupts the natural flow of the production process, causing delays that might start small. Eventually, however, it might end up becoming a massive setback that prevents everything from moving further forward.

That said, a company must take their time to fully understand their flow systems to eliminate waste effectively and completely. The concept of flow in Lean manufacturing is all about creating a series of steps that are in sync with each other — one that hardly ever gets interrupted.

## Setting Pull

One of the most significant waste involved in manufacturing is inventory. To solve this, a pull-based system must be established. This system aims to minimize inventories and works in progress as much as possible. Relevant materials should always be available to maintain the company's flow.

Instead of creating products way ahead of schedule based only on market forecasts, a pull-based system encourages you to begin working on something only when a customer expresses the need for it. Thus, you'll only begin production at the moment of need only in the quantities requested.

This allows you to develop the most efficient way to assemble a product, as you need to deliver your promise within a reasonable timeframe.

## Pursuing Perfection

The first four principles of Lean manufacturing are all about identifying and reducing waste as much as possible. This last principle is the crucial point that holds all Lean thinking concepts together. Perfection based on company standards helps deliver products in the best state possible to the end user.

Although a perfect product can never technically exist, pursuing perfection is what inspires companies to continue serving their customers to the best of their abilities.

This is what ultimately sets them apart from the competition. After all, if small mistakes can be removed from the value stream every single day, there will come a time when errors will be close to non-existent.

The shift towards Lean thinking may not exactly be an easy task, especially if you've just realized that you have major roadblocks in all the steps of your value stream. But when you've identified what exactly your problem areas are, you've already taken the first step in creating a more efficient business. Applying the principles of Lean thinking and Lean manufacturing gives you a more competitive edge, simply because you've addressed all of your waste.

# Chapter 4:
# How to Identify the Value of Your Enterprise Using Lean

Lean businesses always identify ways to maximize the value for their customers, which is the core objective of Lean thinking. Most people are under the notion that Lean thinking can only be implemented in sales and marketing departments since those departments work directly with customers. This is not true since Lean thinking is now being used to deliver value products to stakeholders of all departments.

Most businesses still believe that Lean thinking is a way for the demand side since they are not looking at the value stream. These businesses can make better profits since the demand for their products exceeds their supply. Therefore, businesses must remember that Lean is not only about removing waste from the process but also about identifying ways to enhance the value stream to maximize the value of the product.

There is no company in today's economy that rejects more prospects or refuses orders. The business must always look for ways to drive revenue. Therefore, a business must improve continually to enhance and improve the processes in the value stream.

How does a business use Lean thinking to identify value?

- Understand the demands of stakeholders and customers.

- Identify elements in the process that are waste contributors and those that affect the quality of the product.

- Defining the internal customers or stakeholders. These internal stakeholders are members of each department that use outputs of one department as input to achieve their business goals and objectives. Regardless of whether a business is working with internal or external customers, it must focus on how the customers are satisfied rather how well they are satisfied.

Most businesses are product-focused. These businesses cannot view the market or access the market to become the best. They also make the mistake of looking at the value of the product or service and how it will help the customer. Businesses must remember that the idea of value is abstract and has no real definition. The business must always identify ways to create, identify deliver value to its customers.

It is important to remember that value to a company begins and ends only with the stakeholders or customers. If a customer requires a specific product or service from your company, you must use all the resources you need to deliver the product within the stipulated time. It is essential for every business to identify the products or services that will add value to its customers.

## VALUE STREAM MAPPING

When a business identifies the products and services that provide value to its customers, it should map every process and procedure that the company must follow to manufacture or produce that product or service. It is during the mapping process that the business can identify the steps that contribute to waste or add no value to the goal. For instance, if the business discovers the process to place orders by employees is complicated, it must either eliminate that process since it is a waste contributor.

### Flow

When a business creates the process map, it will identify the steps that are unnecessary or contributors of waste. The business must then remove those processes or steps to create a flow. This flow will ensure that there are no obstacles that will hinder the delivery of products or services to customers.

### Pull

Lean processes always produce based on the demand from customers, which makes them "pull processes." Pull processes are those that call for the production of products and services on an as-wanted or as-needed basis. In service businesses, the delivery is always dependent on the workforce.

### Perfection

A business should continually refine the first four principles to ensure that processes have minimal or no waste in them. The idea behind this principle is that any waste that goes unnoticed in the first four stages is always exposed over time. It is important to eliminate that waste to help a business adapt to the changing needs of its customers. Therefore, it is essential to understand how Lean thinking can be applied to help a business develop a holistic approach to the delivery of products and services.

# Ways to Add Value to Your Business?

### Faster and Better

The business must identify ways to deliver products of high quality to customers either before the promised time or on time. Every individual is impatient and a person who has finally taken a look at a product will want it yesterday. If the business can deliver faster, more customers will flock towards the business since there is a direct perceived correlation between the value of offering and the speed at which it is offered.

### Better Quality

The key is to remember that every customer wants products that are of better quality. Therefore, every business must develop products that are of greater quality when compared to the products of its competitors. A business must remember that the customer defines quality. A business must always find out what its customers want and develop products with high quality for them.

### Always Add More Value

Always add value to the product. Most businesses in an industry deliver the same or similar products. For any business to stand out, it must offer something that other businesses do not offer. Apple is an excellent example of this point.

### Increase convenience

You have to identify ways to eliminate processes that make it difficult for customers to place their orders with ease. There are issues when the customer needs to go through elaborate processes to place an order. If that is the case, customers will choose businesses where it is easy for them to place their orders. Lean thinking plays a key role here since the business will need to identify waste contributors and remove them thereby adding value to the process.

## Improve Customer Service

It is important to remember that human beings are emotional and this is a factor that every business must include in its customer service. The business must identify a way to tap into the emotions of its customers by being warm, friendly, cheerful and helpful. A business must ensure that it always helps its customers regardless of how big or small the request is.

## Offer Discounts

Planned discounting will add value and wealth to a business. If a business has a surplus of products, it must identify ways to sell those products in higher volumes. Most supermarkets, like Costco, give customers the chance to buy large volumes of a product at a lower rate. The business can also pass on the savings to the customer and also make profits by selling more significant volumes of some products.

When a business wants to identify ways to enhance the value of its products and services, it will look at ways to increase the speed at which it delivers products and also find ways to improve the quality of the products.

This is when they begin to innovate and identify new processes that can maximize the value of a product for the customer. Businesses must always function with the customers in their minds since they define the business.

If a customer believes that a business is honest and the products delivered are of great quality, word will spread across the market and more customers will switch to that business. Therefore, a business must always identify ways to enhance value for its customers.

# Chapter 5: Creating a Lean System for Your Enterprise

To create a Lean system that lasts, the first thing you will need to do is consider the absolute simplest means of getting your product or service out to the public and put that system into effect. From there, you will need to continuously monitor the processes you have put in place to support your business to ensure that improvement breakthroughs happen from time to time. The last step is to then implement any improvements as you come across. While there are plenty of theories and tools that can help you go on from there, the fact of the matter is that creating a Lean system is that simple. Many of the chapters in this book will consist of deep dives on various tools that will make this process as easy to set up and as most likely to stick as possible.

## There's More to Business Than Profits

When using the Lean system, the end goal is to determine the many ways that it might be possible to improve the efficiency of your business. While an increase in profits is often a natural result of this process, this should not be the primary motivating factor behind undertaking a Lean transformation. Instead, it is important to focus on streamlining as much as possible, regardless of what the upfront cost is since you can confidentially expect every dollar you spend to come back to you in savings.

There are limits to this at a certain point, the gains won't be worth the costs. To determine where this line is, you can use a simple value curve to determine how the changes will likely affect your bottom line. A value curve is often used to compare various products or services based on many relevant factors as well as the data on hand at the moment. In this instance, creating one to show the difference between a pre-and post-Lean state should make such decisions far easier to make.

## Treat Tools as What They Are

When many new companies switch to a Lean style of doing things, they find it easy to slip into the trap of taking tools to the extreme, to the point that they follow them with near-religious fervor. It is important to keep in mind that the Lean principles are ultimately just guidelines and any Lean tools you use are just that, tools which are there to help your company work more effectively. This means that if they need to be tweaked to better serve your team and your customers, then there is nothing stopping you from doing just that. Your team should understand from the very beginning the limits and purpose of the Lean tools they are being provided and understand that they are not laws.

## Prepare to Follow Through

Even if you bring in a trained professional to help your team over the initial Lean learning curve, it will still ultimately fall to you, as the team leader, to ensure that the learned practices don't fall by the wayside as time goes on. It takes time to take new ways of doing things and turn them into habits it will be your job to keep everyone on until everything clicks and they start operating via the new system without thinking about it. Likewise, you must make it clear just why the Lean process is good for the team as a whole and for the individual team member as if they are personally invested in it. This will ensure that they will stick with it, even if the going gets tough.

## Lean Leadership

With so much emphasis placed on improving efficiency, the Lean process naturally puts a lot of emphasis on team leaders who work hard to directly inspire their teams to adopt the Lean mindset. In the end, many Lean systems live and die by the leadership involved, which means it is important that those who are put in charge of leading the Lean transition can not only explain what's going on but are truly committed to the work that is being done as well.

Some of the things that Lean leaders should strive to emphasize include:

### Customer retention

It is important to understand what a customer will accept, what they will enjoy what they will stop at nothing to obtain. The Lean leader should also work to truly understand the many ways the specific wants and needs of their target audience throughout the customer base.

## Team improvement

To help their team members be their best, Lean leaders should always be available to help the team throughout the problem-solving process. At the same time, they will need to show restraint and refrain from going so far as to take control and just do things themselves. Their role in the process should be to focus on locating the required resources that allow the team to solve their problems. Open-ended questions are a big part of this process as they will make it possible for the team to seek out a much wider variety of solutions.

## Incremental improvement

One of the major duties of the Lean leader is to constantly evaluate different aspects of the team to ensure that it is operating at peak efficiency. The leader will also need to keep up to date on customer requirements, as this is something that is constantly changing as well. Doing so is one of the only truly reliable ways of staying ahead of the curve by making it possible to streamline the overall direction of the company towards the processes that will achieve the best results.

## Focus on sustained improvement

It is also the task of the Lean leader to ensure that improvements that are undertaken are seen through to the end as well. This will often include teaching the team members the correct Lean behaviors to use in a given situation and also approaching instances of failure as opportunities for improvement and innovation.

# Chapter 6: Lean Concepts and Tools for Your Enterprise

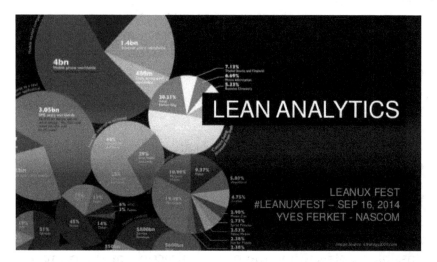

Lean companies employ the support of many concepts and tools that support the principles and also help to eliminate waste from the processes. This section covers some of the most critical tools that every business must be aware of.

## TAKT TIME

A Lean business must always look at ways to optimize processes to ensure that its customers and stakeholders are happy with the rate at which they have received their products. Takt time is the average rate at which any business must produce or execute products or transactions respectively based on the customer's requirements and in the stipulated time.

Takt = (Time available to produce a product or service) / (Demands made by the customer)

## Cellular Manufacturing

Cellular marketing aims to reduce the time taken to meet the customer or market's demand and also to bring processes that produce similar products together. Workstations and equipment are arranged to bring different teams to manufacture similar products.

## Continuous Flow

This tool ensures that the batch size is reduced to eliminate some constraints in the system. The business must identify a method by which it produces products or information that moves at a consistent pace from one step that adds value to the next with zero delays or waste in between.

## Standardized Work

The business must create a document that lists out the processes or methods being used to produce goods and services to meet the calculated takt time. This helps to standardize tasks and enhance the full value stream.

## Kanban and Pull Systems

Kanban is a tool used to schedule tasks and also instruct different departments with the tasks that it must complete to produce or manufacture different products and services. This tool was developed by Taiichi Ohno to improve the manufacturing process of Toyota automotive in the late 1980s. Every business must include a customer process that signals the manufacture or supply process to deliver the final product.

## The Why's

A business must always ask the question "why" to get to the root of any problem that may arise during the process cycle. For example, if there is a delay to receive the raw material from the supplier, the business can ask the following questions:

- Why are we sticking to this supplier only?
- Why is there no backup supplier?

## Level the Workload

Customer patterns are often variable the processes in every business are consistent in the sense that every process must be built to manage a defined quantity of work. This strategy can be adopted by many businesses to plan different types and volumes of work.

# Chapter 7:
# How to Foster Innovation and Develop New Ideas in your Enterprise with Lean

There is a lot of talk about innovation and how companies have started to innovate their processes to work efficiently. But, what is the impact of using Lean to foster innovation in business? The potential is huge it is essential that every business harness that potential.

The word innovation can either excite or terrify us. Many people are skeptical about the innovation of processes in their company but others are embracing this innovation with open arms. The former group is stuck in their old ways while the latter are willing to unlock their creative potential to improve the business. However, there is one thing that is certain – the leaner a business, the easier it is to innovate the business.

The debate on how Lean thinking can foster innovation is one that has gained popularity. Innovation can be defined as the process of changing or transforming a process or an idea into something new, which will make the lives of the employees in the business easier.

Regardless of what process the business is transforming – manufacturing technology, products, services, software and business models – any innovation should always lead to the maximization and creation of value for the stakeholder or customer. This means that the business should meet not only the needs and demands of the customer but also anticipate them. Lean is one process that is customer-driven every principle and tool is based on the idea of freeing up the business's resources by removing waste and also maximizing the customers' value.

This helps to include newer projects and also allocate some resources to those processes. Many people believe that a Lean business can innovate processes since it encourages the employees to identify innovative ways to improve its processes.

The business community has realized that Lean thinking is one model that should be used to foster innovation in business. Many organizations have used Lean thinking as a foundation to innovate their ideas and processes.

It is also important to remember that it is not only businesses that can benefit from Lean thinking. Social, economic and environmental problems have become driving forces behind innovation. People and businesses should be respectful and mindful of the resources of our planet before they begin to innovate.

This innovation should contribute to solving the challenges of our time. Toyota Automotive has taught the world that Lean thinking improves the society. This is further proof that Lean thinking and innovation are a perfect match.

It has been proved that Lean thinking is more superior to traditional manufacturing. But, one has to remember that Lean thinking is more about improving the management system and leadership behavior. Lean drives innovation and is an approach that is based on learning. However, certain conditions have to be in place for Lean management to succeed.

## ORGANIZATIONAL STRUCTURE FOR LEAN INNOVATION

An organization must have the right structure to foster innovation through Lean thinking. Companies must always be inclusive in the sense that every stakeholder must participate in the decisions that the company makes.

For example, employees, engineers, suppliers, scientists and customers must agree upon every decision that is made by the company to maximize value for the customers. Every function that takes place in a business must be included in innovation this is what Lean thinking teaches us.

The phenomenon of "open innovation" arises when every team in an organization is included in the process of innovation. This concept suggests that every innovative idea must be welcome even if it is coming from outside the organization. Businesses can take ideas that were coined by college students, scientists, young entrepreneurs and sometimes amateurs as well.

A company that is open to innovation must have a flat organizational structure since vertical structures have been known to fail. Business leaders must always identify the processes or layers in the structure that add value to their customers. There are a few strategies that a business can use to foster innovation through Lean thinking in their organization.

## HOW TO START THE PROCESS OF INNOVATION AND EXPERIMENTATION?

### Understand Why

Most businesses have started to innovate their processes. This does not mean that a business should always choose ideas from outside the organization. If the business is unable to sketch or draft an idea that can maximize value for the customers, it does not understand the process fully. Additionally, it cannot implement new ideas successfully if it does not understand how those ideas benefit the company and the customer.

## Business Factors

The management must always look at the business factors in their business and their competitors' businesses. If the factors used to conduct processes are the same, no innovation has been made to the process. This reduces the competitive advantage that the business may have over its competitors.

## Business Model Diagram

If there are any competitive barriers, they must be removed to start improving and innovating processes. The management must outline the key activities, partners, cost structure, revenue stream and value propositions and observe them keenly to understand if any changes can be made.

## Value Matrix

If there are any products or services that the customers do not appreciate or want, these can be removed from the value stream to enhance the process. This allows businesses to invest in fewer resources and add more value to the products and services. Businesses will be able to elevate the elements of the business that are bringing in more value and also create different purchases that are in line with the demands of the customers.

## Strategy Profile

Businesses must revisit their business strategies and their competitors to identify areas where they can innovate and newer areas of business that can be tapped into. This will help the business identify new areas of work and also develop products and services within that area of work.

### Experimentation

Every business is allowed to fail. If there is a new concept that has been developed, the business should put it into action to see how the customers view it. There is a possibility that the idea may fail but it is all right to fail. This helps the business identify what can be done better the next time an idea is implemented.

### Renewal

Ideas that have been implemented should never be ignored. The business must revisit the ideas and see what can be improved to enhance customer experience. Always make upgrades to existing ideas since innovation is an ongoing process.

## HOW TO FOSTER LEARNING AND EXPERIMENTATION THROUGH LEAN?

A learning organization is not different from Lean management. Learning is a process that is embedded in Lean management. An organization where teams learn from everyday processes and also experiment with innovations and changes made to a process is called a Lean and learning organization.

Every employee in an organization must learn every day about the processes and enhance their knowledge of the processes. This will enable the employees to cater to any problems that may occur during the process.

What every business must remember is that learning provides the business with an environment where employees are given the freedom to think and also embrace the idea that solutions to work-related problems are found in their mind.

The employee must always tap into his or her knowledge base and use that knowledge to develop concepts and ideas that will improve the process.

In a Lean business, learning is not restricted to training only. Training does help the employees develop some skills and also grasp and understanding of how the company functions. But, through learning, the employees will develop better skills and more knowledge that can enhance the profitability of the company.

## Learning Model

The following learning model can be implemented in businesses to enhance learning.

### Level 1

Every employee must learn the process, procedures, understand why a process is being done the way it is and also some essential facts about the process. This is a level of learning that applies to processes where only minor changes can be made.

### Level 2

Learn new skills that can be transferred to situations at work. If the employee is in a new situation or has been shifted to a new process, he or she must be able to respond to changes in the process. The business can also choose to bring in outside expertise for this level of learning. There can be training that will help employees enhance their skills.

### Level 3

Employees must always learn to adapt. This is a level of learning that applies to situations that are dynamic and where every solution must be developed. Experimentation and learning from failure are two ways of learning in this level.

## Level 4

This is where an employee learns to learn. This is about how an employee can be creative and innovate processes. He or she can learn to design processes for the future. Knowledge is reframed at this level every assumption made by an employee is challenged.

Learning organizations set employees free. They are not required to be passive players in the business but can learn to express their views and ideas and also challenge those ideas and their skills to improve the work environment. Employees can create an environment where they can create and achieve the results that they truly desire.

## Establish a Learning Culture

It is difficult to establish a learning culture in organizations that are not Lean since they are comfortable in old practices and rarely find the necessity to change their processes. That being said, it is hard to establish a learning culture in any business. This section provides some aspects that a business should consider when it is keen on developing a learning culture:

### External or Future Orientation

Organizations that have external or future orientation can understand their environment. Some teams comprise of senior members of the organization who take some time out of their busy day to develop a plan for the future. Additionally, the business can also choose to employ advisors who can help them plan their business.

### Free Flow and Exchange of Information

There should be some systems in place that ensure that there are experts available whenever needed. Employees must have the chance to expand their horizons and also network with employees or professionals from other companies. This will give them an opportunity to enhance their knowledge of different processes, which will help them become experts in the process.

## Commitment to Personal Development and Learning

With the support from the top management, employees must have the chance to learn. Employees who make an effort to learn regularly must be rewarded. This act will ensure that other employees also step forward and learn more. The employees must also be given the time to learn and also be encouraged to think Lean which will help to remove waste from processes.

## Trust and Openness

Views should be challenged but every individual must be encouraged to develop or create ideas that will improve processes. They must also be allowed to voice their opinion, even if it is different from what other employees think, since that gives rise to diversity.

## Valuing Employees

Any idea that is developed by an employee should be tried and tested. An employee must be valued his or her thought process must be stimulated. If the idea is experimented and fails, the employee must learn from that failure and develop an idea that overcomes any errors.

In simpler words, a learning organization does not only implement ideas developed by senior management. It also allows employees to express their views.

## Lean thinking is about creating a learning organization

It is important to remember that Lean businesses are not only about the processes; it is also about learning. Every process is a great tool to transform an organization into a learning organization. This should be the goal that every organization must achieve in the current market and economy.

The disruption, complexity and change will continue the rate at which these phenomena are occurring will only increase with time. The only competitive advantage that any business has in this economy is the ability to adapt the only way a business can adapt is by learning continually.

A learning organization embraces change and creates reference points that help to rebuild the structure. Learning organizations are healthier since they:

- Increase the ability to accept and manage change
- Garner and encourage independent thought
- Improve quality
- Give employees hope that things can always get better
- Develop a committed organization and workforce
- Stretch and expand perceived limits

To create a learning organization the management or leadership must be effective. This means that leadership cannot follow the traditional hierarchy but must consist of a mixed group of people from different levels in the system.

The business must also accept that every employee can solve some problems that may occur in the organization. The business must give employees the benefit of doubt and encourage them to voice their opinion, which will help the business forge ahead and create a bright future.

An organization must never consider itself separate from the world. It is only when it connects to the world that it can build a learning culture and environment.

One of the biggest challenges that every business must overcome is the way it identifies people within the organization. Only when every employee is considered equal is there a possibility to develop a learning organization.

# Chapter 8:
# How to Set Lean Goals to Achieve Success in Your Enterprise

To help you to make the best changes to your business and get the most out of Lean, the first thing you should do is make sure that you have the right goals in place for your business. Each business is a bit different, so determining these goals and picking out the ones that are best for you can make all the difference. To make sure that you are picking out goals that put your particular business on the right track to seeing results with Lean, you must pick out SMART goals. SMART goals refer to specific, measurable, attainable, realistic timely.

Let's break these all up and learn a little bit more about each one!

## SMART Goals

### Specific

The first part of our SMART goals journey is setting goals that are specific. This means that you must pick out a goal that is extremely clear this is never more important than when you start with Lean. Vague goals may be easier to come up with, they aren't ones that you can measure to see whether you have attained them or not. Keeping goals that are specific in mind can make it easier for you to power through and succeed with any task that you are trying to accomplish.

### Measurable

Your business also needs to make sure that it is setting up goals that are measurable. SMART goals are ones that can be broken into small and easy to manage chunks so that you can take each chunk and work on it one piece at a time. A measurable goal should make it easy to determine the exact point when you are about to head off track. This makes it easier for you to go through and self-correct as quickly as possible. When you can effectively measure your progress it is easier for you to keep going the right way and see the success that you want.

### Attainable

The next thing that we need to focus on is picking out goals that are attainable. If you set out with goals that are unattainable, especially if it is your first goal with Lean, then you will waste a lot of valuable energy and time, while also creating some negative patterns in the business that can end as failures. Another issue here is that you will reinforce fixed mindset ideals, making this a horrible choice no matter the way that you choose to look at it.

### Realistic

You also need to pick out a goal that is realistic. This means that you will be able to expect success for the goal without something extremely unlikely being required to push the reality into your favor. A good goal is one that will require you and your team to put in some work to achieve it but there shouldn't be so much difficulty with it that it's impossible to reach.

### Timely

Finally, the last part of creating SMART goals for the Lean system is to be timely. Studies show that the human mind is more likely to actively engage in behaviors of problem-solving when there is some sort of deadline or time limit involved in the successful completion of the task in question. What this means is that when you pick out a goal, you need to have a firm date of completion in mind for when you need to reach and succeed with this goal.

Setting good goals with the Lean system can make a big difference in the amount of success that you are able to see. Many companies go with Lean thinking that it will be easy and things will just fall into place themselves. But as you can see, you need to think about some SMART goals that you can use with Lean to get it off the ground, to ensure that your team is striving to be the best and that there are deadlines and other guidelines that you have to follow to push yourself, without being overworked in the process.

### POLICY DEPLOYMENT

Policy deployment is a way of ensuring any SMART goals that are set at the management level ultimately filter down to the rest of the team in a measurable way. Making proper use of policy deployment will essentially ensure that anything you are planning to put into effect doesn't accidentally end up creating more problems than it ultimately solves. It will also help to ensure as little waste as possible is generated as a result of things like inconsistent messaging from management or all around poor communication. The goal in this instance should not be to force various team members into acting in a specific way. It is about generating the type of vision for the business that everyone can appreciate and understand how it pertains to both the team and the customers.

## Implementing the plan

Once all of the relevant SMART goals have been finalized, the next thing you will want to do is to group them together based on which members of the team will ultimately be tasked with solving them. Keep in mind that the fewer number of goals, the more likely it is that they will be acted upon in a reasonable timeframe. If your goals cannot be generalized in such a way, it is important to instead begin with the ones that are sure to make the biggest difference overall and work down the list from there.

Regardless of what goals you ultimately settle on; you must take special care to ensure that there are no goals that do not have one person specifically assigned instructions to keep tabs on the overall progress while providing status reports when needed. This person should also be someone who can be counted on to make it clear to the other team members how important the goal is for the business as a whole and how it will make things easier in the long run.

## Consider your tactics

Those who will be responsible for making the goal a reality should be the ones who decide how the goal can best be completed by the team as a whole. However, this process should still include back and forth interaction between all levels of the team just to ensure that the tactics and the goal align properly. Tactics are likely to change as the goal heads towards success, which means it should be studied from time to time to ensure they remain appropriate for the goal in question.

## Moving forward

Once the tactics have been agreed upon by all parties, it will then be time to put them into practice. This will be the stage where the team can take over, though quality goals should still require buy-in from relevant parties. During this period, it is important to ensure all communication from management is on message, to properly ensure that actions and broader goals will continue to align.

## Review from time to time

It is important to keep in mind that once the action is in progress, the team leader will need to change the action as needed. This means that they will also be monitoring things as they proceed, hopefully, according to plan. Remember, Lean systems are always being improved upon, which means your goals and their implementation should be no different.

# Chapter 9:
# Understanding the 5S System and How You Can Apply it in Your Enterprise

When it comes to determining what processes your company has that are considered wasteful, it is important to ensure that the work environment is in optimum shape for the best results. The 5S organizational methodology is one commonly used system based around several Japanese words that are first-rate when it comes to improving efficiency and effectiveness by clearly identifying and storing items in the right space each time.

The goal that comes with this kind of system is to allow for more standardization in your company across more than one process. When you can do this, you will notice that there is a significant amount of savings that show up in the long term. The reason that this method can be so effective is that when you have the human eye work to track across a messy workspace, it can take a bit of time, even if that time period is short, for the person to locate what they want and then process everything that is in the room. While this amount of time may seem small at a glance, if it happens constantly and the whole team is doing it then it results in a ton of time that is lost. Finding ways to reduce this and keep your employees at the job can help save you time and money in the process.

Lean Six Sigma and Kanban are tools that improve work process efficiency by eliminating waste and applying necessary changes to the current value stream. Both of them tend to be more mental in nature — meaning, the changes usually come from a gradual shift in people's understanding of company-specific workflows. Given that, can waste be eliminated in ways other than changing the mindset of the whole workforce?

## WORKSPACES AND PROCESS EFFICIENCY

Applying physical changes to your current office setup can also improve your workflow significantly. We're not just talking about eliminating transport and motion waste, in which layouts are modified to simplify the movement between processes. We're also talking about putting everything in its rightful place.

This is exactly what the 5S process is for. Each S in the cycle aims to organize workspaces such that all tasks can be performed safely and efficiently. It operates on the idea that if the workplace is kept clean and things are where they should be, it will be easier for employees to accomplish their tasks without wasting their time on non-value adding steps or exposing themselves to safety hazards.

5S is a concept that started out as a tool at the Toyota production floor. 5S is regarded as a foundational component of the Toyota Production System because it helped keep the workplace neat and highly organized. This methodology was put in place because they knew how difficult it was to produce consistent results when a place is utterly messy.

Mistakes, delays accidents are probably not immediately blamed on all the clutter in the workplace. However, if you think about it, all the mess usually prevents people from focusing on their jobs. Consequently, this only impedes the flow and it's only a matter of time before everyone gets stuck on the same spot.

How do we work with the 5S organizational method? There are five parts that come with this and they include:

## Sorting

The first part of this method is sorting. Sorting is all about doing what you can to make sure that the workspace is as clean as possible that nothing that isn't required to complete the work is kept out. When sorting, you need to make sure that the space is organized so that you can remove anything and everything that could potentially create an obstacle when it comes to your team completing the task that they need to do. You will want to ensure that the items that are critical to the process have their unique space, one that is labeled and easy for everyone on the team to find.

You don't want to make your workspace a mess. If things get easily lost, if there are items there that aren't necessary to the production phase if you run into issues with items always being somewhere else, even in other parts of the building, then this can slow things down. Taking some time to organize things and putting them in the locations that are the most convenient to find later on can make a big difference in how well you will be able to find them how well the team can get the work done.

After you organize the area, it becomes so much easier to keep the space free of any new distraction. Your leader should encourage the team members to prune their personal workspace regularly to ensure that no new obstacles end up getting in the way.

## Set in Order

When you are trying to organize the items in your workplace, it is important to ensure that all of the items are organized by which are used the most. While doing so, it is so important that you and your team take care to make sure that all of the items and tools that you need for the most common steps are nearby and easy to get. Your goal here is to reduce the amount of movement waste for getting items as much as possible.

You will find that over time, keeping the items that you need in the same space each time will help you get faster and faster at completing the project each time. Muscle memory can take over the team members can reach for and grab things without even needing to think about or look at the item that they need.

You need to have an open mind when you are working on this step because you may find that promoting the ease of workflow can be more than just organizing the area. It could even require some serious reworking of the facilities and how they are laid out at this point. Also, you must make sure that all the items are arranged correctly to make it easier for you to create steps for every part of the process. You want it to not only be easy for the people who are already on the team but also for those who are new to the team so they can catch on and not slow down the process.

## Shine

The next thing that we will take a look at is known as Shine. Keeping the workspace as clean as you can making sure that there isn't a lot of a mess around so that you maintain the most effective workspace possible. You want to talk to your team and emphasize how important it is to have some kind of daily cleaning to ensure that the overall efficiency of the team is boosted and to ensure that everything stays where it needs to be.

This is also a good time for you to set up a schedule for regular maintenance, if any is very needed, which will serve to ensure that the whole office stays as safe as possible for everyone. The end goal here is that any member of the team should be able to walk into the workspace and understand, within five minutes or less, where the key items in the process are located.

## Standardized

The standardized step in this methodology is all about ensuring that the processes in the organization itself stay in line in such a way that you can take these same ideas and apply them throughout all the areas, the departments everywhere else throughout the whole business. The reason that you want to do this is to make sure that order is maintained, even when things get hectic. It makes it so that everyone is held to the same standards of quality and reliability.

## Sustain

Finally, we will look at the idea of sustain. Sustaining the process is vital because it could take a week or more to set up this process. If you spend that much time learning about the process and getting it set up, you don't want to have it fall apart in just a few months. This makes all that hard work a waste of time it can be discouraging overall.

It is important to make sure that this new organizational method becomes a vital part of the business starting from day one and moving into the future. If things are truly sustainable in this kind of regard, then the team will successfully move through the process, without the management or the leader expressly having to ask them to do it.

While sustainability is something that you should strive for with this method, it isn't something that you can expect overnight. It requires lots of training and adoption of the ideas of Lean and more, to become a part of the culture for your business. This does take time as everyone gets on board with the ideas and as they start to learn more about the process. But once it happens, you will start to see all of the benefits that come with this method.

## WHY THE 5S' ARE A GREAT STARTER TOOL

If you have some big plans for your business and these include transitioning yourself to more advanced concepts of Lean over time, then working with the 5S method is a great way to help move employees in the right direction to make this happen. This method can be effective with any employees who seem to be stuck in their ways. Once these individuals get on board, they will find that it is hard to deny all of the benefits of the Lean system and these organizational versions they will jump on even more. When they see these benefits, they are more likely to jump on board with some of the additional changes that you want to add in the future.

One thing to remember when you are rolling out a new system like this one, you may find that the team members are only going to care about two main things. These include the way that this kind of new system will affect them specifically and whether the Lean process will provide some results.

These concerns are also what make the 5S system a great place to start. It comes with some answers that are easily understandable for anyone who has a question and who wants to see if Lean and the other methods we have discussed in this guidebook will provide some results.

## IS THE 5S SYSTEM A GOOD CHOICE FOR MY BUSINESS?

While the 5S system is a good choice for many businesses, no matter what kind of industry they are in, it isn't a solution that fits everyone. This is why it is so important for you as a business owner to have a good idea of both the strengths and weaknesses when you get started. One of the biggest strengths with this system is that when it gets implemented properly, it will help your team define their processes easier while helping them to claim some ownership on the processes that come.

Remember that with Lean the goal is to not have one manager or one leader calling all of the shots. The point is to bring in all of the team members and hear their opinions and get everyone on board. When the team gets their voice heard and can have a say in what happens, it will add some more accountability in the process. And when everything goes according to plan, it will lead to performance that is improved even more, which then leads to better conditions of work for everyone on the team.

Also, implementing this process has the potential to make long-term employee contributions thanks to an internalized sense of improvement. In an ideal world, this is something that will continue on until the main ideas of continuous improvement start to become the order of the day. When the company and the team can use the 5S system in the proper way, it can provide them with some bigger insights into the worlds of work standardization, equipment reliability value analysis.

However, while there may be a lot of things to love about the 5S system, there are also some drawbacks that businesses need to be prepared for. One of the biggest weaknesses that occur with this is that if the system and its purpose are not communicated to the team properly, then members of the team can sometimes make some mistakes. This is because they may see the system as more of an end goal, rather than as a means to an end.

The 5S system needs to be the flag-bearer of any kind of success that will come in the future, rather than the sum total of the journey the company made with the processes of Lean. Specifically, businesses whose movement is constrained quite a bit by some external factors (which they are not able to control), may find that it is hard to use the 5S system companies who run into lots of storage problems right now may need to solve these issues before they try to transition into the method.

Also, just because this method is a good fit for many different kinds of companies doesn't mean that it is automatically going to fit in with your business and your team. This can be seen when we are talking about some of the smaller teams, or for any team that has all of their members take on many roles at the same time. Just because the 5S system is seen as a very popular way to implement the Lean principles doesn't mean that it will fit for everyone.

Choosing to ignore this information and moving ahead anyway and enforcing organization just because you think you need to, or just because another business has done it, won't do much of anything when you take a look at the results that it generates. If you try to implement this system into a process where it doesn't belong, you are just going to generate more waste in the long run.

This is even more true for any kind of business that works with a large variety of interactions with humans, various styles of management other management tools. However, when the different aspects work together properly, they may be able to generate some extra value to their customer, which is seen as a very vital part of a business that can see success in the market.

While the 5S system can be a great way to help your business, if you blindly press forward with it, you will find that it is easy to lose sight of the proper outcome for your customer because you are trying to pursue the perfect outcome or a perfect implementation of the 5S principles. If this method isn't going to help you to serve the customer properly it waste more time than it is worth, then don't worry about implementing it into your business.

Finally, when you are trying to implement this system, you must take the time to stress to all the members of your team that 5S is something that needs to be a part of their natural routine and the best practices that are standard for the business. It should never be seen as any kind of additional task that they need to do outside of their daily work. The goal of the 5S system is to enhance how effective the workflow for your business is at every step of the process. If you try to separate out this system into a new layer that is in addition to the work, rather than going along with the work, then you are doing the complete opposite of what the process stands for.

# Chapter 10:
# How to Carry Out the Production Process in Your Enterprise with Lean

When you are working on putting a Lean system together for your company, you will be able to determine where all of the waste has been hiding in the processes that you use. This means it is time to look into what you can do about the flow of the process to make things better. Often the answer will come either in the form of a batch model or a continuous flow model.

## CONTINUOUS FLOW MODEL

The ideal version of the continuous flow model sees the customer order a product or service before the necessary steps are taken to generate the product or service that is being paid for. The product or service is then delivered to the customer who then pays for their order. The end result here is that there is no downtime between when the customer puts in their request and when it is completed. Furthermore, every step will smoothly flow into the next as a means of ensuring that overall downtime is reduced as much as possible.

The biggest upside to the continuous flow model is that it allows business to make assumptions and plan for the future based on a profit level that prioritizes continuity and stability. A continuous flow setup also features less waste than other types of processes. The biggest downside, however, is that this type of scenario can be difficult to produce reliably as every step in the process is rarely equal, regardless of how clear the value stream map might be. If you are striving to create a continuous process scenario, then you should be aware that new problems can also appear quickly if your available margin for error begins to shrink.

To persist despite these drawbacks, you will want to do your best to attack these problems head-on and be determined to push through them if you hope to find success. Additionally, if you hope to choose this route, it is important to start your journey to a Lean system with this in mind as a continuous system is only going to work if every part of the system is completely in sync with all the rest.

Heijunka is a useful tool when it comes to facilitating this process as it promotes leveling out the quantity and quality of the process over a prolonged period in hopes of making everything as efficient as possible and, what's more, to expressly prevent batching. While it might sound complicated, in reality, this process can be as simple as making sure your team has all of the storage space they need to organize the various parts of the project. They store them in folders that are organized based both on the frequency of use as well as the due date. Folders that are currently in use are stacked vertically on top of one another while those that are idle are stored horizontally out of the way somewhere. There are also numerous other types of organizational methods that promote Heijunka, so it can be helpful to explore them all to see what offers the most benefit to your business.

## Batch Production

This method will have all the steps for creating the product or service be done in bulk one after the next. This can be a good choice when you are in a situation where what the process is generating is evergreen because this allows it to be stockpiled as a direct counter to erratic customer demand.

Depending on the specifics that come with your business, this batch production model can also decrease some of the costs of production as just a few members of the team can move from one step to another instead of having all of your steps working at the same time. it can also provide you with a lot of opportunities to do cross training.

However, you will usually find that batch production can be less productive when you have a lot of individual steps that are needed to finish the process. This is because the starting and stopping times need to be calculated each time this can add up if there are a lot of steps that you need to complete. It can also cause some potential delays if one of your customers places a big order that is customized and the batch is in the middle of production.

## Takt Time

Takt time is something that you can use to measure time and it is often used in production environments, though it can be beneficial no matter what kind of task you need to perform. Takt time is the time that it will take your team to start up a new process after they complete the last one. It assumes the production rate is the same as the rate of customer demand.

Let's take a look at how you can determine the Takt time. If your team is working to complete one process at a time throughout the day, the Takt time of that process is determined when you take the time that elapsed between those two processes, with the assumption that the demand is being met. This means that you can write out the formula for Takt time as $T = Ta/D$. T is the Takt time, Ta is the amount of time that is available to finish the process and D is the demand that the process is experiencing.

Once you have figured out how to determine the right Takt time for the processes you are using, you will find some benefits to you. First, this can clarify which steps in the process are causing the bottlenecks, which helps you to take the necessary steps and actions to mitigate them specifically. If you find that there are any processes that tend to go off track, that problem is shown as well.

Takt time is not a set-it and forget-it type of affair which means that if you find that your demand changes dramatically, then you will need to recalibrate all of your takt time to adjust for this fact. This also means that if your demand isn't relatively stable, then determining your takt time might not be very beneficial on its own. If you try and force your process into a takt timetable and it isn't a good fit, then all you will end up doing is causing even more waste in the long run.

Likewise, you will need to be aware of the way in which the products or services produced by your processes fit together or else, you risk creating bottlenecks anyway which will throw off the accuracy of your takt time. As a general rule, the shorter the takt time, the greater the amount of strain that resources including both machinery and people will regularly experience.

Generally, this Takt time will place a lot of emphasis on steps that can add value to the process, which can help you to learn what to remove from the process. Once the team starts to use the idea of Takt time and gets more familiar with it, they will find that it is a fantastic way to track how productive they are being.

Also, you must be aware of the way in which the various products and services that are done by your process can fit together.

# Chapter 11: Kanban and How It Fits into the Lean Enterprise

Kanban is a method of scheduling that can be used in the Lean system after it has been started in your company. It is a type of inventory management system whose end goal is to minimize waste in the supply chain. It can also tend to come in handy when it comes to pinpointing problems as it makes these problem areas stand out more than they otherwise would. Many companies find that Kanban is useful when they want to figure out the upper end of work related to inventory that is underway to ensure that the process doesn't overload.

Kanban is a system that is driven by demand. It is often implemented as a means of ensuring that the turnaround times are faster while still limiting the amount of inventory that you need and increasing the overall level of competitiveness between the implementation team.

Kanban was first used by Toyota in the 1940s after the company did a study about supermarkets and decided to use similar practices that they saw in those stores to help them keep their factories stocked at optimal levels all of the time, without having too much stock sticking around. This eventually turned into the core ideas of Kanban to help companies keep their amounts of inventory level and balanced with the current consumption rates of their customers.

From this system, any additional supplies are added based on some predetermined set of signals to ensure that the stock was able to stay near the ideal level at all times, rather than overflowing or dipping at irregular intervals. The signals in question are all based upon the signals from the customer, which means that if customers demand changes, either going up or down, then the signals to the inventory will change as well.

## Rules of Kanban

There are a few rules that you need to keep track of when you get started with Kanban:

- Each process that you work on will create an amount that is set by the Kanban.
- The following processes will collect the number of items that the Kanban will set.
- Nothing is moved or created with a Kanban.
- Kanban is attached to the related goods.
- Defective products won't be counted in the Kanban.
- The fewer the Kanban, the more sensitive you will be when you work on the system.

There are several different parts that come with the Kanban system. First, are the Kanban cards. These are the signals that are used to help keep the whole team on track when they are moving through the process. When the system was created, these Kanban cards were actual cards that would make their way through the system but today, there are software programs that can help to send out the right signals as needed.

These Kanban cards often represent the consumption through a lack of cards in one area, which drives another part of the process to do what needs to be done so that the relevant cards can get passed on and will make the process be efficient and keep moving on.

Many companies who use the Kanban system rely on the electronic version. You will find that the electronic Kanban system is even more effective than physical cards. This is because the software will make sure that the right signals and cards are sent out at the right time. This system marks set types of inventory with specific barcodes that can be scanned at the right times during the process. When the barcodes are scanned, they send out a specific message out to the program about the routes that are needed.

## THE KANBAN SYSTEM FOR BACKLOG REDUCTION

Most of us have gotten stressed at one point because of delayed projects. Such issues are usually blamed on a person's lack of time management skills. While that is a logical cause of delays, sometimes the inability to manage time isn't the problem. It's more of the inability to minimize works in progress (WIPs).

This is similar when you have multiple tabs open all at once. Even if you know the order in which to get to them, the right sequence will eventually be lost on you. This is how workplace waste usually start. When employees are always switching tasks, they never stay at one task long enough to progress to the next step.

As a result, most of them will always be "busy", yet they are rarely every productive. In such cases, applying the Kanban system may just be what you need to eliminate employee unproductivity and backlogs once and for all.

# Kanban: The Original Scheduling System for Lean Manufacturing

Kanban means "card" or "signboard" in Japanese. It first came into existence as the scheduling system used by the Toyota Production System to properly execute their just-in-time product workflows.

Because the production line relies on customer demand, they needed a system that could help them visualize the entire flow across the value stream. Hence, they used actual cards to signify which tasks are already done which ones are still awaiting completion. This ensured that no one was doing too much at any one point.

## The Core Principles of Kanban

Kanban's primary focus is to ensure that everyone's tasks are accomplished on schedule and that no backlogs will cause a significant impediment in the workflow. The following principles highlight how Kanban succeeds as a Lean tool:

### Workflow Visualization

If you want to see how every checkpoint in the value stream is related with each other, a Kanban board will show you how tasks move between stages. By pulling and moving cards from the "In Progress" column to the "Finished" column, employees can find it a lot easier to recognize which tasks should be prioritized which should already be delivered.

This is usually done using an actual board that's subdivided into columns, with tasks written on cards. It can also be a digital version, using a customized program or app.

### WIP Reduction

When an employee or a whole team's focus shifts at the middle of their current tasks, it typically harms the whole workflow.

Kanban reduces the WIPs allowed in every stage so employees can work on tasks only when the Kanban board says they're free to do so.

## Flow Management

Kanban is mainly fueled by its goal of making workflows as smooth and as trouble-free as possible. By revealing the whole process in visual form, it becomes easier for managers to see how the process can be sped up sustainably.

Instead of keeping employees busy, Kanban allows the manager's focus to shift to the workflow and figure out how tasks can move through the value stream at a faster rate.

## Feedback Loops

Regular updates are also scheduled to keep everyone in the loop. These short meetings are generally done in front of the Kanban board to let everyone know what their tasks are, together with those tasks' current status.

Feedback loops put everyone in the same page. Additionally, operations reviews, service reviews, and risk reviews are also conducted at regular intervals to further encourage process improvement.

## INTEGRATING KANBAN INTO THE WORKPLACE

A Kanban board that is filled with employees' necessary tasks is one of the simplest solutions you can apply if you want to know where your bottlenecks usually lie. The effort to do this change is also simple enough to overcome any resistance. Overall, Kanban simplifies the route your tasks will take.

Kanban boards usually come in 3 to 5 columns. The 3-columned ones are usually labeled with "Requested", "In Progress" "Finished". The 5-columned ones have the "In Progress" column subdivided into three parts: "Working",

"Waiting" "Review". Depending on what your organization needs, your Kanban board can be as simple or as complex as you need it to be.

Since Kanban is a highly visual system, it immediately reveals what's delaying the entire work process. Hence, managers and employees can work together to find ways on how these cases can be minimized — especially when it's happening too often.

Fortunately, Kanban is flexible and versatile enough to be integrated into your current work system without causing a company culture shock. The changes can be small enough that it wouldn't even take extreme efforts to sustain. It may not be the cure-all for your workflow problems but it can at least encourage people to take the necessary steps to improve how tasks are done and delivered.

# Chapter 12:
# How to Run a Lean Office?

One of the truly great parts of the Lean system is the potential it holds when it comes to standardization, specifically when it comes to minimizing waste. Much like when it comes to setting goals, setting work parameters that are clearly standardized makes it easier to answer specific questions about the process. This should include things like who will follow through on the process once it has been outlined, how many people will it take, what will the end result be, what the metrics for success should be, what is required to meet them, how long the process will take and more. These are all questions that ultimately need to be asked to guarantee your standardization measures don't end up creating new problems instead of solving existing ones.

Workflow standardization is not expressly designed to ensure that processes are completed as quickly as possible. Rather, it is about utilizing the most effective practices possible to ensure they are completed with the same level of reliable quality every time. You will also do well to remember that standard practices will naturally change over time as improvements to safety, quality productivity are found. You will want to take care to avoid becoming so reliant on a single type of standardization that you end up allowing it to hold you back from future progress.

With that being said, it is also important to avoid falling into the trap of undertaking a round of standardization solely for standardization's sake. Instead, it is important to consider if standardization is the right choice by considering the various processes already in place and asking yourself if they would be of a higher quality, performed to a higher safety standard or completed with less waste. If you move forward this is not the case, then all you are doing is inviting in waste.

Furthermore, standardization should involve more than simple instructional documents. It should be created from the input of those who perform the processes on the regular and then combined with a fresh round of customer feedback to ensure all bases are covered. The reasons for the standardization process should be clear to everyone involved before getting started for the best results.

## KPIs

KPIs, also known as key performance indicators, are extremely useful when it comes to determining the ideal steps to take during the standardization process. KPIs are also useful when it comes to measuring the overall success of the process as a whole based on numerous different metrics. Choosing the right KPI to focus on is a matter of considering what metrics you value most at the moment as well as in the long-term. There are a wide variety of indicators to choose from, all of which are useful in different circumstances and when it comes to accurately defining specific values. Essentially, each KPI can be considered an object which is useful in various value-add scenarios.

## Choosing indicators

When it comes to identifying the KPIs you want to use for your business, the first thing you will need to do is ensure that your process is already well-defined as this will help you have a true handle on the specifics of every aspect of the process as well as the best ways to determine the ideal means of completion. It is important to only stick with indicators that are relevant to the goal you are currently working towards. Otherwise, they can easily be altered dramatically by factors that are literally outside of your control.

Much like with your goals, you must make sure your KPIs are SMART and that they clearly indicate specific information for a specific purpose. You will also want to choose options that are easily measured while still providing accurate results if at all possible. Much like goals, KPIs are useless if they are not realistically achievable. The most effective KPIs are those that are relevant to the success of the business in the moment or in the future while also including an element of time that has specific periods as they relate to the data.

## Be Aware

It is also important to keep in mind that while determining specific KPIs isn't too difficult, keeping track and compiling the relevant data can be more difficult than it first appears. Furthermore, additional values, including those for things such as staff morale, are difficult to gauge accurately. Before you invest resources into generating KPIs, it is important to first make sure they are adequately measurable and useful. Otherwise, you will be on your way to creating even more waste.

You will also need to ensure the focus remains on keeping the KPIs on the data that they are detailing and use it as a means of determining the overall health of the business as opposed to a set of numbers that can only move one way. If your team ends up too focused on reaching a predetermined KPI, the data they return will be biased and inaccurate.

## CREATE YOUR VALUE STREAM MAP

Now that we have taken a quick look at this, it is time to learn how you can create a value stream map. A properly constructed value stream map is so important to your business. It allows everyone on the team a chance to see the big picture because it maps out the entire flow of resources from their starting points all the way through to the part where the product is put together and then given to the customer.

Since they take on such a big picture approach, this will make it a much more manageable task to determine the points in the process that are ending in a bottleneck and are reducing the efficiency of the whole process. This is the area where you need to concentrate your focus on first.

While one person can go through the steps we are about to talk through, the value stream map is the most effective the most useful when the whole team can work on it together. This allows you to see all of the different parts and where the problems are and can help the team to not only be involved in the process but to ask questions and see why some new procedures are being put in place.

The first step that you need to work with when creating a value stream map is to consider the exact process that you should be mapping. For a business that is just using the Lean system for the first time, you must begin by considering the various processes that will need to be shown so that you can pick which one needs the most work at the time. You need to take a look at all of the different processes that you need to go through each day and then figure out the ones that are of the greatest importance and work down from there.

If you still aren't able to decide where to start, then you may need to spend some time talking to your customers. Ask them questions and consider what they are telling you as important. This can help you to figure out which areas seem to be getting the most complaints you can work from there.

What is known as the Pareto analysis can be a great tool to use at this point. It can make it easier for you to know the exact place to start if you aren't sure where your efforts are put to the best use. It is known as a statistical analysis technique that can be useful for those who are looking at a few tasks that are all going to generate serious results. Usually, with Lean, you just want to focus on one task at a time. If you end up looking at a process that has a few steps that would be equally beneficial to help with, then the Pareto analysis can help you figure out the one that will work. The goal here is to focus on the 20% of your business that, if taken care of the right way, could help to generate 80% of your total results.

Next, we need to choose the shorthand. The value streaming map is not big enough to write out everything you may need to use symbols and colors to help you talk about the different stages that occur in the process. You can pick out the shorthand that seems to work the best for you and your team then make sure that it is consistent overall.

You also need to set limits. If you take things from a scope that is broad enough, virtually every value stream map can be connected to other value stream maps, or go into bigger detail. But you don't want to spend weeks working on this process at some point or another, you must set some limits on what the value stream map will account for. This ensures that only the most important parts make it and that you can then move forward to making changes.

Once the value stream map is done, you should start with the steps that are the most clearly defined. This is the point where you will need to make a list of all the steps that should be taken, going from the start to the end, to see success with your goals. This doesn't need to be incredibly in depth, or a look at every link in the chain but it should contain all of the major stages that you will then need to look at more closely to help you get started all the way through to completion.

During this time, you also need to consider the flow of information. You will find that one unique aspect of this is that it is also going to account for the way that information can flow through the process from beginning to end. It will chart the way that information passes between each of the members of your team as well. You can add to this the different ways that customers interact with your business, in addition to how frequent these interactions can occur.

From here, we need to focus on collecting the data. When it comes to outlining the initial value stream map, you may find that you are looking at a few aspects of your process you will find areas that need more data before you can make any decisions. The data that you may need to track down at this point includes:

- The total working time available
- The number of shifts that you need to plan to get the process down
- Uptime
- Transition time
- The availability of the service
- Total inventory that is on hand
- The cycle time

When you are collecting all of this information, you must remember to head straight to the source and find out the details, rather than just making assumptions. You also need to keep up to date on the information, rather than looking at outdated figures just because it is easier and more readily available.

The next thing to concentrate on is watching the inventory in your business. Even if you are pretty certain about the requirements for inventory in the process in question, you must stop and double check before you add anything to your map. Even a small miscalculation could skew your overall results and could nullify the hard work that you did. You should adopt a measure two times or more to ensure you get the best results. After all, it is common for inventory to build up for a wide variety of reasons there is a high likelihood that you will not know about this until you look at it a bit closer.

After you have been able to collect the data and have a visual representation of the work, it is time to use this information to figure out where some of the points of the issue may be. You should also watch out for any of the processes that would include redoing any of the work that was completed before, anything that needs a longer period of resetting before work can start up again, or any long gaps where one part of the team isn't doing anything but waiting.

And finally, you need to generate the ideal version of the ideal stream and how you would accomplish these goals. You can use the information that you have and then make some changes to avoid the issues and the bottlenecks that are already occurring in your process. With this in mind, you can then work out a future value stream map that is the plan that you will follow to improve the processes along the way. You simply need to figure out what needs to be done first, second, third and so on to make this ideal map into reality.

# Chapter 13: How Six Sigma Can Make Lean Enterprise Even More Effective

Six Sigma is the shorthand name given to a system of measuring quality with a goal of getting as close to perfection as possible. A company operating in perfect synchronicity with Six Sigma would generate as few as 3.4 defects per million attempts at a given process. Zshift is the name given to the available deviations between a process that has been completed poorly and one that has been completed perfectly.

The standard Z-shift is one with several 4.5, while the ultimate value is a 6. Processes that have not been viewed through the Six Sigma lens typically earn around a 1.5.

## ZSHIFT LEVELS

A Six Sigma level of 1 means that your customers will get what they expect roughly 30 percent of the time. A Six Sigma level of 2 means that roughly 70 percent of the time, your customers will get what they expect. A Six Sigma level of 3 means that roughly 93 percent of the time, your customers will be satisfied. A Six Sigma level of 4 means that your customers will be satisfied more than 99 percent of the time. A Six Sigma level of 5 or 6 indicates a satisfaction percentage of even closer to 100 percent.

## SIX SIGMA CERTIFICATION LEVELS

Six Sigma is broken into numerous certification levels depending on the amount of knowledge the person in question has regarding the Six Sigma system. The executive level is made up of management team members who are in charge of actively setting up Six Sigma in your company. A Champion in Six Sigma is someone who can lead projects and be the voice of those projects specifically.

White belts are the rank-and-file workers; they have an understanding of Six Sigma but it is limited. Yellow belts are active members on Six Sigma project teams who are allowed to determine improvements in some areas. Green belts are those who work with black belts on high-level projects while also running their yellow belt projects. Black belts lead high-level projects while mentoring and supporting those at other tiers. Master black belts are those who are typically brought in specifically to implement Six Sigma and can mentor and teach anyone at any level.

All businesses have components that they can improve on. If you have never thoroughly assessed your processes before, it can indeed be difficult to determine which areas are ripe for improvement. It therefore becomes essential to streamline your workflows first so it's easier to identify where the process bottlenecks are.

## LEAN SIX SIGMA

The first part of this book focuses on the most important Lean concepts that can transform your business into a more efficient manufacturing machine. In this chapter, we will discuss another tool that seeks to eliminate waste: Six Sigma.

Lean and Six Sigma are waste elimination systems that are both popular in manufacturing. In essence, they share the same end goal of process efficiency — they just have different approaches in getting things done. One of their key differences is their waste identification methods. Lean identifies waste by examining the company's 8 Deadly Waste (DOWNTIME). Meanwhile, Six Sigma does this by using the DMAIC (Define, Measure, Analyze, Improve, Control) method.

## LEAN VS. SIX SIGMA

Lean primarily focuses on eliminating steps that don't add any value to the final product. Value is regarded as anything that customers appreciate enough to pay for. For instance, motion or movement isn't something that customers would willingly pay for when they get their product. One of the goals of Lean is to limit such waste as much as possible, as they aren't value-adding.

Six Sigma, on the other hand, relies on data to solve problems within work processes. It puts a heavy emphasis on customer satisfaction by minimizing product defects. At its core, Six Sigma aims for a 99.99996% defect-free rate. You can expect a Six Sigma workflow to only have 3.4 defects or less out of a million outputs. Defects are any factor in the product that doesn't satisfy customer expectations.

As you may notice, both Lean and Six Sigma care about what the customer ultimately wants. The focus of their approach is what mainly sets them apart. Lean works toward increasing the flow (or reducing traffic) within the value stream, while Six Sigma chases consistency in their processes and outputs.

Essentially, here's how Lean and Six Sigma go about eliminating waste:

Lean lowers total production time and limits the use of resources to ultimately maximize customer value.

Six Sigma aims for product perfection through reduced variation to ultimately reduce costs and improve customer perception.

## LEAN SIX SIGMA: WASTE ELIMINATION TOOLS COMBINED

Here's where it gets exciting. What if both of these systems are combined? What if you use Lean principles to make your tasks flow as efficiently as possible then use the Six Sigma system to create processes that are consistent across the board?

This is where Lean Six Sigma comes in. Lean is a system that goes for defect detection, while Six Sigma goes for defect reduction. Combined, Lean Six Sigma brings you defect prevention — a methodology that prioritizes both the product quality and customer satisfaction by reducing waste, production cycles product variations, all while standardizing work processes and flow.

In a nutshell, Lean Six Sigma is a system that not only improves flow and efficiency but also enhances the quality of the whole process. This is because Lean's emphasis on reducing waste supports Six Sigma's focus on quality, thereby eliminating most opportunities to have defects. By the same vein, Six Sigma's value for the highest quality supports Lean's goals on process efficiency, as consistency plus the absence of reworks leads to faster cycle times.

### IMPLEMENTATION

Giving your team a compelling reason to try Six Sigma is vital to the overall success of the process. To ensure that Six Sigma is properly implemented, you must properly motivate your team by explaining how crucial the adoption of a new methodology is. The most common choice in these situations is to create what is known as a burning platform scenario.

A burning platform is a motivational tactic wherein you explain that the situation the company now finds itself in is so dire (like standing on a burning platform) that only by implementing Six Sigma is there any chance of long-term survival for the company. Having stats that back up your assertions is helpful, though, if times aren't so tough, a bit of exaggeration never hurt. Adapting to Six Sigma can be difficult, especially for older employees and a little external motivation can make the change more palatable.

## Ensure the tools for self-improvement are readily available

Once the initial round of training regarding Six Sigma has been completed, you must have a strong mentorship program in play while also making additional refresher materials readily available to those who need them. The worst thing that can happen at this point is for a team member confused about one of the finer points of Six Sigma to try and find additional answers only to be rebuffed due to lack of resources.

Not only will they walk away still confused but they will also be rebuffed for trying and not rewarded for taking an interest in the subject matter. A team member who cannot easily find answers to their questions is a team member who will not follow Six Sigma processes when it counts.

## Key principles

Lean Six Sigma works based on the common acceptance of five laws. The first is the law of the market which means that the customer needs to be considered first before any decision is made. The second is the law of flexibility wherein the best processes are those that can be used for the greatest number of disparate functions. The third is the law of focus which states that a business should only focus on the problem the business is having as opposed to the business itself. The fourth is the law of velocity which says that the greater the number of steps in a process, the less efficient it is. Finally, the last is the law of complexity which says that simpler processes are always superior to more complicated ones.

## Choosing the best process

When it comes to deciding what process to apply the Six Sigma treatment to, the best place to start is with any processes that are already defective and need work to reduce the number of times they occur. From there, it will simply be a matter of looking for instances where takt time is out of whack before looking into those steps where the number of available resources can be reduced as well.

## THE METHODOLOGIES TO WORK WITH

When you are ready to work with the Six Sigma process, there are two main methodologies that you can choose to work with. Both are efficient and can work, it just depends on which kind of industry you are in and what works the best for you. The two main methods are DMAIC and DMADV.

First, we need to take a look at the DMAIC. This is an acronym that will help you and your team remember the five phases that come with it. This is useful when it comes to creating a new process and fixing any processes that need some extra work to be more efficient and deal with less risk. The way that DMAIC works includes:

- Define what the process needs to do. To figure this out, you need to get some input from the customer and then work from there.

- Measure: This is where your team needs to measure the parameters that the process will adhere to. Once this is done, you can ensure that the process is being created properly by gathering all of the information that is relevant.

- Analyze: Here you will need to analyze all of the information that you have gathered. You may be able to see some trends coming out of that information or find out that you need to do some more research and analyze it before continuing.

- Improve: This is where the team can take that information and the analysis that you did make some improvements to the process.

- Control the process. You need to work to control your business process as much as possible. You can do this by finding ways to reliably decrease how many times a delinquent variation starts to make an appearance in your process.

In addition to working with the DMAIC process, you can work with the DMADV process as well. This is very similar to the method that we just talked about before the five phases will correspond with the DMAIC process as well. The five phases that come with the DMADV method will include the following:

- Define the solutions that you want the process to provide. You can look at your mission statement, how the product is supposed to work input from the customer to help figure this one out.

- Measure out the specifics of the process so that you can determine what parameters need to be in place.

- Analyze the data that you and your team have been able to collect up to this particular point.

- Design the new process with the help of the analysis that you have.

- Verify any time that it is needed.

Both of these methods can be very effective at helping you to see results when you try to implement Six Sigma into your business. Often they work similarly but you will need to consider the situations around your process and what deficiencies you need to fix to help you determine which process is the best one for you.

## IS SIX SIGMA THE RIGHT CHOICE FOR YOU?

While this process is something that can work for many different businesses across a wide variety of different industries and Six Sigma has something to offer for teams of all sizes and shapes, it doesn't mean that this process is the best fit for everyone. This can be apparent as implementing it successfully means that several specifics need to come into play. This will start with the conviction of those who are looking to implement the system in the first place, as well as the overall culture that is found in the business and how open it is to the new change.

This is why many companies decide to ease into the process and will start with the 5S method that we talked about earlier. This is seen as a lower impact method that can adjust the team to what you want to happen before you move into some more advanced techniques, like what you find with Six Sigma. Once the team has accepted what you are trying to do, it becomes so much easier to implement all of Six Sigma and all of Lean into the business and its culture.

When you are taking a look at the Six Sigma method and trying to determine if this kind of transition is something that you can do, you must make sure that no one in the business, especially upper management, sees this as a fad or a trend that the business is just trying out. , Six Sigma the whole Lean philosophy needs to be seen as an evolution of the ideals that the company already put in place.

In most cases, the more involved you can get the leadership of the team right from the beginning, the more onboard the team will be the more participation you will be able to get out of everyone. This is why it is so important to get all of the employees on board, whether they are in top management or hold another important position within the company.

Also, it is so important for the culture of your company to be seen as one that is in full support of this kind of positive change to remember that if your upper management, or anyone on the management team, isn't able to come up with a consensus on the new program, that it is better to hold off a bit to reach that consensus. Jumping in when not everyone is on board, especially if some of those are the upper management, means that the idea and the process will be dead from the start.

This doesn't mean that every single person on the team must be committed to the idea of Six Sigma or the Lean methodology right from the start. But it does mean that the changes that occur need to be seen as institutional. This ensures that the front that you send to the public shows that everyone is united under the ideas of the method.

Implementing Six Sigma into your business can take some time but when you add it together with the ideas of Lean, then you will see a big shift in the company culture and so much more. But when both of these ideologies are used together, you will find that it results in more satisfaction with your customers, less waste, more efficiencies in the process more profits in the long term of your business.

## WHO WILL GAIN FROM LEAN SIX SIGMA?

When applied correctly, Lean Six Sigma will clean up the messes of your business' entire workflow. As a result, it creates a bigger infrastructure for various processes, thereby allowing tasks to move without getting caught up in a bottleneck.

The benefits of Lean Six Sigma aren't limited to the company's owners or managers. It also extends to the following groups:

- **Employees**: When cultural resistance has been overcome, employees become more accepting of the upcoming company changes. As a result of the renewed openness to change, Lean Six Sigma is bound to improve your employees' job performance. Consequently, the goal for continuous improvement means that they'll constantly undergo training to keep their skills and knowledge updated. This can be fulfilling even on a personal level.

- **Customers**: When efficiency and defect reduction are combined, customers will always get products that improve their lives.

- **Suppliers**: Variations and defects usually come from raw materials. Lean Six Sigma can help suppliers determine the root cause of these variations and work on eliminating their occurrences in the future. This lowers the overall costs of creating the materials.

- **Stockholders**: Consistency in materials, products workflows can significantly reduce the costs needed for reworks, capitals, storage capacities staffing.

Just like Lean, Six Sigma and Lean Six Sigma are effective tools in minimizing the need for additional resources. It operates on the premise that high standards can be achieved by maintaining the consistency of products and processes. Diversity is typically celebrated but in Six Sigma, the lower the variation, the better.

# Chapter 14:
# How to Simplify Lean
# in Your Enterprise

All of the products and services that are generated by your business have a mixture of three different value streams that can ultimately be used productively if you take the time to understand them fully. These include the concept to launch stream, the creation of customer stream, and the order to customer stream. To ensure you are getting the greatest overall value out of all of the processes your business finishes, it is important to look at a value stream map as it is an excellent way to ensure you are maximizing efficiency at every turn.

The average value stream map will include everything that ultimately comes together to generate value for the customer including activities, people, materials information. To properly visualize a value stream, you will want to follow the Plan/Do/Study/Act process, also known as the Lean cycle.

To get started, you will want to plan out the task ahead by focusing on one goal at a time. From there, you will want to make a list of everything that will need to be done to ensure the task is finished successfully. This is then followed by the step of following through, the results being studied acted upon as required.

## Value Add

Regardless of what your business does, you will find that Lean principles can be implemented to improve the overall amount of value you are providing for your customers while also showing them you appreciate their business and respect them as individuals. What's more, you will be able to address the potential for waste in your organization while also maintaining flow and work to achieve perfection.

Often, you can manage this by doing something as simple as listening to your customers' specific wants and needs which will make it easier for you to determine what they value the most when it comes to the niche your company habits. Value is most often generated by adding on something tangible that either improves or modifies the most common aspects of the good or service being provided. The goal is that this improvement is something the customer is willing to pay for, so when they receive it for free, they see this as a viable reason for your service to cost more out of the gate. It is also very important that the added value is very easy for the customer to claim because otherwise, they will feel that you have misled them.

## Cost Reduction

As the Lean system is already quite big on cutting down on waste in all of its forms, it should come as no surprise that it has some ideas when it comes to cost-reducing measures. For starters, it is important to understand that when it comes to

Lean, all the different types of waste can be broken down into three types.

Muri is the name for the waste that forms when there is too much variation within common processes. Muda is the name given to seven different types of waste including:

- Transportation waste is formed when parts, materials or information for a specific task are not available because the process for allocating resources for active products isn't where it should be.

- Waiting waste is created if a portion of the production chain has ideal time when they are not actively working on a task.

- Overproduction waste is common if the demand exceeds supply there is no plan in place to use this situation to the business's advantage. The Lean systems are designed to ensure that this number reaches zero so supply and demand are always in balance with one another.

- Defective waste is known to appear when some segment of the standard operating process generates some issue that needs to be sorted at some point down the line.

- Inventory waste is known to appear if the production chain ends up remaining idle between runs because it doesn't have the physical materials needed to be constantly running.

- Movement waste is generated when required parts, materials or information needs to be moved around successfully to complete a specific step in the process.

- Additional processing waste is generated if work is completed that does not generate value or adds value for the company.

A commonly added eighth muda is the waste created by the underutilization of your team. This can occur whenever any member of the team is placed in a position that doesn't utilize them to their full potential. It can also refer to the waste that occurs when team members have to perform tasks for which they have not been properly trained.

Muda also comes in three categories, the first of which is muda that doesn't directly add value but also cannot be easily removed if the system will continue working properly. When faced with this muda, the goal should be to work to minimize it slowly as a precursor to removing it completely. The second type of muda is that which has no real value, whatsoever you should work to remove it directly once you've become aware of it. Finally, the third type of muda doesn't directly add value but is required for regulatory purposes of one type or another. While it may be annoying, this type of muda is unavoidable in most instances and the best that you can do is ensure you are always updated to any relevant policies.

## CREATE YOUR VALUE STREAM MAP

A properly constructed value stream map is a vital part of the process as it will allow you to see the big picture by mapping out the entire flow of resources from their disparate starting points all the way through when they come together and eventually make it into the hands of the customer. As such, it then makes it far more of a manageable task to determine the points in the process that are bottlenecking the overall efficiency of your business's process and thus, taking the first steps towards adopting Lean processes.

While one person can certainly work through the following steps, the value stream maps that prove to be the most effective are often those created by the entire team, so that those who are the most knowledgeable about each step will be able to give their two cents as well. Your initial value stream map should be thought of as a very rough draft and should be constructed as such, which means planning it out in pencil and expecting lots of rewriting as you go along.

## **Consider the process**

The first step in this process will be to consider exactly what it is you will be mapping. For businesses that are first starting out with the Lean system, you will want to begin by considering the various processes that are ultimately going to prove to be of the greatest value to the team as a whole and then work down the list from there. If you still can't decide where to start, then you will want to turn to your customers, consider what they have to say and start with the areas where you regularly receive the most complaints.

What is known as a pareto analysis is an effective tool at this juncture as it can make it easier for you to find the right place to start if you aren't sure where your efforts will be best put to use. It is a statistical analysis technique that can prove especially useful if you are looking at a few different tasks that are sure to generate serious results if only you could decide which one to use first. The goal, in this case, is to focus on the 20 percent of your business that, if nurtured, could ultimately generate 80 percent of your total results. Your initial value stream map may focus on only a single service or product or on multiples that share a significant portion of the process.

## **Choose your shorthand**

The symbols you use to denote various stages of the process you are mapping don't have any hard and firm guidelines as they are unique to every project and every business. Regardless of what you and your team ultimately choose, it is important to create a list of all of the symbols you are using and what they mean so that anyone who comes in after the fact can easily get caught up. From there, it is important to stick to the designated symbols and not make anything up on the fly. Additionally, if the business is working on more than one value stream map at a time, it is important that the symbols correspond between the two. Otherwise, things can quickly spiral into illegibility.

## Set limits

If taken from a broad enough scope, virtually every value stream map for your business can be connected to other value stream maps or go into greater detail. At some point, however, this is counterproductive and you will have to set limits on what the value stream map will account for if you ever hope to successfully move forward. Likewise, if you let this part of the process get out of hand, then the map can lose focus and become less useful as a result.

## Start with steps that are clearly defined

After you have a clear beginning and end for the process you are mapping, the next thing to do is to make a list of all of the logical steps that need to be taken from start to finish. This shouldn't be an in-depth look at every link in the chain but instead, should be an overview of the major stages that will need to be looked at more closely as the process moves towards completion.

## Consider the flow of information

One important step in the value stream mapping process that sets it apart from other similar mapping processes is that each value stream map also accounts for the way that information flows throughout the process from beginning to end. What's more, it will also chart the way information passes between team members as well. You will also need to ensure it takes into account the ways the customer interacts with your business, in addition to how frequently such interactions occur. You will also need to ensure the communication chain includes any suppliers or any other third parties the company deals with.

## Further details

When it comes to breaking the process down to its most granular level, you may want to include a flow chart with your value stream map as well. A flow chart is a great way to map out the innermost details of how a given process reaches completion. This is also an excellent way to determine the types of muda you are dealing with, so you can consider if they can be removed from the process.

## Collecting data

When it comes to outlining your initial map of a value stream, you may find yourself with certain aspects of the process that require additional data before anything can be determined with any real degree of certainty. The data that you may need to track down will include:

- cycle time
- total inventory on hand
- availability of the service
- transition time
- uptime
- number of shifts required to complete the process
- total available working time

When it comes to collecting this data, it is important to always remember to go to the source directly and find the details you are looking for rather than making assumptions. Furthermore, it is important to get the most updated numbers possible as opposed to looking at older, more readily available figures or hypothetical benchmarks. This may mean something as hands-on as physically keeping an eye on every part of the process in question so you can take relevant notes.

## Watch the inventory

Even if you are relatively certain about any inventory requirements for the process in question, it is vital that you double check before you commit anything to the value stream map. Minor miscalculations at this point could dramatically skew your overall results and essentially nullify all of your hard work if you aren't careful. This means you need to adopt a measure twice to see the best results. After all, inventory is prone to building up for a wide variety of reasons and there is a good chance that you won't know it until you take a closer look and do a once over on what's on hand. You can also use this step as an excuse to take stock of exactly what the team is working with and determine how far it will stretch effectively.

## Using the data

After you have finished visualizing the steps found in your most important process, you are now ready to use it as a means of determining where any problem points might be. You will especially want to keep an eye out for processes that include redoing any previously completed work, anything that requires an extended period of resetting before work can begin again, or long gaps where parts of the team can do nothing except wait for someone else to finish, those that take up more resources than your research indicates you should or even just those that seem to take longer than they should for no particular reason.

## Generate the ideal version of the value stream

After you have determined where the bottlenecks are occurring, you will want to create an updated value stream map that represents how you want the process to proceed once you have everything properly sorted. This will provide you with an A to C scenario, where figuring out the pain points represents B. Ideally, it will also provide a clue as to how you can go about eliminating the waste from the process to create an idea, which you can strive for both in the short and the long-term.

Once you have determined the ideal state for the process, you can work out a future value stream map that will serve as a plan on how to take the team from where you are currently to where you need to be. This type of plan is often broken down into sections that last a few months, depending on what needs to be done. Additionally, most future value stream maps will come with multiple iterations because they will need to change several times as the project nears completion.

When working through various variations of the value stream map, it is important to pay close attention to the lead time available for various processes. The lead time is the amount of time it will take to complete a given task in the process and, if not utilized as efficiently as possible, it can easily lead to a wealth of bottlenecks. Remember, when it comes to creating the best value stream map possible, no part of the process is beyond scrutiny.

# Chapter 15:
# How to Use Lean to Improve the Process of Large Programs in Your Enterprise

The key for any business willing to apply Lean thinking is to identify a plan and start. It is not an easy task to transform a business into a Lean business overnight and the process to become Lean does not end.

Most businesses make the mistake of trying to become perfect as soon as they can. They forget that they must first improve their processes and become better before they can achieve perfection. This section covers some ideas to help you implement Lean management in the organization.

### WORK IN PROCESS RELATED TEAMS

Instead of working in financial roles or teams, process operators must work with teams that are process oriented. In most businesses and processes, the management is notified of any problem that may have arisen in the process and the management identifies a person who can solve that problem.

However, it is better to have teams that are self-directed, in the sense that people address problems and solve them. A business can start with the necessary tools but it should also understand that both thought and management must be changed for the organization to become a Lean business. Often businesses do not transform into Lean businesses not because of the failure to understand how Lean tools and techniques need to be used but the failure to change the management.

## CORRECTLY COACH STAFF

If a business selects a few people to coach on how Lean thinking can be implemented to improve processes, it will create a management group that can work with different teams and facilitate change and removes waste from the process.

The staff must first do and then be trained. It is unfortunate that staff cannot be trained to think or learn Lean through PowerPoint. The principle of Lean or the Toyota way is always to learn by doing and there are different approaches to applying Lean thinking in business.

The team must create a process map and also identify steps that may be waste contributors. Additionally, they are also asked to create a plan and a budget using Lean thinking. Another common approach is the Toyota approach where some members of a team are put into difficult situations that they must overcome. They are expected to identify a solution to the problem.

## DEVELOP FEEDBACK AND COMMUNICATION CHANNELS

Through communication channels, people at different levels and in different teams can share their ideas and build synergy, which will help the business move towards a profitable future.

Feedback channels allow customers to share their views about products and services, which enables the business to improve.

## Use Value Stream Metrics

You must eliminate non-Lean metrics that wreak havoc within teams and use those metrics that adhere to the value stream. This change will ensure that every employee in the organization works to the best of his or her abilities and delivers products and services of high quality.

## Create a Positive Atmosphere

Most businesses will make mistakes when they switch to Lean thinking and management. It is crucial to accept those mistakes and learn from them. The managers and staff in the business must be patient with the progress being made.

## Collect and Collate Data

Every business is driven by the analyses conducted on different types of data that are collected by various departments in the business. The business must use this data to change processes. This helps to remove the bias, both professional and emotional, out of decision-making and ensures that every employee in the business accepts the changes made.

It is also good to track the performance of every team and store that data for future reference. It is crucial to remember that Lean management is not a project but is a way of business. You must track every process and review the flow regularly to remove any waste contributors.

## SET A BENCHMARK

It is always good to learn from businesses that have implemented Lean thinking to understand and gain an idea of how it can be implemented in your business. Most companies are willing to present their change from being a non-Lean company to a Lean company. Every member in the management should network with the management from other businesses to understand how Lean thinking and management can be implemented in their organization.

## NEVER GIVE UP

It is difficult to change from a non-Lean business to a Lean business since most staff members are unable to accept change. Over time, they realize that Lean thinking improves the processes that are performed in their business. They learn that they can optimize processes and remove useless or redundant processes from the flow that most customers are unwilling to pay for.

As a business, you must strive to transform both your management and your processes. Remember never to give up since the aim is to build a business that constantly improves to enhance profitability.

# Chapter 16: Benefits of Introducing Lean in Your Enterprise

Becoming Lean as an individual can make a big difference in your tasks as an employee. When you apply its concepts consistently enough, they're bound to affect your life's other aspects positively. Over time, you'll find that you're able to process decisions in a more systematic way. If Lean concepts can have such a profound effect on a personal level, you can imagine the possibilities if you scale the leanness all the way to an enterprise.

Lean thinking encourages people to apply doable changes in small increments. The ultimate goal is to speed up all the workflows within a system without compromising product or service quality. Lean is certainly not a quick fix for eliminating company waste. It involves being in a long-term commitment with continuous growth and improvement.

Even if a particular Lean technique has been proven effective by many companies, changes certainly didn't happen within a few months of applying the methods. It usually takes far longer than that for anything significant to be noticeable. It's also understandable how people may feel discouraged to stick with the new methods if the benefits aren't that obvious. To help you stay lean when you're tempted to think that it doesn't work, here's a list of its short-term to long-term benefits:

## Short-term Benefits

- **Improved Management:** Even though problems will still come up every now and then, Lean makes the work environment more convenient to deal with if you're a manager. With better task standards in place, it will be easier for you to pinpoint anything that's disrupting the flow of the value stream. Most of the time, you will be able to figure out that something isn't quite right just by looking at an area's set-up or layout.

- **Improved Efficiency and Productivity:** As a result of standardizing every piece of the workflow, it becomes automatic for employees to know what exactly they need to do — and when they need to do it. It reduces a lot of redundancy and overlaps that stem from task confusion. It also ensures that they are doing their work correctly every single time. They no longer have to constantly ask whether a particular task is under their responsibility. They can just focus on their task list without worrying about anything else.

- **Safer and More Convenient Layouts:** Since literal waste will be decluttered, turning Lean gives your company more space to move around. This will instantly make task movements a lot more convenient. Additionally, it will provide your staff a safer space for working when the layout is reorganized to eliminate hazards.

- **Involvement from the Whole Company:** Lean is something that isn't applied only to one team or department. When a company decides to go Lean, every level of the hierarchy is involved — from those on the top all the way to the ones on the bottom. After all, Lean systems depend on the cooperation of everyone involved.

## MEDIUM AND LONG-TERM BENEFITS

- **Improved Cash Flow:** Once you get rid of downtime you can now focus your energy on ensuring that the value-adding steps of your value stream flows as smoothly as possible. In the absence of roadblocks, workflow bottlenecks delays, not only will you be able to deliver products just-in-time but you'll also improve the cash flow within your company.

- **Customer Satisfaction and Loyalty:** Customer satisfaction is one of the most immediate results of applying Lean, so they become more likely to trust your brand again in the future. If you keep on doing what works, you're bound to gain their loyalty in the long run.

- **Employee Satisfaction and Loyalty:** While Lean systems are mainly focused on the desires of the customer; it also promotes better mood and morale among employees. The changes may be met with resistance at first but once they see that it takes them far less time to complete tasks compared to before, they'll become more open to the overall idea of Lean.

- Additionally, since Lean is all about constant improvement and collaborations, they tend to feel better about themselves because they're part of a team that cares about others. Lean systems give them a safe space to voice out their concerns and provide suggestions for further improvement.

- **Marketability for Collaboration:** What makes something marketable? In terms of companies, marketable companies are usually the unproblematic ones. You need to be that company if you wish to be a part of a Lean enterprise. After all, Lean is all about efficiency you need to be an efficient team player to ensure that you don't disrupt the flow of the entire system.

Lean is not merely an exercise in cost-cutting. It is more of a long-term opportunity for consistent growth. Once you have smoothed out your Lean processes within the company, you will eventually become the preferred suppliers of particular products and services.

That's because your consistency and standards translate well to your products — something that lets both customers and collaborators know that you're a company that they can trust.

## What Are the Challenges of applying Lean Methodology in Your Enterprise?

Lean thinking all sounds good in theory it can be exciting to continue applying it once you've seen how great it can be in practice. However, as Figure 8 shows, the tasks between teams or entities cannot always be as conveniently executed as getting from Point A to Point B in a clean, straight line. Their involvement with each other goes back and forth, which emphasizes how every component must be free of waste to ensure a smooth flow.

Shifting to Lean has its issues and challenges. Like any other form of change, you should resist hoping that it would do its "magic" in just a few weeks or months.

Technically speaking, when every factor is ironed out right from the beginning, it can be possible to have everything sorted out in just a short time. But that only applies when the scenario is ideal. Experience will tell you that situations are rarely ever ideal, especially when transitions are concerned.

Here are some issues that you might have to deal with on your way to Lean:

## Cultural Resistance

This may be the biggest hurdle that you have to get through when transitioning from wasteful to Lean. When a status quo has already been set, most people are resistant to any change in the company culture. That's usually a result of staying in their comfort zones for so long. They feel that change is unnecessary since they already like the current workflow.

To gradually ease the workforce into the Lean system, training (or retraining) people must be prioritized. Here's what you need to clarify with them:

- The changes that you'll be implementing
- Why you are implementing them
- How they will benefit from these changes
- How it will benefit the whole company

Although all four of these are important considerations, they're likely most concerned about the third point, as this involves their role in the company. However, if you can clearly explain the good things about these changes, then people will be more inclined to accept it.

## Costs and Upkeep

On a personal level, there are cases in which you'll need to spend money today to be able to profit or save more money in the future.

Going Lean requires the same thing. Eliminating waste will need money, because going for the long-term fix requires money. Eventually, however, the money you spent will eventually go back to you in the form of increased profits from minimized defects.

And, just like your home needs yearly maintenance, Lean also requires upkeep. Proper planning and execution will ensure that you won't have to worry about running out of certain parts or having outdated systems.

## Talent Gaps

Since Lean processes may now require updated technologies, companies that are going Lean must bridge the talent gap. This means that they may have to let go of general-labor employees in favor of those who have licenses and certifications to operate Lean system equipment. These employees are adept not only at handling these systems but they are also capable of performing maintenance, inspections, repairs designs.

## Technological Hurdles

One of the initial costs involved in Lean is investing in newer software and technology. Since Lean encourages automation in almost every area, it is crucial that you choose the system that doesn't keep you stuck in your old ways. Not all systems are created equal, so you must go through your choices carefully to ensure that you ultimately get the one that is reliable enough to sustain your Lean methods.

Implementing Lean will not be as straightforward as it seems to be. While Lean is there to make processes a lot simpler, going against the usual grain might complicate things at first. This is especially difficult when you already have a set system among your various teams. After all, when you already know how to communicate with other members in a certain way, it does take effort to change all of that into a process that might be the total opposite of what everyone is used to.

The most effective companies and enterprises know how to mobilize the entire workforce to create the best products or services for their customers. Lean thinking can help you do just that, because you'll no longer be caught up in problem-solving all the time. Your focus can now shift towards your company's biggest asset, which are your employees' talents.

# Conclusion

When it comes to implementing Lean techniques successfully, it is important to be realistic as to the timeframe required to not just ensure the entire team is up to speed but that they have internalized the core Lean principles you are trying to instill. You will need to take a long hard look at your team and your business as a whole and decide where the most work will need to take place. Every business has limited resources, after all. It is important to think wisely before allocating them.

While you can easily get sucked into a pattern of changing everything, to ensure your business is as Lean as possible you should keep in mind that discretion is the better part of valor and you should be sure to start by focusing on those things that will end up doing the most good before moving on from there. Don't forget, change for the sake of change won't do anyone any good and will likely serve to create more waste than it will eliminate. Ultimately, it is important to remember that creating a Lean business is a marathon, not a sprint, which means slow and steady wins the race.

The next step is to start implementing the Lean system into your business. There are many benefits of the Lean system learning how to get it started in your company can mean happier customers, more profits less waste overall. Many different types of businesses, in a variety of industries, can benefit from the Lean methodology. Using this can make so many differences in your business and how well it can work. When you are ready to get started with the Lean system, check out this guidebook to help you get started.

Lean thinking is a way of business and not just a business project. There are only some businesses that have begun to use Lean thinking to enhance and improve processes and also maximize customer value. The group of businesses that do not implement Lean thinking is afraid of change. However, change is the only constant in the market and life.

Lean thinking requires a change not only in the processes but also in the management and leadership since the business has to be open to new thoughts and ideas. A business must always work towards maximizing value. This book covers some points that a business must consider to do that.

Through Lean management and thinking, a business can encourage its employees to identify ways to improve processes and also innovate or develop new processes that maximize value. This creates a sense of equality in the organization since every employee has the right to voice his or her opinion.

# LEAN SIX SIGMA

*The Ultimate Step-By-Step Guide to Learn Lean Six Sigma Method to Improve Mindset and Performance, Maximize Process Efficiency and Increase Profitability of Your Work Team*

**By Adam Ross**

# Table of Contents

Introduction .................................................................... 547

Chapter 1: Introduction to Lean Six Sigma ......................... 549

Chapter 2: Fundamentals of Lean Six Sigma ...................... 561

Chapter 3: The Key Players in Six Sigma ............................ 567

Chapter 4: Tools Used in the DMAIC Process ..................... 573

Chapter 5: Six Sigma Certification: Learn and Leverage Your Career .............................................................................. 580

Chapter 6: Why Lean Six Sigma is Worth the Effort ........... 589

Chapter 7: Beneficiaries of Lean Six Sigma ........................ 596

Chapter 8: Why Some Companies Are Not Taking Advantage of Lean Six Sigma ............................................................. 601

Chapter 9: Design for Lean Six Sigma ................................ 605

Chapter 10: Deployment Planning .................................... 611

Chapter 11: What Leaders Should Note in Readiness to Implement Lean Six Sigma ................................................ 620

Chapter 12: Implementing the Lean Six Sigma Methodology ..................................................................... 626

Chapter 13: Tips for a Successful Lean Six Sigma Implementation ................................................................. 633

Chapter 14: Challenges to Anticipate in Lean Six Sigma Implementation ................................................................. 639

Chapter 15: Getting Top Management Support ................. 646

Chapter 16: How to Improve Customer Satisfaction .......... 652

Chapter 17: The Process Improvement Team .................... 658

Chapter 18: Value Addition and Waste Management ........ 665

Chapter 19: How Good is Lean Six Sigma for Small and Medium Sized Companies? ............................................... 674

Chapter 20: Effective Application of Lean Six Sigma ..........678
Chapter 21: Lean Six Sigma in Government Operations.....682
Conclusion..................................................................................686

# Introduction

Thank you for downloading this book. Here is everything you need to know about how to reduce costs and optimize processes through Six Sigma certification! In a crisis scenario such as reducing demand and increasing competition, investing in innovation and increasing productivity are vital strategies for the success of organizations. Its main objective is to provide financial gains to companies through the improvement of existing processes. For this, a structured and quantitative method known as the DMAIC Method is used.

This book shows you how you can get a select number of your staff trained and then use them to pioneer change in your institution. It takes you through the main training stages, showing you the importance of certification in this area. You will even be able to see marketable professionals who are versed in the workings of Lean Six Sigma. You will be able to see how you can streamline systems in a way that causes services to flow efficiently and clients feel satisfied to the extent of giving your organization a vote of confidence. This book goes a step further and shows you how it is possible to improve processes within government as well, improving staff performance while lowering government expenditure. And you can even see how making the health sector efficient impacts the wider society with things like reduced sick leaves and so on.

When you read this book, you will see that it is possible to have a great working environment and still keep costs low and yields high in all areas of operation. You will also appreciate the importance of Lean Six Sigma, especially considering it is an area that is already tested internationally, and has a credible certification process put in place. It is now your opportunity to take up the Lean Six Sigma approach that has propelled many companies to the top, allowing them to become pacesetters in their respective industries.

Learning Six Sigma skills will allow you to make the change that you need in your organization, no matter what your position is. By using this problem-solving method to improve your organization's technical and business performance, you will be able to deal with any challenges that you may face.

For this reason, top corporations around the world have adopted this methodology, allowing them to enjoy a massive profit of over $100 billion for the last decade. Having Six Sigma competency will also give you leverage when you are trying to move into a higher management position.

If your organization is considering starting a Lean Six Sigma initiative, then this is the book for you. You will discover how different industries can adopt strategies and techniques to improve production, service delivery, and growth; all in the name of satisfying customer needs and achieving the company's goals.

The intention is to prepare the reader adequately before the book dives into the nitty-gritty aspects of Lean Six Sigma. This book breaks down the basic components of Lean Six Sigma such that people who have never studied Lean or Six Sigma will grasp the concepts with relative ease. If you have some knowledge about Lean Six Sigma, you will still find this book extremely useful.

You can achieve a lot more by making yourself aware of the benefits of Lean Six Sigma. This book is key to open new doors for your business by giving you the knowledge of efficient methodologies that can be implemented in your business. Before we go into it, understand that no change can take place overnight and every great journey starts with a single step.

Happy Reading!

# Chapter 1:
# Introduction to Lean Six Sigma

## WHAT IS LEAN SIX SIGMA METHODOLOGY?

Lean Six Sigma is a tool used to identify which areas and processes of a company need to be improved and how it should be done effectively. Through this method, we study the failures that have been repeated in the internal activities of the business, the necessary advances and the strategies to increase the performance of the company.

Lean Speed or Lean Method is a collection of tools used for reducing waste produced by the flow of information and materials. The primary objective of Lean is to determine and get rid of non-value-added and non-essential steps of the business process to streamline production, gain customer loyalty, and improve quality.

In short, Lean Six Sigma calls for systems whose performance can be measured. And after gauging your performance against what is expected, you deduce where losses are occurring in terms of wasted inputs and so on; and then you correct that.

Lean Methods used within the DMAIC framework can support the tools of Six Sigma that improve the efficiency and speed of the business process. Consultants in Six Sigma and Lean Methods realized the synergy of the two strategies in the 1980s. Lean Six Sigma boosts the strengths and reduces the weaknesses of each of the strategies. It emphasizes the use of tools and methodologies to determine and get rid of waste and maximize process speed. Furthermore, it identifies and minimizes or eliminates process variation.

It is ambitious in a way and it would enforce accountability, from the stakeholders down to the most common worker. The methods of Six Sigma would take any organization out of its comfort zone for a definite amount of time. When projects are creating profit and the organization feels the benefit of change, everyone would embrace the cultural change that this methodology provides. The initial difficulty of laying out Six Sigma would soon be replaced by recognition of opportunities out of problems discovered, and all errors unearthed from old processes would provide leverage when it comes to adhering to better practices.

## YOUR EXPECTATIONS FOR LEAN SIX SIGMA

At the end of the day, what you seek to achieve when you introduce this methodology of doing things into your organization is the alignment of projects with the organization's strategic objectives. This you do by having defined roles for everyone involved and having set protocols for measurements

## WHY MANY FAIL AT SIX SIGMA?

If you think that many companies that have been introduced to Six Sigma are doing so well in minimizing errors (and enjoy impressive ROI because of this), then you think wrong. Many companies do not even reach five sigmas, or fewer than 233 errors per million opportunities in their final products since there are too many processes, tools, people, materials, and machines that they have to check.

When you look at all possible inputs that organizations do to achieve a product, you will observe that all of them should operate in sync within a particular level of variation that the system will tolerate producing a desirable or satisfactory outcome.

Now, if any step involved in conceptualizing, managing, and producing is compromised or is not performed as expected, you can already infer that the risk of error spreads throughout the system. Since there are many steps and areas to check in a vast system, you can think that the entire process of product creation serves as a huge hide-and-seek playground for errors.

A problem that happens to a specific area may be caused by an action that happened to another time or place. The gap between these occurrences makes it harder to find where the error originated.

Six Sigma practitioners often refer to the reality of having to fix these errors as the hidden operation or the hidden factory. You can almost see all the rework and cover-ups that need to be done, as well as the cost of days that are wasted when you need to constantly make corrections in your company.

However, you cannot accept mistakes or treat them lightly – once you begin thinking that "this is the way it is," you will mentally hide all the things that are hampering your organization's growth. It does not mean, however, that you need to accept that you need to re-do and revise work again. You simply need to eliminate the error.

Six Sigma seeks to eliminate hidden factories that run in secret in all organizations. Because you do not need to have to allot another set of resources to correct mistakes, you can be confident that all the time and resources that you usually waste will return to the business.

## THE MANAGERIAL PERSPECTIVE OF LEAN SIX SIGMA

Six Sigma can occur at two different levels: technical and managerial. When you take Six Sigma from the managerial perspective, the initiative will include all people, projects, details, units, and technologies that should be accounted for. For all these components to work harmoniously with each other and make sure that Six Sigma would work well with the technical elements, you need to set up the right orientation for the management.

Six Sigma makes it possible for the management to predict behaviors and gain control of performance by using scientific methods to leadership. It works similarly to the methods used in producing cars – set processes are followed and by allowing repeated processes to be optimized, products like cars can be created with little variation from each other.

It is even possible to mass-produce these products without requiring advanced education to the workers – as long as their skills are honed to perfection when it comes to mass production, the personnel can still create near-perfect products.

To achieve management results using Six Sigma, the following traits are built right into the management system orientation:

### Clear Value Proposition

Any Six Sigma project is designed to achieve an improvement of 70% or more for every business trait, and when this development takes place, operating margins experience stimulated increase. This improvement goes hand-in-hand with the increase of value that customers experience. Measurable and direct financial impact and focus becomes an important contribution of Six Sigma projects.

## Accountability and Commitment

Six Sigma initiatives begin right from management and organization leadership. By making sure that every authority within the business is committed to setting performance goals and creating strategic implementation tactics, and sticking to the Six Sigma initiative, the management becomes accountable for making the organization realize improvement goals that they set for teams or business units.

## Customer Focus

There is no process, operational, or business change that should happen without truly seeing who the customers are along with what they want to buy or need to have in their lives. Because Six Sigma sticks to the requirements of customers, this focus allows the business to grow and enjoy better profits.

## Process Orientation

Six Sigma is designed to improve how each business process performs by looking at how these processes can efficiently and effectively turn any material into a desirable output. This focus allows Six Sigma to be very reliable in improving the characterization, optimization, validation, and the overall design of a process.

## Tools and Technology Enabling

When you need to use Six Sigma in an entire organization or when you need to manage data banks, training activities, personnel, processes, and projects all at the same time, you should have the ability to use technology and tools.

## Change Infrastructure

Having a Six Sigma management system requires that you have an infrastructure or a system that would enact tactics of process improvement and project implementation.

## Culture Change

Six Sigma initiatives often begin with consultants from the outside. These consultants will provide tools, methods, and training until the knowledge is applied and internalized within the organization. Over time, Six Sigma methods will grow organically within the organization.

## THE TECHNICAL PERSPECTIVE LEAN SIX SIGMA

The objective of Six Sigma's technical side is to see to it that products, transactions, and services meet a highly-desired level of quality and reliability. Just think of how car manufacturers operate: they do not only build cars but also provide services that they profit from and encourage people to buy from them.

For them to ensure that they are getting the results that they want out of everything that they provide to their consumers, they need to see to it that all other services and transactions are as efficient and effective as possible.

In Six Sigma, characteristics that organizations need to pay attention to are called CTX. The letters CT stands for "critical to" while X is any characteristic or value, such as satisfaction, time, or quality.

## HOW DOES SIX SIGMA WORK?

It can be said that it occurs through the definition of goals and the application of specific actions so that the objectives of the company are achieved.

The success of the technique is directly related to the mobilization of the professionals and the participation of all the members of the organization. To do so, a DMAIC strategy (Define, Measure, Analyze, Increase and Control) must be defined, seeking to establish the right steps to obtain the best results.

## Define

This phase is characterized by the planning and definition of goals and desired improvements, that is, of the strategic objectives of the company. The definition is nothing more than the establishment of clear goals for the execution of activities, which clarifies the main points of improvement. The goals under analysis are the strategic objectives of the company.

## Measure

After defining the objectives, one must measure the reality of the existing processes. This is the time to understand each step of them, as well as all the problems that are occurring. The measurement step is critical to understanding how Six Sigma works. First of all, you need to understand how the company's internal processes are being carried out. From then on, you can determine the most important and reliable metrics. This facilitates the monitoring of the progress of activities and consequently the pursuit of the objectives defined in the previous step.

## Analyze

It's time to identify the steps needed to get out of the current situation and achieve the strategic objectives. This analysis should be done using statistical calculations.

The analysis process must be performed on top of the organization's current system. Its main objective is to detect the paths that can be followed to eliminate the existing distance between the current situation and the goals that were previously defined.

In the case of an engineering company, this stage is ideal for complete planning of both the actions and the services that must be performed.

## Improve

Once you have defined where you want to go, what changes are needed, and the steps to achieve your defined goals, it is time to improve and increase existing processes and services.

This is the most challenging step since improvements need to be thought of within the company's reality, and you need to analyze the flaws. Also, it is time to standardize the work, eliminating the flaws.

In engineering, it is often impossible for the services performed to have the same standard. However, processes must follow this rule.

## Controlling

It is necessary to continuously monitor and control the company's processes to avoid the occurrence of errors and defects, ensuring that the goals and objectives achieved are maintained.

From the moment an engineering process is standardized, improvements are made and flaws eliminated, maintain statistical and mathematical control. Spreadsheets and management programs are great tools for this.

## THE LIFE CYCLE OF A SIX SIGMA INITIATIVE

When you perform any Six Sigma initiative, such as a project, it does not happen all at once. It has to go through these stages:

## Initialize

Since initiatives are programs, it makes sense that you make the right preparations before you dive right into your task. For that reason, you need to have an initialization stage which includes choosing who would be in the project core team, preparing any support system, and enabling the processes that you want to implement to enable deployment activities.

When you initiate a project, you want to track down your first deployments to keep them in check. You will want to have a deployment scope that is limited to select business lines or activity divisions.

## Launch plan

This will be a document of your Six Sigma leadership system, scheduling of activities, strategies for tracking and reporting, and implementation layout plan.

## Deploy

The structure that you have created, composed of finance practices, software tools, process optimization, training materials and training schedules for Belts, and management communications, will be deployed by your core team. At the same time, performance and project tracking will also be launched on this stage.

Once the deployment plan is complete, you can begin assigning the initial waves of Belts that have completed training to Six Sigma projects. Since deployment also involves training, you can consider the deployment of Belts as part of their training, since it will create immediate ROI.

## Implement

Once your organization has finished training the first Belt training waves, the early success that the training has created will create traction and momentum within the organization.

Once the implementation stage has begun, you will see that people will begin collecting performance data, characterizing process performance, and identifying indicators that are critical to quality. That means that your company will begin rooting out the causes of waste and start increasing productivity, lower costs, and decrease process cycle times. At this point, you will see Six Sigma work.

Take note that not all Six Sigma projects may work if you are just starting. For this reason, you must start out with projects that have a manageable scope, little risk, and better promise of getting returns for the company.

## Expand

When you experience success in implementing a Six Sigma project, you can take this achievement as a sign that you can take your initiative to new locations or lines of business. Once you gain traction with Six Sigma, you are ready to expand its scope and implement it where it can be applied.

## Sustain

Since Six Sigma is a problem-solving methodology, you need to deploy projects that are designed to apply tactics that solve problems and business challenges. That means that you need to make sure that your initiative is designed to address performance, technical, quality, and other kinds of challenges that you meet in your organization.

When you turn Six Sigma as a tool for your organization to self-heal, you will see that your initial initiatives change your organization's character. You will realize that efforts geared towards fixing issues will address any other similar problems that may arise in different lines of business. Since Six Sigma is also designed in such a way that its traits are spread over the organization, Six Sigma becomes part of the culture when you get new hires, acquire a new process, or have new contractors.

## THE BEST PRACTICES OF SIX SIGMA

To achieve better results using Six Sigma, it is very important that you adhere to several practices. Even if you have been doing Six Sigma for a while, you should compare and contrast what you do with the best practices in the methodology that has found to be most effective.

### Set Stretch Goals

A stretch goal is defined as a goal that aims for a 70% improvement over a given current performance. For example, if your business now has a profit margin of a measly 7%, then you would want to aim for a profit margin of 11.9% which is a 70% increase of what you used to make.

Six Sigma, in itself, is not designed for the less ambitious manager – it is made for those who want to make breakthroughs in their processes. By combining Six Sigma tools and techniques with stretch goals, you would be able to reach goals that may even sound to be too optimistic or aggressive.

### Strive to Achieve Tangible Results

Six Sigma is known to be a methodology that makes organizations cut costs by 20 to 30%. At the same time, it is designed to create 10% or more revenue.

### Define Outcomes

Every output or result that you produce in an organization is set by the inputs that you have, which tells you that every product that you produce and the success that you can gain can be very deterministic. By being able to have the necessary adjustments and control with your inputs, you would be able to create consistent outputs with consistency.

## Use Critical Thinking Before Taking Action

There are too many occasions wherein people jump into action against a problem to solve it. However, you should not confuse action with effectiveness – they are never the same, and unwarranted action may even cause a problem to continue. You would never want a subpar, band-aid solution that may cause defects in the long run.

## Have Faith in Data

Six Sigma practitioners have a rather apt saying: "In God we trust, all others bring data". This is a belief that is worth putting faith in when you are in business – the absence of data is a cause of doing everything based on guesswork and wishful thinking. Data will help you become objective, have reasonable goals, and work out the best solutions with empirical evidence that is bound to work.

# Chapter 2:
# Fundamentals of Lean Six Sigma

It is not always easy to determine what to improve even when the organization decides to do so. There are so many things to check and many issues to point. It is always hard to know how to start and where to start. The Six Sigma approach is considered to be the best in the world as it answers all these questions. Lean Six Sigma covers every step of processing in a systemic manner – here are its core principles:

## GIVING PRIORITY TO CUSTOMERS

It is the first principle is related to customers in Six Sigma as they hold much importance in its functioning. The business advice of the past is considered true today that a customer is always right. Therefore, no matter what business you do, you should give priority to your customers always. Keep in mind that without fulfilling the demands of the customer, your business might stop to grow further.

## DETERMINING THE CAUSE

People, especially organizations, will always want to look at the results and learn how the results happen. As the law of nature dictates, all outcomes are results of inputs and processes applied to them. These outcomes also include errors that create variation.

When you understand how a process can change results, you can use the way inputs are added together to create outcomes as leverage. Looking behind every possible result and examining the inputs, processes, and the variations will help you find out what truly caused the outcome. Once you know what the cause is, you can put yourself into a better position to assume full control the next time you are in the same situation.

## GETTING THE SIX SIGMA WAY

When you adhere to the thinking that you can always produce the best possible results by controlling and configuring inputs in a particular manner, then you are adhering to the principle called determinism. In Six Sigma, you need to analyze inputs and processes and do the best possible combination to achieve goals.

When you follow this principle, you are controlling your environment, rather than being reactionary and simply let your environment take over. When you are not aware about the relationship of causes and effects in your environment, you will be unsure about how you are getting results in the first place.

## ELIMINATING WASTE WITHOUT COMPROMISING QUALITY

When you have assembled your present value stream, you can distinguish issues with your work and tackle them. Remove activities that have no value at all. Lean Six Sigma philosophy is tied in with finding where issues emerge, fixing them, and averting future events. There is no need to showcase the sectors that are working flawlessly as it will diverge the attention from the main problem. Though it will make your employees happy to see progress, it is better to remain focused.

## FOCUS ON THE PROBLEMS YOU HAVE NOW.

You must be very well grounded when it comes to the project manager in Lean Six Sigma encourages you to think of the real-world problems that impact your customers and your processes at the moment. This will create a sense of urgency for your problem-solving processes, and it will give everyone the chance to feel like they are truly part of the team.

## TEACH TEAMS TO PRIORITIZE.

This is closely connected to the aforementioned principle but it is extremely important as well. If your team knows how to create priorities, you will not have to always micromanage them (which, in all honesty, can be annoying and counterproductive not just for them but for you as well). When your team has to handle multiple tasks or projects, be sure they know which ones are a priority - otherwise, they might pick up the easier or, the less important tasks first.

## TEAMWORK AND ANALYSIS.

When you analyze the various issues of a problem in your processes, be sure you involve the entire team. The underlying concept behind this is that in Lean Six Sigma, every team member must help any other team member at any time. This includes analysis tasks as well - because who else would be more suitable to help you run proper analysis, other than your very own team members who are there, in the middle of the production process, and who can spot the most common mistakes.

## CREATE CROSS-FUNCTIONAL TEAMS.

, the content writing department might not be able to pick up the slack from the web development one when the latter one is missing in action. However, a more cross-functional team is important because it helps everyone feel part of the bigger project - and thus, it makes it more likely that everyone is more satisfied with their work.

## YOUR ANALYSIS IS FOCUSED ON THE PROCESS, RATHER THAN THE PRODUCT.

Even when you may have spotted a problem that is visible on the product, it is still recommended that you focus on the process. This will help you eventually determine not only the symptoms of the "disease," but also its root cause - and thus, it will enable you to eliminate that cause.

## TRY TO CREATE A MAP OF THE PROCESS.

As we were saying earlier in the book, people are much more likely to understand the information you provide them when the information is presented in a visual format. Therefore, your process will be easier to understand, and it will make it easier for your team to spot variations in the process.

## YOUR ANALYSIS SHOULD ALWAYS BE BASED ON DATA.

This might come without saying for many but when you analyze a process and want to spot the mistakes in it, be sure your analysis is based on actual historical data. Anecdotal evidence is fine but only if it can be fully backed up by the data.

## ADDRESSING THE TRUE CAUSE OF A PROBLEM.

There are many problem-solving techniques out there - and while some are great, others start with the wrong assumption (e.g., that a problem is a common occurrence within a process, which may or may not be true, ). However, Lean Six Sigma encourages you to control the unique cause underlying an issue by spotting if it is a recurrent one or if it is a special case. This way, the correct problem-solving strategy can be employed.

Every solution you propose should come with a control system. In other words, once you fix a problem, you should make sure it doesn't happen again too.

## HAVING A SMOOTH WORKFLOW

Labor will continue to work or not work; they will continue the similar undertakings until someone from the management chooses something else for them. Convey new guidelines and practices to follow if you want the change. Be certain that every representative or worker gets proper training and look out for criticism. Otherwise, the problem will not be solved.

The work must go smoothly. The obstacles should be managed beforehand to gain the best results.

## MAKE THE CHANGE ACCEPTABLE THROUGHOUT

Lean Six Sigma requires a ton of progress and change. You have to welcome a change and ask your workers and labor to accept it too. If you'll put yourself in your labor shoes' you might fear or panic by hearing the news of change. As so much of work is now computerized, it could result in losing their job. Make things clearer from your end on how these computerized operations will help workers in making things much easier. Show them how convenient you have made their work.

## HAVING A SYSTEMATIC AND SCIENTIFIC APPROACH

On a basic level, the motivation behind why Six Sigma is so popular approach is that it defines a framework through which your company can improve its processes. It's the era of information; Six Sigma has a logical quality that takes advantage of the information drive world. It only seems fair to take the benefit of the collected data and use it for making enhancements and improve further processes through it

# Chapter 3:
# The Key Players in Six Sigma

Six Sigma is not done by a single person – it needs a large group of people that are devoted to performing tasks and roles on technical and managerial levels. Most of the time, these people are taken within the organization and trained to develop necessary skills for Six Sigma.

Since Six Sigma is a very rigorous framework, the people who are tasked to train in doing Six Sigma projects are often the organization's very best. If you are chosen to do a Six Sigma project, then you can expect yourself to work with the cream of the crop.

## EVERYBODY'S A LEADER IN SIX SIGMA

These are tasks that are required of every leader and are fundamental to everyone who wishes to implement Six Sigma.

Six Sigma initiatives, however, begin with business leaders and executives that approve every Six Sigma deployment product, endorse Six Sigma projects, and are held accountable for the results that they bring.

However, you can try and introduce Six Sigma from the bottom up if you think that you have the right vision for potential improvement on your area of business, or if you think that your boss doesn't get what is supposed to happen. You can also be successful in managing your tasks by troubleshooting possible problem areas.

However, if you want to make sure that the entire organization benefits from the changes that you can do in your area, you may want to talk to your senior management.

## THE LEADERS IN SIX SIGMA

Different personalities are responsible for making Six Sigma initiatives work in the entire organization. These are the following:

### Six Sigma deployment leader

The deployment leader, who is often an executive who makes direct reporting to the corporate level person responsible for launching and sustaining Six Sigma initiatives, is the most important person in the deployment process. He ensures that the corporate goals and strategies align with any deployment plan. He monitors how different areas sustain or improve their performance when Six Sigma begins execution.

In a nutshell, the deployment holds the following responsibilities:

- Holding accountability for Six Sigma results throughout the organization
- Driving vision and mission for Six Sigma into different levels of the organization

- Removing any barriers that may prevent successful implementation
- Publicizing Six Sigma progress, plans, results, roles, and best practices
- Updating the executives on the progress made by different business units.

If you belong to a large corporation, then you may need to have different deployment leaders that may operate on different business units, since the role requires that leaders report to their business executive leader. However, if you have a smaller organization, the Six Sigma champion and deployment leader roles can be fulfilled by a single person.

## **The Six Sigma core team**

This team is composed of members that perform benchmark products and services, conduct detailed gap analyses, make the operational vision, create implementation plans, and conduct the organizational assessment. The make sure that the deployment of Six Sigma programs is complete by doing the following:

- Promote and install a measurement system that will allow progress tracking, create accountability for initiatives launched, and create a visible dashboard that will allow everyone to monitor efforts and progress
- Benchmark services, products, and processes for the organization to see its marketplace's relative position
- Set stretch goals that are focused on creating change on processes that allows work to get done, rather than simply revising existing methods, to create higher improvement rates
- Promote success stories that show how Six Sigma tools and methods that are used have achieved significant improvements

Core team members include the following departments and people:

- Business unit Six Sigma leaders

- Human resources

The human resources department representative performs the following tasks:

- Writes job descriptions for every Six Sigma position and prepares a chart that identifies all Six Sigma roles
- Creates a compensation package for all positions and tasks with the business leadership to create rewards, recognitions, and career development plans for all Six Sigma participants
- Coordinates every Six Sigma-related activity

## Finance Department Representative

The finance department representative sees to it that the following tasks are done:

- Validates how costs and savings will be defined, valued and reported
- Creates a project savings audit and leads its department's participation in selecting projects and reviewing their processes
- Defines budgeting and accounting prerequisites for any expenses related to Six Sigma
- Holds accountability for any Six Sigma finance-related activities and is the point person for finance issues and coordination of all project validation and auditing tasks

## Training department

The training department's representative sees to it that the following tasks are done:

- Develops all training courseware and curricula to ready training for Six Sigma.
- Coordinates and develops schedules for all tracking, reporting processes, supply and logistic materials, and Six Sigma training
- Holds accountability for all training and coordination of similar activities for the entire organization

### Communications department

The communications department representative performs the following tasks:

- Organizes the communication channel for broadcasting successes, as well as coordination with suppliers, partners, investors, customers, and stock analysts
- Lays out the distribution of information, references, and Six Sigma materials throughout the organization

### Information technology department

The IT department representative performs the following tasks:

- Arranges for and initiates the purchase, installation, and distribution of hardware and software necessary for Six Sigma training, knowledge transfer, analytics, process improvement, and project management
- Lays out and executes plans for providing user support for Six Sigma software usage
- Serves as the point person for Six Sigma IT activities and issues

### Functional representatives

These are members of the senior corporate staff who run their departments and perform a large amount of responsibility. These leaders are capable of driving short-cycle initiatives for change in their departments.

### Belts

Six Sigma projects require applied statistics knowledge in varying degrees. The amount of skill depends on these situations:

- Considerable statistical expertise is necessary for solving complex organizational problems
- Existing problems that have moderate complexity, or having to need to assist in solving complex problems, may require a medium level of skill
- Every day routine work may require a minimum level of applied statistics skill

In Six Sigma, karate belts define the number of skills and areas of performance for those that underwent training for Six Sigma project development and implementation. Black Belts are awarded to those that have the highest amount of skill and could produce projects for the most complex organizational situations. This is followed by the Green Belt, which is awarded to those that have medium skills, and then by the Yellow Belt, which applies to those that know everyday level statistics.

# Chapter 4:
# Tools Used in the DMAIC Process

Lean Six Sigma uses DMAIC as a roadmap to provide a structured way to resolve business and process problems. The tools and methods used in DMAIC are extremely useful in determining, analyzing, and improving problems. However, most practitioners often apply these tools indiscriminately, not realizing that every tool is linked to a specific phase of DMAIC, and should, therefore, be used separately and sequentially.

That is why it is important to always refer to the concept of $Y = f(x)$ whenever the DMAIC process is being used. This mathematical equation is translated to "Y is a function of x." In other words, the output of the business process (Y) results from the inputs (x's) within the process. DMAIC seeks to identify those few variables and process inputs that are primarily responsible for influencing the process output. Every DMAIC phase should, therefore, be considered based on how it helps achieve this goal.

## PROCESS MAPS

A process map is a tool that is used to graphically depict the steps, inputs, outputs, and other relevant details about a process. It helps to illustrate the practical relationships between the different elements of a process. There are two types of process maps:

- **Process Flowchart** – It is a simple logical sequence of activities within a process.

- **Deployment Flowchart** - It is also referred to as a Swimlane flowchart and is used to describe the various roles of each stakeholder or department involved in a process.

## SIPOC DIAGRAM

This is a diagram that illustrates the cross-functional activities undertaken within a process. It enables the team to identify suppliers, process inputs (x), process owner, outputs (Y), and customers. It also helps to identify and create limits for the process. It incorporates five elements:

- **Supplier** – The entity providing inputs for the process.

- **Input** – The data or product used within a process to deliver output.

- **Process** – The activities undertaken to deliver output and satisfy customer needs.

- **Output** – The results of a successful process.

- **Customer** – The entity receiving the outputs.

## Voice of Customer gathering

This is the statement the customer makes regarding a specific product or service.

## Critical-To-Quality drilldown tree

A CTQ drilldown tree is an effective tool used for converting the needs and requirements of customers into measurable characteristics. It is what creates a link between the project and the business, and helps manage the project.

## Sampling

This is a data collection strategy that involves picking a select number of elements out of a larger target group. All the elements that are of interest to the study constitute the population. The group of elements that are studied is the sample. For example, the population would be all the employees in an organization, and the sample would be a small group of randomly chosen employees. Sampling methods include:

- **Simple random sampling** – Every element has an equal chance of being chosen.

- **Stratified random sampling** – Groups are formed depending on certain characteristics, and then elements are chosen randomly from each group.

- **Systematic sampling** – Every nth element is chosen from the population.

- **Cluster sampling** – Clusters of elements are chosen after a specific interval.

- **Convenience sampling** – It is dependent on access and convenience.

- **Judgment sampling** – It is dependent on the belief that the elements chosen fit the requirements.

- **Quota sampling** – It focuses on the representation of particular features.

- **Snowball sampling** – It depends on references made by others with similar characteristics.

## MEASUREMENT SYSTEM ANALYSIS

This is a technique used to understand the variations that possibly arise due to the measurement system being used. The aim is to determine the most suitable tool for analysis depending on the type of data. For continuous data, Gage Repeatability and Reproducibility (R&R) is used, while for discrete data, Discrete Data Analysis (DDA) is used.

Two types of variation cause variations in a process. Actual Process Variation is the result of controllable factors or uncontrollable factors. Variation from Measurement System is the result of errors made by the operator or a flaw in the measurement instrument used.

## PROCESS SIGMA CALCULATION

Process Sigma is a measurement gauge used to assess the output of a process and compare it to the performance standard. The higher the process sigma is, the higher the capability of the process. Process sigma enables the project team to have a common platform for comparing processes that may normally be measured using different tools.

## PROCESS MAP ANALYSIS

It helps to understand the inputs that are used to generate outputs. It helps explain which inputs are controllable and which ones are not. It defines the value-added activities and those that are non-value-added. Process map analysis also helps provide information regarding the location of bottlenecks in the process.

## WHY ANALYSIS

This tool involves asking a series of "Why?" questions to determine the possible solutions to process variations and defects. For example, a lending institution may be interested to find out why its loan application process requires more than 14 working days for a customer to be declared creditworthy. The Why Analysis would be as follows:

- Why does the loan approval process take longer than 14 days? Most application forms are returned with blank fields.
- Why are the fields blank? Customers failed to fill in the required details.
- Why did the customer not fill in the required details? They didn't understand the information that was required.
- Why couldn't the customer understand the requirements on the form? The directions on the form are not clear.
- Why aren't the directions on the application form not clear? The print is too small to read.

## HYPOTHESIS TESTING

This is a tool that can be used to detect whether there are statistical differences between data sets. The aim is to determine if the data represents diverse distributions. The steps include:

- Determining an appropriate hypothesis test
- Stating the null and alternative hypotheses
- Calculating test statistics

- Interpreting the results – accepting or rejecting the null hypothesis

## PILOT SOLUTION IMPLEMENTATION

This is a technique used to test the effectiveness of a potential solution prior to implementing it in a process. It can be used to test a portion or the entire solution. Piloting is always a good idea in cases where the scope of variability is large, which may result in unforeseen consequences. Once a solution has been implemented and the process has changed, reversing the solution can be difficult. Piloting helps to avoid situations such as this. The steps involved include:

- Top management leadership and control
- Choosing a pilot team
- Holding meetings with the pilot team
- Planning strategies for effective execution
- Selling new ideas to affected employees
- Training relevant employees for execution of a pilot program
- Implementation of a pilot program on the shop floor
- Debriefing and expansion of a pilot program if initially successful

## BRAINSTORMING: OPPORTUNITY MATRIX

Before process improvement is conducted within an organization, there must be effective brainstorming to generate ideas on it will be done. The steps include:

- Gathering experts from diverse departments
- Identifying a long list (25-150) of potential root causes of a problem. The aim is to come up with as many root causes as possible and may take a couple of hours. No judging of others' ideas.
- Interviewing contributors who were not included in the brainstorming session, for example, former or

present operations personnel. Additional root causes are collected.
- An Excel worksheet is generated showing every root cause, its ID number, initials of the proposer, and any further comments. The file is sent to all team members who are then asked to rank the root causes in order of importance - 1 represents "not important at all" while 10 is "extremely important." They are also asked to rate the estimated cost of every root cause, as well as indicate who should be considered a Champion for attacking a specific cause.
- The team leader receives the files back for collation. The cost, importance, Champion, and proposer rankings are calculated. The standard deviation of the importance rating is also calculated.
- An opportunity matrix is created, showing the importance ratings on the y-axis and the cost rating on the x-axis. The root causes are depicted as bubbles within the matrix and are indicated using their ID numbers. The size of the bubble represents the standard deviation of the importance ranking. The smaller the bubble, the greater the consensus. The root causes to be looked into further are picked according to their level of importance and consensus.

# Chapter 5:
# Six Sigma Certification: Learn and Leverage Your Career

Demand for Six Sigma Certifications is increasing in the job market. Certified professionals can deliver better results and are viewed by the best employers. The methodology is recognized for eliminating the main flaws in a process and optimizing it, always seeking better results.

In the courses, you are taught how to use the available resources more efficiently, creating a constant quest to increase productivity and effectiveness.

This type of knowledge can be used in different sectors simply because it covers administrative and functional processes.

It aims to produce products more efficiently with less waste. It is a methodology developed to identify defects and bottlenecks in production, administrative, manufacturing, and other processes, correcting them and thus eliminating them. It always aims at the continuous improvement of both professionals and procedures.

Six Sigma is a project management methodology that is there to help increase profits, ensure product quality, boost morale, and reduce defects. Many companies use it to help them strive to be as close to perfect as possible. Although there is no governing body that dictates the rules of Six Sigma, many organizations are going to offer certification in this methodology. By becoming certified with Six Sigma, you will find that you are someone to take seriously and that could provide more value to the company you are already with. Some of the things that you need to do to get Six Sigma certification includes:

## DETERMINING THE MANAGEMENT PHILOSOPHY

Consider what the organization needs: What kind of management style is going to benefit your organization the most? Is it dealing with too much waste or overhead in the supply chain? Are there some issues with staying consistent to get things done? What is the overall culture of the business?

Decide how you would like to optimize the process: You may be someone who thinks that the best way to make sure quality is there is to ensure that all the processes are consistent with as few variations as possible. Others may want to opt for efficiency or producing a quality product without as much waste as overhead.

## GETTING CERTIFIED

**Find a training program**: It is likely that you will have to do some classroom instruction, so look and see if there are some near you to avoid travel. Always make sure that the program is accredited. No, there are no formal standards right now but there are some accreditation organizations that can make sure you learn what you need.

**Enroll in the program**: You will attend the right classes and learn the material that you need to get the belt that you choose.

**Take the written test:** Once you are doing with the training, the next step is to do the written test. This will check to see if you have learned what you need about Six Sigma. These tests can take some time. The Yellow Belt can be two hours, the Green Belt about three hours, and the Black Belt about four hours.

**Complete the projects**: The final phase of being certified will be the process of completing a few projects using the Six Sigma methodology. This is like the "lab" to make sure that you can implement what you learn.

## THE TYPES OF CERTIFICATES

One constant question that comes up when a student is looking to learn more about Six Sigma certification is the difference between the belts. They serve as a way to make the candidate's learning process and commitment gradual. Each has its own peculiarities and characteristics to prepare it for the responsibilities that will come.

They are divided following this gradation, in which different levels of knowledge are achieved: white, yellow, green, black, and master black. We will review how the training is performed for each step and what is learned by going through them.

### White Belt

This stage is characterized as the candidate's first contact with the Lean culture and Six Sigma methodology. He will know where it came from and in what way it is made. You will have a sense of the importance of continuous improvement within a corporate environment and how a project that is created by promoting the establishment of that purpose in the company succeeds.

Every beginning requires a process of familiarity with what is being learned until the student absorbs every theoretical part and is aware of all facets of the subject explored. Therefore, the White Belt will need more training to access the tools and have some responsibility in a project. However, they can accompany the teams giving support.

## Yellow Belt

After learning and already being aware of the basics of this methodology, the next step in Six Sigma certification is the Yellow Belt. An important action that is learned at this level is the creation of an improvement road map. Through training, he learns the processes that are executed by completing this document and can lead a small project to deploy it.

They are always easy to understand projects in which the collaborator already knows the environment that will undergo the implantation. For example, the department of the company of which the Yellow Belt is a part or in the organization of the procedures within their routine of work. He will have access to and will know how to use the analysis tools that were not explored in the White Belt certification and that deal directly with quality.

## Green Belt

After gaining small-scale experiences, the Green Belt is the Six Sigma certification stage in which the candidate can achieve and gain a greater understanding of continuous improvement. He can take projects of medium complexity, which can include both the segment in which he is already accustomed and other areas. This level allows him to utilize a broader skillset.

Although he cannot yet achieve a position in which he manages teams, the collaborator will serve as a supervisor for some projects. In comparison to Yellow, the Green Belt's capacity for data analysis and process mapping is of an intermediate degree. The Green Belt also shows a competence that helps in developing more effective statistics.

## Black Belt

Although some confuse it with the Green Belt, there are differences between the stages. At this stage of Six Sigma certification, the employee has the ability to teach the methodology to those interested. Because of his efforts, he already has a familiarity with the subject that allows him to transmit knowledge in relation to everything that concerns continuous improvement.

With the achievement of this title, he can manage projects of great importance within the company. The Black Belt has total mastery of quality tools and will know which ones are appropriate in solving and seeking improvements. He facilitates and conveys his vision in the projects of those who are Yellow and Green, acting as an advisor.

## Master Black Belt

Although the Black Belt fully dedicates their time to the continuous improvement of projects of great importance within the company, the Master has the final say in the ultimate level of Six Sigma certification. However, it can only be achieved when the candidate already has a vast number of projects that he has managed in his portfolio.

The Master Black Belt can lead all employees from previous levels because he has the competence to know exactly what he is doing, what tools will need to be used and the best ways to achieve the desired result for the brand. The Master Black Belt is considered as the propagator and incentive of change because their management is totally committed to the organizational culture.

## WHAT IS THE STRUCTURE OF A GOOD SIX SIGMA COURSE?

There is a myriad of options for undergoing the Six Sigma course and the quality of each is measured based on the results of the professionals who passed through it. Knowing which of the currently available courses are the best deals is not a simple task but there are some criteria that should be evaluated.

A good Six Sigma course should have a minimum duration of:

- 5 hours/class (for the White Belt certification - directed to professionals who have no knowledge of this methodology).
- 60 hours/class (in the Black Belt certification - ideal for those who want to manage projects improvement and become a professional).
- The programmatic content needs to encompass the DMAIC strategy, detailing all the steps and explaining how to perform each of the steps.

Some topics that can be addressed are:

- The sigma levels of a process
- Continuous improvement
- Real data on the methodology
- Comparison of 3-sigma and 6-sigma services, among others
- Last but not least, a quality Six Sigma course should include a step-by-step training for the student. The following points are required:
- Theoretical training
- Practical application of the concepts taught
- A pilot project
- Conduct a test validating the approval and certification within the methodology
- Understanding how Six Sigma works is of great value to a professional's career. The course must contain the aspects mentioned above.

Thus, whoever passes the certification obtains:

- The knowledge necessary to apply the method in the companies in which they work
- The ability to improve the results of the company in which they operate

- The certifications to leverage their career

## THE BENEFITS OF SIX SIGMA CERTIFICATION

Obtaining a Six Sigma certification brings several advantages to your career and professional life. In addition to deepening your knowledge in matters related to your profession, it is a great way to know the news that are emerging in the market and tools hitherto unknown. Below are a few advantages.

### Employability

In an increasingly competitive job market, obtaining a certification, such as Six Sigma, brings the professional a huge competitive advantage and puts them ahead of competitors.

During times of crisis, companies seek professionals to certify projects even faster than normal. And the explanation for this is quite simple: in troubled times, the search for professionals capable of reducing cost and waste through process analysis and adaptation is critical.

Being able to bring together in your curriculum the characteristics of a professional capable of increasing the productivity of the company while reducing their expenses is to add differentials that will enhance their employability.

### Higher wages

According to a survey of the American Society of Quality (ASQ), a certified Six Sigma professional earns up to 12% more than their competitors in the same area. This can bring a great differential in the life of any professional, right?

Recently, studies have also shown that Black Belt professionals have an average salary that can be 15 to 20% higher than those who do not have any type of certification. As it is still rare to find professionals with this type of qualification and knowledge, the market tends to value them even more, since the potential of aggregation to the company is always very great with certificates like this.

## More versatility

Six Sigma certification levels (Green and Black Belt) offer the professional a wide range of actuation options. In this sense, a professional with Six Sigma certification is qualified to identify, analyze and eliminate wastes in various sectors and productive processes of any company. From improving the financial sector's cash flow to reducing logistics and transportation costs, Six Sigma can be present throughout the business environment.

## Improved Analytical Skills

Six Sigma certification presents a very important and arduous training, in which the professional will know and learn all the precepts and theoretical concepts. But it also consists of a practical part, in which you will have the opportunity to put these teachings into action.

One of the key features of a Six Sigma certified professional is their high analytical capability. It is part of your training (and will be part of your professional performance) to use analytical skills capable of solving problematic situations and generate satisfactory results.

This type of competence is part of the high-performance professional profile that is cultivated in the courses. And, more than any other characteristic, the market tends to value and always have open doors for professionals with high analytical capacity. Knowledge is irreplaceable!

## Credibility in the curriculum

Becoming certified in Six Sigma is therefore, a step ahead in your professional career. You will be recognized by companies in national and international territory. An opportunity for those who want to explore new markets and learn the culture of the company from another location.

That said, it's clear how much this type of certification adds to a professional's resume. Even more, if we consider that many positions in several organizations already require a certain level of Six Sigma certification in the curriculum, gaining this qualification becomes even more important.

## Problem-solving authority

Because of all the knowledge gained from Six Sigma certification, the employee will thoroughly understand the aspects of continuous improvement and will bring more knowledge to each new challenge that a project proposes. As it progresses, problem-solving becomes something that is no longer difficult to present.

## Participating in a variety of projects

Even if you are starting out as a White Belt within Six Sigma certification, your approach to the project environment will bring you more opportunities to get to know different areas of your business. This helps strengthen your knowledge of other markets and understanding of aspects of another segment that can bring benefits to yours.

## A Greater understanding of data analysis

With each level gained in Six Sigma certification, the student has a better perception of data analysis. Companies are looking for professionals who can handle critical situations and who can analyze certain statistics to maximize their profitability and avoid wasting stock. Being certified, you will have the chance to be an expert at it.

# Chapter 6: Why Lean Six Sigma is Worth the Effort

Customers are sensitive to quality and will pay handsomely for fine stuff. However, you have got to put in the effort to refine your product and make it stand out from the mass in the market. And when you have an order, you have got to make the customer wonder: Why would I go anywhere else? In short, you make your customer's product in such a way that you are leaving no room for someone else to make it better. That is what Lean Six Sigma makes you do – produce the best that could be.

Let's see why else your effort is worth it:

### ABILITY TO GIVE YOUR CUSTOMER THE BEST VALUE

You see, as you give your customer the best product he or she could ever get, the customer gets easy on the purse. Customers who understand quality are prepared to pay for it. In any case, you do not add any features and functionalities or anything else whose cost the customer does not foot. So essentially, you are not eating into your revenues while refining the customer's product or service. At the same time, you are making yourself irresistible to the customer in a way that makes the price of the product almost inconsequential.

## Makes the Organization Adaptable

When you are working with Lean Six Sigma, there is clear data and clear processes. And when it comes to implementation, it is clear who is in charge of what. Every type and amount of input is known to the detail. So, whenever something crops up in the market that has a direct impact either on the product or service or even the market itself, your organization can analyze what is happening and promptly make necessary changes to accommodate the new changes. In short, this methodology makes your enterprise strategically placed to handle unanticipated variations in the business environment.

## Reducing Costs

By eliminating errors and using unnecessary elements in production, waste is also eliminated. In this way, the costs related to the processes and the execution of the services are reduced.

## Develops an Effective Workforce

Everyone from the most junior employee to the highest of executives develops a feeling of ownership and hence responsibility. Each one of them feels accountable for everything that transpires all the way to the project end.

## It Enhances Efficiency

Since wastage is curtailed, output per employee is higher and better and the organization begins to attract more clients; and business booms.

## It Drastically Cuts Down on Operational Costs

High efficiency is one way of bringing down costs. There is also the aspect of producing output that does not need to be reviewed and modified. Costs also come down whenever loopholes are sealed and pilferage is eliminated.

## Revenues Shoot Up

All the aspects of DMAIC lead to increased revenue. This means that each one of those aspects of management is worth implementing because every organization works towards achieving a huge and consistent flow of revenues.

If you are seeking to identify an organization to emulate in flourishing through Lean Six Sigma, you may wish to look at General Electric; Boeing; Dell; and such other companies that today have a place of prestige in their respective industries.

## High Productivity

Since tasks and processes are planned and controlled constantly to avoid the occurrence of waste, they generate higher quality products in less time, with a very low incidence of problems and inadequacies.

## CUSTOMER SATISFACTION

The Six Sigma methodology has as one of its main objectives customer satisfaction, as it analyzes their impressions and desires and applies them to the production process.

With the reduction in errors and consequent increase in quality, deadlines are fulfilled and this makes the customer feel more satisfied with the product.

## YOU GAIN MORE LOYALTY FROM CUSTOMERS

You see, with improved processes that lead to fewer defects, what you are saying is that you are making your customers happy almost to the point. And with every customer knowing how difficult it is to reach perfection, your near perfection is more than anyone could ask for. And it is unlikely that such customers would wish to shift to another manufacturer or even service provider. This is how your customer retention level gets to soar. And their loyalty gets to draw other people's attention and in many cases pulling them in as new customers. Then you get people wondering how your business seems to be unaffected by increasing competition in your industry – it is that loyalty you have managed to cultivate, courtesy of Lean Six Sigma.

## TIME IS MANAGED BETTER

Did you know that time wastage contributes immensely to final losses? For instance, you get to pay wastages for hours not worked; you get to lose customers just because your employees continue to continue chatting as they sluggishly respond to the customers; and such other uneconomic ways of spending working hours. you can even trace some product or service defects to poor time management – like wasting so much time that when you get to doing the actual work you are literally rushing it through. How can you surely be thorough and make a product to the customer's satisfaction? You may not even have time to check for quality at different stages!

For great time management, you need to set goals that are dubbed SMART – Specific; Measurable; Attainable; Relevant; as well as Time-bound. Then, , you use the data based principles of Six Sigma.

## INCREASE THE CASH FLOW

Cash flow is important for every type of business under the Sun - so always have proper cash flow in your company. While Lean Six Sigma may not directly influence this, it will definitely help with the Days Sales Outstanding processes. The DSO should be as high as possible - so you can use goals related to this when setting up a Lean Six Sigma project. For instance, you could aim for invoicing process variation time reduction, for inventory management process variation reduction, and so on.

## YOU HAVE A MOTIVATED WORKFORCE

Do not imagine that workers keep smiling when they are sweating it out for nothing. They will do that when they know that they are being appreciated. And why are they being appreciated? Because under Six Sigma they are producing results that are pleasing to the customer and thus prompting the customers to place more orders. As a result, revenues are increasing without the counter effect of returned defective goods. , as you may recall, Lean Six Sigma is one interactive methodology where everyone involved has a say. That in itself has been seen to raise productivity to a range within 25 and 50 percent.

## ENABLING BETTER MANAGEMENT OF YOUR SUPPLY CHAIN

Just imagine a scenario where you have a supplier for every component of a particular product with multiple parts! You would have just as many people to depend on for the efficiency of your process. This is because delayed deliveries can affect your working process in an adverse manner, just as defective supplies can. However, with lean Six Sigma, what you strive to do is reduce your number of suppliers. If you analyze the whole scenario further, you will realize that not only will you reduce DOWNTIME but you will also have a chance to negotiate more favorable credit terms for your organization.

## SMOOTH PROCESSES

These smooth processes result in increased speed and accuracy. Can we not just call that faster processing and increased efficiency? And, , those are the aspects that most customers consider when thinking of whether to stick with you or go searching elsewhere. In this working environment, the resources you need to put in are always on the decline and that is because the idea of waste is almost superficial now. And with happy customers keeping their accounts running, the revenue side keeps getting heavier. On the overall, your organization then begins and continues to stand out in profitability.

## DEVELOPING AN EFFECTIVE WORKFORCE

Did you know that a lot of hours are lost at the place of work as employees await the so-called 'orders from above'? When using Lean Six Sigma, nobody dictates to anybody. How can it happen when everyone was part of the team that laid things on the table; identified existing weaknesses and prescribed solutions?

## YOUR ACHIEVEMENTS WILL BE MARKED BY HIGH STANDARDS

Excellence is a fundamental factor of Lean Six Sigma. And with this, you get to reap, not just cash rewards but also respectability. That is why marketing agencies are reaping millions to give companies a facelift; to reflect excellence. But with you working with Lean Six Sigma, you do not need to convince anyone that your products or services are worth a try. Excellence in this regard comes with the territory. Achieving excellence in all spheres – production, packaging, delivery.

## PROVIDES ROOM FOR INNOVATION

How can you not be innovative, employing your imagination and creative knack to come up with progressive ideas, when you never have to firefight or strive to do damage control? When you are counting decimals as your degree of failure, as an organization it reflects a scenario where processes are flowing smoothly and where every face is glowing with satisfaction. And you want that for growth, continued stability, and also expansion.

# Chapter 7:
# Beneficiaries of Lean Six Sigma

Do you think any organization or enterprise is too big or too tiny to cut down on waste and increase profits? Obviously, no – every organization is faced with situations of scarce resources and bigger revenue figures in their strategic plans, and so they would be glad to be part of Lean Six Sigma, a process that is geared towards reducing costs and increasing revenue. Here are some of the beneficiaries of Lean Six Sigma

### EMPLOYEES

Employees are the ones in the action and determine whether the organization is moving downhill or up in profit-making. Therefore, the participatory nature of Lean Six Sigma makes the employees feel valued and leaves them with the feeling of ownership as far as implementation of changes goes. And even when the employees are faced with challenging processes, the fact that they already feel accountable keeps them determined and happy to be part of the challenge.

## The Health Sector

Have you realized you have fewer requests for sick off as an employer when your employees are happy? That is a pointer that with many organizations implementing the Lean Six Sigma management style, health facilities are bound to experience less pressure. At the same time, it means that the efficiency that comes with Lean Six Sigma is bound to have patients enjoy better services, the aged more quality time with their minders, and health workers spending less time dealing with unnecessary paperwork and such matters that do not impact on quality. So, we have higher quality services and fewer resources injected into mundane and unnecessary chores.

## Technology

The technology sector is an obvious beneficiary of Lean Six Sigma in that more technology is going to be utilized the more evidence continues to come out that technology has a lot to do with increasing efficiency. With manufacturers being able to produce items of a high standard and lower defect count, people are bound to be attracted to investing more in technology.

## Financial Sector

There is less time spent enrolling new customers when you have Lean Six Sigma in place. Even the time it takes to deliver services to customers is greatly reduced and that means attracting more customers while retaining the old ones. That points to guaranteed continuity and expansion of your income stream; and increased financial activity just coming from the spillover effect.

## EVERY INDUSTRY

What this essentially means is that whatever industry you are in, you will find it important to put in place means of earning profits, minimizing cost, or both. So, Lean Six Sigma is the efficient tool for all, irrespective of their industry.

For one, more and more companies are getting into the mode of hunting for anything and anyone progressive as far as profitability is concerned. And that is how Lean Six Sigma has gained popularity. And hence the rise in demand for qualified and certified people to lead and drive the process. Needless to say, without having worked with someone before, the only way you can be sure they are competent is if they can pass as duly certified. Today, you can see advertisements of companies seeking to nab people who have been certified as professionals in Lean Six Sigma.

## SALARIES AND LEAN SIX SIGMA

You do not get vacancies being filled by the likes of GE and imagine the salary would be low. Yet the positions linked with Lean Six Sigma have the element of uniqueness and rarity, that making them even more marketable. So, if anyone had any doubt about the value attached to qualifications of Lean Six Sigma, they are about the erase them after going through the salary indications:

It is said that if you are a Green Belt professional, your salary will be higher than some other professional from the same field who does not have Lean Six Sigma certification. The figure given as a premium for the Lean Six Sigma professional is 42%. Here we are saying that if you are an engineer with Salary X, when you get the Green Belt certification your market value will soar and your salary offer is likely to be 142X% of what you were earning before.

Salary for Green Belts holders in the US is particularly high, and the average pay is something to the tune of $72,000 annually.

For Black Belts, employers are known to put $98,000 on the table. Then when it comes to Master Black Belts, the salary for one individual comes to around $113,000 annually.

As such, you will find a good number of employees today enrolling for training in matters of Lean Six Sigma, as they strategically endeavor to make themselves, not only viable but also highly marketable. , for this you need to begin from the Yellow Belt certification.

## Salaries of trainers?

Surely a teacher must be better paid than the fresh graduate. In that case, trainers of belt holders earn relatively higher salaries. you should not be surprised to come across a Lean Six Sigma trainer earning something like $100,000 per annum. And you should also not lose sight of the fact that these trainers are often available for consultancy. The long and short of it is that when you get the necessary training and earn the relevant belt or belts, you find doors opening faster to let you take advantage of big-time income-generating opportunities.

Here are various industries where Black Belts are paid exemplary high salaries:

- Industries related to IT
- Industries associated with food and beverages
- Industries that deal with energy and utilities
- Amongst all these industries, bear in mind that Master Black Belts are the highest-paid.

## Is the Lean Six Sigma training expensive?

Well, someone said many days and decades ago that should you want to have the real feel of cost, try to compare the implications of being ignorant with the impact of being well informed and skilled. With ignorance, you might find yourself paying through the nose and without prior planning. But with knowledge, you can reach sky high in performance as well as in imagination.

Anyway, brace yourself to pay something between $4,000 and $7,000. The consolation is that you will be saving on transport cost and time as the belt certification courses are readily available online. And also, many employers will be ready to sponsor you if they find you competitive, focused, and loyal to the business.

# Chapter 8:
# Why Some Companies Are Not Taking Advantage of Lean Six Sigma

### LACK OF RELEVANT INFORMATION

Well, for one, this methodology has not penetrated the general market. It is safe to say that it is still with the pacesetters. So, the reason some companies who would otherwise make huge strides in growth do not even talk about Lean Six Sigma is a sheer lack of knowledge. Apart from coming across the term when trying to Google something, or hearing it from word of mouth, there are few other sources of information on this cutting edge methodology.

## BELIEVING LEAN SIX SIGMA TO BE A FAD

There are many reasons why some companies lead while others follow. However, often you find CEOs who are close-minded and not willing to do anything that seems to challenge the status quo. That is why you find a sudden structural overhaul of a company's top management by the board when some forward-looking member introduces the idea of change of management style. In short, some dub the relatively new management style a fad simply because of the fear of implementing something new.

## TIME MANAGEMENT THAT IS WANTING

Have you ever taken into consideration the fact that time spent, no matter how well or poorly, cannot be salvaged? This, , as opposed to an exam failed – you can always do a re-sit. Even a product not well completed – final touches can usually be made later. Anyway, some executives who know about Lean Six Sigma keep it at bay citing lack of adequate time to implement it when it is a shortcoming in time management.

## UNDERRATING THE SIZE OF THE ORGANIZATION

This business of ours is too small for big methodologies! Do you think you could be too tiny for a fat bank account? If not, how then can you dismiss an improvement tool that does not come as a whole mass but as a combination of implementable principles? If you are small or just medium size but you acknowledge that reducing product defects is worthwhile and you are ready to use reliable data to improve your processes in a way that can be objectively assessed, then you are ready for Lean Six Sigma. In short, you could embrace Lean Six Sigma but implement it in phases.

### SOME COMPANIES HAVE NOT HEARD OF LEAN SIX SIGMA.

Although it is becoming popular, Lean Six Sigma is not part of the mainstream. A manager needs to search for it in Google so that he can start learning about it.

### SOME COMPANIES BELIEVE THAT LEAN SIX SIGMA IS FOR LARGE CORPORATIONS ONLY.

They may be experiencing problems within the organization. However, they do not think that Lean Six Sigma can help them. They must realize that they can implement important Lean Six Sigma principles to improve customer satisfaction.

### SOME ORGANIZATIONS THINK THAT LEAN SIX SIGMA IS FOR MANUFACTURING ONLY.

Although it started in the manufacturing industry, the Lean Six Sigma principles apply to service and transaction scenarios. The service industry can use the principles to reduce its waste. Repetitive processes with high volume can be good Lean Six Sigma projects.

### SOME BUSINESSES PREFER LEAN STRATEGIES FIRST AND THEN JUST USE SIX SIGMA LATER.

This decision cheats customers, businesses, and employees. Lean and Six Sigma are complementary. Lean simplifies business processes and improves throughput and speed. On the other hand, Six Sigma reduces variation and defects and improves product or service quality. Combining these two strategies can produce effective and efficient results.

## SOME COMPANIES FAILED TO IMPLEMENT LEAN SIX SIGMA CORRECTLY IN THE PAST.

It is best for these organizations to analyze why they failed and to strive to correct their mistakes when they try implementing Lean Six Sigma again.

## SOME COMPANIES FEAR FAILURE.

Only a few people can acknowledge this fear and do something about it. These companies must realize the paralyzing affect this fear has on their business processes. They must strive to stay in the business by innovating.

## THE MASSIVE STATISTICS AND ADVANCED MATH

Have you also misconstrued Lean Six Sigma to be all about big math; statistics and probability? Well, it is not. You can still make a big improvement in the success of your business entity without involving yourself with complex figures. Even a business that deals with customer care and not anything like engineering can do with the reduction of waste. It can also do with happier customers. Can you identify obvious duplications and redundancies in your organization without holding a calculator or mathematical table? Yes, you can. Can you identify obvious wastage without doing number related calculations? If it is yes to both questions, then you surely can apply Lean Six Sigma without having to employ a statistician and still reap higher revenues.

# Chapter 9:
# Design for Lean Six Sigma

When an organization says that it is using Lean Six Sigma, it is usually assumed that the methodology in play is DMAIC. This is true in most cases because many organizations have existing processes that are generating a lot of waste. However, there is an alternative approach that is used primarily by organizations that are looking to design a brand new product or process, and want to ensure that it meets quality standards. This approach is known as Design for Six Sigma (DFSS).

## DFSS

DFSS enables an organization to enhance the rate and quality of its design process. DFSS can be implemented when designing or redesigning a product or service from scratch. It is expected that a product or service designed via DFSS will have a process Sigma level of at least 4.5, which translates to not more than 1 defect in every 1000 opportunities. However, depending on the product, the Sigma level can sometimes be as high as 6 or more.

## DFSS Methodology

The first step in the DFSS methodology is identifying and analyzing gaps that may negatively affect the performance of a new process, product or service. The main focus is on how customers respond to the new item. Once this information has been obtained, it is then possible for the organization to establish a project to deal with the problems.

There are several variations of the DFSS approach. These include DMADV, DMADOV, DCCDI, IDOV, and DMEDI. They may differ slightly from one another but they essentially follow similar steps and aim to achieve similar objectives. DFSS approaches are a way of designing processes, products, and services to minimize development costs and delivery time, improve effectiveness, and enhance customer satisfaction.

The basic procedure is as described below:
- Capturing of customer requirements
- Analysis and prioritization of requirements
- Development of the design
- Tracking the capability of the process, product or service at every step
- Exposing gaps between customer requirements and product capabilities.
- Establishing a control plan.

## Implementing DFSS

Most organizations that implement DFSS tend to focus too much on financial accountability at the expense of implementation accountability. It is important that organizations that choose to implement DFSS place emphasis on staying true to the DFSS process. This should be translated into the disciplined and thorough application of DFSS tools, for example, QFD (Quality Function Deployment), transfer functions, tolerance allocation, expected value analysis, and others. Refusing to apply DFSS tools in a design process will not produce the expected benefits.

When implementing DFSS, the organization must believe that the powerful tools that form part of DFSS will bring the intended benefits. However, there are signs that most companies are reluctant to implement DFSS yet they expect to reap savings directly. This fear of putting in the hard work that is part of DFSS leads organizations to take shortcuts that do more harm than good in the long run.

The business world is constantly buzzing with talk of the desire for culture change. If the powerful tools available are not being implemented, this culture change will happen very slowly, even with top management pushing the agenda. Achieving breakthrough improvement and change go hand in hand with using the tools available. When deploying DFSS, it is important to remember that using the tools will produce results, which means implementation accountability must be pushed to the fore. It bears just as much importance as financial accountability and is much easier to monitor.

## Benefits of Implementing DFSS

DFSS has been proven to provide a gain of one sigma quality level over previous designs.

It is a very cost effective-way to eliminate defects from a system. Costs of production are usually lowest during the initial phases of design, thus giving DFSS a high-performance/cost ratio.

It offers a disciplined approach when it comes to accountability of implementation. The DFSS scorecard enables an enhanced and more consistent collection of data. The DFSS data and scorecard help to highlight the potential causes of failure rather than depending on assumptions.

## Differences between DFSS and DMAIC

DMAIC is used when improving a process that is already in place while DFSS is used when developing an entirely new process.

DFSS is considered a preventative approach rather than a curative one. Organizations implement DMAIC methodology only when they identify flaws in the process and try to eliminate waste. With DFSS, the defects are eliminated while the process is being designed.

DFSS is considered to be more economically viable than DMAIC since defects are eliminated during the initial stages of process/product/service design.

The tools used in the implementation of DFSS are quite different from those in the DMAIC methodology. the reason why DFSS was created was that DMAIC tools could not be used to optimize a process beyond three or four Sigma without having to redesign the fundamentals. The best option was to design for quality from the start.

## VARIATIONS OF DFSS

### DMADV

This is a popular DFSS methodology that has five phases:

**Define** – Customer goals and project goals are defined.

**Measure** – Customer needs and requirements are determined. Industry benchmarks are also set.

**Analyze** – Options are analyzed to satisfy customer needs.

**Design** – Detailing how customer needs are to be met.

**Verify** – Verification of whether performance will be able to satisfy customers.

## DMADOV

This is a slight modification of the DMADV methodology. It contains an Optimize phase where advanced statistical models and tools are used to optimize performance.

## DCCDI

**Define** – Definition of project goals.

**Customer** - Completion of customer analysis.

**Concept** – Development, review, and selection of ideas.

**Design** - Detailing how customer needs and business specifications are to be met.

**Implementation** – Development and commercialization of the product or service.

## IDOV

This methodology is well known in manufacturing circles.

**Identify** – Finding out the customer CTQs and specifications.

**Design** – Customer CTQs are translated into functional needs and further into potential solutions. The best solution is chosen from the list.

**Optimize** – Advanced statistical models and tools are used to optimize performance.

**Validate** – Ensuring that the design will satisfy customer CTQs.

## DMEDI

**Define** – Identifying business problems and customer desires.

**Measure** – Customer needs and requirements are determined.

**Explore** – Analysis of the business process and exploring options for designs that will meet customer needs and specifications.

**Develop** – Delivering an ideal design as per customer needs.

**Implement** – Putting the new design through simulation tests to check efficacy to meet customer requirements.

# Chapter 10: Deployment Planning

Deploying Lean Six Sigma is a decision that has to be taken seriously. Tough questions must be asked and answered before taking those critical first steps. One of the first steps that have to be taken is creating a plan that addresses the key issues affecting organizational processes. The executives and leaders must also consider potential challenges that may be faced.

## THE DECISION TO DEPLOY

The level of success of Lean Six Sigma initiatives will depend on whether certain conditions are met. Before a deployment decision is made, there are a few questions that need to be asked:

## Are there any compelling reasons for Lean Six Sigma deployment?

Compelling reasons could include the organization suffering huge quality losses, poor customer satisfaction, or even new rivals entering and dominating the market. A burning platform is a great way to motivate people to embrace a continuous improvement initiative.

## What are the explicit goals of the initiative?

A burning platform is a great way to develop the push required to deploy Lean Six Sigma. However, it is also necessary to develop a pull. This pull comes in the form of goals that are specific and designed to show how the organization will look in the future. These goals should highlight the business case for Lean Six Sigma and may include:

- A fundamental change in business culture and management.
- Effective conversion of strategy into results.
- Solving problems throughout the organization.
- Reduction of costs while improving customer satisfaction.
- Increasing revenues.

Management must agree on the goals before deployment to make planning easier and avoid false starts.

## Is top management strongly supportive of the initiative?

Leadership has no substitute. There must be high-level executive involvement to steer the deployment process, hold managers accountable, and tear down any organizational barriers. The executive who is sponsoring the initiative must be determined and willing to sacrifice to make Lean Six Sigma work.

## Will Lean Six Sigma resolve the problems plaguing the organization?

Most organizations tend to believe that Lean Six Sigma is the solution to all their problems. However, there are certain issues that this initiative simply cannot fix. If the organization is faced with bad leadership, financial restructuring, or a poor business strategy, then Lean Six Sigma isn't the answer. It may provide the tools to understand and improve the process capability of the organization but some underlying issues have to be fixed separately before deployment.

## INTERNAL CUSTOMER REQUIREMENTS FOR DEPLOYMENT

In most business processes, the customer always comes first - deployment is no different. The customer can see the solution to their needs and pay for it and that determines the value of deployment. It is, therefore, important to understand internal customer requirements when using Lean Six Sigma tools.

One way of accomplishing this is by creating a Critical-To (CT) tree. This will enable the organization to refine its general deployment goals into precise and measurable performance specifications. A CT tree is developed using the following steps:

- Identification of deployment customers. These are people within the organization who decide to allocate resources toward Lean Six Sigma or have the authority to influence such decisions.
- Establishment of a rigorous and structured process to understand customer requirements. This can be done through focus groups or interviews.
- Obtaining measures and specifications. This involves determining how much money the initiative will save the organization and the time frame for doing so.
- Clarification of what a culture change means to the customer and ways of measuring it.

A CT tree helps to provide the necessary clarity and gain solid top management support. It is usually easy to get people to agree to something if it is vaguely described. Once the process has been specified and measured, however, everyone knows exactly what they are getting into. This avoids misunderstandings, assumptions, and hidden agendas. In the end, it is much easier to design a deployment plan if expectations are clear.

## Choosing a Deployment Model

A deployment model refers to the structure, scale, scope, and focus of the deployment. Many models that can be used but it is recommended that the model chosen be appropriate for that particular organization. There are four general deployment models, each highlighting issues that need to be addressed:

### Organization-wide model

This is the traditional model used by most organizations. It requires strong central management and is driven by top leadership. Every sector of the organization is involved and results are rapidly produced. It is easy to improve multiple functions at once since they are all involved. Deployment obstacles are easily broken down by strong top management, and the business can be transformed due to the model's scale and scope.

The biggest problem with this model is that there has to be strong, focused, and persistent leadership. These are features that are usually rare in the majority of organizations. There must also be a committed deployment team. This model is resource-intensive and other initiatives may suffer. It can be very challenging to execute.

The organization-wide model has been proven to be the most sustainable and with the greatest impact. If there is a powerful and committed leadership, and the deployment is done quickly and comprehensively, there will be enough momentum to override the resistance to change that plagues most organizations.

## Business unit model

In this model, Lean Six Sigma is deployed in only one particular business unit of an organization. It is less complex than an organization-wide model as it requires a smaller and simpler infrastructure to support functions like project monitoring and training. Due to its size and nature, it is easier to get management to adopt it. This is a suitable model to use in organizations where people are very skeptical about Lean Six Sigma. Though it requires a strong business unit leader, it is not necessary to get executive support early on.

The disadvantage with the business unit model is that it does not impact the organizational culture. It is also difficult for the deployment team to work across business units to improve processes. This model has to prove itself first before it can be transformed into an organization-wide initiative, which may take years. Finally, the people involved in the deployment team are only exposed to one business unit, thus limiting their ability to gain organization-wide experience.

## Targeted model

In the targeted model, Lean Six Sigma is deployed to attack specific problems that may exist within one business unit or throughout the organization. It is a fast and effective model due to the ease of implementation. Due to the limited scale of the initiative, a lot of infrastructure is not needed and not many changes have to be made. The problems are the focal point and motivation action.

On the other hand, this model is so narrowly focused that it cannot transform the business. Since there isn't much infrastructure put in place to support this model, it becomes very difficult to later expand the initiative throughout the organization.

### Grassroots model

This is where a few individuals in the lower ranks of the organization decide to deploy Lean Six Sigma to solve a specific problem. There is not much infrastructure support due to the scale and it is easy to start.

Since there is little infrastructure support, it is not easy to expand the narrow scope. Ultimately, the results obtained are usually very meager relative to the whole organization, thus making it very difficult to capture the attention of the top leadership.

## ACCOUNTABILITY FOR DEPLOYMENT

It is extremely important to resolve accountability issues from the get-go. Managers and executives must be held accountable for Lean Six Sigma results. If they are not made to be accountable, they are likely to marginalize the initiative. To improve accountability for results, the organization can link the achievement of Lean Six Sigma goals to some form of significant compensation. This will reinforce accountability and ensure that resources are allocated where needed.

There must also be accountability for deployment execution. Someone must be held accountable for the procedures, policies, training, selection of Green and Black Belts, and project monitoring. These functions are best centralized to ensure efficiency. The individual responsible should report to a high-ranking executive such as the CEO to link the deployment to the organization's overall strategy.

## CHANGE MANAGEMENT

Mastering the tools of Lean Six Sigma is important but what influences its success is the ability to manage change. People do not like it when the status quo is altered. All of a sudden, there is an emphasis on data rather than personal opinions, performance problems are brought to the fore, and process owners are forced to be accountable for improving the way they work.

This is why it is crucial to create a change management plan early. Quickly assess the stakeholders and their relevant departments and ask them the following questions:

- Is the value proposition for Lean Six Sigma well understood?
- Is the deployment plan understood?
- Do you support the Lean Six Sigma initiative?
- Do you have enough business knowledge and resources to support deployment?

Change management requires diplomacy and personal contact. Resistance can be rooted out if people feel that their opinions matter and have been taken into account. Even the most hardheaded stakeholders can be convinced if they are engaged early on

## DEPLOYMENT MISTAKES TO AVOID

Deploying Lean Six Sigma produces great rewards for an organization. However, there are times when the whole deployment program fails, resulting in a lot of wasted time and resources. This is usually because of deployment mistakes that were not handled well. These mistakes need to be recognized and avoided at all costs.

### Too Broad a Scope

Whenever a Lean Six Sigma project fails, it is usually because of scope creep. If the scope is too broad from the beginning, there will not be enough focus to guarantee the improvement of a process, product or service. Sometimes the scope can even increase in the middle of the project. To avoid this problem, the team must concentrate on maintaining a narrow scope as possible so that they do not bite off more than they can chew.

## Poor Deployment Strategy

The aim of having a deployment strategy is to ensure that organizational goals are aligned to deployment outcomes. If there is no alignment, the stakeholders will fail to see the point of the entire process. The solution to this problem is to make sure that the deployment results and business goals are aligned. The deployment strategy must take into account planning, employee training, project execution, information management, and achievement of operational excellence. There must be a periodic review of the progress made on every strategy and its impact on business results. By monitoring these two elements, the team will be able to perform adjustments when necessary. When positive changes start to be seen, the organization begins to believe more in the effort.

## Too Much Emphasis on Training and Certification

It is easy to fall for the notion that everyone involved in a Lean Six Sigma project must know every detail about every complex statistical tool and technique. There are a lot of training and certification courses out there, with trainers and consultants competing heavily against each other to corner the market. As a result, there has been a lot of focus on teaching advanced tools and getting certified. The truth is that not every tool has to be used in every project. The solution is to place more emphasis on learning expediency and application of knowledge. An organization should remain focused on the execution of the projects rather than how many certified Belts it has.

## Poor Project Selection

If the project improvement team loses focus from the beginning and does a shoddy job of selecting and prioritizing projects, disaster will strike. The project may be scrapped or delayed, thus causing cynicism among the Belts. The solution to this mistake is to make sure that data and goals are the key elements to focus on when selecting and prioritizing projects. There must be regular meetings to review data and customer, business and process goals. The team should also make sure that every project that is selected has a sponsor who will monitor and give approval for the project.

## Not Appointing a Deployment Leader

Some organizations have tried to get away with deploying Lean Six Sigma projects without designating a deployment leader. Without a deployment leader, the individual teams will engage in improvement activities in their areas but there will be no real synergy or unity of purpose. This will lead to confusion and failure. The solution is to appoint a deployment leader whose responsibility is to train team members, assign projects, and select the tools to be used. A deployment leader is the one who provides direction and ensures general progress.

## Isolated Implementation

What point is there in improving a product's design but leaving the manufacturing process intact? Deploying small, localized improvement projects is not a smart strategy. It may be a good place to start if resources are minimal but isolated and disconnected pockets of improvement will not realize the full benefits. With Lean Six Sigma, the best organizational results are achieved when a pervasive implementation strategy is adopted. After all, organizations are made up of interconnected processes.

# Chapter 11:
# What Leaders Should Note in Readiness to Implement Lean Six Sigma

The methodology is meant to keep you on track; consistently evaluating processes, measuring achievements at every stage while at the same time measuring any losses and taking instant measures to return to perfection; or, at least, near perfection. So, you cannot afford to drop Lean Six Sigma just because you are now leading the pack or your shareholders are smiling all the way to the bank. You need it to maintain that success and the only way to do that is to keep following the basics of Lean Six Sigma.

In any case, you may be in the lead today but who says a competitor is not already employing the best brains versed in Lean Six Sigma to try and edge you out?

## LEAN SIX SIGMA IS A STRUCTURED APPROACH TO MANAGEMENT

In short, you need to brace yourself for order and working systems and not just a structured system on paper. You need to give in to employee active participation even in terms of ideas because that is what Lean Six Sigma entails. The management system where employees are simply labor providers is out of date and will not help you minimize losses in your organization.

## DECISIONS ARE, BY DEFAULT, MADE BASED ON ACCURATE DATA

In short, this is not a situation where you make decisions based on whims or emotions, or even your gut feeling. In Lean Six Sigma, everything is data-based, and so you as the CEO, like your employees, are set for strict accountability. And you need to be aware that success in Lean Six Sigma is measured to the decimal and the margin of error that denotes success is very small.

## WORKING UNDER LEAN SIX SIGMA CALLS FOR STRICT DISCIPLINE

Did you know that once you get accustomed to acting in a disciplined manner you no longer need much effort to do it? This is what organizations that have achieved success via Lean Six Sigma are experiencing. Working with precision becomes part of them no matter the magnitude of the task. And as you can appreciate, the total of numerous completed tasks is the overall success of your project and exhilarating for the customer. What then would make a happy customer go anywhere else? You can only revel at the expansion of your customer base and smile at your bank account.

## Lean Six Sigma Projects take a Process at a Time

What is the logic? Well, if you implement different processes at the same time, how will you know which one helped you positively and to what degree? If one process is creating losses, how will you tell which one it is that is doing that? In short, you will be sabotaging your efforts by implementing different processes concurrently; and you may find yourself reverting to acting on maybe's and likelihoods – nothing close to what Lean Six Sigma advocates.

## Define the Team that Will Participate in the Project

After identifying failures that undermine the company's performance or opportunities to improve tasks that are not yet at an expected level of excellence, it is time to form teams that will participate in the improvement projects.

## Stipulate Meeting Frequency for Problem Discussion

In some situations, flaws or defects, as well as causes, are evident. In others, the team needs to focus on the problem in a focused way until it fully understands it. To do so, it is necessary to establish the frequency of meetings to discuss the case that needs to be resolved.

In this context, the support of the company's top leadership is fundamental. After all, if the management feels that it is not worth "wasting time" to correct problems or seek improvements, the improvement projects will not even get completed.

## Mapping the Process

A company functions as an open system, so there are exchanges with the "outside world". In the middle of the field between the inputs and outputs, there is the processing of the inputs. At this stage, it is possible to identify a set of processes that contribute to the organization achieving the desired results.

## Define the Indicator and Assess How It is Measured

It is no wonder that improvement projects should be conducted in a scientific and not just empirical way. After all, as we pointed out before, it is not enough to solve the problem but to prove how it was done.

In this sense, the project team should define the indicator that adequately portrays the issue to be faced, for example, the reduction of cycle time, the number of defects to each of the units produced, the number of customer complaints, etc.

## Stick with the Changes That Worked

Once you've tested the suggestions you've previously selected, the team should define the ones that provided the expected results. In this case, it is important to keep in mind the operational definition of improvement, according to which "improvement is a positive, relevant, and lasting impact (in project indicators) produced by intentional changes."

## You Need a Reason That is Compelling Before You Introduce Lean Six Sigma

If you do not do that and you pretty well know that your projects will require the participation and unequivocal support of everyone involved, you may not get much success. You need to have everyone in your organization buying into the idea of change.

## YOU NEED TO GET YOUR TOP MANAGEMENT IN YOUR CORNER

From the onset, you need your colleagues at the top to understand what changes you have in mind. This is especially important because you do not want to have your senior managers feeling like they are losing power to ordinary employees. You need to give them a brief on what Lean Six Sigma is about and the wonders it has done to organizations that have embraced it.

## A SPECIAL VOTE FOR RESOURCES TO FACILITATE LEAN SIX SIGMA PROJECTS IS NECESSARY

If you think you will need to hire new personnel with knowledge of Lean Six Sigma and relevant experience, put that on the table when making your proposals at the top level. If there are materials required, technology to be acquired or modified, or any other thing that will demand resources, let that be clear. Otherwise, a project can easily fail if it is not supported by the relevant resources. And then the organization ends up worse than it was in the first place.

## ANYONE WITH A STAKE IN THE ORGANIZATION NEEDS TO BE ON THE LOOP

Take the case of a customer who has been casual with his or her specifications or even non-committal with timelines. These are the kind of customers who tell you the product can be delivered any time you have it ready, only for them to call in sounding an emergency. You cannot afford that with Lean Six Sigma. Product specifications need to be defined and stated because that is the benchmark for the success of the process being used.

## IT IS CRUCIAL TO SET ASIDE TRAINING FUNDS

While training funds need not run into millions of dollars, you still need a couple of thousands to give your staff, particularly those who will be actively involved in projects, some insight as to what to expect of this new management style and methodology of working. Note that you have the option of bringing in an expert to give your staff in-house training.

# Chapter 12: Implementing the Lean Six Sigma Methodology

Implementing the Lean Six Sigma system is not difficult - but you have to pay attention to how you do it. As we were mentioning before, deploying Lean Six Sigma correctly is crucial for the success of this methodology.

## THE SIX SIGMA CULTURE

The Lean Six Sigma Culture is all about understanding your customer, what they need, and how you can meet those demands, requirements, and needs with your cost planning, with the quality of your product, and with the timeliness of your delivery.

To create this kind of culture, you must be yourself a strong believer in everything the Six Sigma Culture brings along. And when it comes to the "technicalities" of the implementation of the culture, it all starts with the so-called "5S System".

## The 5S System

The 5S System is an acronym-based system that will allow you to keep in mind the absolute basics when it comes to the Lean Six Sigma culture:

- Sorting. All the unnecessary items should be removed from your workspace.
- Set in order. All the items that are usually easy to use should be arranged and put away.
- Shine. Make sure your work area is clean and neat.
- Standardize. Repeatable processes should be consistently approached.
- Sustain. Keep on maintaining the right procedures.

## STEPS TO LEAN SIX SIGMA IMPLEMENTATION

Use these tips as a set of guidelines to help yourself create the right process of implementation for your particular situation!

## The Burning Platform

You shouldn't start considering Lean Six Sigma without having a proper reason to do so. As the old saying goes, why change something that works?

Sure, Lean Six Sigma is attractive and cool - but if you don't have a compelling reason to implement it, you might find that there is no point in doing it.

The compelling reason is sometimes referred to as a "burning platform" - the catalyst behind the Lean Six Sigma implementation, to be more specific. For instance, if your process has generated quality losses, you will find that Lean Six Sigma is a good idea. Likewise, if your competition is way ahead of you, then this means there might be a problem with your processes - so Lean Six Sigma is, again, a good idea.

## Bring Your Resources Together

Like it or not, you cannot implement Lean Six Sigma if you don't have your resources in place. This means that you might have to make new hires - and when it comes to this, it is quite important that you find just the right person(s) to make sure your process is handled by people who are experienced enough for their complexity.

Furthermore, bringing your resources together might also mean that you will have to purchase new equipment, new technology, or new material.

When selecting your resources, be sure you are very clear about what you are looking for - be it experience or skill in the case of a new employee or be it features in the case of a new piece of technology, for example.

## Share the Knowledge

As we were mentioning earlier in this book, you need to be a mentor for your team. As the one who holds the know-how in the art of Lean Six Sigma, you should make sure to share its philosophy and methodology with those around you.

Furthermore, you should also aim to continuously improve yourself in this methodology, and then bring back your knowledge. This is a long-term goal, though - for now, focus on the proper implementation of the information and techniques you have at the moment.

## Define the Ownership

The Lean Six Sigma ownership **must** go to someone - it might be you; it might be one of your PMs, or it might be one of the executives in the company. Whoever it is, it is important to establish the ownership right from the very beginning.

## Measure the Processes

Lean Six Sigma will only work when applied to processes that can be measured. Without measurement, there's no such thing as improvement. Moreover, your measurement system should be quite standardized, and it should help you determine the baseline performance of your processes.

The key to successfully measuring data is to make sure the quality of the data is at its highest.

## Create a Governance Program

Your program should be fully governed if you want to be able to sustain the momentum. Any kind of poor governance mistake (too much governance, too little) can lead to success when it comes to Lean Six Sigma implementation.

## Reward and Recognition

As the person managing the Lean Six Sigma implementation, you are more than a teacher: you are a leader and a mentor.

If you want to make sure your team will follow you out of respect and appreciation, rather than simply because they "received some orders from above," you should always encourage them. Reward and recognition are crucial in Lean Six Sigma - both through its implementation and through its use.

## MISTAKES TO AVOID WHEN IMPLEMENTING LEAN SIX SIGMA METHODOLOGY

Here are the main mistakes you should avoid when implementing Lean Six Sigma in your organization:

## Poor leadership.

As a leader, you must hold the knowledge, and you must be willing to share it and mentor those in your team as well. Apathy just doesn't bode well with Lean Six Sigma, precisely because this entire method relies a fully motivated team, a team that can listen, and a team that wants to do better not because KPIs are hovering above them but because they are inspired to do so.

Leadership in Lean Six Sigma is a source of support, a source of information, and a source of motivation. Team members should come to their leader to seek advice, and leaders should, in their turn, emphasize the importance of implementing the main Lean Six Sigma concepts.

The more motivated your team is, the more efficient your process will be!

## Poor deployment strategy.

Like everything new, Lean Six Sigma should not happen overnight - you should carefully deploy it so that you can see the best of it. If your deployment is poor from the very beginning, you will most likely end up failing. To make sure you deploy Lean Six Sigma properly, you should constantly analyze the way things are going with its deployment and implementation, and you should always be aware of any problems you might have. The sooner you can implement the necessary changes, the better it will be for everyone: for you, for your higher management, and your team members as well.

## Focusing too much on training and titles.

The hierarchical structure of Lean Six Sigma is very well built, and every type of "belt" holds a different set of responsibilities. It is only natural that you want to advance and grow on this hierarchy - but when you have just started the deployment and implementation of Lean Six Sigma, you don't have to focus on constantly growing your status and changing the color of your belt. Instead, focus on applying what you know now and take it slow when it comes to achieving new certifications. This will allow you to concentrate on making Lean Six Sigma work for your team and on truly making the most out of it.

## Putting too much pressure on the team members.

Yes, you want your deployment to be successful but straining your team members (and much less without helping them understand the benefits of this) will only lead to exhaustion, frustration, and a break in the project. Make sure you align the company goals with those of the individuals working in your team and with those of the Lean Six Sigma deployment. Balance is key!

## Not knowing your resources.

Every Lean Six Sigma project is a team effort - so, you should first and foremost make sure you have an actual team to work with. Most often, the "Champion" is the one that will handle the resources in a Lean Six Sigma project. However, as a project manager, you will also have to make sure you have enough skilled workforce in your team to accomplish your goals, as well as make sure that they will stay there for the entire duration of the Lean Six Sigma deployment.

## Not minding the actual business impact

You cannot manage a Lean Six Sigma project properly if you don't know the actual impact it will have on the business.

## Not having the support of the higher management and the other stakeholders.

Lean Six Sigma is a bit of a disruption in the "normal" way of doing things - so you must have the support you need before you begin. Getting the key stakeholders on your side will help you prioritize the deployment and implementation, and it will help set clear goals and expectations for the team as well.

## **Lack of responsibility taking.**

Lean Six Sigma is a collaborative effort, indeed. However, every single participant in the project should take responsibility for the things they do. Without this, you will not be able to foster an ambiance of growth and prosperity within your team, and the Lean Six Sigma will eventually fail. Encourage people to take responsibility even when they make mistakes by being gentle in explaining them and by focusing on improvement, rather than reprimand.

# Chapter 13:
# Tips for a Successful Lean Six Sigma Implementation

Keeping these tips in mind will most likely improve your chances of success in Lean Six Sigma implementation. However, there are times when you may not know exactly what to do to ensure you get the most out of Six Sigma. Some of the tips that you should follow when you first get started include:

### BEHAVIOR IS JUST AS CRUCIAL TOOLS.

You might need the right tools when implementing the Lean Six Sigma method. And while you should make sure you have them with you when you start the implementation, it is also quite important to make sure that you and your team's behavior is fully aligned with the values of Lean Six Sigma.

The main mindset people will most likely have to change is related to the fact that most of us are tempted to find a workaround when we encounter a problem. However, Lean Six Sigma advocates for the exact opposite: facing the problems and logically solving them.

## BRING LEAN SIX SIGMA TO THE CORE OF YOUR BUSINESS.

This might be difficult at first but if you get your Champion on board and if you ask him to lobby for your business, you can bring Lean Six Sigma to the core of your business. The main reason this will work out well is that Lean Six Sigma will "irradiate" the knowledge and the methods you should get familiar with.

## TAKE THE TOP-DOWN APPROACH.

This means that you should not implement Lean Six Sigma from the lower levels of the organization to the highest. Believe it or not, a lot of senior managers and executives are these days much more friendly when it comes to the implementation of systems and methods (and more specifically so when these systems can be appreciated by higher management.

## WHEN YOU ARE JUST STARTING, TAKE SMALLER PROJECTS

The ones that have a high profile and can provide you with a quick win. This will encourage you and your team to understand that lean Six Sigma can give you the very best results.

Your company culture cannot be fully in accordance with the ideal Lean Six Sigma standards. Therefore, acknowledge the fact that the ideal company culture may not be fully attainable. Aim for what is doable and go with it! The company culture will change under the influence of Lean Six Sigma, in time.

## CONTINUOUS COMMUNICATION MAKES A DIFFERENCE.

Always talk to your team, your stakeholders, your higher management - tell them if you have concerns, listen to theirs, and constantly work to make the Lean Six Sigma process implementation as smooth as possible.

## BRING PEOPLE TOGETHER.

If you cannot necessarily bring all the participants in your Lean Six Sigma project together physically, do make sure you create discussion group chats that will help them support each other when they need it. This will foster a collaborative culture, which is extremely important to lean Six Sigma.

## MAKE SURE THAT LEADERSHIP COMMITMENT IS THERE.

Make sure that the top management of the business is committed by getting them trained.

Elect the right person to train all the belts. There are tons of programs out there that promise to be the best but most of them are mediocre. You want to pick out one that will teach your employees and help them to do well when Six Sigma is implemented.

Double-check to see what the return on training investment is going to be. If it is not at least 20 times, then you are going to be wasting money or you may need to find a new project to work on.

## DEVELOP A MENTORING PROCESS

This can make sure that the right guidance is done to ensure that all people are trained. Also, it can help make sure that course corrections are made regularly and that all projects are done on time. Always ensure there is some financial validation of the project. There should be a financial leader who will sign off on how much the project will help the business save money. This can be done during the control phase.

## CREATE A GOAL YOU SHARE IN COMMON

Once you have decided that it is time to implement Six Sigma, the next thing that you should do is make sure that all of your qualified team members are on the same page. This common goal can be shown through an executive directive and it needs to be established for all employees. The point of doing this is to reduce the variability to help reduce waste.

## STANDARDIZE THE METHODOLOGY THAT YOU WANT TO USE

To make sure that your Six Sigma project is going to be successful, you need to have it define a standard approach. If you do not do this, then many individuals on the same team are going to spend their time redefining it again.

## MAP THE PLAN

To make sure that the program you are doing is focused and keeps running on time, you need to make sure that the plan is mapped out completely. You also need to make sure that your teams for each project are identified and that the process is scheduled. The organization needs to be aware that process improvement programs are not going to be implemented within a few days. It can take a few months to a few years to do this. During this time, you must make sure that you invest your resources of money and time wisely.

## SET TIMES TO PRESENT THE DATA

Throughout the implementation of your new program, there should be frequent reviews and audits. This is done to ensure that there is some progress being made through implementation. The data needs to be presented and each team needs to be able to describe their milestones, progress, any roadblocks, and the needs and findings that they have.

## PICK THE RIGHT PROJECT

Go with a project that meets your company goals. There may be many projects from which to choose. However, if you are going to one that does not align with the goals you have for the organization or seems to go against what the organization values, then it should never be picked, regardless of what the Six Sigma process tells you. Make sure that you implement a project that works with your business, or it is going to end up failing, no matter how hard you work in the process.

## EVALUATE THE HISTORY OF DATA AND INITIAL INFORMATION

Imagine reaching the end of your project and finding that the data that was used for decisions were not true. The statistical tool used to ensure that information used in your Lean Six Sigma project is consistent is called Measurement System Analysis (MSA). It costs nothing to check in advance if the project has an adequate database and information, right?

## ESTABLISH PERFORMANCE METRICS

Performance metrics are the popular KPI'S (Key Performance Indicators). In this step, it is worth using any metrics that allow you, at the end of your project, to compare the results before and after. The 6 Sigma, CPK, and OEE indicators are very common in the industrial environment.

## TRUST THE SPONSOR

Every project in Lean Six Sigma has a sponsor involved. This professional is responsible for ensuring that relationship problems and investment needs are resolved as quickly as possible, not impacting the delivery times of each stage of the project. You must gain the trust of the designated sponsor for your project since it is he who will help you with hierarchical and communication problems - if such needs exist. To gain their confidence, to demonstrate autonomy in the subject, and to always reveal in advance the gains he will have in his industry can help.

# Chapter 14: Challenges to Anticipate in Lean Six Sigma Implementation

It is easy to appreciate that you can do better when you are aware of the most common problems that people encounter in trying to effect changes. It is even more challenging when these changes are geared towards perfection as often people look at you as a person who exaggerates things. Here are some of the issues:

### LACK OF COMMITMENT FROM LEADERSHIP

Six Sigma is not a methodology that you can read about once, handoff to the employees, and hope that it goes well. There needs to be a big effort among the whole company to make Six Sigma work, and getting a commitment from everyone in management is one of the most important steps.

If you just choose to use some random people in the business who are available but do not have the right training, then you are already starting the project off on the wrong foot. Moreover, this can reduce how likely it is that the project will be a success. A successful Six Sigma project is going to require leaders who have the dedication to provide money, talent, time, and resources to this new endeavor.

## NOT UNDERSTANDING HOW SIX SIGMA WORKS

It is hard to get a methodology to work well if you do not have a complete understanding of how it works. Some organizations try to do it simply because they think they should. Some do it because they see that someone else was successful, and they want to be successful too. Others just rush into the project because they are so excited but they do not have a firm grasp on what it requires to implement Six Sigma successfully.

## POOR EXECUTION

Even if you have some expert guidance to help with this process, there are times when the project is not going to go well because it was not executed properly. This poor execution will happen when the improvements are not aligning with the goals of the organization.

If Six Sigma is used properly, you are going to see some amazing results. You will be able to cut out wastes, help your customers out better, and make more profits in the long term. However, there are times when a business will take considerable resources to work on Six Sigma, and they will not see the results they had hoped for. Making sure that these top issues are not a part of our project can increase your chances of seeing success.

## PROCESS OWNER NOT BEING TOO ENTHUSIASTIC

Such people may tell you they are with you in the whole change business, yet when you arrange for a meeting to chart the way forward they do not avail themselves.

## NOT BEING ABLE TO IDENTIFY THE REAL PROCESS OWNER

Some organizations are run so unprofessionally even when they are reasonably big, and without properly defined roles it is difficult to tell with certainty the right person to deal with.

## PROJECT CHAMPION NOT RENDERING NECESSARY SUPPORT

If, for instance, you have a Project Champion who was chosen amidst acrimony from some top executives, they may not be exactly motivated.

## FRICTION WITH DIFFERENT DEPARTMENTS

Lack of support from some heads of the department is something that leads to frustration of process implementation. Sometimes the daily routine needs to be adjusted and sometimes downplayed, for the Six Sigma project to continue smoothly. Now, if the heads whose departments are affected are not co-operative, bottlenecks are bound to develop.

## ENCOUNTERING BARRIERS IN LANGUAGE

If you have some stakeholders who do not speak your common language, things are bound to go slower than necessary. This is because when working as a team, some things need to be responded to spontaneously to capture the mood of the moment. But with a language barrier, all these factors have to be ignored as you get a translator to pass the message both ways.

# HAVING PEOPLE RESIST CHANGE, HENCE SLOWING DOWN THE PROJECT

Lack of support from top management. You are doomed from the onset if the organization's executives are not with you a hundred percent. Is there anything you can do without resources authorized by them such as cash, access to company vehicles, exclusive working areas, and all that?

# LACK OF UNDERSTANDING

There are those companies that go for what seems to be in vogue just to be seen as progressive. some are cases of the executive wanting to impress shareholders. And what does that tell you? That they do not comprehend the need for organization assessment as in DMAIC; they cannot visualize how adopting the Lean Six Sigma methodology is going to change the way things work in the company; and even the need for extra resources. In short, you have an executive that is bent on making some cosmetic changes; that is, without changing the status quo.

# POORLY EXECUTED PLANS

It is not enough to have great Six Sigma plans and a great champion. If things are not done smoothly and properly, nothing will fall into place. And the results cannot be great.

# TOO MUCH FOCUS ON THE ULTIMATE RESULTS

Some processes are sustainable while other ways of forcing outcomes are not, and the Lean Six Sigma methodology works through sustainable processes which are measurable and easy to define. So, once you use them to succeed, you will be able to replicate them over time. And you need to know that an organization is not termed successful from an assessment of one year. That goes over a span of time.

## HOW TO OVERCOME COMMON LEAN SIX SIGMA CHALLENGES

### Display wins quickly

You may not be a showoff but you have seen the public fall for the person flaunting success from the onset. Do they take time to evaluate the chances of that success being short-lived? Nay! So, flaunt what you have. Let stakeholders begin to see the positive impact of the project the soonest.

 show the impressive results to the top management fast and you see them fall head over heels trying to inquire if you need any more resources – even without you asking. And the rest of the organization begins to talk about the project with pride and a sense of ownership. This is a great boost for you!

### Try and create a good rapport with all concerned

The thing is: good as you may be, you cannot succeed solo – it is either you and the others or nobody at all. So, the wise; the unwise; the bold; the timid; the cheerful; the grumpy; if you are all in this project, you have got to find a way to work with them smoothly.

If you have never noticed, some people try to sabotage your work just because you do not put them in the loop. It injures their ego and because they have some of those funny personalities, the only way to feel better is to mess you up.

### Resolve issues quickly

Can you just get into the habit of visualizing the anxiety on the other end once someone has inquired into something regarding the project? Curb that anxiety by answering the question or responding appropriately as soon as you can. If that happens to be the product owner, you will be winning his or her confidence. And if that is top management, you will be affirming that they did the right thing to approve of the project. Nobody likes to be kept waiting and you know it.

## Achieve impressive results

Do they say something about actions speaking louder than words? Well, nothing beats this than the actual results of the actions. When your project doubles revenues while not increasing costs of operation, you get top dogs in the industry who are headhunting for go-getters narrowing down to you. And how nice it feels to be hired on your terms!

## Go easy on IT solutions

While it may be tempting to request for some software upgrade or overhaul, this may not be what you need for the quick implementation of your processes. And having that may not necessarily be a panacea for problems of efficiency. So, if you can stick to simple solutions as far as IT goes, the fewer challenges you will face.

## Make use of your Champion

You are much better off referring to the Project Champion whenever you cannot find a solution amongst team members. That is the reason you have been assigned a Champion – better informed and more experienced than the rest of you.

## Ensure you have a project implementing team

This is formed by members of your team who ensure that every activity is going as per plan. In this role, then, they can notice problems promptly and to seek remedies the soonest. This way you do not have simple problems escalating to big ones or even getting out of hand.

## Have charts to indicate progress

The idea is to have people outside your project know what your team has been up to and to get them appreciating the benefit of having the project work. And what a better way that let them visually follow your progress through scorecards or charts? In the end, everyone feels upbeat and your team particularly feels highly motivated.

## Educate top management first

Even before you get to the small fish, it is the big sharks you need to educate in matters of Lean Six Sigma. They need to appreciate the benefits of the methodology and embrace the concept. they need to reach a point of being excited about it because that is necessary to have them facilitate its successful implementation.

# Chapter 15:
# Getting Top Management Support

Top management must be fully onboard before beginning a Lean Six Sigma program. However, there are some instances where improvement efforts are driven by lower or mid-level managers rather than the top brass. The top management may be unwilling to invest the time and money to improve processes when there are many financial pressures to be dealt with. This may make it very difficult for process improvement measures to spread throughout the entire organization. There are two approaches towards turning top management reluctance into support for Lean Six Sigma initiatives:

## STEALTH APPROACH

This is where some managers or departments begin implementing Lean Six Sigma on a small-scale under the radar. The aim is to actualize the significant benefits of improving processes while keeping a low profile. There are several variations to this approach but the general technique is as described below:

- **Identification and clear articulation of the gap that separates actual and desired process performance.** This should be done by a small (1 to 3) core group of people who believe in the mission to improve the process. It is recommended that at least one of these individuals be knowledgeable about Lean Six Sigma. This step should take about 2 days.

- **Articulation of the needs for the project.** The group should come up with reasons why the improvement is beneficial to the organization. These could be financial and customer reasons. They could also be emotional reasons, such as reduced job frustration, workmanship pride, or getting rid of bureaucracy. This should not take more than 3 days

- **Utilization of project selection criteria to assess potential projects.** These criteria include quick payback, the high potential for success, business strategy support, availability of data, and a self-contained process that won't require arbitration from senior management. The team should also consider adding other criteria that will highlight the value of Lean Six Sigma to management. This step should take around 2 days.

- **Completion of project organization.** A champion should be selected to resolve any minor political battles. Every team member should receive training. This should take 1 to 2 days.

- **Addressing the problem using DMAIC where suitable.** It should be noted that the focus is to be placed on the achievement of quick results rather than adherence to the methodology. For example, the team should pick simple Lean Six Sigma principles and tools like waste elimination, check sheets, and Pareto charts. Complex and lengthy tools like FMEA should be avoided. If

DMAIC is used, the team must not take too much time undertaking the DMA phases. This step should include 4 additional people on top of the core group and must take no more than 5 weeks.

- **Presentation of results.** Top management is shown the results and a request is made for implementation of Lean Six Sigma throughout the organization.

## LIMITED INITIAL COMMITMENT APPROACH

The goal of this approach is to fix several problems that are of interest to top leadership and demonstrate improvement quickly. If this is done, it will be easier for senior management to commit to a broad rollout of Lean Six Sigma in the organization. The steps for this approach include:

- **Engaging with top management to identify around 2-4 problems or opportunities.** The team should consist of three core members, with one of them being knowledgeable in Lean Six Sigma. This should take 1-5 days.

- **Collaboratively developing criteria for project selection and then establishing three projects that meet these criteria.** Some of these criteria include: supporting the business strategy, supporting a minimum of one senior management problem, rapid payback, readily available data, high potential for success, and easy establishment of milestones for the long-term projects. This step should involve the core team as well as top management. This should take 1-4 days.

- **Finalizing of project organization.** Some mid-level managers and frontline employees should be involved and trained accordingly. This should take 1-5 days.

- **Identifying the critical stakeholders and creating ways to get them to commit to the success of the team.** This should involve the core group and about 15 others who will be split into three sub-teams. This can take 1-3 days.

- **Where appropriate, DMAIC should be used to address the problem.** As before, the focus should be on the rapid achievement of results and not adherence to the methodology. This activity should take 2-9 weeks.

- **Conducting regular status checks to make sure of project progress and financial gains.** If progress has been made, interim celebrations should be conducted and gifts (cash bonuses, stock options, etc.) awarded. This step involves the improvement team and top management. The status checks are to be conducted throughout the project.

- **Presentation of final results** to senior management and subsequent rollout of Lean Six Sigma organization-wide.

It should be noted that the Limited Initial Commitment approach is not the same as the Pilot approach. Firstly, unlike the pilot approach, this approach has active top management involvement. Secondly, this approach is intended to generate further interest in improving the processes, and therefore, the initial "fixes" are not supposed to be final. Finally, this approach includes a mini-portfolio of diverse projects and Lean Six Sigma tools rather than just a single project. Pilot projects are not as versatile in terms of fixing different problem situations.

## HOW TO OVERCOME TOP MANAGEMENT RELUCTANCE FOR LEAN SIX SIGMA?

- **Ensure rapid results** – The benefits of the project must be seen quickly and exceed costs. The team should try to maintain a timeframe of five weeks' maximum and a 30% minimum return. The aim is to turn the heads of top management, show an ability to keep costs low and generate momentum for future improvement.

- **Use good project selection criteria** – This will help the team pick the best projects possible and demonstrate value to top management.

- **Define project scope well** – The scope should be narrow enough to ensure fast completion and broad enough to bring real benefits. The team members must keep their eyes fixed on the original project goals to avoid scope creep.

- **Set own goals** – A team that sets its own goals will find it easier to stay motivated and committed to the successful completion of projects, despite the daily pressures of work.

- **Get Lean Six Sigma experts** – The team must find people, whether internally or externally, who understand how to use Lean Six Sigma principles. This will increase the chances of deployment throughout the organization.

- **Monitor interim progress** – It is important to create a work plan that has key milestones, clear deliverables, and allocates responsibilities. This will ensure fast and high-quality results.

- **Target processes that are people**-intensive rather than machine -intensive – Improvement projects that involve a lot of people tend to bear faster results because humans have greater variability than machines. People will not do the same task the same way all the time, and different people will perform the same task in different ways. It will be easier to make quick gains in processes that tend to be people-oriented rather than machine or chemical-driven.

- **Create a conducive team atmosphere** – The way team members interact with one another has a big effect on project success. The project leaders must be able to regularly bring teams together to improve working relationships.

## TIPS FOR ENSURING LEAN SIX SIGMA WORKS FOR THE ORGANIZATION

- **Secure top management commitment.** The senior managers must first be trained by introducing them to Lean Six Sigma. They must be convinced that it is beneficial to the organization.

- **Train and educate all leaders to become Lean Six Sigma Champions.** The Champions should include functional managers, process owners, and the steering committee.

- **Incorporate Lean Six Sigma into the company's next business operating plan.**

- **Choose training consultants who have practiced Lean Six Sigma rather than those who only know how to teach theory.** Get the right consultants for the Belts.

- **Create a mentoring program where experienced practitioners help the new trainees.** This ensures that projects are finished on time and regular course corrections are made.

- **Ensure that the returns are at least 20 times the training investment.** Defining the project well and allocating the right practitioners will help achieve this.

- **Validate the financial metrics of all projects.** The finance leader should verify any financial savings that accrue from the project, and the finance department must check the metrics during the control phase.

- **Start a thorough and genuine certification process.** Once a candidate completes a project and displays an ability to use tools and techniques properly, they should get certified. The certificate should be signed by the Lean Six Sigma reviewer, the finance leader, and the functional manager.

# Chapter 16:
# How to Improve
# Customer Satisfaction

One problem of using the Six Sigma model to improve customer service processes is to search for ways to measure improvement. Customer experience is not quantitative but qualitative therefore, it is difficult to search for the right metrics to monitor progress accurately. As such, the company must choose the metrics for its Six Sigma model.

## FACTORS TO CONSIDER IN CHOOSING CUSTOMER SERVICE METRICS

First, the business must consider variability. It must be able to adjust its metrics to consider the differences between its customer service and the other businesses.

Second, the business must ensure that every person providing customer service is on the same page when it comes to measuring progress. It must create a positive environment within the department to effect the changes.

Third, the business must employ quantitative metrics, if possible. It can monitor the time spent by customers waiting for a customer service staff or the number of complaints received.

Fourth, the business must use sales figures by repeat customers in measuring customer loyalty. It can also use different metrics to measure abstract goals and customer satisfaction.

Fifth, the choice of metrics will depend on the customer service area that the business wants to focus on. As such, it must be able to narrow down the processes to at most two at a time so that it will not overwhelm the customer service staff, as well as those who will supervise the Six Sigma process.

The identification of improvement areas in customer service is just one process of Six Sigma. A business must be able to monitor the metrics precisely and carefully so that Six Sigma will be effective.

## How to Use Lean Six Sigma to Get Good Customer Service

There is a very simple answer to the question posed in this subtitle: simply eliminate the factors that make your customer service bad!

Lean Six Sigma can provide you with the help you need when it comes to this. As an approach that focuses on discipline more than anything, it can help your company focus on creating and delivering products that are as close to perfection as possible.

Lean Six Sigma will help you identify those factors that are critical when it comes to providing your customers with products that are very close to their standards of quality. The efficiency, capability, and stability of your service will be improved as a result of embracing the Lean Six Sigma approach.

## Understanding Customer Needs

The quickest way to gain positive feedback from multiple customers is to just treat the very first customer with care and respect. Once that is done the word of mouth from your very first customer will reach more people and the chain goes on and on. Marketing is something that creates a mutual relationship between a supplier and a customer.

## Problems in Measuring and Improving Customer Service

Customer service is important in most companies. A business allots a large part of its operating margin in service processes. As such, most efforts of Six Sigma are in these processes to improve, modify, measure, and model them. The usual problems in these processes are in the choice of quantitative and qualitative measures that are right to the service process, in particular, and to the business, in general.

Another problem is how to balance the various qualitative aspects with the rates of response that the customers expect. Most clients do not want to answer long surveys. They may decline or abandon them.

An issue in measuring the service processes for Six Sigma purposes is the characterization of a defect, which can be quantitative or qualitative. Data measurement can be continuous or discrete, depending on the context. There must be a conversation from qualitative customer satisfaction measurement to its equivalent quantitative measure.

Usually, a business can rank overall satisfaction from one to seven. If the rank is below six, it can consider it as a defect if customer service is critical in the operations. On the other hand, it can be acceptable if customer service does not play an important role in the business process.

Lastly, a defect can be context-sensitive. A newspaper delivery business must be able to bring the morning newspapers to its customers within the cutoff time. On the other hand, delivery of mail to the mailbox must be within the day for it to be timely. Customers of the Postal Service do not require delivery of their mail within a specific period during the day.

## HOW TO MAKE SENSIBLE MEASUREMENTS OF THE SERVICE PROCESSES

One way to measure service processes is to use the right measurement level. Service processes also use the 80/20 rule, which means that 20% of the processes contribute to 80% of the time it needs to implement the service processes. The rule also means that 20% of customers account for 80% of customer dissatisfaction. If it focuses only on some important elements, the business may be able to generate an excellent result. Detail usually does not create significant incremental value.

Another way to measure service processes is to take into account important variations in the execution of tasks. For example, an underwriter in an automobile insurance underwriting can consider a regular car for a driver with no record of accidents as a regular case. On the other hand, it can consider a customized vehicle or motor home as a special case.

Assessments of the cases for Six Sigma purposes can differ significantly. Not all measurements are applicable to all cases. Therefore, the business must make the necessary adjustments in terms of deciding what and how to measure service processes.

It is also possible for a business to emphasize quantitative instead of qualitative measures strategically. Some businesses can emphasize qualitative measures when their customer service representatives have face-to-face encounters with their customers. On the other hand, they can put more value on quantitative measures if the service processes focus on quick service.

Lastly, a business can emphasize managing support and communication. There are large-scale service processes such as insurance claims processing that require various groups of people. As such, these groups can resist any improvement in the processes through Six Sigma methodologies. These people may be doing the same process for a long time so they may feel confused about their role in the process improvement.

To remedy this problem, the company can offer information sessions to these groups to explain to them the bigger picture. This way, these people will not feel threatened. It is also important that the management provides significant support in the implementation of the process improvements.

## THE CUSTOMER-ORIENTED APPROACH

Large companies like Motorola, Citibank, and General Electric adopted the Six Sigma methodology successfully because they adhered to the customer-oriented approach instead of the product-oriented approach.

The customer-oriented approach has for major steps: quantifying customer satisfaction; gap identification between customer needs and the company's performance level; analysis of why the gaps exist; and developing a plan to eliminate the gaps.

The customer-oriented approach gets rid of mistakes; improves product quality; and initiates product changes. To eliminate mistakes, it empowers the Six Sigma project team to offer solutions in important matters. It aims to encourage employees to do things right the first time.

For assembly line projects, an error can add to the cost of production and can affect product quality. It can influence customer satisfaction directly thereby affecting customer loyalty significantly. For example, if it employs the product-oriented instead of the customer-oriented approach, the Six Sigma model can make delivery time faster by changing the process of packing.

However, a change in the packing process can have an impact on product durability that can affect customer satisfaction.

# Chapter 17:
# The Process Improvement Team

Improving the processes within an organization is not an easy task for most managers. There are numerous responsibilities to take care of and fires to put out. The resources to implement the improvement is lacking in most cases. Indeed, numerous obstacles prevent organizations from effectively deploying Lean Six Sigma. However, one way to leverage available resources and apply the methodology is to assemble a cross-function improvement team.

On the other hand, some organizations choose to apply a management-led initiative, where managers start the process improvement themselves. They meet and discuss issues regarding process improvement and cost reduction. Once they come up with ideas, management communicates the improvements that need to be implemented all over the organization. The recommendations trickle downwards, with supervisors policing the initiative and workers executing the orders.

## DISADVANTAGES OF A MANAGEMENT-LED PROCESS

Compared to a team-led improvement process, this strategy has many innate weaknesses.

The managers who are brainstorming for solutions are not in direct contact with the process in question, which means that they are likely to address perceived rather than actual issues.

Since responsibility for success is placed on management and supervisors, they will have to deal with a bigger workload.

Frontline management and the workforce are ignored and feel no sense of ownership of the initiative. This may lead to a lack of enthusiasm to see the project succeed.

Information moves from senior management downwards, thus creating room for confusion and miscommunication.

## BENEFITS OF TEAM –LED PROCESS

The people who generate ideas and solutions for improvements are those who know the process inside out. They want to see these issues resolved.

Ideas move from the bottom upwards. This makes the frontline staff feel as if they own the process and enthusiastic about the initiative.

It emphasizes teamwork and makes the workforce feel appreciated.

The team can quickly recognize easily implementable solutions, thus saving the organization money and improving the process immediately.

## How to Create a Good Team?

For a team to be successful in its endeavors, it is important to have a good structure and composition.

The team should comprise people who know the process well and are diverse in their thinking. There should be some process experts as well as suppliers and customers.

The team should be manageable in size. Ideally, there should be no more than eight members to ensure full participation by all.

Meeting times should be established in a way that allows everyone to attend.

The first meeting should be about the establishment of ground rules. All members need to be informed about what is expected in terms of attendance and participation.

A team recorder should be appointed. Their job is to record any good ideas that members come up with.

## Guidelines for Selecting Lean Six Sigma Candidates

If a Lean Six Sigma project is to provide the intended benefits, the right candidates need to be selected. The guidelines described here can also be helpful when choosing which Green Belts are ready to transition into Black Belt status.

### Traits for Green Belt Candidates

These candidates must have shown proficiency in starting and finishing projects while solving problems using a data-based approach. Their traits include:

- Interest in Lean Six Sigma – It is critical to have an interest in improving existing processes. This is shown by participation in improvement programs and a proven track record of doing quality work.

- Process orientation – A Green Belt needs to visualize the entire process and how the various components interact to produce the required output.
- Knowledge of the process – You must understand how the project will impact the organization as a whole.
- Passion – The candidate needs to show excitement and dedication in being part of the initiative.
- Enthusiasm to learn – A Green Belt usually learns about many tools and techniques. These need to be practiced, not just during training hours but even beyond. This will only be possible if the individual has the zeal to learn.

## **Traits for Black Belt Candidates**

This role places more emphasis on leadership qualities, which makes it a bit different from that of a Green Belt. Middle managers can make good Black Belts. A Black Belt is required to possess the same traits as a Green Belt as well as satisfy the criteria described below:

- Possess technical skills – This is a critical factor, as a candidate needs to be able to apply high-level technical skills during a Lean Six Sigma project.
- Have business acumen – As a leader, a Black Belt must be knowledgeable about the current market the organization exists in, identify the daily challenges the business faces, and thus push the program in the right direction.
- Be an influential personality – When leading teams, the Black Belt will need to give direction to people, communicate well with the different management levels, and help the organization implement change.
- Possess problem-solving skills – A Black Belt must have proven their data analysis skills in past projects.
- Have a mentorship attitude – A Black Belt is responsible for training and mentoring Green Belts. They are required to provide expertise and help eliminate any potential obstacles. In some cases, they will have to conduct training for Lean Six Sigma awareness.

## PROJECT DEFINITION AND IDENTIFICATION OF ROOT CAUSES

Once the team has been created, the team must establish a charter and define the project. This is a document that explains and quantifies the problem that needs to be solved, the team's goals, and the time allocated for every step in the project. At this time, the team leader needs to identify every member's strengths and interests and assign responsibilities accordingly. It is much easier for people to execute tasks if those tasks are aligned with their strengths and interests.

The metric that represents the performance of the process should be identified. For example, if the team has identified throughput as a problem, then the metric could be defects. A Pareto chart is an appropriate analysis tool for this as it illustrates defects by type as well as the total number of defects. The team also needs to make sure that the metric used is an actual indicator of process performance. Assumptions should not be made as this will lead to wastage of time.

Other tools that can be used during the brainstorming session include a cause-and-effect diagram. Every team member needs to be encouraged to take part. Every idea should be recorded and ultimately rated according to impact. In case any ideas can be implemented quickly, the team should inform the project sponsor so that quick action can be taken.

## PLANNING, MONITORING, AND CONTROL

The team needs to allocate resources to the tasks that will lead to the improvement of the process. Timelines must also be set for every task. The team can use a Gantt chart or a spreadsheet to monitor tasks, members responsible, target dates, and status of tasks. The Gantt chart is a good way to develop an agenda for future meetings. Task progress must be tracked weekly and any roadblocks eliminated.

One of the simplest ways to track the impact that an action is having is by correlating the start date of every task with the performance of the process. Activities that are implemented to minimize defects will display themselves on the control chart as process shifts. As the tasks are implemented one by one, the control chart should be indicating that the process is moving closer to what the team established at the beginning.

The team must develop a transition plan once the goals of the project have been achieved. This should be the responsibility of the process owner.

## THE ROLE OF THE PROCESS OWNER

These people deserve credit for how they used their Six Sigma credentials to help the company. However, there is one group of people who do an excellent job but are never recognized enough. They are the ones who are truly responsible for maintaining the gains of Lean Six Sigma long after the Belts have left the scene. These are the process owners.

The process owner is an individual who is tasked with determining how a process runs and bears responsibility for ensuring that it continues to satisfy the customer and business needs now and for years to come. Every organization that wants to keep the Lean Six Sigma momentum going needs to recognize the role of the process owner.

- They understand the critical aspects of the process. The process owner knows the elements of the output that the customers and the business value the most. They also need to deeply understand how their process aligns with the goals of the company.
- They track the performance of the process using data. The data used needs to be input metrics as well as output measures. Input metrics are useful because they help to predict performance from an early stage. In most instances, the process owner tracks data that is already compiled by other process operators.

- They ensure that the process is well documented, and the documentation is standardized and updated often. An organization must always strive to reduce variations in the way employees operate a process. The process owner is responsible for identifying best practices and standardizing the process to guarantee output quality. The best practices must be documented in the form of flow charts or other visual methods and updated regularly.
- They establish a process management plan that everyone working with the process can see. This plan also contains a response plan in case signs of trouble are detected.
- They hold reviews regularly. These include a process review, where questions are asked regarding customer satisfaction, control of input/output metrics, and persons assigned to deal with any process problems. Another type of review is the process management review, where questions are asked about how effective the process monitoring and managing methods are.
- They ensure that all solutions that the improvement team identified are integrated and sustained in the process.
- They ensure that the process operators are well trained and have enough resources to perform their duties effectively.
- They provide the vital link between the process and customers. The process is the one person who must stay connected to everyone else, whether it is internally or externally.

The role the process owner plays may seem boring and routine but it is extremely critical to the organization. They do not work alone, and the process operators that work under them also help to manage the process. However, at the end of the day, the process owner is who has the authority and responsibility to make decisions regarding the process.

# Chapter 18: Value Addition and Waste Management

In business, a value-added process can be described as a series of activities that meet the following three criteria:

- The activities must in some way change the product or service.
- The customer must be willing to pay for the output of the process.
- The process activities must be performed the right way the first time.

## TYPES OF WASTE

Waste is a by-product that can be produced by almost every business activity within an organization. Waste exists in many different forms – some are obvious while others are hidden.

This can make the identification of waste a problem. In Lean Six Sigma, waste can be categorized into seven groups:

## Defects

This type of waste includes products or services that do not conform to the standards of quality that the customer expects. For example, if the client ordered 1,000 pairs of shoes and the company delivered 1,000 shirts, the mistake in delivery is a defect. The client will reject the delivery. The company wasted time and resources. In some cases, the client may accept the erroneous delivery at a discounted price. It also includes any raw materials that a product manufacturer rejects due to their poor quality. Such factors translate into longer production times and increased dissatisfaction among customers, both internal and external.

To help reduce defects, the company must ensure to use the Six Sigma tools and employ good quality management.

## Overproduction

If there is excess production, there may not be enough buyers to buy the additional quantity of products. The old production belief that a company must always make full use of its resources is not true anymore. This old practice forced the sales team to sell additional products even at a discount. However, this strategy entailed more costs and cash flow problems.

This is the type of waste that occurs when production processes are allowed to continue despite there being no need to do so. Once the production targets have been met and goals accomplished, the process is allowed to continue, leading to the manufacturing of excess products. This form of waste also includes the production of goods before they are required, not to mention the excess transport costs incurred.

Overproduction also causes other wastes like non-value added processing and inventory. At present, smart companies manufacture products depending on customer demand. If the demand does not cause 100% utilization of resources, these companies perform other tasks like factory cleaning or training. They employ task time analysis, demand leveling strategies, and pull production systems to minimize waste.

## Waiting

There is waste when there is waiting. There is no value added when a product waits in line for completion. There is value if this product undergoes processing. Also, there is waste if invoices remain unsigned on the table of the manager. There is waste when an employee waits for his turn in a multi-step process so that he can do his task. This is waste that results from an assembly line or subassembly process that is not moving. In other words, it is a period of inactivity where a machine or worker has stopped working. For example, an employee leaves their workstation to get raw materials yet another employee is waiting to receive a product part from the first employee. The time wasted does not add profitability to the process and costs the organization money.

Waiting is easy to identify and eliminate. A business that reduces or eliminates waiting time becomes more efficient. It can take advantage of pull production and workflow balancing to minimize or eliminate this kind of waste.

## Non-value Added Processing

A company has different processes. However, it may not need many of these processes if it searches for ways to fix the root causes that cause extra steps. For example, it may order an inspection of all its products at least once. Inspection is a non-value added process because if the company requires everyone to do things right the first time then there is no more need for inspection.

A business that uses the Six Sigma strategy can get rid of inspection because the methodology will reduce the defects to three pieces per million. Therefore, there is no need for inspection. Aside from production, services and office processes can also have non-value added procedures. However, it is difficult to recognize size non-value added processes in an office environment. Transactional mapping tools can help highlight these processes.

For example, there is waste if a single request requires various signatories. It can take hours or days to route a single document for signatures. The company must search for the root cause of this waste to enhance lead-time and not irritate management with voluminous documents to sign. Root cause analysis and value-stream mapping can eliminate non-value added processes.

## Unnecessary Transportation

This is where there is excess transportation of products in the form of unnecessary movements within the facility. It is a result of poor design of the production facility, where processing is done by several different departments rather than within one cell environment. This type of waste also includes damage to products during transportation, as well as unnecessarily long transport times.

During transportation, there is no value added to the product. A company must think of ways to eliminate or minimize this waste. Today, the transport of products has become faster. In an office environment the transport of information is also faster because there is fax, phone, telex, and internet. A company can use linear programming, supply chain optimization, and value stream mapping to reduce this kind of waste.

## Inventory

Inventory is also a waste because it can result in different kinds of waste. It can lead to waiting, defects, overproduction, and non-value added processing. It is a result of uncertainty or inefficiency. It takes up space and capital while it sits in the warehouse. In a factory setup, it is the easiest waste to see. This is waste in the form of excess inventory. Capital is needlessly tied up in raw, work-in-process, as well as finished products. The inventory does not add value to the current production order in any way. The main cause of this type of waste is a lack of storage space. The organization should only produce what it can sell according to current customer demand, or else it will end up with excess products that no one wants. This can also lead to obsolescence and damage to products.

However, it is more difficult to see inventory in a transactional or office environment. For example, unread mails are also inventory. Piles of unattended purchase orders are also a form of inventory. Although it is ideal, zero inventories are almost impossible to achieve because of uncertainty and variation. However, it is possible to optimize inventory by handling uncertainties and variations well.

A company can use inventory modeling, capability studies, supply chain optimization, and variation studies to minimize this kind of waste.

### Motion

By limiting motion, a company can minimize the energy and time needed for a process. It may encounter difficulty in reducing motion significantly because it does not have a great impact on the value stream like the other wastes. However, motion is still a waste so the company must take steps to eliminate or reduce it. It is possible to limit motion by time and motion studies. This is waste from excess motion, probably due to employee ergonomics that are not ideal. Employees, machines, and raw materials waste time moving pointlessly from place to place.

### APPLYING THE WASTES TO TRANSACTIONAL PROCESSES

The wastes can be used in manufacturing as well as transactional processes. However, when it comes to transactional processes, they can be applied more simply and logically. For example, assume that there are two departments involved in a transactional process, with an activity conducted by Department A ending up being reworked by Department B. A team is tasked with improving the process to eliminate waste. The team examines the current process and comes up with these questions:

- Are all process activities performed correctly, consistently, and in a sequential manner? Does each activity add value?
- Have the interfaces within and between departments been defined? Are they working? Is it clear who owns a particular interface?
- Are the decision-making criteria clear and well understood?
- Are there any dangling process steps? Some steps could lead nowhere, either because there is no clear customer or process output.
- Does the process include rework to fix defects? Where do the defects originate?

These key questions can help practitioners improve the process. To illustrate how these questions can be used to eliminate the seven wastes and improve a process, the following problem scenarios and their improvement actions are presented:

### **Activity performed inaccurately or inconsistently.**

According to the payment process of a company, customers were supposed to match payments to the right accounts before the next billing cycle. However, this was not possible 10% of the time, forcing the funds to go into a suspense account. The company had to get 16 people to work on nothing else but investigating these suspended payments.

The process was mapped and a total of ten different ways to resolve the issue were discovered. The solutions were explored and most found to be inefficient. The improvement team picked the best solution and all the employees were trained on the new method. The company was able to cut the staff investigating the suspended payments by half.

Improvement actions: Guidance and work instructions were provided. Trained personnel were held accountable.

## Activity not performed in the right sequence.

Employees in most organizations today are required to show their ID badges when entering a building. In some cases, they have to use their badges to access the company's computers. Though similar information is scanned for the two processes, they are usually viewed as distinct processes. The outcome is that the company loses productivity through new recruits or individuals transferred to different departments.

The company decides to combine these two ID requirements and instructs new employees accordingly. Before they start work, HR ensures their security information is uploaded. When new employees arrive for work, they are immediately dispatched to IT and security departments to begin the ID badge process. Then they are directed to sign up with payroll. Finally, they receive their badges.

Improvement action: The sequence of activities was changed.

## Too much cycle time for the loan application process.

A financial institution discovers that it takes 21 days for a loan application to be approved. A loan application form is usually sent to different departments for approval. An improvement team tracked one document and found out that it traveled all over the building. They measured the linear distance the document traveled and discovered that it moved a whopping 5,000 feet! It was decided to locate all the relevant departments around one area of the building. This led to a 4,800-foot reduction in distance traveled. The loan approval period was also cut to 3 days.

Improvement action: Elimination of the biggest non-value-added steps.

## Inoperable interface

A team was tasked with improving the document-scanning process, with the goal being to minimize overall costs. The team found out that one of the document feeders of the scanning machines stored all the relevant information in electric form but the organization still required the documents to be printed and sent to the scanning department. This led to a huge surge in workload for the scanning department, and also cost the company a lot of money in terms of paper. Its carbon footprint also increased. This indicated failure by the company to map the whole process from start to finish.

Improvement actions: Clear definition of the interface and assigning accountability and ownership.

## Improper decision-making processes

Sometimes organizations fail to define the decision criteria that should be used in a transactional process. This can easily lead to variation in the way employees interpret policies. An improvement team conducted a review of a mortgage company's audit process. It was discovered that different auditors used different criteria to approve mortgages and the underwriters were also using diverse criteria. The result was that some people whose loans should have been declined received approval, and some who should have been approved were declined. It also led to time being wasted reconciling audit results.

The team reviewed the company's risk models and credit policies to define terms. All the underwriters were also trained and random analysis checks conducted to ensure consistency in decision-making.

Improvement actions: Clarification of operational definitions, training of employees, and reviewing decisions.

## Redundant Processes

These are processes that may have been of value long ago but are no longer required. They have been in place for so long that nobody has noticed that they are adding no value in a process. This is why Lean Six Sigma Belts need to challenge the status quo and eliminate processes that lead nowhere. A good example is the fact that most organizations have in place a system where expense reports must be approved by several departments. This causes unnecessary delays and breeds mistrust.

Improvement action: Eliminate redundant steps

## Rework Loop

There are numerous cases of rework in transactional processes. One department prepares official documents and sends them to another department. The receiving department discovers that some of the documents have not been filled in properly. This forces employees there to stop their work to fix the problems. This can easily become an institutional problem. The rework loop can only be eliminated by changing the organizational culture. Employees must be trained to take responsibility for the quality of their work rather than always expecting other people to check it for them.

Improvement action: Identify the root causes of rework, eliminate them, and track the changes.

# Chapter 19: How Good is Lean Six Sigma for Small and Medium Sized Companies?

The following benefits can be derived by small and medium businesses from Six Sigma:

- Providing a standard toolkit to improve business processes
- Making processes transparent, manageable
- Allowing fact-based decision making
- Providing a platform for profitable growth
- Aligning organizational and process goals
- Helping to establish a focus on the client
- Establishing a common language and facilitating communication between people and internal suppliers and customers

To ensure the success of Lean Six Sigma and therefore, ensure its great contribution to achieving results, it is necessary to train people with the appropriate profile and we have already proven here that this does not mean there is a need for specific training. Duly trained employees will become sponsors of the program and specialists in methodology and quantitative and managerial tools, which will have a great impact in their areas of action and in their chances of reaching new goals and paths. By committing to learning, the consequences will be visible in your activities. Lean Six Sigma can be a possible system for many, just by wanting and having willpower.

## LEAN SIX SIGMA IN GOVERNMENT OPERATIONS

As problems do not distinguish businesses, they occur in the most diverse economic segments and sizes of establishments and in almost every company there is a need for improvements. In the food industry, for example, there may be bottlenecks in the production chain, which can increase the cost of the commodity and generate several negative consequences for the organization. In the financial services sector, the difficulty of doing the credit analysis of clients can be an obstacle even to the survival of the business, because this segment is very competitive.

## SIX SIGMA IN THE INDUSTRIAL AREA

In the industrial area, a manufacturer of auto parts must have a high degree of accuracy to meet the needs of automotive factories. Otherwise, defective items will represent a major loss to the business. In a credit card company, a challenge may be to increase sales to ensure the financial health of the company. Therefore, practically any type of company lives in search of perfecting some process to leverage its results. What many of them do not know is how to do it.

The differential of Lean Six Sigma methodology in the search for improvements is that it has a very structured method, capable of scientifically proving whether the changes implanted in an organization have resulted in improvement of productivity and quality. Therefore, by having a method, Lean Six Sigma can be applied to different realities with satisfactory results.

When they do not have this methodology, companies tend to want to solve their production system failures. However, many of them take very inefficient and costly paths to the business, such as putting pressure on employees to get better results. Another unsuccessful way of raising performance is to find scapegoats internally but without any scientific criterion of performance analysis. In such cases, the company walks in circles without finding solutions to its problems.

By using an improvement road map and using statistical tools to prove or reject hypotheses, the Lean Six Sigma methodology seeks to combine efficiency and effectiveness in the search for better business processes. From the point of view of the projects, it is much more advantageous to invest in this type of work to solve and to prevent problems than to bear the consequences of perceived failures by the clients.

## SIX SIGMA IN SERVICES

A service provider whose quality is evaluated during the execution of the activity can suffer damages due to defects in the processes. In the case of a bank, if the customer is dissatisfied with something, he can try to solve it at first by self-service, either over the internet or by telephone. If he cannot, he may consider going to an agency to talk to the manager. If this still does not resolve the situation, the customer can complain on consumer protection websites or file a complaint. If all this happens, the banking institution will create a great liability for the institutional image, not counting the possible sanctions of the supervisory entities. Therefore, it is much more advantageous to proactively decrease the rate of complaints than to learn to live with negative results.

## Six Sigma in Health Organizations

Other companies that perform closely with their customers are those of telephone companies and those of the health sector. In these cases, the consumer already forms an almost automatic value judgment regarding the enterprise. Therefore, such organizations should be careful not to sacrifice their business because of a lack of "listening" to complaints and the observation of opportunities for improvement.

In the case of the health sector, the needs of companies are increasing due to a series of factors, such as increase and aging of the population, growth in costs to maintain adequate structure and technology for care, risk of damages to patients, etc. Because this sector deals with the highest good for a person, which is life itself, the degree of excellence in business performance must be enormous.

## Six Sigma in the Public Sector

It is necessary to mention that even in the public sector it is possible to have applications of Lean Six Sigma. Entities and government agencies have a great history of dissatisfaction on the part of users of the services. Cases of friction between these parties are common.

To overcome this dissatisfaction in the public sector, managers must lead improvement policies in their respective areas of activity, to bureaucratize processes and speed up service delivery. proactive initiatives presuppose a certain degree of political will on the part of those responsible for the operation of the public machine, yet they demonstrate that Lean Six Sigma can operate in this sector. In Scotland, for example, the model of improvement is a state policy in the country, so it transcends the political plans of some rulers.

# Chapter 20: Effective Application of Lean Six Sigma

Do you realize that there is a lot that can go right if you view your profession as your business? For one, you will begin to look at the people you are attending as your customers; customers that you value and not people at your mercy. And how does that change your behavior? Well, you begin to look into ways of serving them fast and effectively.

Do you now begin to see the overall impact on your career? The minute you begin to serve your clients fast is the minute you begin to save the institution's time. The minute you begin to offer high-quality services is the minute you stamp your authority over those people you are serving because inevitably, they will find themselves coming back in future for consultancy. So, you do not have to go out to the field and look for clients but instead, they come to you en masse. If you are within the funded category of organizations, do you think you will need to do much convincing to attract more funding? not – the flow of clients is bound to speak for you.

## IS LEAN SIX SIGMA HELPFUL IN TIMES OF APPRAISAL?

If you have been practicing the Lean Six Sigma model of management, and there is an appraisal underway, you are assured of either a promotion or upgrade without much ado. Whatever institution yours is, being upgraded from one level to another one above that is a big plus that comes with material benefits and prestige. If you are a service provider like a hospital, you easily become the institution of choice, a very invaluable position to be in.

## HOW BEST CAN INSTITUTIONS IMPLEMENT LEAN SIX SIGMA?

Good question this one is because theoretical knowledge will only help if it is implemented and implemented well. We begin with structures and systems. You need to know whom to entrust with what.

- Create working teams
- Build teams within your organization and teach them how Lean Six Sigma works
- Organize so that each of your teams has a project that is defined
- Let your team members understand the correlation between every move that they make and the bottom line of the organization
- Train key personnel

Identify key persons within your teams and train them in all aspects of statistics at an advanced level. That way, they will lead the team in the documentation of data and also in data analysis. Surely you cannot tell the extent to which you are deviating from set standards unless you can calculate standard deviation with accuracy.

## USE DMAIC TO TACKLE PROBLEMS

DMAIC is an acronym that helps you to remember the steps to take in tackling a problem. It goes thus:

- Define
- Measure
- Analyze
- Improve
- Control

### Defining the Problem

You see, once you have defined exactly what the problem is, you are one step in the proper direction. Otherwise, as long as you have not put your finger on what is ailing your organization you could spend unlimited resources moving in circles and not correcting the situation.

### Measure the extent of the problem

Here no assumptions are made. In Lean Six Sigma you cannot afford to say, for example, the customer wants bread and we know how bread is made so all we do is bake and deliver to the customer – no way! Workings here are customized. This particular customer may require bread with nuts or dates or anything else like that dotting the inside of the ready bread. The customer may even wish for a certain level of brownness. It is your business, your role, to listen to the customer and write down those specifications.

### Analyzing the Problem

This is the analysis bit where you trace the steps to how you got off track in the first place and how you are doing currently. It is clear you are not doing very well today; the reason you still are not earning as much as you would like. You have not captured the market within your capacity and shareholders are not having a smile worth writing home about. In short, you are not very proud of your overall performance.

Now, you need to be clear if the problem is becoming more serious or it has reached a point of stagnation. That particular analysis also entails weighing your options because every move you make is bound to have an impact on the staff and possibly other stakeholders.

## **Improving the Situation**

Once you have gone through these fundamental stages, it then gets to a point where you have to take action to rectify the situation. Here is where you need to be well focused because you could rub some people the wrong way while trying to improve the situation. But as they say, the finest gold just does not find itself glittering – rather, it absorbs a lot of heat in the process of refinement.

## **Controlling the Situation**

It is the time to ensure you have people to report progress and hitches in short regular intervals. It is also the time to make every team member know the extent of his or her responsibility. That is because if you leave the body of workers to feel like sheep whose work is just to follow, they are likely to watch as things go wrong, and sometimes even fuel a bad situation a little more.

## WHAT TO DO WHEN YOUR SIX SIGMA PROJECT HITS A HITCH

Things can be overwhelming at some stages of the project as not everyone you want support from may be helpful. And sometimes things beyond your control just happen. As the perfectionist that you are your instincts are the try, try again business – not giving up.

# Chapter 21:
# Lean Six Sigma in Government Operations

Do you think governments need Lean Six Sigma? And then you will need to figure out whether this methodology of Lean Six Sigma is even doable within institutions of government. The government is a mammoth institution that is actually a conglomerate of institutions.

The question of whether this methodology of running organizations can do well, or can even be exercised within government can only be answered when you have a clear understanding of what the methodology entails. And that you know. But just to be sure you remember, think about **lean** and what it represents.

# LEAN

This is a set of working methods that are geared towards identifying and eliminating anything that does not add value to the organization. It is just the same way you get the butcher to trim that fat on the meat that you are not going to cook, anyway, once you get home. Why carry it home?

Does the government do well with wastage? No! Wastage of resources can even bring down a government. How many times have you heard of governments being toppled because of a scarcity of necessities? And those placards that begin waving on the streets as a preamble to the more serious action of ousting the government leader include sentiments of government waste.

Here are the two categories of lean the government could take:

- Value Stream Mapping (VSM)
- Kaizen Rapid Process

This is simply a way of representing the steps of waste elimination visually. In short, you could have some form of diagram or chart showing the entire process you intend to follow to produce the most appropriate product or service while spending the least of resources.

## KAIZEN RAPID PROCESS

Kaizen is not originally English but has now been assimilated into business English. Kaizen is what brings the point home when you are looking at continuous business improvement. Kaizen comes from two words: **Kai** – Taking apart; and **Zen** – Making good. Here you get to deal with imperfections as you go along. In Kaizen, the changes are not drastic but are rather small, sustained, and often incremental.

You can appreciate that different institutions within government can opt for different ways of streamlining their operations for better performance.

## SIX SIGMA IN GOVERNMENT

After all, the delivery of services cannot be improved for efficiency without analyzing the prevailing weaknesses first. And in our case, there is DMAIC to base our evaluation on. In short, the Lean Six Sigma methodology of running organizations is as good in government just as it is good in business organizations.

Only beware that the greatest mess in government is within administrative processes. They can be painfully slow, and sometimes ineffective.

The administrative waste in government often comes in the form of:

- Accumulation of pending work – talk of backlog
- Typographical and factual errors in documents
- Work overlap – work often duplicated
- Redundant paperwork– serving no gainful purpose
- Unnecessary process stages
- Long hours of accumulated waiting time
- Movements that can be avoided; purely wasteful
- Unproductive shuffling of paperwork

However, once you modify or even overhaul the existing processes and bring Lean Six Sigma into operation, you end up with government bodies rendering services like they were in business; accounting for every minute of their day and all the inputs that they consume.

This is how Lean Six Sigma does in government:

- Rendering great services while drastically reducing the cost of that delivery
- Streamlining and improving operations by increasing their speed; people's agility; and overall efficiency.
- Building a high-performance working body that is strong enough for the institution
- Managing assets better; reducing risks and actual losses; while delivering real excellence.

Even when not taking on the whole concept of Lean Six Sigma, some government institutions have already begun to implement some strong principles from this methodology.

# Conclusion

Lean Six Sigma is developed from two separate but very much alike improvement methods: Lean and Six Sigma. Although there is a lot of difference in how both methodologies help to attain the organization's goal, both have the same aim i.e. to improve the processing. Both methods when combined produce a better outcome than the one method alone.

In the professional world, certifications, courses, and qualifications are always welcome. Six Sigma certification is an excellent choice in this area. Nowadays, companies must be aware of the construction of a competitive differential to remain active in the market and have a good engagement with their consumers. This also serves the purpose of attracting them through strategies that a skilled employee will easily create.

The effectiveness of the combination of both methods is evident from the experience of the companies who have gained the benefits from them. Though there is a lot of research already conducted on the matter, still more research will be able to identify the problems and challenges that an organization might face. Research should be conducted for every sector separately to give an insight of Six Sigma implementation.

The book has defined all the basics you needed to get started with Lean Six Sigma in your organization. The journey you are about to take is a long one with something new to learn on every step but before we close this book for good, let us look into the aspects that will give a brief overview of the book.

Now that you understand what the Lean Six Sigma method of management is, you can start living it every day. Start with implementing the various aspects of waste reduction. There is also the aspect of problem-solving that you have learned in the form of DMAIC. As you embark on practicing those systematic steps of problem-solving, your processes will be improving and your revenues will increase as a consequence. That will show you that cutting waste and solving problems in the way prescribed by the Lean Six Sigma approach gives fast and progressive results. You will also see the benefit of having more of your people trained in matters relevant to Lean Six Sigma.

With this powerful knowledge, the ball is now in your court. Work towards helping your organization reach its potential and do not hesitate to congratulate yourself for a job well done when you are finally a leading light in your industry!

# SCRUM

*The Definitive Step-By-Step
Guide to Learn Scrum Process FrameworktTo
Manage Complex Works and Advanced Projects
With Your Team and Achieve Your Goals Faster*

By Adam Ross

# Table of Contents

Introduction .................................................................. 693
Chapter 1: Understanding Scrum ........................................... 694
Chapter 2: Why Use Scrum in Project Management? ......... 705
Chapter 3: Scrum Core Roles ................................................. 709
Chapter 4: How to Put a Scrum Team in Place ..................... 714
Chapter 5: Sprint Cycle ........................................................ 719
Chapter 6: Scrum Events ...................................................... 727
Chapter 7: Scrum Tools ........................................................ 732
Chapter 8: Difficulties Faced when Making the Scrum Transition ............................................................................. 735
Chapter 9: Scrum Artifacts ................................................... 738
Chapter 10: Scaling Scrum ................................................... 741
Chapter 11: Agile Estimation Techniques ............................ 743
Chapter 12: Scrum in Project Management ......................... 748
Chapter 13: Scrum Implementation Steps ........................... 753
Chapter 14: Project Planning ............................................... 761
Chapter 15: Release Planning .............................................. 773
Chapter 16: Scrum Key Metrics Breakdown ........................ 782
Chapter 17: Scrum in Software Development ..................... 787
Chapter 18: Scrum Mistakes to Avoid .................................. 792
Chapter 19: Optimizing Sprints ........................................... 798
Chapter 20: Careers in Scrum .............................................. 806
Chapter 21: Tips for Scrum Mastery .................................... 809
Conclusion ........................................................................... 820

# Introduction

Scrum is a framework that guides a team of developers towards creating software that is relevant and useful to the end user by the time of release. Scrum not only ensures that the products are viable, it also ensures that the development team has leverage by allowing members to self-manage and explore the limits of their creativity in resolving problems. Scrum need not be limited to the software world; other teams can take up the framework for their unique production processes.

Scrum is a project development framework which can help an organization achieve all of the above and it is great because of its simplicity. The framework can provide the organization with the best way to coordinate all efforts and resources needed to complete a particular project. The best aspect with this framework is that it can be applied to any type of project under development.

Learning to succeed as a team is extremely important, and these attributes are needed if the project is to be a success. Not just the team is involved; Scrum Framework emphasizes how important feedback from the customer is because it saves time and money in the long run. Any and all feedback during the development stage is welcome, because it helps the product to be the best possible quality before the end of the project timeline.

The following chapters will discuss what exactly Scrum is, the process behind using it, and how it can help you and your business. The last thing is trying and incorporate Scrum into your company or business! Scrum can seem very confusing at first, with a lot of little details to remember. However, it is an incredibly valuable method which can really help simplify your workflow.

# Chapter 1: Understanding Scrum

## What Is Scrum?

Scrum is one of the various Agile Frameworks that is mostly used in developing complex projects. Initially, the Scrum framework was formalized to be used in software development projects, but it can now be applied in any innovative and complex project.

Scrum is a control and management process which cuts through the challenges and complexities of project development to develop a product capable of meeting the business needs. The Scrum Teams are allowed to deliver working products in an incremental manner. Scrum can be seen as a simple framework which provides an effective team collaboration during the development of complex products.

Scrum isn't a technique or a process for development of products, but it's a framework in which one can employ many techniques or processes. With Scrum, the efficiency of product development and management processes can be made clear for project development teams to be able to show improvements.

The framework is very simple, and any individual or organization can choose to implement it easily. The framework can be adopted by anyone, including those with limited knowledge in project management. If your organization develops projects, this is the time for you to adopt this framework. The framework is scalable and flexible, making it applicable to various kinds of projects. If you are developing a project for the first time, this is the right framework for you due to ease of use and ease of adoption. Other members who will be participating in developing the project will also find it easy to learn the framework.

It is essential for the Scrum Team to have the ability to adjust to each of the various changes the procedure will go through. The buyer may change their mind, the Scrum Team could improve just how they wish to finish a job, or the product owner could make alterations on the product backlog.

Each product goes through a lot of changes throughout the procedure, and it is crucial to be adaptable. If you can't adjust, the item is going to fail to be created and the whole system will need to be reworked.

It's useful when there are many different types of projects to complete each project in a timely manner while ensuring the value of the product doesn't change. Scrum has a strong collaborative and connective philosophy, which also helps each project to be completed in the best possible way.

## Scrum Pillars of Improvement

The three pillars that uphold the scrum framework are transparency, inspection, and adaptation.

## Transparency

The success of any project is achieved by getting all parties engaged, working together, and committed to the project's goals and objectives. For this to happen, each member needs to feel wanted and that they are an important asset in the project by having access to all the information that pertains to the project. Therefore, all parties must present the facts as they are and be transparent in their relationships with others which cultivates trust and collaboration.

Scrum encourages healthy communication through Scrum ceremonies within the team and using demos across teams. Sharing information across teams helps engage others in resolving issues or offering alternative methods to tackle particular tasks. It makes sense to share information with other teams in the project or department because you will be working towards the general good.

Transparency also makes it easier to resolve problems. Needless to say, it is very difficult to identify an issue if not all the cards are on the table. However, with transparency in an organization it is easy to follow the course of activities and identify a mishap. If issues are resolved this way without assigning blame, the organization gains a competitive advantage because it is able to address issues very fast, preventing more complications and possible damage.

## Inspection

In Scrum, inspection does not refer to the assessment done by an inspector but the evaluation that is done by everyone on the team. Team members are obliged to inspect the processes, practices, products, people issues, and the improvements being made.

The Scrum users should be allowed to inspect the progress of the development process as well as the deliverables. This way, they can identify any undesirable aspects. However, the inspection should not be done so frequently such that it will interfere with the project development process. It is advisable that such inspections be done by individuals who are skilled. If not done well, a wrong product could be developed which will be rejected by customers. Always inspect the product being developed.

Being critical is not being judgmental, fault finding, negative or looking for someone on whom to place blame. Inspection is only done with the intention of improvement. Scrum's projects are only required to improve with time to deal with the issues that a team could come up with and increase productivity by making incremental changes.

Inspection is done during the daily scrum and the retrospectives and requires transparency within the team and across the organization. Without full knowledge, the inspection would prove difficult.

Inspection does not only benefit the development team, but the product team as well. After a careful inspection of what has been produced so far, the product team may decide to start rolling out the project into the hands of the consumers and get useful feedback. The feedback allows them to make changes to ensure that what is being produced is right and that it will meet needs in the market.

The most important thing to remember when doing a Scrum inspection is doing it in a non-blaming and non-judgmental way. The key is not in finding out whose is at fault; but it is in finding out what has happened, what can be done about it, what the team can learn from it, and how to make improvements in the future.

During the inspection process, the inspector may find that some aspects of project development are not in line with what was agreed. This can result in a product which is unacceptable. This calls for the process to be adjusted so that it can be in line with what was agreed. Such adjustment should be made immediately so that further deviations can be prevented. If adaptation is delayed the deviation may go too far, and it may become hard to correct it.

## Adaptation

Unless the team has all the tools they will need to make changes to what they have done, inspection is pointless. It is not enough to identify and point at issues and mistakes correctly, there needs to be a capacity to make changes. Scrum has a 'fail fast, fail often' policy that teams use to address and uncover issues very fast. It allows the team to see the incredible contribution it is making and only work towards enhancing that.

Therefore, as the project progresses, a Scrum team increases its pace while an ordinary team will slow down and lose interest. Adaptation for the team, just like inspection, means that the team looks at its progress so far and identifies places that would require improvement as a team and how to pursue this success going forward.

Another reason for adaptation is the fact that many factors shift during the development process. There could arise a crisis, new priorities, upsizing or downsizing, leadership change, market disruptions, and world events that will shake up the course of the project. A traditional team would have a difficult time restructuring the already planned work and adapting to the constantly changing realities. The team will have to renegotiate budgets, change requests, make new contracts, and other activities that derail progress. However, teams using the Scrum framework can adjust to changes easily and hence deliver relevant valuable products.

It is critical to take note of the fact that the three pillars are not just useful for addressing problems, they are also used to measure successes and help the teams capitalize on their strengths. The pillars also help teams identify their strengths and take advantage of their competitive advantage.

## SCRUM PRINCIPLES

### Evade formality on Agile projects

Scrum project teams that see the most success are those that embrace creativity and spontaneity in their processes, as opposed to formality. Remove formality in your processes by eliminating and rooting it out where possible. This will be achieved if the team looks for ways to make their activities less formal. For example, instead of having to wait until the daily scrum to ask some questions or discuss issues that can be resolved easily, it is easier to walk over to a team member and ask the question directly.

### Act and think as a team

Team members work for the benefit of the entire team and hence should work towards ensuring that the team as a whole is productive. Whenever individual performance metrics are introduced in a team, collaboration, communication, and performance go down. Instead, team members should seek to work as a team through failures and successes. In a Scrum project, the responsibility of working towards the goal of the project, defining the scope, and sticking to the assigned time should be the responsibility of the entire group, not individuals.

### Visualization over writing

Visualization works better than writing in boosting thought and memory. This is because retention improves when you visualize compared to when you write. Successful teams use drawings, diagrams, and modeling tools to help their members conceptualize the project. The goal is to make the material as visually consumable as possible.

Visualization makes it easy to process raw data into information. Simply reading reports on the progress of a sprint is ineffective and unlikely to demonstrate the progress fully. However, adding a visualization such as a burn-down chart increases the ability to retain information and allows the team to measure the project against trends and timelines. It is also easier to identify problem areas at a glance than having to read about them.

## Scrum uses

While Scrum was initially used to develop products, for nearly 30 years it has been used in a wide variety of industries to do things like:

- Determine viable markets, products and technologies
- Identify products ripe for refinement or enhancement
- Iterating and producing new versions of products or additions as quickly as possible
- Sustain existing operational environments and create new ones including cloud environments
- Renew and sustain existing products

Due to its rapid iteration process, Scrum has been used extensively when it comes to developing hardware, software, embedded software and the like. It has also been used for almost everything, including autonomous vehicle creation, governments, schools, marketing strategies and organizational operations too numerous to mention.

While it was created nearly 30 years ago, as the interactions between environmental, market and technological complexities have grown; Scrum has proved its utility when it comes to dealing with life's complexities on a near daily basis. It has also proven especially adept at improving processes related to incremental and iterative transfers of knowledge.

## SCRUM VALUES

Scrum values are the values upon which the Scrum framework is formulated. These values relate to ethics, which makes scrum from a social perspective, a value system. The values are commitment, focus, openness, respect, and courage.

## Courage

Scrum members work together as a team and feel more supported with all resources available to them. As such, Scrum teams can undertake even the most challenging tasks. It is through courage that the Scrum team can see change as a source of innovation and inspiration. Training, resource provision, and support are essential for any team to remain courageous.

## Commitment

They are committed to show an improvement and deliver a working product. Scrum teams are self-organized, and this requires a lot of commitment. A committed team has a higher chance of achieving a goal.

When team members commit they commit to the team, to quality, collaboration, learning, the sprint goals, self-organization, excellence, and doing the best they can. They also commit to coming up with working software, constantly improving it, adhering to the Scrum framework, creating value, finishing the work, inspecting, and adapting. Challenging the status-quo and transparency are also critical commitments in Scrum project implementations.

## Openness

Due to the empirical nature of Scrum, openness and transparency is very important. It helps the team inspect the facts as they are so that appropriate solutions can be developed. The work, progress, problems encountered, and lessons learned changes in a project due to the unexpectedness and unpredictability of the world.

Openness is encouraged in Scrum projects, particularly in regards to how Scrum teams should work together and express to each other how they are doing. Any team which faces concerns should raise them for handling. Inspection should be done on what is real so that any adaptations made are sensible.

Scrum teams should also be open and ready to collaborate with other teams even from other disciplines within the organization.

## Respect

Scrum teams work together and share their successes as well as failures. They help each other in times of challenges and this brings about respect. Each member in the Scrum should be ready to respect the background and experience of other Scrum members. Diversity in the team should be embraced and respected. Respect should be accorded to the project sponsors by developing the right product. Money and time should not be wasted doing things which were not initially planned for. Any changes to be made to any aspect of the product under development should be communicated to all stakeholders.

## Focus

Focus is paying attention to the most important aspects without being bothered by sideshows, even when they may prove to be important. It is important to focus on what is clear now rather than on other changes and adaptations that may or may not happen in the future. The now is important because it resolves problems that consumers are experiencing at the moment. The future is highly uncertain, and the best lessons for tomorrow are best learned from the issues of today.

The Scrum team should focus on few things each time so that they can work together in a bid to produce excellent products. Due to the iterative and incremental approach of Scrum, the Scum team should be focused. At any particular time, the Scrum team has to be focused on what is important without being worried about what will be important at some time in future. The future is uncertain, so the team should focus on what they know currently. This helps them learn something so that they can show an improvement in the future. The Scrum team has to focus on their work to get things done.

The above values are related to the Scrum ethics. They give direction to the kind of work done by the Scrum team, as well as how they behave and act. Anything done in Scrum, whether implementing changes or coming up with new decisions, should reinforce and uphold the above values instead of diminishing them. Each member should commit themselves towards upholding them.

## SCRUM RULES

No project methodology can be successful without rules, and Scrum is no exception. Scrum rules are the glue that binds the Scrum Team to the roles, events, and artifacts within the overall Scrum Framework. While some methodologies have extremely rigid rules that govern them, what sets Scrum rules apart is that they are more inclusive and flexible in nature.

While some of these rules are guidelines for adopting Scrum best practices, others take the form of general norms that should be encouraged within a project setting. Together, these rules and norms will then govern the interaction between team members and stakeholders.

Here are some key Scrum Rules that Scrum practitioners must be aware of:

- Sprint lengths should be of the same duration
- No Sprint should exceed 4 weeks in length
- Teams shall not take inter-Sprint breaks (Sprints must follow a continuous, unbroken cycle)
- Each Sprint must start with a Sprint planning meeting
- Sprint planning meetings must be time-boxed (2 to 3 hours)
- Each Sprint review meeting should then be followed by a Sprint Retrospective, which all team members must attend
- When prioritizing Product Backlog Items (PBIs or User Stories), no two items can have the same priority

- If there exist any defects in the previous Sprint (Iteration), those must be prioritized for resolution at the highest level in the upcoming Sprint
- Team meetings must be open and fair, with all members (and stakeholders) allowed to express their points of views
- When a team member is facing a challenge delivering his or her commitments, he or she shall actively seek out assistance from others who can support him or her
- Scrum Team members who complete their assignments ahead of time must actively volunteer for additional tasks from the "Open" list
- While rules will certainly help bring order and discipline within project teams, no number of rules can actually prevent chaos - unless everyone on the team abides by the rules.

The key principles behind Scrum Rules are:
- Everyone must be consulted before a rule is proposed
- All Team members and stakeholders must agree to abide by the rules
- The rules must be well publicized
- There should be consequences for not following a rule

Ultimately, these rules and norms are high-level guidelines for project managers to refer to when managing their projects. Common sense should be used when adopting them, and they should be tailored to adapt to a specific project's needs if required.

Transitioning to Scrum requires adjusting to cultural changes and hence new mindsets. And like all change, it will not come easy; but we assure you from experience that as teams fully commit themselves to Scrum they discover a new sense of creativity, flexibility, and inspiration which leads to better and more efficient results.

# Chapter 2: Why Use Scrum in Project Management?

Using Scrum is applying the very best part of software growth, that is a mufti-faceted and creative exercise that actually works best when everybody is doing the share. Additionally, there are many instances when Scrum is able to help a company in quite unique ways. All things considered, perhaps your business is doing all right, and you feel it does not need a change. Nevertheless, think about this – organizations that apply Scrum experience positive changes in their organization's culture. They are more team oriented and create even more quality for the buyers. Would you rather operate a business which is concerned only about profits or one which cares much more for its employees?

Businesses using Scrum teams show results which are greater than normal teams. But how about the opposite side of issues?

Let's say there is a company that may be in deeper trouble and needs help to be successful. If they are prepared to follow the Scrum system they can get back on their feet and back to wherever they'd love to be.

Scrum is a good way to prioritize to do lists into things that are manageable, helps to enhance teamwork, improves communication abilities, and also creates faster results. When working with Scrum, an individual will become more agile, they will understand how to respond faster and ways to react better to modifications that inevitably come their way.

Here are some of the benefits of using scrum:

## Simple to use

Scrum is very easy to use and can be introduced into an organization with minimal hassle. Although there are several roles and different regulations to follow, one person isn't taking on all that responsibility. It's spread evenly throughout the entire group, which makes doing your job super easy!

## Using Scrum Enhances Client Perception

Though clients are only concerned with the time of delivery of the deliverables and not about the methodology employed by the business, they do realize the difference if a business is employing a traditional route to management or using an agile Scrum framework.

## Employing Scrum Eases Management

Scrum streamlines the development process and makes it more predictable and amenable to change. This:

- Allows easier management of workforce
- Boosts client/customer relationships

- Enhances visibility of the entire project management process
- Causes team members to become more motivated and inspired

## Perfect Implementation

Scrum has a defined set of roles, activities, artifacts, and rules. Using everything together, you have the ability to implement your ideas in a way that seems almost perfect! As long as every role and rule is followed, the project becomes an amazing streamlined process.

## Flexibility

Scrum is an adaptable practice. Sometimes you don't always start with all the information but must gather it along the way, which Scrum is really good for. Changes can be introduced during the next Sprint and implemented into the process.

## Reduces Risk

Scrum reduces project risk by creating in increments. In doing so, development cost is reduced and the risk of starting over is lessened.

## Optimize Team Efficiency

Scrum is all about a team that works together and gets things done. By following the correct stages and resolutions, the Scrum Team becomes an unstoppable force capable of creating many different ideas.

## Continuously Improving

When one project is done Sprint retrospective meeting happen. That is when the Scrum Team meets up and discusses any constructive criticism or issues that might have happened during the project timeline. By figuring out the issues at this moment, they can prevent any future ones of the same nature from happening again.

## Employing Scrum Benefits For Your Teams

Scrum management reinforces your team's best work. Scrum's focus on self-direction, collaboration, autonomous decision making, and continuous and immediate feedback benefits your team by:

- Allowing them to discover creative solutions and unlock their true potential
- Establishes a safe environment where people thrive on respect, peer-acknowledgement, and a sense of self-accomplishment
- Team members realize their sustainable pace as a group, allowing all members to remain predictably productive over the long haul.

# Chapter 3:
# Scrum Core Roles

There are 3 important roles in Scrum: The Scrum Team, the Scrum Master, and the Product owner. Each one of these functions carries a certain duty that they must satisfy to enable everything to be successful. Additionally, they have to work very closely together in a symbiotic relationship for the very best effect.

## THE PRODUCT OWNER

The Product owner tends to be focused more on the business side of things, representing the customer and stakeholders. The role itself is represented by just one person, since having a team trying to run things would get confusing.

The item proprietor is likewise liable for managing and posting the item build-up. He is likewise engaged with the arranging of the discharge.

An item Owner is regularly the venture chief or can likewise be a business examiner who has specialized abilities. An effective item proprietor is required to have abundant specialized information and needs to have an area expertise and ought to be effectively open to the advancement group.

## THE SCRUM MASTER

The Scrum Master has his/her attention on the advancement of the procedure and furthermore is known to manage the scrum group. The Scrum Master are the people in control and also the ones which arrive at the big ideas.

It is their responsibility to produce the vision and also hire the Scrum Team to get it done. In reality, nobody else is permitted to tell the Scrum Team what they should do! The Product owner will be focused much more on the business side of items, representing the buyer and stakeholders. The job is represented by only one individual, since having a group attempting to run things will get confusing.

It's a fine line, but an extremely important one! A Scrum Master also has to deal with the issue of being in charge but having no actual power over the Scrum Team. They can keep the team on task, and help to facilitate issues, but can't fire or hire anyone. They're there to help the team specifically with the Scrum but can only work with the team as members. This means that they can't point out one specific person and have that person do something. The Scrum Master's authority has to be over the team as a whole.

To do all these responsibilities effectively, the Scrum Master should be skilled in coaching, moderation, and development know-how. Each skill will be used in various ways throughout the sprints, and it's important that the Scrum Master is capable.

The Scrum Master is answerable for arranging the dashes and organizing the run build-up. He/she is likewise associated with overseeing the improvement process. The Scrum Master likewise helps in recognizing and taking out the obstacles that block the execution of the group

The Scrum Master is answerable for setting up the torch outline and aides in good correspondence among everyone in the undertaking. The scrum ace empowers the gathering to pursue the work process and guarantees that the errands in the dashes are finished on schedule. A Scrum Master can either be the group chief or go about as the task director. A scrum ace is required to have a wide variety of abilities such as specialized skills, problem solving, and people skills.

## THE SCRUM TEAM

A Scrum group doesn't mean the commonplace advancement group. A scrum group has its own extraordinary abilities.

Expressed below are highlights of a Scrum group:
- Cross-utilitarian groups: the group has individuals from different specialty areas so as to help accomplish the goals. Programming engineers, software engineers, designers, investigators, framework administrators, analyzers and so on could be the individuals from the groups.
- Self-arranging groups: the groups accept an approach assignment to be finished and how to finish the undertakings.
- Business portrayal: The business delegate is the voice of the client, and furthermore the voice of progress.
- Build-up driven: work is done according to overabundance.

The duties of the improvement group:
- To accomplish dash objectives
- To set self-up made objectives

- To sort out their time

It is possible for there to be many different Scrum Teams, depending on how much work needs to be done. It's important to keep each team in a lower number to ensure the work gets done correctly, but sometimes there is a larger project, which calls for more than one Scrum Team. It's extremely important for all of these teams to coordinate to ensure that everyone is on the same page. In order for this to happen, they have meetings called "Scrum of Scrum Meetings". Each team picks one member, someone to represent them, and all these representatives meet for cross-team coordination. Having someone as the team representative helps them to be even better at working together to get the project done. It's sort of an elite team that reports back to their own respective teams.

Each individual Scrum Team member has a particular set of skills, and they train each other in these skills, so everyone will know what to do. It means that each team is balanced with many different specialties, which the other members need to acquire at least a little bit of knowledge in. Doing this ensures the project doesn't become hindered, and that everyone can help each other with each project. In order for everyone to work together in a proficient manner, each member follows the same rules, has a common goal, and shows respect for one another.

When first putting a team together, there might be complications along the way. A new team won't deliver the best possible outcome at first; it takes time to adjust to each other and figure out how to work together. Typically, it takes about an average of 3 sprints before the team works out all the kinks.

There are several rules that the members come up with and agree to. This will allow for everything to flow a little more smoothly.

Just as you will find core roles that are essential in Scrum, there are non-core roles. While these roles aren't mandatory for a Scrum task and may not even be as needed as the various other roles, they are now really significant since they can play a major component in the projects. These are the Stakeholders, Vendors, as well as the Scrum Guidance Body.

The customer is the individual who buys the project 's service or product. It is possible for an organization 's project to be for clients within that very same business (internal customers), or may be clients outside that business (external clients). A user is a person or maybe organization which uses the project 's product or service.

# Chapter 4:
# How to Put a Scrum Team in Place

Putting Scrum into action isn't an "all or nothing" proposition. However, one should realize that individual organizational restrictions will hamper the adoption of some of those tips in their entirety. In such cases; adapt, tweak and bend them until they fit your individual needs.

In the real world, Scrum Teams are a collective name given to several sets of roles that are performed by individuals and groups working on a Scrum driven project. The key to a successful Scrum project is to ensure that you put the right team in place, and that everyone on the team:

- Agrees to pursue common goals
- Embraces a common set of rules and norms
- Respects each and every member on the team
- Values all input given by every member

- Without these prerequisites in place, a Scrum project is doomed to failure from the outset.

Scrum teams are, by definition, cross-functional in their setup. That means you will likely have people on the team with diverse skillsets, many of whom have never worked together as a coherent team, and some that will probably only be part of the team for a very short duration before being replaced by others.

It matters not how well one is trained in various Scrum disciplines or if you have all the knowledge of project management on your side; unless you are prepared to be flexible in your approach, you won't get very far in implementing Scrum in real world project settings.

## BUILDING THE TEAM

At the heart of a successful Scrum project is a successful team. And the success of the team itself is not in what individual contributors can do, but in what the team is collectively able to deliver. And therein lies the challenge for Scrum practitioners. One may have the best and brightest individuals assigned to a project, but if they don't, or are not able to, work together towards a common goal their brilliance will mean nothing to the project.

And that gives rise to yet another team challenge; given that Scrum teams are devoid of any formal and specific "project manager" role, how does one actually manage to get a team of individuals, some of whom may never have worked together before, to successfully deliver all of the Product Backlog Items? The answer is in using a bit of human psychology and some cunning and craft.

### The Individual's Mindset

In the real world, individuals who are Scrum project team members are unlikely to respond to some of the stimuli that might motivate individuals in the general workforce. Ideals like "job security" and "promotions" are not something that will drive a Scrum Team member to give his or her best to the team. To build effective Scrum Teams we need to look into the mindset of potential team members.

Way back in 1954, Abraham Maslow, the "Father of humanistic psychology", came up with a pyramid that depicted a hierarchy of human needs. According to Maslow, individuals have 5 sets of distinct needs that must be satisfied. Maslow's findings are important to us today because somewhere along that pyramid we will find what motivates individuals on a Scrum Team. If we wish to build effective teams, then we must understand the mindset of potential Scrum Team members.

Maslow theorized that physiological needs such as food, water and other bodily needs formed the bottom of the human needs pyramid. Next comes Safety needs, which in the context of a project team member might equate to job security, security of income, owning a home and prospering from decent employment. Then comes love and belonging needs which speak to an individual's need for social relationships. The last two types of needs, self-esteem and self-actualization are what should interest Scrum practitioners the most, because that's what will drive Scrum Team members. These are human needs that determine feelings like:

- Self-fulfilment
- Self-contentment
- Self-motivation
- Confidence
- Peer respect
- Creativity
- Open-mindedness
- Dedication
- Commitment

If you want to put Scrum into action in the real world, then it is those individual needs that must be fulfilled so that Scrum Team members can contribute to the project's goals.

## Creating and "Managing" The Team

So, given that Maslow's assessment of human needs theory is accurate, then how does one go about choosing individuals to build a successful Scrum Team?

Here are a few practical suggestions for building the team and making it function effectively:

- Scrum Teams draw strength from collective performance. That means, even if he/she is a strong contributor individually, if a team member is unable to function in a group setting, his or her inclusion in the Scrum Team could be potentially disruptive
- When selecting team members, be sure to ensure that they can be genuine contributors. Individuals that have no value to offer will only be a drag on the team's efficiency.
- Scrum Teams must be built with breadth of expertise rather than depth. Scrum Teams are cross-functional groups. Having three business analysts or four structural engineers with the same experience profile on the team won't work. Identify as many unique skill sets required to deliver all of the PBI for the project, then go about selecting your team

## Team size

Teams that are too small can lead to individuals carrying too much of the burden and therefore burn out quickly but too large a team size can lead to inefficiencies. Most modern day Management Scientists agree that the optimal span of management is between 5 to 8 individuals. It is to avoid all of these distractions that Scrum teams are recommended to be smaller in size compared to teams in other methodologies like Waterfall. While the core team size should be kept manageable, there is no harm in adding temporary members to balance the team's skill set.

A team size larger than that will mean:

- Many more points of friction amongst team members
- Greater coordination and communication overhead

## **Clairty of Purpose and Objectives**

Just as clarity of team rules and norms is important, so too is clarity of purpose and objectives. The daily Scrum meetings should be used as a forum for reiterating the purpose and objectives the team has before them. The more they hear about them the more driven they will be to accomplish those goals

## **Team Dynamics**

As someone who is responsible for forming a Scrum Team, you must also be aware of some famous management theories governing team dynamics. The most famous of these is the Tuckman model which simply stated can be interpreted as: "Teams don't just 'hit the ground running', they need time to form themselves"

Scrum Masters will need to play a big role in encouraging healthy team dynamics. It might therefore help if the Scrum Master has some background or experience in coaching and counseling. Negotiating with individuals is what works for Scrum Team members, not commanding or directing!

# Chapter 5:
# Sprint Cycle

Creating a team of individuals to achieve a thing as advanced as the Scrum procedure can be a tough task. It is required that you make sure that everybody is working towards the same goal, and also involves a certain procedure known as the Group Development Process. This procedure is a five step system which ensures the Scrum team is as effective as they can be.

The first four stages are Forming, Norming, Storming, as well as Performing. These stages are needed for the Scrum Team to develop and applying this method will help them to assess difficulties, find solutions, plan work, tackle problems, as well as provide the very best outcomes possible.

It is interesting to be aware that, especially in Agile application development, teams will display a behavior known as swarming. This is when the team comes together to focus and collaborate on solving a singular issue. This action is adapted from whenever a swarm of bugs is centered on the same event, like a swarm of wasps attacking someone because said person determined it will be a good idea to hit the wasp's nest with a baseball bat.

Using the Group Development Process strategy results in maturity along with a very effective Scrum Team. It is important to remember that at times a procedure done this way can take time. Many businesses are definitely more concerned with quick results and jumping into things instantly, without worrying about just how vital team development is. Using a technique this way is going to lead to good results.

## Forming scrum teams

For a Scrum project to run successfully, the Scrum Master should identify the right team members. A Scrum team should be made up of several members with each member possessing some expertise in a particular field. The members of the development team are expected to be independent, customer-focused, self-motivated, collaborative and responsible. The team should be capable of creating an environment which accommodates group decision-making and independent thinking so that they can reap the maximum benefits from the structure.

The Scrum Master facilitates the formation of new teams.

The following are the steps necessary to form a new Scrum team:

## Initial Meting

In this step, the assembled team has to discuss the roadmap, development vision and high-level features. Initially, they have to work independently on their work and act like a group of people instead of a team. At this stage, there is no clear alignment and trust, so the team members must avoid conflict and focus on agile planning and information collection.

The Scrum Master has to work to promote positive behaviors of the team. Teaching and directive style of leadership is used at this stage. The activities given below are done:

- Orienting all members of the Development Team through a kick-off workshop.
- Creating a conducive working environment capable of aiding collaboration.
- Engaging with customers, businesses and stakeholders.
- Encouraging and guiding the team on how to handle challenging topics.

## Storming

The members begin to air their opinions and challenge any situations they feel to be wrong or unfair to them. Arguments and personality clashes raise tensions in relationships. It is hard to make decisions at this stage due to the high level of uncertainty. The Scrum Master jumps in to help the team members resolve their conflicts and disagreements. The style of leadership changes to provision of guidance through coaching and mentoring. In the storming stage, the Scrum Master has the following roles:

- Facilitating workshops during which conflicts will be identified and resolved.
- Showing the value in diversity and differences and empathizing tolerance.
- Promoting values and principles of Agile.

## Planning the Sprint

Any work that is going to be generated during the Sprint should first be discussed during the Sprint Planning portion of Sprint. This plan should be created in a collaborative fashion and include the entirety of the Scrum team. Sprint Planning should be kept to less than eight hours each month, with shorter Sprints having shorter planning periods as well.

When it comes to determining exactly how the work in question is going to be completed, the development team determines this aspect of the process after the Sprint Goal has been created and the next round of backlog items has been chosen. The development team has complete control when it comes to determining how best to add the chosen functionality to the next increment. This work will naturally require varying levels of effort and work from smaller groups within the development team of various sizes.

Any backlog items that are chosen should all work to deliver on a single element of the products function, which is often reflected in the goal for the specific Sprint as well. It can also be any other type of coherence that serves to keep the development team working together towards a common goal as opposed to splintering into numerous smaller, more personal, goals.

While the development team is in the midst of a Sprint, it should also keep the Sprint Goal and what is required to see it completed successfully in mind. If during the Sprint, the work takes an unexpected turn it is then the responsibility of the development team to speak to the product owner to ensure that the Sprint can proceed successfully.

Daily Scrums are vital when it comes to ensuring open communication between the development team, often to the point that they remove the need for other meetings entirely, thus naturally increasing productivity as a result. They also make it possible for the entire team to be aware of any impediments to the Sprint as quickly as possible. Their daily nature also ensures the team has the ability to make decisions quickly while improving their knowledge at the same time. As such, it is a key component when it comes to the Sprint's ability to improve thanks to adaptation and inspection.

## THE NORMING STAGE

After reaching an agreement and a consensus, the team begins to show cooperativeness and cohesiveness. Each member understands his or her role, and the ground rules are laid. The team members begin to take responsibility and show togetherness towards a mutual success. Due to accountability, they start to understand the contributions of each member.

Now that the team is empowered, they begin to assume authority, and the leadership style is changed to emphasize facilitation and support to the team. The Scrum Master's tasks include:

- Organizing the customer workshops.
- Organizing the external activities so as to increase socialization.
- Developing a community of mentoring and practice.
- Focusing on incremental improvement and constant innovation.
- Preventing conflicts from occurring.
- Helping and facilitating the organization as a whole to support the team.

This stage is actually about cohesion within the team. It is essential for every part to accept each other's efforts and to undertake in community building while making an effort to resolve team issues. Team members should be prepared to alter their prior opinions and ideas when presented with information from various other team members by asking questions of one another. The team acknowledges that leadership is discussed and there's no demand for any cliques. Having all of the members get to find out about one another as well as discuss with one another is essential in strengthening trust, which then contributes to the improvement of the group as a whole.

It is also crucial that you have established rules for the way the team operates in every meeting. The workers have to talk about strategies, like place of the conference, how long the conference usually takes, and what time it begins. They have to discuss how the conference is going to flow and what you should do in case conflicts happen. Inclusion plays a crucial job within the Scrum Team. Every group member must feel that they belong, so they really participate in all of the activities. The primary objective is finding a set of rules that everybody is able to agree to and really follow. Doing this can assist the team to work as best as possible.

The team is going to feel a sense of companionship and relief whenever interpersonal conflicts are resolved. In this particular stage, imagination is high; there is a feeling of sharing and openness of info, both on a private and job level. Everyone feels great about being a part of a team which gets things done. The one downside at this point is the fact that the users resist change of every type and fear scandals that could lead to the future breakup of the team. They might determine the sole method to stay away from said breakup is by resisting forming it in the first place.

## THE PERFORMING STAGE

Once the roles have been established the team is capable of focusing on a similar goal, which will in turn lead to success. A skilled and motivated team working in a self-organized way can address issues quickly. The team is now empowered fully and capable of providing solutions to any problem on their own.

The following are the roles of the Scrum Master during this stage:

- Encouraging a high level of autonomy.
- Supporting the team members to grow in alignment with the project goals.
- Facilitating disengagement activities and development review.

## ADJOURNING STAGE

This stage was not initially a part of the task and was inserted in later years. But because it had been put in at a later period does not indicate it's any less critical! At this stage in time, the team has almost certainly fulfilled the task vision. While the complex side of things is finished, the team has to determine points on an individual level. They have to focus on just how they worked together as a group and see if there can be some improvements which may be made.

The team also recognizes achievements and participation. They could also use this as a chance to say private goodbyes. The team worked closely with each other on a rigorous project. It is essential to wrap things up on an individual level, or else there may be a sensation of incompleteness. And what if the team gets back together on any future jobs? It is crucial they go over the procedure and methodologies that succeeded and also aspects that failed.

The team is able to go through and decide in case there is anything that could be salvaged with a small amount of change. Information gathered during this particular time could even be utilized for performance evaluations. Thus, it is crucial that the team takes this stage seriously. At times it can be hard to stay within the stages. There may be a person that's particularly stubborn, or perhaps some folks simply do not particularly work effectively with others.

There are a few distinct measures that a team is able to take to make sure they build correctly through the various stages. The team has to ensure they change up the duty of team facilitator. Each person must have an opportunity to be in charge as well, as doing this creates a sensation of equality and inclusion. The mission and purpose of the group has to be clear to other members involved. And the quest really should be looked over often.

Individuals are likely to respond much better and are even more accepting of other 's in the case that they feel they have had the opportunity to be heard. Each session must end with criticism that is constructive rather than destructive. It is essential to lift one another up and be useful towards one another rather than putting one another down. And it is also essential to keep in mind that the constructive criticism needs to be about the group approach and be nothing personal. Everyone should contribute as well as perform the work.

The above steps should produce a working Scrum team. Keep in mind that the teams may have to revert to the earlier stages of the model in the case of unexpected market conditions or the addition of a new team member.

# Chapter 6:
# Scrum Events

Scrum projects are carried out through a series of events, which are geared towards producing all of the project deliverables. Additionally, there are other Scrum Events which serve to manage timelines and quality of the deliverables, as well as conduct self-appraisals of the overall Scrum (and Sprint) processes that were followed, and adopt measures to streamline them where necessary.

The Scrum Agile Framework uses artifacts to be able to offer information that is accurate about the product; what occurs while it is under development, the tasks currently being planned, and also the activities currently done. You will find numerous artifacts which could be feasible in a task, though the primary are: The product Backlog which is list of all the specifications, features, functions, and repairs that would must be produced on the item for any later releases. As the product is consumed, feedback is provided and also the backlog changes and gets bigger.

It is actually easy for the Backlog to change totally based on technology, business needs, and market conditions. It is ever evolving; so as long as the item exists, so also will the item Backlog. Usually the things in the item Backlog possess a description, order, estimate, and value given to them. It is not a completed list, and continually changes based on what the item requires at the moment.

The Product owner may be the only person in control of the backlog, though the team does make a thing called Product Backlog Refinement. This is when the Scrum Team provides details, priority order, and also estimates on the list, and determines how and when refinement must be completed. Normal tasks while in the refinement include: reviewing the highest priority products in addition to the backlog, asking questions of the Product owner who has to deal with products which are not necessary much more, writing in items that are new, ranking and prioritizing the things, redefining the approval requirements, refining items to prep for later Sprints; knowledge that the item design may well improve when the backlog emerges. The greater number of information a program backlog product has, the more up the list it is. It's essential to have precise estimates to complete the project.

It is a listing which is customized throughout the process; anytime new work appears; the Scrum team provides it with the Sprint Backlog. Usually things on the Sprint Backlog are deemed not needed, therefore it's likely that various regions of the program may be taken out of the list. Just the Scrum Team can in fact modify the Sprint Backlog during a Sprint. It is created specifically for everyone on the team also allows them to stay on course and focused.

They normally use this info after the task is done. And this info is likewise used-to assist the team to determine the number of Product Backlog objects are selected during Sprint Planning.

The Sprint's objective is delivering Increments which clearly show the products likely functionality when launched, and also an Increment of product functionality is presented with each Sprint. And also, as the Scrum Team usually spends more hours working in concert, the definition of Increment should grow to incorporate stronger criteria for increased benefits.

It is common practice for everyone and any items to get an Increment for any work carried out on them. The primary takeaway from this is that the Product Backlog and also the Sprint Backlog are being used to describe work that has to be completed, work that will bring value to the venture.

Here are the scrum events:

## The Sprint

Within the Scrum Framework, all project activities designed to deliver items in the Scrum Product Backlog are performed via an event known as the Sprint (or "Iteration"). Sprints are usually confined to durations of between 1 and 4 weeks.

The objective of the sprint is to create the ideal conditions so that the project team "sprints" to finish all of the deliverables that are on the Sprint Backlog.

## Sprint Planning

Team members are allowed to freely express their views on whether the commitments can be met, or if they see potential hurdles in delivery. Once the team has agreed upon what is to be included in the current Sprint, they commence discussing HOW to deliver on the WHAT.

The HOW session takes all of the WHAT deliverables and breaks them down into specific tasks, estimates timelines for them, and assigns responsibilities for each task to individuals (or groups) on the project team.

The Scrum Team meets at the start of every Sprint, and also it's below exactly where they determine and commit to some

Sprint Goal. The Product owner provides the item Backlog, clearly shows the tasks, as well as asks the team to buy the tasks they wish to focus on. The Scrum Team also figures out the demands which is utilized to help stated purpose and can be utilized within the Sprint. Additionally, the Scrum Team is going to identify the single jobs it'll take for each particular requirement.

## **Daily Scrum**

A short, fifteen-minute conference which is held every single day in a Sprint and also with the Scrum Master. During this particular conference, the Scrum Team members coordinate on the priorities. They discuss what's most crucial to get accomplished throughout the day, what they finished in the past, and in case there can be some hurdles they may encounter when practicing the present day 's work. Doing this aids the streamlining of everything, and also prevents some problems showing up unexpectedly. The Scrum Master facilitates the Daily Scrum Meetings and participation of all team members is mandatory. These meetings are "stand up" sessions, and should be no more than 15-minutes in duration. If there are significant items flagged during the session, they should not be ignored due to lack of time. "Off line" meetings could be scheduled to deal with such items separately.

## **Sprint Review**

Since each Sprint is meant to culminate with completion of certain deliverables, this implies that the Sprint Review will be held once those deliverables have, in fact, been completed.

Sprint Retrospectives are sort of similar to a Sprint Review, this is a conference which happens after every project or Sprint. Nevertheless, it's not led by the item owner, but by the Scrum Team themselves together with the Product owner. They explain what went well, what changes which are possible that they can make, and also how they can create all those improvements. Additionally, they discuss the way to make the team work more effective in case there are issues taking place.

It is essential to speak up about problems, otherwise, it can create problems later on which could stop the project from continuing.

# Chapter 7: Scrum Tools

Scrum tools are responsible for facilitating planning and tracking in Scrum projects. They provide a single place where the management of the sprint backlog, product backlog, tracking and planning of sprints, conducting of daily Scrum meetings, showing burn-down charts and holding of Scrum retrospectives can be done.

There are various types of Scrum tools. Some of these tools are open source, while others are paid. You can also get distilled versions for some of these tools. However, for you to be able to enjoy all the features of the tool, you will have to purchase the full version. These tools will make it easy for you to complete each iteration. They can also help you deliver high-quality Increments.

The following are the available Scrum tools:

## **Acunote**

This is a fast tool, and it's easy to use. The tool can provide your team with the actual progress instead of wishful thinking. For those who are in need of data-driven management, this tool will provide you with powerful analytics. This tool can also help in facilitating collaboration across the whole Scrum Team. Small teams can use the tool to keep the items to be accomplished. Large companies can use Acutenote to track the work done by many employees. The tool can also be integrated with other tools, such as source control systems, Google apps, bug trackers, etc. The good thing about this is it's an open source tool.

## **Redmine Backlogs**

This tool comes with several features which can help you manage your team effectively. It can help you sort stories in the backlogs. The tool can also give you a mechanism to display burn-down charts. It provides a task board through which you can track the tasks. With this tool, one can track down any impediment for each sprint.

## **Scrumwise**

This is the easiest Scrum tool for you to use. With this tool, you can make the teams happy and productive. You will be able to manage the tasks done by different members and track the way things are being done. The tool facilitates the creation and management of backlogs. You can also plan for sprints and releases and know whether you will deliver an Increment at the sprint's end. You can create a task board which you can use easily, and you will be able to track the events in real time. The tool can help you know whether your progress is on the right track or not.

## **Axosoft**

This is a good tool, especially if you are developing a complex and large project. It helps you assign work effectively to the members. This tool will help plan for your project early enough. The progress of the project can be tracked visually by use of burn-down charts. Finally, you will be able to release the right product in time, which will increase your confidence. Any deviation from the right path of the project will be detected early enough for corrections to be made.

# Chapter 8: Difficulties Faced when Making the Scrum Transition

While there are any number of reasons that could be the turning point when it comes to your decision to transition your team to the Scrum framework, it is important to keep in mind that this transition is not without its share of difficulties as well. This chapter will look at many of the most common difficulties often associated with the transition and discuss the easiest ways to avoid them.

### Team members resisting change

When it comes to the challenges that are often going to be faced when making a Scrum transition, perhaps the most frustrating for a future Scrum master is the covert, overt, passive and active resistance that you will likely face from the team. For starters, active resistance is the easiest to spot as it is often limited to a handful of jaded and grumpy individuals who don't like anything that gets in the way of how they do things. However, if this issue is not dealt with on a one-on-one, personal level then these agitators could generate a galvanizing message that could spread to other team members until there is an active block to prevent the change from moving forward.

Perhaps the most challenging part of dealing with resistance, however, is that it might be a subconscious response that occurs in a team member who appears to have completely bought into the process at first glance. Remember, just because a team member might know that Scrum is the right thing to do doesn't mean that it is the easiest thing to do, which is where the mental disconnect might come into play.

To break through this mental, disconnect, the goal should be to create the feeling within the organization that this type of change is inevitable. If team members understand that Scrum is already a done deal, then they will be more likely to spend less time fighting it and more time learning how to make the change as easy to handle as possible.

Motivation is another key factor, as it is important to create a sense of urgency in the transition as well. Selling Scrum as a way of helping the company which is struggling, whether this is actually the case or not, can be an effective means of quelling doubt very quickly.

## **Misunderstanding of the process**

As the Scrum process is so very different from many of its alternatives, it is extremely easy for team members to become confused, despite their best intentions. In order to help get them in the right mindset, the first thing the team needs to understand is that what is occurring amounts to a true culture change for the company that will alter how every member of the team spends at least a portion of their day. One of the most common misunderstandings that are sure to arise is the idea of deadlines as opposed to estimates, which are very different things and can take some getting used to. It is important to keep in mind that true reeducation involves learning to think of production as a process which means learning to think in increments and manage expectations differently as a result.

## Meetings

Depending on how the workplace was previously broken down, getting used to the idea of a cross-functional team where everyone understands the project can be quite a lot to swallow. If a strict policy on meetings isn't implemented early then you will find that people still attend far too many meetings each day and the team's productivity suffers as a result.

To properly address these issues, it is important that the team does a full transition to Scrum all at once as trying to go slowly will only further complicate the issue.

## Intimidation factor

When teams start managing their own work, it means that each member will naturally have much more responsibility when it comes to decision making, prioritizing, and scheduling which can feel like a lot of extra pressure. To counteract this fear, you need to make it clear that nearly all of these decisions are going to be made by the team as a whole. Another way to make this part of the process seem more manageable is to start with smaller teams right off the bat. This will keep the individual number of moving pieces quite low, which will make the entire process seem less intimidating right from the start. If you have a larger team and you are starting off with smaller teams to make the process more manageable then it is important to also ensure that they always remain as cross-functional as possible.

# Chapter 9: Scrum Artifacts

In archaeological terminology, an artifact describes a man-made object, like a vase or a tool. Essentially, an artifact is something which we people make to be able to fix an issue or even produce something.

Like any good process or methodology, Scrum prescribes certain tools, called Scrum Artifacts, which help practitioners document the overall project. The Scrum Team and other stakeholders also use these artifacts as visual aids to manage and keep track of progress being made on the project as well as individual Sprints (Iterations).

## Sprint Backlog

The Sprint Backlog is yet another powerful tool that helps Scrum Teams stay on top of what needs to be done to accomplish their goals.

The Sprint Backlog provides a visual picture of:

- The PBI (or User Stories) that are scheduled for delivery during the current Sprint
- The list of open tasks that must be completed in order for each PBI to be considered "done"
- A subset of those "open" tasks that have been assigned to a developer and are actively being worked upon
- A list of development tasks that have been completed ("done") When a team member is assigned a task, the task is removed from the "Open" queue and entered in the "Dev" queue, with his/her name alongside it.
- Scrum Teams own and manage the Sprint Backlog, and it is updated daily (often several times a day). It is reviewed during the daily stand-up meeting, and updates made for everyone to see.

## Burn Down Chart

Managing projects requires keeping a keen eye on what's happening, in terms of how work is being finished, and what is expected to happen, in terms of forecasting future outcomes.

This tool helps PMs and other stakeholders see exactly how quickly the Scrum Team is "burning" through the Product Backlog (User Stories). The Burn Down chart is a visual aid that helps show progress made on completing various milestones to deliver the final product. It compares how the team is doing (Real Burn Down), in terms of effort in finishing deliverables. It projects what completion will look like (Estimated Burn Down) if the current rate of progress is maintained and plots the progress rate (Velocity) of the Scrum Team. PMs can use various formats of Burn Down Charts to focus on various metrics, such as "Total Effort versus Work Done"; "Total Effort versus Work Remaining"; "Effort versus Velocity". These views will help the Scrum Master and Product owner decide how to manage slippage (if any), or reprioritize PBIs in a more realistic way.

The Burn Down Charts should be reviewed during each Daily Scrum Meeting, and Team Members should be allowed to comment on why things aren't progressing as planned.

# Chapter 10:
# Scaling Scrum

Scrum was first created as a strategy used primarily for smaller sized jobs. Many thought it had been great but did not truly know if it was easy to scale since it had never been done before. So can Scrum be scalable? It really is feasible, through a thing called Scrum of Scrum Meetings.

Scrum Teams usually have between six and ten members. Nevertheless, if there's a necessity for over ten individuals, then several teams are formed. This is wonderful for bigger projects and needs communication that is open and synchronization between every team. Each group picks a representative, who then meets with all of the various other associates. They update one another about progress, challenges that are currently being faced, and coordinate activities.

How frequently Scrum of Scrum Meetings occur is driven by the color of the task, just how complicated the project is, inter-team dependency, plus the suggestions of the Scrum Guidance Body.

So how can the meetings work? It is suggested the teams have face to face interaction between them. However, that is not very often possible, because numerous businesses have different teams operating in various time zones and locations. If this happens, then social networking and video conference calls may be used.

Since it could be hard to get everybody collectively at exactly the same period, it's essential that important things be reviewed anytime the meetings take place. Before the conferences actually take place the Chief Scrum Master announces the agenda and the separate teams consider and consider other products that have being talked about. Any problems, modifications, as well as risks that have the potential of impacting the numerous teams must be brought up and discussed during the conference. Even challenges facing the teams must be brought up, since there is usually the potential of it affecting several teams. The individual representative from each and every group must update the other teams.

It is recommended to comply with these four guidelines: What work has my team accomplished after the final conference? What will my team be working hard on until another meeting? Is there anything that is still unfinished that other teams want to be done? And, can what we are engaging in affect additional teams? The most crucial rule of Scrum of Scrum Meetings is ensuring there's exceptional control across the various Scrum Teams.

There are many instances of things which involve inter-team dependencies; meaning a single team's task might depend on a different team's delivery of an additional task. Thus, it's essential that each group is open in the communication and everybody works together. Carrying out this ensures the very best results with no problems along the way.

# Chapter 11:
# Agile Estimation Techniques

Within each Sprint, the team can discover ways that are different to decide on a nimble estimation of a gadget. There's no completely wrong way, every team has to choose whichever one is most effective for them. Using any kind of cards, the workers write specific figures on them to vote for an estimation. In case the votes do not match up, and then it carries on with a talk therefore everybody is on board; which helps to keep going until the votes are unanimous. this is a great technique when finding out estimates for a few products.

### The Bucket System

This method utilizes the same number sequence as Planning Poker, but rather than playing cards, they calculate items by placing them in buckets. The bucket does not need to be a real bucket; the team can use some item which will hold the estimates. The team starts by talking about only several of them together, after which uses the divide and conquer method to assign work to themselves. This method is deemed some casual and is beneficial if the info is required rapidly and there's a bigger number of products. The sizes wish with a collaborative and open discussion. In case there's a stalemate, and then the team can vote where size they believe fits best. After the estimate is completed, the sizes may also be given number values in case it is needed.

### Planning Poker

Using play cards, the team members write specific numbers on them to vote for an estimate. If the votes don't match up, then it continues with a discussion so that everyone is on board; and it keeps going until all the votes are unanimous. This is a good technique when figuring out estimates for a small number of items.

### Big/Uncertain/Small

This is a great technique when the Scrum Team needs a much faster Agile estimation. The items that need estimates are put into three different categories: big, uncertain, and small. The team begins by discussing just a few of them together, and then uses the same divide and conquer technique as The Bucket System to go through whatever is left.

### TFB/NFC/1

This technique is very similar to Big/Uncertain/Small but adds the idea of a specific size to it. The sizing categories are TFB (Too F-ing Big), NFC (No F-ing Clue), and 1 (meaning 1 Sprint or less).

### Dot Voting

A simple and very effective technique that is best when used for estimating only a small number of items. Each team member is passed a small number of dots and uses them to show the size of the item. The more dots an item has, the bigger the estimate.

## T-shirt Sizes

The team members put the items into t-shirt sizes: XS, S, M, L, XL. This technique is considered a little informal and is good when the information is needed quickly and there is a larger number of items. The sizes are determined with an open and collaborative discussion. If there is a stalemate, then the team can vote on which size they think fits best. Once the estimate is done, the sizes can also be given number values if it's needed.

## Divide until Maximum Size or Less

The team chooses a maximum size, such as a 1-person day of effort, for each item. They must determine if each item is already that maximum size or is less. If the item ends up being larger than the predetermined size, then the team breaks up the item into sub-items. The process is then repeated with the sub-items and continues until every item is in the minimum to maximum size range.

## Affinity Mapping

This method is about putting together the things depending on how similar they are. Sometimes there should be a talk on the meaning of what similar often means to the team, regarding the products. Affinity Mapping works very best when there's a small number of products, primarily since it is an extremely physical action. Numerical estimates may be contributing to the groupings after everything is sorted, in case needed.

## Ordering Protocol

Using the simple scale of low to high, things are set up in order. After they are within an order, every group member takes a turn creating changes. They can often replace the order of a product by transferring it one spot lower or maybe one spot higher, they'll make use of the turn to go over the product in question, or maybe they can pass on their turn. In case everybody decides to pass and then changing the purchase is done. This method even offers a few variations: The challenge, Override, Estimate, and the Relative Mass Valuation method. Divide until Maximum Size or even Less The group chooses a maximum size, like one individual day of energy, for every product.

They should decide in case every product has already been that maximum size or perhaps is much less. If the product ends up being bigger compared to the predetermined size, then the team breaks up the product into sub-items. The procedure will be repeated with the sub-items and carries on until every product is completed.

Along with these strategies, you will find specific concepts to observe when accomplishing an Agile Estimation. The team should keep in mind that the tactics are claimed to be collaborative, meaning everybody is required is provided at the same time. These methods likewise encourage a feeling of unity; They are created to ensure that no one individual could be blamed for an incorrect quote since it's not possible to trace who estimated what. They are also intended to be faster than regular traditional techniques.

Estimation is recognized as a non-value added activity, therefore these techniques are being used to minimize it almost as it potentially can be. Heading more into this specific, Agile estimation does not involve the estimation of real days or dollars. Instead, points or perhaps labels are utilized, as well as goods are compared with one another, and that stays away from the trouble when comparing anything to an abstract idea.

In addition to these techniques, there are certain principles to follow when doing an Agile Estimation. The team must remember that the techniques are supposed to be collaborative, which means everyone is involved is included in the process. These techniques also promote a sense of unity; they are designed so that no one person can be blamed for a wrong estimate because it is impossible to trace who estimated what. They are also designed to be faster than normal traditional techniques. Estimation is recognized as a non-value added activity, so these techniques are used to minimize it as much as it possibly can be. Going further into this, Agile estimation doesn't require the estimation of actual dollars or days. Instead, points or labels are used, and items are compared with each other, which avoids the difficulty when comparing something to an abstract concept.

# Chapter 12:
# Scrum in Project Management

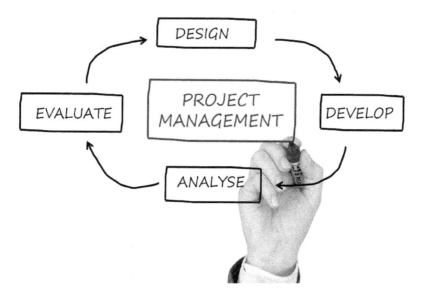

Adopting Scrum means fundamentally changing how the organization perceives clients, employees, processes, project managers, and management. It is nothing less than restructuring your organization's existing culture.

But with Scrum, your organization empowers itself with self-reliant, self-managing teams and a predictable and repeatable release schedule for your projects.

## Project Phases

Projects are typically conceived as a process that must be followed to achieve a final output successfully. This is an important consideration as project managers tend to make an effort to systematize processes to remove as much risk and uncertainty as possible.

While it is true that risk is an inherent part of any project, working with clear guidelines and within a proper framework can reduce a great deal of risk. However, projects tend to have dynamic natures in which anything can happen.

As such, projects generally have five phases. Let's get into detail regarding each one:

- **Planning**. The first phase of any project is the planning phase. In this phase, project managers will sit down the project sponsors and stakeholders to determine what the objectives are intended for the project. This is the part where interested parties will sit down, hammer out contracts, and come to agreements on what is going to be delivered, under what timeline and what the acceptance criteria for the project will be. This phase also considers the formation of project teams.

- **Initiation**. The second phase of a project involves the necessary prep work that will go into putting the project into motion. This could include the purchase of equipment, hiring of staff, and the acquisition of any other materials which will be needed to make the project happen. Also, negotiations may be conducted with suppliers as needed.

- **Execution**. This phase is all about getting the job done. So, the project teams will come together to work and get the project moving. Depending on the project management methodology, you might get some early results such as in the of Agile, or deliverables will be seen until the end of the project such as in the case of more traditional project management approaches. This is the phrase in which the objectives begin to come to fruition.

- **Monitoring and evaluation.** When the project reaches this phase, it is because the final output has been released and is undergoing testing. It is at the point that the final deliverables are tested to make sure they meet the required specifications before the final acceptance of the products. This phase may lead to the customer rejecting the final product and requesting changes before the final product is accepted.

- **Closing.** Once the products have been accepted, then the project will go into the closing phase. When the project enters this phase, any final changes are made to the deliverables, and the customer gives the final acceptance to the products. This is where the ribbon is cut, and all the applauses come. The final release of the product is issued, and there are high fives all around. The project team then begins to wind everything up and either move on to the next project or say goodbye.

## Key features of Scrum Management

- Measurable productivity
- High visibility of progress
- Customer involvement and regular feedback
- Development and empowerment of cross-functional, self-organizing teams
- Predictable rhythm and a framework where inspection and adaption occurs simultaneously
- Time-saving due to reduced bureaucratic overheads (documentations, meetings, etc.)

## Benefits of Employing Scrum Management

By employing Scrum Management techniques, you will gain newer roles, and realize the following benefits for your organization and your role as a manager:

- Transfer of decision making to the people who are at the forefront of development (team-members)
- Employing a customer-centric approach
- Early identification of problems
- Ability to respond to change easily

- Improved team productivity
- Ability to maintain a predictable schedule for delivery

Let's diversify our answer to "Why use scrum in Project Management?", by realizing its benefits to your clients and teams, and its impact on management:

## Using Scrum Enhances Client Perception

Though clients are only concerned with timely delivery of the deliverables, and not about the methodology employed by the business, they do realize the difference if a business is employing a traditional route to management or using Agile Scrum framework.

Primary benefits for clients include:

- Quicker delivery of functional products
- Flexibility to change in client priorities, and agility to incorporate these new requirements
- Bringing value stream back to the business instead of the client
- Employing Scrum is easier for management
- Scrum streamlines the development process and makes it more predictable and amenable to change.
- Allows easier management of workforce
- Boosts client/customer relationships
- Enhances visibility of the entire project management process
- Causes team members to become more motivated and inspired
- Employing Scrum benefits your team
- Scrum management reinforces your team's best work. Scrum's focus on self-direction, collaboration, autonomous decision making, and continuous and immediate feedback benefits your team by:
- Allowing your team to discover creative solutions and unlock their true potential

- Establishes a safe environment where people thrive on respect, peer-acknowledgement, and a sense of self-accomplishment
- Team members realize their sustainable pace as a group, allowing all members to remain predictably productive over the long-haul.
- Employ Scrum Management for a better product lifecycle, all of which is dependent on the efficiency and reliability of your product development lifecycle.

By employing Scrum Management, you gain the following product-lifecycle benefits:

- **Improved Credibility** — Collaborative efforts and inspect-and-adapt loops result in higher quality products

- **Improved Predictability** — Early feedback supports higher predictability of development process

- **Improved Productivity** — Sprint Reviews reduces risks and averts extensive scope revisions. It leads to products that satisfy clients

# Chapter 13:
# Scrum Implementation Steps

If you are done with the current project management methods you are using, or just desire some form of a shakeup to give your organization some life while improving functionality, then it is time to try Scrum.

You will not require any special training on how to implement Scrum because you can learn everything by yourself. Getting to know the basics is easy, but mastering the technique can be a tad difficult. Some people compare Scrum to poker, saying that although you can learn it in under 10 minutes, it may take you awhile to excel at it.

However, do not let that deter you because you do not need to be a master just yet, most things are learned slowly, and you will be proud of yourself when you do. That said, here are some preliminary steps you can take to prepare for the implementation of Scrum in your workplace.

## Commencing a Scrum Project

As you begin implementing Scrum in your project, ensure that you have done the following:

### Assess the need to use Scrum in your project

First, you need to understand Scrum and how it is used before determining its suitability for your project. As detailed in previous books of this series, Scrum is a lightweight framework that is used for managing the process of developing software. Companies use it to boost their competitiveness in the market, have an incremental system for developing what is needed, to ensure transparency to stakeholders, and to enhance the quality of the product by testing the progress made after every sprint.

Scrum is also suitable for companies that want to recognize their risks in time and to implement a systematic risk management process and as a system to make embracing change easier. Scrum makes the working environment fun, helps to keep the costs down, promotes customer satisfaction through effective collaboration, and makes working on long and complex development systems easier.

Once you are convinced that your project will be better off when using Scrum, it is now time to inform and convince the stakeholders of the same.

### Seek the approval and support from the Stakeholders

You will need to identify the stakeholders up-front. A stakeholder is anyone who has an interest in the product but is not part of the team. Approach this group and explain how the project stands to benefit if you implement the Scrum system.

Take the time to train the stakeholders on the Scrum implementation process and clearly explain the potential benefits that would be realized were the system to be implemented. For this to be clear, key stakeholders should be included in almost all demos, sprint reviews so that they can give their opinions, reservations, and seek clarification. Their feedback is quite important.

Each stakeholder should be encouraged to be an active participant in the implementation process and not an obstacle which they will inadvertently become, if not involved correctly.

## Define any possible risks and their significance

Take note of uncertain events that could deter your progress and keep you from realizing your intended purpose. In Scrum, the team and the stakeholders are instrumental in identifying the risks that could affect a project, a sprint, the implementation process, and the program development process.

## Train all your people on how to use Scrum

While it may have been easy for you to learn how to use Scrum by yourself, other people in the organization may need a little help. These people are concerned with other items on their job description lists and will potentially consider learning Scrum a difficult task. Leaving them to learn by themselves also increases the possibility of experiencing resistance from them. Therefore, an introduction and a guide into how Scrum works will go a long way into rousing their interests in the new program. In addition, change always faces considerable resistance, and you proving by example that the change is positive will convince a number to have a positive attitude towards it.

## Plan for facilities

You are already aware that Scrum calls for daily meetings, and by default, you need to set aside enough space where the team will be meeting. This space needs to be one that can support software development, with the required hardware, software, visual aids, boards, charts, seats, and other utilities you may need. Also, ensure that space supports software testing, integration, and simulation.

## Produce the first product backlog

Once you have completed the training and have set up the proper equipment, you are now set to try out the first project and hence, coming up with the initial product backlog. When coming up with this backlog, ensure that you take into consideration all the customer's or the user's needs and preferences. Also, come up with a definite project scope because the items on the backlog are a reflection of the project scope.

You do not need to come up with a list of all the resources that will be required because Scrum leads you on a journey of discovery. In addition, the team that will be working on the backlog items will take care of that, in collaboration with the main stakeholders.

## Write the Project's Storyboard

The project storyboard is a detailed report of the approach the project will take. In software development, the storyboard is a detailed plan of software development. In this plan, including the project's vision, performance goals, deliverables, project activities, release strategy, retrospectives, sprint strategy, demos, daily Scrums, metrics, possible risks, and the mitigation measures to take. The details of the storyboard should arrive in consultation with the customer and the key stakeholders.

## Take note of personnel with the required skills set

When launching the Scrum model, ensure that you get the best of the best talent, because the success you experience on this first attempt will determine whether your project will go forward or not. The team chosen should have full knowledge of all project planning processes. Their input is also of untold benefit especially in the planning for product releases and other processes. The team should also be included in the process of defining and estimating work in the project. Ensure that you collaborate and negotiate with the management so that you can retain some of the best talent through the cycle.

## Execute

Once the planning process is complete and the resources are set in place, it is time to get going. Analyzing the situation too much paralyzes progress and once everything has been determined, there is no reason to delay the implementation itself. The details of the top 2 or 3 sprints should be so detailed that they can be done in one single sprint. The product roadmap becomes a guide determining the order of activities and to check what has been completed and what is yet to be done.

## Structuring the Vision

A vision is a detailed sketch of the solution to be achieved in the future. The solution is developed based on the needs of the stakeholders, the customers, and the capabilities of those who are destined to provide it. A clear vision inspires and motivates the team, the consumers, and the stakeholders. It also acts as a guide directing people towards the desired destination. In addition, the vision enables the product owner to make sound decisions when deciding the direction, the team ought to take in production.

Structuring a vision with the intent of producing a worthy product takes up a lot of energy and time. Below are a number of steps you can take to come up with an effective product vision.

## Decipher the inspiration driving you to create the product

Having a revolutionary idea that introduces a new product into the market is commendable, but this is not enough. You need to have a vision that speaks to everyone involved. The vision becomes the primary goal that the team will be aiming for and the main driver towards creating the product. It provides the reasons for consistency in pursuing the purpose even when things change in the shaky world. In essence, it becomes the true north (or compass) for the product.

To come up with the right vision, begin by asking yourself, "What is the main driver giving me an interest in working on this product? Why do I care about that? What positive change will the product bring to the existing problems? How will the solution I intend to come up with shape the future?" Questions like these are likely to cause you to think deeper about the vision of the project.

## Create a separation between Product Strategy and Vision

The product vision and the product strategy are two separate entities. The vision should not indicate the plans you have made to reach the goal. This separation allows for a change in strategy, which happens a lot in Scrum while maintaining your vision.

Furthermore, the vision is a prerequisite that enables you to come up with the right strategy. If you do not have a definite goal in mind, then it is difficult to know how best to get there. A handy tool that would help you and your team clearly distinguish between the two is a product vision board. The row indicates the vision while the columns below that indicate the strategies to be taken up to realize this vision as you can see in the image below.

## Choose a Shared Vision

One of the best ways to come up with a shared vision is through a collaborative visioning workshop. Instead of coming up with a vision and then trying to sell it to the people, it is easier and more effective to collaborate and make it together. During the workshop, submit the product idea and request the attendees to envision the use of the product. As they come up with different visions, write them down and look for the common theme. Combine these goals into a simple new goal that every member will agree to. This can also be done for existing projects and products.

## The Vision ought to inspire

A vision that focuses on creating solutions for others often creates better and lasting motivation and inspiration. You will find that you relate better to it, especially in times of doubt, better than one that would focus on your own needs. Although money is a good driver, people are pushed to succeed more because they find meaning and benefit in what they are doing than because it earns them something.

Avoid stating the goals of the business as a product vision, and instead, capture the goals when coming up with the product strategy. If unsure, just state the beneficial changes your business and other people can expect from what you are producing, without having to go into details on those benefits. Otherwise, your vision will not be a source of motivation, uplift, and drive.

## Go Big

The best visions are so ambitious and broad that people begin to envision great change. It even influences creativity when coming up with the product strategy. The advantage in this is that the team can come up with different strategies and ways to get to the intended destination, and if one strategy fails, the team can come up with another while remaining rooted in the vision.

## Precise and Sweet

Since the product vision is the definitive reason for coming up with the product, it should easily communicate the direction the product is taking, and be easy to understand.

## Make the Vision the benchmark for all decisions

The vision should guide all decisions and cause everyone in the organization to focus continuously on the true reasons for developing the intended product. Although by itself, the vision is not adequate, it becomes the initial filter for all new ideas and requests for changes so that all helpful changes can be taken in. Anything that does not, is discarded.

# Chapter 14:
# Project Planning

Project planning is not a top-down activity. It is not about the Product owner or the Scrum Master handing out responsibilities or supervising the work after coming up with the development plan on their own. Rather, the entire team does project planning. For example, the section of the team that is handling a particular task is the one that provides an estimate of how much time it will take to complete it. They also determine the features to be executed in each sprint. Therefore, project planning in Scrum is a collaborative exercise.

This list is not exhaustive. The best practices will be a lot clearer to you once you're aligned with the vision of Scrum and its benefits. You'll find that a lot of these points become obvious once you start thinking the right way!

## Treating the Product Roadmap Correctly

A product roadmap is an elite planned document that describes the reasons why the product is being developed. It is also described as a visual summary that maps out the product vision and the strategy to be taken over time.

The roadmap is an important component of the production process for many reasons. It enables concerned parties to come to an understanding of why and how to prioritize certain aspects of the product development process. It enables the manager to understand and better organize the product's strategic vision.

The roadmap is an important tool that aids product managers to communicate more persuasively their strategic vision to all parties including the developers, the organization executives, customers, and other relevant parties. Lastly, the roadmap becomes the all-important guidepost throughout the development process, allowing everyone handling the product to check in regularly to ensure that the products being created still serve the needs and purpose they were intended to.

Some of the things you will want to avoid when creating or using a product roadmap include:

## Mistaking the roadmap to be a list of features

Just like listing several features does not make a product; it does not create a roadmap either. Therefore, when creating one, dwell on themes and not features. A theme is an assurance that you will resolve a customer's problem. It requires you to conduct extensive research to identify the business values, the levels of effort, and the need for urgency in certain areas of your plan so that you can correctly know what to prioritize when creating the roadmap. Themes are also important because they shift your attention from the competition and the individual needs of the stakeholders to focusing more on the value you intend to bring to your customers.

## A product roadmap is not a release plan

The product roadmap ideally provides direction for the next two, three years while a release plan focuses only on the next two or three sprints.

## A product roadmap should not contain any dates

Since a product roadmap does not dwell on releases, it should not contain any dates. Changes and distractions come up every time, and the Scrum model encourages the team to take in all changes in the making of the product. Therefore, if you insert dates in the roadmap and the project timelines are changed as you change strategies, the stakeholders will not be interested in the narrative, they will consider the project a failure. This is also quite damaging to a team's reputation. However, if you cannot avoid dates, make the scope as broad as can be so that the time therein accommodates changes and allows you to deliver before or at the time promised.

## The tool is overrated

The product roadmap tool is overrated. You do not need it to come up with a roadmap. Index cards and a whiteboard are fine, and so are Google Docs, Excel, and Keynote. Choose what best suits you. Only the content matters, the presentation is not as important.

## Requirements

A requirement is simply a function, feature, or service that a user desires. Requirements present themselves as constraints, functions, business rules, and other elements that must be available to meet the needs of the users.

For example, if a customer wanted a custom-made car, the requirements of coming up with this would be based on the features of the car such as a comfortable seating position, a propulsion system, a steering capability, etc. The solutions to these requirements would be bucket seats, an engine and a steering wheel, in that order.

When stating requirements, ensure that they do not point to a particular solution for as long as you can because tying the project down to one thing limits its flexibility. A solution developed too early easily becomes an impediment to creativity, time, and the budget.

Requirements fall into three categories:

## Functional Requirements

Functional requirements are those that express the feature or function and provide a description of what is required. For example, the requirements 'find a venue for the meetings' and 'visit the customer's site' do not indicate how the solution will be achieved. However, 'rent a conference hall' and 'drive to the customer's site' are possible solutions. However, these solutions do not negate the possibilities of taking alternatives. You could walk, fly, or take a train to see the customer. You could also choose to construct a conference hall. Therefore, stating the requirements without providing a definite solution provides room for innovation and flexibility as the project progresses.

## Non-Functional Requirements

Non-functional requirements indicate how well or to what extent the solution needs to reach. These requirements primarily describe the attributes of the solution such as its reliability, availability, security, maintainability, and other adjectives that have to do with responsiveness and performance. For example, availability for 24 hours each day or a 2-second response time.

## User Story

When a requirement is expressed in the voice of the end-user, it is called a user story. These requirements are also called features, epics, and themes.

User stories are becoming more popular in Scrum and other Agile methodologies for many reasons. They help to unleash the true motive behind the requirement. They express the requirement in a meaningful user-friendly language. They focus on priority requirements without having to delve into minor issues earlier on. They express the need from the viewpoint of the people that the solution is expected to influence.

## Steps of Requirement Handling

An honest gathering of the requirements is the foundation of the successful execution of a project. The following steps are critical in ensuring that all the deliverables of the project will meet the expectations the customers have.

### Identify all the stakeholders of the project

The first step towards developing the requirements is identifying the key stakeholders of the project and the effect they have on the outcome. Identifying these stakeholders is easy, beginning from the primary to the secondary and to the tertiary level stakeholders.

You will need to brainstorm with the team members, the sponsors, and the functional group leaders. Involving these people is meant to help you avoid leaving out any relevant stakeholders and avoiding gaps in the requirement handling process.

### Provide the stakeholders with the right questions

Now that you have identified the rightful key stakeholders, it is now time to ask them the questions that will allow you to understand their most basic expectations from the project. Knowing the right questions to ask is an art that you will need to learn, but you will get better at it with time. The questions also help the stakeholders to refine their expectations because many of them may not even understand what they are looking for, but asking them the right questions gets them to the core of the matter. It may take several attempts to get to the right answers.

## Identify the best requirement handling techniques

Techniques like groups, surveys, brainstorming, reverse engineering, prototyping, one-on-one interviews, and direct observation are used as avenues for gathering requirements, each offering unique benefits, which are also dependent on the nature of the project. You will need to choose a suitable technique for the specific project by weighing out the cons and pros of each.

## Put it down on paper

Since Scrum has a free flexible model, it is easy for people to overlook the need for appropriate documentation. In the management of projects and requirements gathering to be specific, details of all errors, results, changes, and conversations held must be written down. Documenting everything that is discussed is the only way to link the requirements and the deliverables. Without proper documentation, it can be difficult to resolve issues that come up during the course of the project. Documentation also reduces the uncertainty that many have regarding the success of the project.

## Perform a proper analysis of the results

Since you have succeeded in gathering and documenting the requirements, you will also need to analyze the results to confirm the accuracy, completeness, and truthful nature of them. Ensure that you prioritize requirements that fall into the operational, technical, functional, and implementation categories. In addition, you should arrange the requirements in order of their significance.

## Confirm the results

Just before you hop behind the project's steering wheel, take a moment to verify the exceptions made, the obstacles encountered, the findings, feasibility, and other significant matters before going on with the project. This you can do with the help of key stakeholders. Confirming the results helps to avoid misunderstandings and uncertainties once the project is on the road. It also ensures that all parties concerned agree.

## Sign Off

Once the results are out and verified by the stakeholders, it is now time to seek sponsors and to have the stakeholders sign off on the project. The signing off is a physical confirmation and seal to show that all parties are fully aware of the requirements and have accepted to the gathering process used, the terms, and the findings made before commencing the project.

The basic process of recognizing the stakeholders, asking them the right questions and working with them to recognize the requirements before proceeding to document, analyze, verify and sign off, are the critical steps that take place at the beginning of project management. These steps also help the stakeholders to keep track of all activities with the hope that the outcome will meet the needs as intended.

## Product Backlog

Although the team cannot do things outside the scope of the product backlog, the absence of a product backlog does not mean that the team will not deliver. Therefore, the backlog is only an option that the team has for delivering the required result, rather than a commitment.

Adding or taking out an item from the backlog should be very fast and cheap because the order of items on the backlog changes with time, as the team develops a better understanding of the process and the expected solution. This ability to reorder the list, adding new items, removing some backlog items, and the ability to refine continuously the product backlog as the project proceeds is what gives it its dynamism.

## Best Practices for the Backlog

- Always have a clear vision of the product you seek to develop as you manage and maneuver the Product Backlog. Any change that you make must agree with the product vision.

- The order that the items in the Product Backlog take will depend on the urgency, dependencies, risk, value, and the amount of experience or learning to take out of doing them.

- Ensure that the Product Backlog can easily be understood and available to all members of the team. This sounds matter-of-fact but you will find that in many projects, the Product

- Make the Product Backlog a responsibility that requires the input of all the Team Members. While it is the Product owner's responsibility to order and maintain the Backlog, the entire team is responsible for what goes into it.

- Ensure that the Product Backlog remains manageable. It is tempting to want to resolve all user issues and to avoid disappointing the stakeholders by continuously adding items or stories to your Product Backlog. However, having to update the Backlog several times can consume quite an amount of time. It is also not fair to say yes knowing that you surely will not live up to what you have promised.

- Let the stakeholders in on the Product Backlog. Always make the Backlog visible and avoid hiding it in some complicated program or tool. If the Shareholders have access to it, they can continuously monitor the project's status and provide useful feedback. In the end, this communication builds trust that proves valuable especially when you have to make difficult decisions.

- Ensure that all the tools you adopt support your use of a Product Backlog. If using a tool brings about too many unnecessary constraints, try another, or better yet, avoid the tools completely. Most times, teams are overwhelmed by the amount of work using a certain tool creates. Therefore, if you realize that a tool is causing too much work, avoid using it.

- When you need to increase the transparency, reorder or adjust the balance of the Product Backlog, employ the Backlog Prioritization Quadrant technique.

- Ensure that at all times there are at least two sprints of the Backlog items that are ready for the undertaking. For a sprint to be ready, it has to be clear about its agenda, practicable, and testable.

## Estimating Backlog Using Fibonacci

All items on the Product Backlog depend on the team's and the product owner's estimation to plan their release dates and to prioritize them. This means that the project requires an honest estimate of how difficult the tasks are and how long it may take before they are completed. Ideally, the product owner should not attend the meetings where the team is making estimations for the project to avoid applying pressure to the team knowingly or otherwise.

The Scrum Framework does not provide any recommendations or tools to be used when estimating the time, it will take to deliver on certain takes. In fact, in the Scrum Framework, estimation is not even done in terms of time. Scrum uses a more complex metric to quantify the time and effort to be used. Common quantification methods are by using t-shirt sizes like XS, S, M, L, XL, a numeric sizing method that is 1 to 10, or by the famous Fibonacci sequence of 1,2,3,5,8,13,21,34. It does not matter what scale you employ because the important thing is that the entire team and stakeholders understand what the readings of the scale mean.

The Fibonacci system, in particular, is a sequence of numbers that might appear incongruous at first glance, but it has a very scientific significance based on the laws of distribution and physics. In this system, a number is the sum of the former two. Here is an illustration: 1,2,3,5,8,13,21,34,5,89,144,233,377,610,987, ...

When using these numbers to show the immensities and sizes of items on the Product Backlog, embrace simplicity to avoid confusion. For example, you could use only the numbers between 1 and 21, and reserve large numbers like 987 for ludicrous requests, like when a stakeholder asks you to fly them to Mars in a cardboard box, for example.

The key to using this system successfully is to embrace relativity. For example, if a Backlog item is a report and although you have done plenty of them by now, this one shows some complexity especially because of the underlying data. Rate this report as a 3.

If the Backlog has another report, compare it to the first. How does it measure? Is it smaller or larger? If it is bigger, a 5 or 8 would do, and if smaller, a 2 is excellent. Do this for all entries and you will end up ranking the items correctly.

To ensure that the Fibonacci scale works for you perfectly, perhaps you could start by picking what you consider the smallest and easiest task on the Backlog. Assign this item 1 then determine which is the toughest or largest task and assign to it number 21. Now, you have established markers, you have sized the Backlog using Fibonacci numbers, and you can begin working on them from the top.

As you get further along the Backlog, it is likely that some items will begin to get fuzzy and start seeming as low priority tasks. In fact, it is never assured that you will get to the bottom of the list. When this happens, do not feel the need to resize the Backlog again because the list is already in priority order. Only continue to work beginning from the top.

## Teamwork is Important

As you size the items on the Backlog, do it as a team. Working as a team also provides an opportunity for new team members to learn from seasoned team members. Characters who are stronger and more vocal are also denied the chance of becoming too overbearing and exerting their influence on the project and its outcome.

Once you are done sizing the Backlog, present the list to the product owner so that they can see the proportional size of the features they have requested and possibly make changes to their priorities if need be. If the product owner asks for a change in priorities, only move the items' position in the Backlog.

## Estimating Backlog Using Velocity

When used for planning, velocity is conveyed as a range taking the numbers 10 to 15 versus 12 (10-15 vs. 12). A range allows the team to maintain accuracy without needing to be too precise.

When using velocity to estimate the Backlog, it helps to have an experienced team because they have useful data such as the average velocity that can be used to make a close to accurate prediction of the time they will take to complete each item. However, sometimes, team members are new and they will need to come up with a velocity range anyway. The best way to approach the velocity issue with this team is to have them come up with two sprints, with two different velocities. A team that is trying to prove itself and improve its performance will likely increase its velocity over the course of time. However, this velocity eventually plateaus. This is normal, expected, and acceptable. If at this stage the team still desires to improve its performance, the team will require a completely different approach, which will include new training, new tools, a slight tweak in the team composition, and any other changes that could increase the team's velocity. Take note of the fact that when first applied, these changes could cause the team's velocity to dip a little, but as the team adjusts to the new way of working, velocity levels will begin to soar.

The stakeholders and the team are warned against using velocity as a performance measure or as a way to gauge the productivity of the team. Instead, velocity is meant to help the team increase the accuracy of its planning and to improve itself internally. Any other intentions are likely to influence the team negatively.

# Chapter 15: Release Planning

Every organization that uses the Scrum model and other Agile methodologies has established a rhythm for presenting its new products and features to the customers. Some release after a sprint, others compile the outcomes of multiple sprints and present them together, while others release one feature after another in a process called continuous delivery. The majority of the organizations prefer waiting for a while before making a release and therefore need to plan for it.

## Release Goals

A release plan is driven by a business objective or goal called a release goal. The project owner comes up with the release goal and ensures that it is tied to the ultimate goal, the product goal. The release goal acts as an indicator of the functionality that customers can expect upon the release of the product to the world.

A clear-cut release goal speeds up the requirement prioritization process because if a requirement is not in line with the release goal, it has to be pushed back to a later goal to which it aligns. All requirements should earn the right to be part of the current investment and those that do not should remain in the Product Backlog until they can offer support to the priority goal. In the same way, if a requirement does not fit the release goal, it remains in the Product Backlog.

## **Sprints**

A release sprint is one whose primary aim is to release the deliverables. It contains items or stories that are destined to finish the uncompleted work and other release-related activities. It is created when the team brings together the last bits of work before the scheduled release. Normally, a release sprint will not require any additional improvement because the items therein have already been through a normal sprint and now only require final touches.

A release sprint takes a different length of time compared to other development sprints. Its length is dependent on the kind of activities involved and the amount of work needed to get the completed product out and into the market. The team determines this length of time when planning the release. Since the activities and the length of time taken in a release sprint are different from that of a development sprint, the velocity concept does not exist here. Release sprints are used to scale tests, conduct focus groups, create remaining documentation such as user manuals, and to improve performance based on the results of the tests. The sprints are also used to ensure compliance with any regulatory requirements and to assimilate the product several enterprise systems.

## Priorities

Prioritizing is a key element of Scrum and other Agile development processes. For example, a Scrum Project Backlog depends on prioritization to determine the order the team will take when working on important tasks.

The issue, however, is that the process of prioritizing itself does not follow any set rules. The more you work at prioritizing, the better you get at it. Prioritizing is considered an art, and just like any other art, there are tricks and tips to learn it.

The default position of a Product owner is that everything on the Backlog is important. However, the Scrum Master has the duty of helping the Product owner rank the items, starting with items of the highest priority. But how is this done in reality? Let us examine this using a real-life though not project-related example.

You could try assigning values to the items, beginning 1 to 5. In the first attempt, go through the items list and allow the Project Owner to assign numbers 1 through 5 to items randomly as he/she chooses. These values are assigned solely based on intuition. If in doubt, assign a 3 and move to the next. Move fast, it will be fun. This first round goes away very fast and you will have prioritized already.

In the second round, take a little bit of caution because this is the refining round. Compare the items which are assigned the same priority and re-prioritize tasks that now appear less important. Those that you are unsure about can retain their positions on the list. When you do this, you will find that refining the previous list is quite easy, and within no time, you will have a prioritized list that carries some relevance.

The last step is the final touch and it requires you to estimate the time it will take per user story. Write this information down. One may take one week while the other will take 7 weeks and another 9 weeks. You will find this even more eye-opening because you now begin to realize the amount of time it will take you to cover the items you have labeled as most important.

However, with a time constraint, try to rearrange this list in the order of priorities.

## **Sprint Lengths**

Little if any advice is given when it comes to determining the sprint length. The definition gives an idea of the length of time but not a definite amount. A sprint is defined as a fixed period of between one and four weeks, and the only advice issued regarding that is that teams should lean towards the shorter time intervals. However, this is not clear advice and teams are left to come up with schedules that work for them.

When using Scrum, particularly the first-timers, it is rational to first experiment with various Sprint lengths before coming up with a definite period that fits the context. There is one trick to going about this: a shorter sprint, one that goes between one and two weeks, will often reveal barriers and impediments faster than longer ones. Although the short span is uncomfortable, they are better at revealing project issues and thereby avoiding them in the future, unlike the longer sprints. This is the Scrum approach because Scrum is intended to bring the problems of the project to the surface.

## **Shorter Sprints**

Lasting between 1-2 weeks, shorter sprints have the following benefits:

- Shorter sprints have short cycles that make planning easier and increase the team's focus and in doing so reduces the amount of 'dark work' and the time wasted.
- Shorter sprints increase the number of retrospectives but still shorten their lengths. That way, the team can try out smaller changes to ensure that the entire process is going on well. This also creates more learning opportunities.
- Since limitations and impediments are highlighted more easily, the team can come to a quick realization of things that could be slowing its progress.

- Shorter sprints force the team to slice its features and user stories into smaller chunks, which enhances the ability of the Product owner to exert control over the process by prioritizing some things and pulling down others.
- The disadvantages of the shorter sprints include:
- Working with very limited time can prove quite stressful at first.
- Some people complain that conducting sprint meetings after just one week is overkill, and not enough will have been done to cover the recommended 2-hour sprint meeting.
- It is difficult to come up with a quality product in only a week or two, most teams can produce quality after about three or four weeks.

## **Longer Sprints**

Longer sprints last between 3-4 weeks. The advantage of this length is that much more can be done in a longer period and the team has a relatively easier time.

The disadvantages include:

- Runs the risk of 'dark work' because new needs and features crop up all the time.
- It can be difficult to plan adequately for each sprint.
- The product owner does not get much opportunity to get the team to make changes.
- This length only allows a few sprint reviews, which reduces the number of opportunities the product owner has to make changes.
- Increases the chances of the team losing focus.
- Problems are discovered and addressed slower than the shorter sprints.
- It can easily lead to the uptake of the waterfall methodology.
- Fewer retrospectives lead to fewer opportunities for improvement.

- Choose between having a longer or a shorter sprint. However, 2-week sprints are the most popular among teams.

## **Planning Sprints**

Doing this effectively requires the owner to take some time away from the team and sort through the requirements, taking out those that do not fit into the same sprint. The requirements left per sprint should be just enough to be covered in the allocated time. The owner needs to be reasonably and consistently ahead of the team.

In Scrum, avoid the scope creeping into and getting the team mired in issues that should not be covered now. Usually, the team will take time to review the issues before they are added to the sprint to give the members enough time to gauge the estimated work to be added. You can compare these valuations against the team's performance in previous sprints using tools like the Burn-down Chart and the Velocity Chart. If you have no previous data to be used to gauge the team's velocity, don't worry, you will have plenty of it once the team starts completing various sprints.

If you choose to move some issues, there are a few factors to take note of. First, you are not allowed to move sub-tasks independently without moving their parents. Secondly, only assign an issue to the current sprint or a future sprint. This means that you cannot move an issue twice; to an active sprint and a future sprint at the same time. Third, an issue will only appear on a particular board, single or multiple, if the issues assigned to it match the filter query of the board(s).

A mistake that keeps recurring among teams happens when a team tries to spring right into action by creating a sprint from a Product Backlog that is yet to be refined and does not have user stories that are actionable at the moment. Others go ahead and plan a sprint without involving the product owner, whose role is to provide insight and input regarding the goals and the work in a sprint. In both cases, the odds of success for each sprint are reduced significantly. A good Scrum Master should guide the team to prevent this from happening.

Scrum teams are also encouraged to spell out complete names instead of using acronyms when documenting the sprint goals, coming up with the definition of done, or when creating a roadmap. It is wrong to assume that everyone will understand what the acronyms mean. Some, particularly the newcomers, may have a hard time extracting meaning from the text. Spelling out the words, instead of using acronyms, causes the members to rethink their use of long concepts and instead of making their goals clear, precise, and easy to understand.

## Burn-down Charts

A Burn-down Chart is a visual tool used for measuring the work that is completed at the end of the day against the projected rate of completion for the scheduled release in a project. This chart is created as a tracking mechanism to ensure that the solution being developed fits within the desired schedule. Its visual appeal makes it popular among people using Agile software, including Scrum users, because team members can easily see and understand the progress report therein.

A Burn-down Chart works well for many teams and many situations. However, teams that make a lot of changes in their requirements will need an alternative chart so that they can practically keep their project on track.

Overall, the Burn-down Chart is a resourceful component of any project because it is a way for the team to measure the amount of work they complete at the end of each sprint.

## Backlog Capacity

The majority of discussions surrounding planning and managing projects mostly focus on the proper way to create schedules and to understand the requirements in the backlog. Although these are fundamental issues, it is important to factor in the role that people play in this development. Projects are done by people with different abilities who are prone to fatigue and whose attention can be diverted by different factors from the main agenda.

If you have a consistent set of persons that see through your projects, which is not always the case, you will need to have an understanding of the amount of work they can do at a given time before you can plan the schedule and the scope of the project.

The Agile approach to projects focuses more on Teams than on individuals. It assumes that the members of the team are consistent and have the right set of skills to carry out the activities of the project. This team orientation means that calculations including those of the resources and the amount of work done are measured collectively rather than on a per-person basis.

The project manager breaks down the work required to implement and validate the requirements into individual tasks based on specifications made in the requirements. Since most tasks are estimated in person-hour units, the goal here is to determine the number of person-hours the team will provide in a specific length of time, like a sprint.

The resource model we use requires you to have the following facts at your fingertips:

- The number of team members
- Numbers of working days in a given period say a week
- The number and length of meetings and activities that will require the attendance of every member, during which no one will be working on the project
- The scheduled off time each member will have during this period
- The availability of work for each member when not attending a known meeting

The rest is simple and can be done using a spreadsheet.

- Get the total number of 'working hours' in the given period by multiplying the number of workdays by eight (estimated number of hours of work in a day).
- From the 'working hours', subtract the total number of hours allocated to team meetings. This will give you the 'net working hours'.
- Get the time off and availability for each team member. Subtract the hours off for each person from the net working hours and multiply what you get by the person's availability to come up with each member's individual capacity.
- Sum all individual capacities to get the team capacity in person-hours. Divide the result by eight to find the capacity in person-days.
- Now, divide the team capacity expressed in hours by the work hours to get the net team resources. This is now the number of effective full-time people you have on the team.

# Chapter 16:
# Scrum Key Metrics Breakdown

Metrics are important tools with Scrum because they are used during the planning, adapting, inspecting, and understanding the progress a project has made over time. Determining the success or failure rate enables the team to decide whether to make changes or whether to maintain the good work. Cost and time are particularly excellent indicators that measure the benefits of using Scrum to develop a new product. It also supports the organization's investments and other financial endeavors.

Metrics that can quantify the level of satisfaction the users get from using the product can help the team determine the area that requires improvement, either areas that have to do with the product or areas related to the team itself.

The following are some of the metrics Scrum project teams use:

## Sprint Goal Success Rates

An effective way to measure the success of a project is by determining the sprint success rate. At a minimum, a sprint does not require that all tasks and requirements in the sprint backlog be complete before being termed a success. This is because a successful sprint only requires a working product increment that meets the sprint goal and fulfills the requirements of the team's definition of 'done.' As such, the sprint must have gone through the stages of development, testing, integration, and documentation.

## Time to Market

The phrase 'Time to Market' is used to refer to the amount of time it takes before a project provides value to its users through its products or its working features.

An important factor to take note of is that value is perceived in two different ways. Firstly, a product is said to be valuable if it can generate income directly, which makes the money derived from its value. Secondly, if the product is meant to be used internally in an organization, its value is realized when the employees can use the product successfully. This value is subjective, based on what each product is designed to do.

Overall, time to market enables the organizations to be aware of and to measure the on-going value of the Scrum projects. This concept is quite useful to companies that produce products that generate revenue because it eases budgeting because it can be done throughout the year.

## Defects

For teams to be completely agile, they must take up agile practices like continuous integration (CI) and test-driven development (TDD). These practices form the bedrock of agile processes and without them, teams that are using Scrum would be ineffective at delivering quality products as quickly as the market is demanding them. This is because the overhead manual testing that is done before each release and the number of defects introduced is easily caught through automation.

The advantage of tracking defects is that the team can know how well it is doing regarding preventing issues from arising and when it can refine these processes. This metric is also critical in sparking discussions around development techniques and project processes during the sprint retrospectives.

## Satisfaction Surveys

The topmost priority for any Scrum Team is to satisfy the consumers by delivering value, early on and continuously throughout the product life. Similarly, the Scrum Team also seeks to motivate Team members and to encourage sustainable development practices.

The Scrum team can gather a lot of valuable data from the experiences of individual team members and customers. This data provides measurable information that helps users to understand how the Scrum team is doing regarding fulfilling its purpose.

Team satisfaction surveys measure the experience the team members have had working for the specific organization, using the processes, working with other project members, the working environment, and other factors that could affect their work. On the other hand, customer satisfaction surveys determine the customer's experience with the process, the project, and the Scrum Team.

Surveys are taken in their traditional form using pen and paper or using online tools.

## Project Attrition

Organizations with a project portfolio of any size should seek to determine the rate at which their projects are cut short. In this, take care not to confuse capital redeployment and the management thrashing teams anyhow and at any stage of the project, based on the senior manager's whim.

Checking the project duration against per-capita redeployment will likely expose a trend of projects ending prematurely, or simply running for longer than was necessary. The former is most prevalent though.

Based on the results of this comparison, the managers can begin to investigate the reasons the projects are cut short. Preliminary findings are likely to indicate cross-functionality, planning, thrashing, impediments, and prioritization issues as some of the reasons for the lack of advancement.

## Return on Investment (ROI)

The income generated by the product that the team has been working on is called the return on investment. In Scrum, return on investment is different from that of other traditional projects because products produced by Scrum can start earning income even after the very first release, which can happen as early as the end of the first sprint. Revenue may also increase after every release.

This metric provides a great way for an organization to take note of the increasing value of the Scrum project. With ROI, you can justify the credibility of the product or feature you intend to create right from the start because most sponsors fund projects based on visible potential.

## Team Member Turnover

Scrum embraces and appraises teamwork and as a result, the team tends to have higher morale than the individual members. One way of measuring this morale is by looking at the turnover. Use the following metrics to determine this turnover.

**Company Turnover**: When the entire company's morale is high, even when it does not include the performance of the Scrum team, it highly affects the effectiveness and morale of the team and others in the company. As the Scrum rollout begins, the company should begin to see a decrease in turnover.

**Scrum Team Turnover**: You can tell that the team environment in your organization is healthy if you notice that the team turnover is low. High turnover is often brought by factors like the incompatibility of the personalities, burnout, ineffective Product owner who dictates and forces commitments on the team or a Scrum Master who does not do much to remove the limitations and constraints, which paints a bad picture of the team in sprint reviews.

## Capital Redeployment

If there are only low-revenue requirements in the backlog, it might prove necessary to end the project before the Scrum team has exhausted its resources. The organization can then use the remaining resources to start a new more profitable project. The act of removing resources from one budget to another is simply called capital redeployment.

## Skills Versatility

Doing this is quite easy. As you start begin, start by capturing all the existing skills at different levels. Assess the skills per individual, per team, and organization. Over time, as the team progresses expect that their levels of skills will increase. These metrics will help measure your progress and also help you determine where your team lags.

# Chapter 17:
# Scrum in Software Development

The creative nature of the software development process makes Scrum a natural fit. Scrum does not provide instructions to be followed but only provides a platform for developers to see everything clearly, before they proceed to act on it themselves. In its empirical nature, Scrum perfectly fits this environment because its framework nurtures excellence and creativity.

The traditional software development and project management methods relied on the ability to envisage the future accurately. They are linear and based on a sequence of events. However, technology developments and the needs of the consumers have long outgrown this rigid framework.

Projects of the past took up the waterfall management system. Waterfall project management is a system that allows a set of requirements to mature progressively in stages where one item must be completed before taking on another. This system requires a prior designing of all the steps and requirements of a project before commencing and the completion of all development work before conducting comprehensive tests.

Lately, as projects have increased in complexity, the limitations of the waterfall system have become even clearer. Code testing was done as the project came to a close, at the time when the team had the least available energy, time, and money. The customers also could not interact with the product until when it was too late to integrate their feedback and ideas into the product. Additionally, projects were consistently delayed or were never completed and they came up short.

Scrum came up in a frantic effort to find a solution and a better way to make software. Its use is not just limited to the process of creating software though, its framework is applicable even in projects in which you can sum up the work and prioritize tasks one against another. As you can see, Scrum embraces change better than traditional methodologies.

## **Embracing Change**

This has created a methodology that accommodates a change in an all-inclusive environment that ensures equal voice and opportunity for all team members.

Interestingly, Scrum has features similar to those of activities conducted in its predecessor, the waterfall methodology, but instead of executing the changes in successive phases, the changes are condensed into iterative sprints to create an operational application. In this way, the project is carried out incrementally, by improving or adding functionality and features created in the initial planning or brought by change.

The Scrum system of software development takes into account the changing landscape and the importance of this change in the market. Change is a factor that cannot be absconded from or discounted. Therefore, the best way to deal with the changes is to assent and become accustomed to it accordingly. This principle of taking in change is embedded in the Scrum framework, which means that by default, embracing Scrum in software development makes a team adhere to changes around them.

The first step towards embracing change is not having a flexible plan or methodology; it begins by changing your mindset and getting ready for any alterations that may come about in the future. Change is an ordinary and normal phase of development. Therefore, the focus of any project should shift from trying to prevent a change in tracking changes and managing expectations. Instead of rejecting change requests, the right response should be informing the customer of the implications of the change such as the risks associated, and the effect the change would have on the project schedule, the project cost, quality, and scope. With this information, the customer can make an educated decision.

## **Business Alignment**

It is now evident that success does not come from coming up with Scrum teams alone, the full benefits are only realized if the organization itself is also built around the software and the new production practices. These days, staying in business is about continuously delivering value, and value is only realized when you restructure the entire business to align with the Scrum methodology.

When scaling Scrum, a software delivery organization will need to align itself on two different levels. The first is the process or product level. Alignment at this level helps to avoid delivery optimization from a single team level and instead promotes local optimization for component teams as they specialize in a specific area. However, this alignment of teams may not offer the best value to the organization and consumers. The second kind of alignment, alignment at a technical level, is important for addressing engineering practices like continuous delivery, continuous integration, and in the implementation of software architecture.

Implementation of a Scrum model in business often starts with one experimental team and if this team succeeds in the implementation process, the organization will then roll out the entire Scrum team-based structure. Despite the structure of the organization, one of the first signs you note after implementation is that overhead communication grows exponentially. Although the need for proper communication between the teams is apparent, the communication inertia that develops after this is interesting even when the teams are situated next to one another.

A successful implementation plan for the Scrum system calls for a proper understanding of what entails Scrum by the team and by all the stakeholders. Even after carrying out proper training, it might still be challenging to achieve the intended outcome. This is the reason the whole organization needs to be aligned with the Scrum model.

A team, in turn, consists of professionals in different fields such as the technical architect, developers, project director, and the quality manager, among others. Because of these variations, it is essential to align the team with the existing Scrum model.

Essentially, it is difficult to determine the resources team members will need for each role. The Scrum model only lays out the roles that the stakeholders play in a project but nothing about the specific individuals who should take up certain roles. Therefore, when aligning the model to the team, you should seek to match the roles among the three job titles effectively.

Resources should be aligned with the product owner. As a product owner divides the resources and allocates them as they are needed, this role is suitable for a person who can stay in touch with the client and communicate the needs of the client promptly. Project sponsors, product managers, business analysts, and project managers are suitable for this role.

The quality assurance (QA) team and the development team are important but should function in a mutually exclusive manner for the success of the alignment. If both teams are in the same sprint, they will cause trouble. Most teams end up arranging separate QA sprints, not allowing them to mix with the development sprints. This leads to an old but beneficial setting where one has to happen before the other commences.

Overall, aligning the overall software development business to the Scrum model is not difficult; it only requires that the right resources are placed in able hands and that structures within the business be made smooth to allow for this change. Each stakeholder has a role to play, and conflicting roles should be played separately.

# Chapter 18:
# Scrum Mistakes to Avoid

## Doing the Practices Without the Principles

Accomplishing simple things like actualizing Scrum gatherings, filling the Scrum jobs, and utilizing appropriate Scrum antiques is great; however, it is just half (or less) of the fight. The Agile standards are what make the practices function admirably, and make them reasonable over the long-haul. Standards are a lot harder to consolidate than rehearses, which is the reason numerous organizations miss the mark – they don't do the hard parts. Utilizing procedures without understanding why you are doing them can prompt disappointment. Lithe is about individuals, collaborations, and culture, not procedures, practices, and apparatuses.

## Complicating the Scrum Startup Process

Try as much as you can to keep the Scrum startup process simple. Scrum will successfully work without the latest and coolest collaboration tool. Spending precious time to get a tool up and running rather than getting people to work together is the wrong focus for your time and energy.

The Scrum framework focuses on individuals and interactions rather than on tools and processes for a reason. Keep it as simple as possible (but no simpler) and put your people first.

## Communicating Through the Scrum Master

A common mistake on a new Scrum team is using the Scrum master as a messenger. For instance, when a certain developer/team member needs to know something about a user story, instead of asking for clear information from the product owner, he/she emails the Scrum master for more information. This is wrong and must be avoided at all costs. You should strive to overcome the culture of indirect communication before it causes miscommunications among Scrum teams and team members.

## Too much planning and preparation

Scrum does not require the regular kind of planning that normal methodologies demand. On the contrary, Scrum teams have the liberty of just jumping in and getting started. The feedback the team receives is used as the means to review and adjust its plans. Some teams even start creating the Product Backlog after starting or finishing the first Sprint.

## Lack of an automated testing system

Without the system itself requiring you to do so, it may be difficult for teams to test out their deliverables within each Sprint. Additionally, most manual testing recommended only wastes time that teams do not have the luxury of.

### Reliance on tools

Most organizations get on a frantic search for electronic tools that can guide them throughout the Scrum process, especially those that are new to Scrum. Looking for a tool is only a means to delay the Scrum process. And besides, the Agile Manifesto does not encourage the use of tools.

### Unproductive Product owner

Today, teams need a Product owner who is adept in matters of business, understands priorities, and can work well with others every day. An indecisive or absent Product owner quickly sinks the entire project.

### Inadequate training

Investing in a class makes all the stakeholders better and quicker in carrying out their roles. Failure to take training shows that the organization itself does not take the Scrum program seriously.

### An unfitting working environment

If members of a team are not working from the same location, they do not gain the advantages of one-on-one interaction. Working together is not enough, the team needs to relate well with each other even in issues outside the project.

### Poor team selection

It's possible to choose some members who do not work well with others, do not believe in the viability of Scrum, or that they cannot manage themselves in their work. All these qualities lead to the quick sabotage of projects and the purported failure of Scrum as a methodology.

## Stretching the goals

No person should pressure the team into doing more and overcommit because it will only demotivate, build resentment, and create distrust among the members. However, you can motivate the team by challenging them with product goals.

## Burning interruptions

The team should not allow even the most pressing interruptions in a Sprint. If indeed the issue is urgent, the team should go ahead and cancel the current Sprint. Otherwise, the interruption should be placed on the Product Backlog and be handled later, possibly at the start of the next Sprint.

## Failure to get Done

This is difficult to prevent entirely and you will find that this happens now and then. However, it can become a habit for a team that overcommits. To prevent this, ensure that Burndown Charts are used effectively and demos are held occasionally to fish out incomplete work.

## Unusable prototypes

Scrum teams should commit themselves to produce quality, 'potentially shippable' software right from the start, in the very first Sprint. Using a prototype code delays the writing of production code. Detailed designs, wireframes, and other tools are not acceptable either.

## Switching team members

The Scrum framework is intent on creating high-performing development teams. If the members are changed, the new team has to redo the forming, storming, norming, and performing sequence all over again. If the team is performing and norming all right, changing the members is impractical and a waste of investment.

## Creating non-scrum roles on the Scrum team

It is common to find that when organizations create Scrum teams, they do so without changing the official duties and titles of the team members. For example, you will find a Project Manager taking on the roles of a Product owner with no accompanying change in the title.

## A Product owner Who isn't Available Or Involved

The Product owner job can be very tedious. Many who are new to the job are not prepared for the responsibility, or simply don't have a clue about what is included. Cooperation is basic in the Agile world. Businessmen and engineers need to cooperate to deliver programming that the business needs. This occurs by steady correspondence, coordinated effort and short input cycles to approve or make course revisions.

## Careless Daily Standups

The day by day stand-up meeting is significant from a few angles. It puts individuals eye-to-eye each day for 15 minutes, powers correspondence and joint effort, and gives transparency and straightforwardness to the task. For such a key gathering, it's essential to set the correct desires in advance so the group pays attention to it. This may sound activist, yet participation at the day by day stand-up is rarely discretionary.

## Not Raising Obstacles Early Enough

The day by day stand-up gives the open door consistently to convey obstacles to completing our work. One of the essential elements of the Scrum Master is to expel snags so the group can concentrate on conveying programming; however, if hindrances are not raised, the Scrum Master can't help evacuate them. Standing by to raise an impediment until it's past the point where it is possible to recuperate from it is unsatisfactory. Until colleagues are familiar with imparting deterrents in an opportune way, remind the group toward the start of each rise up to raise even potential snags, or if there's any opportunity something may defer their work or prompt them to not satisfy their dash responsibility.

## Not Conducting Retrospective Meetings After Every Sprint

Lamentably the Sprint Retrospective is frequently treated like an extra or extravagance, and performed just "if there's time". The truth of the matter is, Agile is about alterations to a great extent, calibrating and reacting to change. It's extremely difficult to alter and calibrate on the off chance that we don't delay to discover where modifications are required. Business as usual isn't Agile; persistent improvement is.

# Chapter 19: Optimizing Sprints

You can optimize your sprints, boost or enhance them based on three different factors, which are the sprint duration, team size, and the number of items on the sprint backlog. Optimization is done by regularly inspecting the processes used in reviews and retrospectives to see the status of the sprint and the project as a whole. To optimize fully, here are some factors you will need to be aware of.

### Daily Scrum Definition

During these meetings, if a person stands and says that they are working on a particular module, you know that in the next day's meeting, the person will be reporting on whether he was able to finish working on the module or not. It is very good for the project for the team to realize the value of these commitments.

The presence of each team member is required and it is preferred that each stands to ensure that the meeting only takes up the scheduled time and not a second past. On the other hand, the team has to address all issues that are raised during the meeting, and none should be ignored based on the excuse that the time is limited. Any issues raised after that need to be recorded and handled after the Scrum Meeting.

## Scheduling

Teams that have taken up Scrum plan and track their work using regular time intervals in a rhythm called the sprint cadence. The sprints are defined in a way that they correspond to the cadence the team is using. The cadence can take 2 to 3 weeks or even shorter or longer. Alternatively, you can come up with a release schedule that puts together several sprints.

Scheduling sprints is the first step in the iteration or the sprint planning process. In the scheduling meetings, the team determines the amount of work it intends to deliver, choosing from the prioritized items on the Backlog and using its velocity history as an indicator of the amount of work the team can handle in one sprint. Other details determined at this stage include the sprint start and finish dates, number of stories or items to be handled per sprint, and the estimated amount of work to be handled in each sprint.

## Conducting

Conducting the sprint in an optimum manner helps abate surprises, refocus the execution of issues, and to aid in acquiring a higher quality code at the end of the project. When conducting sprints, take the following steps:

## Look back onto the roadmap of where you are coming from

It helps to look back and see where your project has come from. The roadmap behind you sets the pace for the user stories and the sprints, which are the backbone of the Scrum program and the delivery of results, particularly those of long projects. This roadmap should have been updated and must be visible to the entire team.

## Hold a briefing before the official meeting

Planning sprints require grooming the backlog and deciding on the deliverable to work towards in the coming sprint. From experience, backlog grooming should be done earlier on in a separate session with both the Scrum Master and the Product owner in attendance, before sprint planning itself commences. Backlog grooming is an activity meant to ensure that the Product Backlog is still healthy. A healthy backlog is one that correctly prioritizes items, has an estimate for the work required for each item and contains well-defined user stories that the team can start working on immediately.

## Team Task Board

When using Scrum, you can make all project activities visible by putting them on the Scrum task board. While it is possible to do this digitally, there is no harm going old school, you only need a whiteboard or a wall, some sticky notes or cards, and tape!

Physical task boards are an excellent tool because they are a quick and effective way for the team and the stakeholders to take in the entire sprint in one glance. Having the board within the team's workspace ensures that they constantly update their progress and stay motivated to stay on course.

When coming up with a task board, ensure that it has the following critical elements:

- The top should be preserved for the **Specific Sprint Goal** and the **Overall Release Goal**. The **Sprint Date** and the **Release Date** can also be included at the top.

- The Columns have several categories. From the left to the right:

- **To Do**: This column is meant for tasks and requirements that are yet to be handled.

- **In Progress**: This column is reserved for the tasks and items that the team is currently working on.

- **Accept**: This column is meant for requirements that are awaiting the Product owner's approval. Rejected requirements are placed back into the In Progress column.

- **Done**: This column is reserved for requirements that are completed and approved.

As you may have noted, the development team can move the requirements from the To Do column into the In Progress and the Accept columns. However, the product owner alone has the mandate of moving the items from the 'Accept' into the 'Done' column.

The product owner should not allow the items in the 'Accept' column to pile up. Ideally, a day should not pass before a card or sticky note is moved into the 'Done' column or is rejected.

## Handling Unfinished Requirements

When asked about the progress of a project, most people will report that they are 40% done, 80% done, or 95% done. These estimates can be reassuring sometimes, but it does not embrace the spirit of transparency that Scrum advocates for. What's more, the status of a project in Scrum and other agile software development methods is either Done or Not Done, and nothing in between.

So, how should you handle unfinished requirements? There are two ways to deal with the situation. The first is that this question need not trouble you much. The inability to finish a user story means that the story is exceptional by itself and no matter how you look at it, it will not impact any of your metrics. However, if this is still intolerable for your team, you have to deal with the underlying issues. Find out what is causing the delays and handle it appropriately.

Delays and spillovers are caused by overestimating the work for the sprint where the team members become too ambitious and commit to more than they can handle. It also originates from not clearly defining the Definition of Done which results in disagreements about whether the story should be considered Done or not.

## How to Correct Course

The first thing to do is to review the entire project and to review the team during the retrospective session. This session is meant to determine what caused the spillover and to go through various options available to the team and to the organization to mitigate the problem. The team must figure out the underlying factors swiftly and not waste much time as it is needed for other issues of the project too. The team must agree on the issue that was spilled over and have the product owner decide whether the issue is still priority or not.

If the story is still considered to be of high priority, it is moved to the next sprint as discussed earlier. It is easier to do it this time because you will have already determined all that it entails during grooming, and it is only a matter of getting it done now. In the event the issue was only done partially, the team should move on to discuss the amount of work that is yet to be done. Analyzing this work may lead the team to create a new user story and redefining Done, in addition to a new way of estimation.

If the story is ruled out and no longer considered a priority, the story is shoved back to the bottom of the Product Backlog awaiting re-evaluation based on priority during the grooming process when it is placed where it rightfully deserves, still based on priority.

To avoid constant spillovers, it makes sense that the Scrum Master takes note of the team's availability for the entire sprint length and then plans the work accordingly. He or she should set aside some buffer time to take care of emergencies, unforeseen events, and the possibility of a story running for longer than planned. It is only logical to devote a considerable amount of time to plan to ensure that all issues included in the sprint align to be reached at the end.

Overall, when spillovers occur, they only need to be managed properly. It is impossible to eliminate them but with proper planning and management, you can reduce the frequency at which they occur.

## Feedback Loop Insights

The Scrum framework promotes an incremental, iterative, and collaborative approach for building software products. As part of enabling collaboration between the development team and the consumers, this process emphasizes short feedback loops.

Frequent interactions and feedback from the end-users keep the creative team focused on delivering on the objectives set, ensuring that they produce a product of high quality, and one with the intended features. The feedback loop also allows the team to take in changes in the development process as they emerge.

This is the reason why Scrum has inbuilt checkpoints to allow for collaboration and feedback. For example, the daily stand up allows the Team to share updates of their assignments and to talk about the obstacles they have encountered on the way.

The Scrum feedback loop has four fundamental steps. The steps are planning, doing, checking for results, and adjusting accordingly in preparation for the next cycle. Scrum has two essential loops: every day and sprint.

A sprint is a major feedback loop. It allows the team to execute plans to help arrive at the intended goal and then measure its progress through retrospectives and reviews. In the sprint review, the team links up with the end-users or the product owner, who is the proxy, to receive feedback on the requirements that have been implemented so far. Once the software is up and running, the team can take note of areas that need improvement and put these changes back to the Backlog.

Conversely, the retrospective focuses on the work and the process it took to complete the work. The team goes over the entire project process determining what went well and what could use a different approach in the future.

## Anti-patterns

Here are a few anti-patterns:

### Point Procrastination

Some teams will avoid tackling the harder, larger, and riskier tasks and move on to the simpler ones in a bid to gain story points to keep the Burn-down Charts looking good, to impress themselves, and stakeholders. This becomes a problem particularly as the project comes to an end and things start shifting and becoming more unpredictable. Additionally, this pattern of doing things could cause the product owner and the management to proceed to reward fast but sloppy team members while getting rid of those whose moves are calculated and careful. Therefore, be careful about measuring the performance of the team using story points because if you focus on points, that is as much as you will get.

### Permitted Mediocrity

In software development, poor quality work leads to bugs that in turn slow the velocity. Bugs also reduce the quality of the user experience bringing up the need to rework. Other times, the team does not want to publicly own up to the bugs and will not look into them properly which could end up causing problems later on, affecting the velocity of the team. Scrum imposes such as a business structure that sometimes, the engineers themselves have no voice over the superiors. There is a need to empower them so that they also have a say in the building process.

## The 'No Plan' Approach

Besides sprint planning, not much else is done to help design or guide the project. As a result, there are constant adjustments, reworks, and realignments throughout the project. True, the point of using Scrum is to adapt and accommodate change, but that does not mean that the team should engage in a guessing game that lacks a clear vision. Some people say that agile processes do not need any form of design, but this is wrong too. No one can achieve success without some form of plan.

# Chapter 20:
# Careers in Scrum

The Agile methodology has gained popularity for changing the landscape of project management and developing software. To that effect, the demand for professionals with a bit of knowledge and experience on the same has heightened.

Scrum appreciation workshops or seminars may be a good starting point. For those team members that are interested in going further with their Scrum training, there are some certification options available as proposed by the Scrum Alliance.

Here are a few to consider:

## Certified Scrum Developer

Scrum product development is unlike the traditional Waterfall phased-project cycle approach. The CSD course will provide developers all the knowledge to sharpen their Agile development skills. Additionally, developers will also master the science behind incremental development as advocated by Scrum, instead of delivery at the end of project lifecycle approach.

CSD has an edge over non-Scrum colleagues in that they not only learn Agile engineering but are also exposed to the basic principles and practices of the Scrum framework.

## Certified Scrum Professional

Certified Scrum Professionals (CSPs) are in-practice CSMs, CSPOs or CSDs that wish to take their Scrum certification to the next level. Every project delivery methodology can be stretched to its limits, and that's when organizations see additional benefits. This training will enable you to acquire additional skills and knowledge to help you challenge your Scrum Teams to extend their current boundaries of Scrum practice.

## Certified Scrum Trainer

When Scrum practice has made you perfect in the science of Scrum, it's time to learn the art of teaching Scrum. As a CST, you'll learn everything there is to know about translating your wealth of Scrum knowledge and experience and passing it on to others.

Every organization that's committed to Scrum should consider having at least one CST on board. CST's will not only help Scrum practitioners in the organization keep their skills current, through continuous training, but could also wear the hat of Scrum Master or product owner if required.

## Certified Scrum Coach

An Agile coach plays a valuable role in the organization and towards effecting change in the organization. The coach assists organizations that are trying to implement Agile methodology by aiding them in the formation of teams and cultivating the culture of change that is needed for agile success.

The coach is also tasked with helping the teams through the process of implementation and encouraging workers and the management to embrace agile methods in all their functions. His ultimate goal is to provide the teams with the rightful tools, knowledge, and training needed to realize the full potential of Agile.

One agile coach says that the responsibility of a coach is to assess where the team lies in terms of its development journey and to offer a complementary approach to support this growth. The main agenda for this team is to improve and this can only be done if the coaches ask the right questions, challenge the people's mental processes, provide a good mental model, and guide the teams in their efforts to build excellent products for their customers.

For CSP's that wish to elevate their Scrum credentials, CSC might be the answer. As a CSC, you must be able to demonstrate that you have all the practical and theoretical knowledge of Scrum to qualify as a Coach to others - individuals, groups and organizations.

One prerequisite to attaining the CSC designation is that you must be able to prove that you have helped at least one organization successfully adopt Scrum in the implementation of real-life projects.

The agile coach is not just hired to help the team embrace this change; the coach also works with the entire organization to aid a cultural shift. As such, for an organization to implement this methodology properly, the coach needs to include the support of other employees in the organization and that of the stakeholders.

# Chapter 21:
# Tips for Scrum Mastery

To become the ultimate scrum master, implement the following tips and strategies:

## Develop a Fun Environment that Your Team will enjoy

Being fun to be around and ensuring the environment you and your teamwork in is fun motivates your team into producing a high standard of work. Fun is, well, fun. If given a choice, every person would opt to work in a place that is fun and with fun people. The prerogative rests upon you, therefore, to create an atmosphere of fun in which your team will unroll and unwind to the fullest potential. Go out of your way to create a fun working atmosphere.

## Psyche Your Team to Achieve the Plan

The Sprint Backlog needs no alteration unless the product owner has negotiated the change with the development team. The leader has to communicate this concept of scrum to the whole team and workshop or the significant organs of the company to ensure that there are fewer conflicts.

Encourage your team to respect this; if anyone says something to the contrary, you are right to get involved as a Scrum Master so you can play your protective duties.

## Apply Collaboration Skills

In scrum, Teamwork is essential. As the scrum master, you should collaborate effectively with both the product owner and the development team for the betterment of the development process.

You cannot be an effective Scrum Master without collaborating with others working on the project. You must collaborate with the team regarding giving them the guidance they need and collaborate with the product owner on issues of the grooming of the product backlog and team dynamics. Collaboration is something you have to choose to do. If you are not good at it, you have to exercise it to improve it. It may take a while, some effort, and lots of commitment, but practice does make perfect.

## Stay Balanced Throughout

A scrum master's work is concise, and so is that of the product owner. Ultimately, you and the product owner have one shared desire: to build an excellent product while maintaining value. Helping each other will help achieve a common goal. Your duty as Scrum Master is to ensure that the quality of the software (or whatever product) you are working on is not jeopardized by your efforts to improve the scrum team. You are there to ensure the team implements the necessary principles in pursuance of quality.

## Maintain the Team's Focus on the Sprint that is Present

Maintaining focus on a short period of work is better than having your thoughts and attention all over the place. The Scrum Master must ensure the team does not stray but remains focused on the present iteration. Developing a product is not a one-sprint job; however, it is of paramount importance that the attention of the team remains at that one sprint and not on a backlog item the team will work on in the future or even something already finished.

## Let Self-Organization and Autonomy be a Culture in the Team

From the time the process starts to the end, you should coach the development team to practice self-leading principles. In the end, even if members of the team were new recruits to scrum, they should be able to self-organize. Doing the team's work will not make things easier because it will make them dependent on you, or it will create resentment when they think you do not consider them good enough to do much on their own.

## Be Aware of the Details of Each Member's Task

It is easier to assist the development team because your main role is to ensure they know and effectively implement scrum rules and principles; you are the expert of that. However, such is not the case with the product owner, yet you and the product owner should work towards a common goal.

## Establish Good Rapport with Other Teams

Scrum collaborations need not be in the individual team; they need to include other teams elsewhere. There may be other scrum teams working on different projects at your organization or in the same area; it would be mutually favorable for you and the other teams if you worked together or merely discussed scrum issues together. You can improve based on their experiences as well as share solutions to common technical or nontechnical problems.

## Make a Point of Not Planning Up-Front

Many teams, especially when they are first getting started with Scrum, still feel the need to do some type of planning before they get started. This can, in turn, lead to what is known as analysis paralysis. This occurs when the planning stage of any given project will often grind progress on that goal to a halt as buy-in is obtained from several different sources for days or even weeks. Don't forget, Scrum was designed to be an adaptable framework for inspection, which means that by its very nature it is antithetical to have several team members sitting around waiting for a single individual to finish preparing so they can get to work.

## Don't Worry About Advanced Tools

It is common for new teams to put off starting the Sprint process while they look through the myriad of different types of tools that are available to help them make using Scrum as simple and easy as possible. While there is nothing wrong with looking into finding a good Scrum assistance tool, it is important to wait to do so until you have a clear idea of just what facets of the Scrum process that you need electronic help with.

## Keep your Product owner Involved

A common problem that many Sprints face over time is a product owner who is energized and eager to contribute at the start of the Sprint, but who then falls off when the time comes to turn ideas into reality. A product owner is just as much a part of a Sprint team as anyone else which means they should ideally be present at every Daily Remember, the Scrum Team model was created with the express purpose of being as beneficial to productivity, creativity, and flexibility as possible, but it can only do this when the product owner is as committed to respect, openness, focus, courage and commitment as the rest of the team.

## Concentrate on each undertaking in turn

You might be fit for dealing with different ventures; however, this could likewise imply that you're mostly dedicated to an undertaking. To give your full 100% and to ensure the undertaking is as effective as it tends to be, handle each task in turn.

## Help the group characterize a reasonable meaning of done

Ensure the meaning of done is unmistakably characterized. It ought to be a rundown containing all things that must be finished to convey quality programming. Help the group to characterize quality checks, with the goal that a colleague realizes how to decide whether an assignment is done true to form.

## Continue learning and exploring

The world is evolving. Ensure you change with it. If you don't, it implies that you're moving in reverse rather than forward! As a scrum ace, you must ensure your group advances and continues improving at their work and cooperation. You can't do this without learning and improving your aptitudes and information. Help your group develop by developing yourself.

## Know your group

Ensure you know each colleague. What are their qualities and shortcomings? What are their characters? Do you know the group's dynamic? Would you be able to name the life partner and diversions? Attempt to find out about your colleagues. On the off chance that you realize them well, you'll figure out how to assist them with functioning better together.

### Get Educated

If this is your first time using the Scrum methodology, do not attempt it without first getting yourself and the team educated on Scrum. While a lot of Scrum is about commons sense project management, there is a vast body of Scrum knowledge that diverges significantly from traditional project management theories. Equipping everyone on the team with that knowledge is the first step in putting Scrum into action successfully

### Be Realistic

Forecasting is always a tricky business when it comes to real-life scenarios. Most new Scrum practitioners are overzealous and, in their eagerness to show how fast Scrum can deliver, underestimate delivery timelines. It is always good practice to add some (not a lot!) extra "runway" to your forecasts to make them realistic

### Celebrate Success

One of the most important ways that one can put the Maslow theory into action is by celebrating team success. Individual's need for Esteem and Self-Actualization can be greatly fueled when they receive praise, accolades, and recognition before their peers for their contributions. That's what will go furthest in cementing an efficient team

### Ensure the group is associated with ceaseless improvement

During the review, the group attempts to discover approaches to improve the procedure given their encounters in the dash. Ensure you propel everybody to ponder the procedure and to continue considering during the entire procedure. This is significant for the group to continue improving.

## Inquire as to whether what you're doing is following Agile standards

As a scrum ace, you are answerable for ensuring the whole group effectively adheres to the standards and standards of Scrum. You're the person who mentors the group every single Agile practice. Along these lines, occasionally, return to the Agile standards and guarantee that what you are doing is in accordance with every one of them.

## Don't Use Stretch Goals

Stretch goals have long been used in many settings as a way of planning out additional goals that can be reached assuming certain conditions are met. They are antithetical to the Sprint methodology, however, and should never be used while on a Sprint for any reason.

Stretch goals that include a predetermined scope and deadline are the most difficult for Scrum teams to work through simply because it requires the team to start with a deadline and then work backward to determine how to complete it, practically the opposite of how things normally go.

## Make it Clear that Individual Sacrifice is Not Required

First and foremost, it is important to understand that the team naturally improves by coming together and solving these sorts of problems, which not only makes the unit as a whole more prepared for the future but more cohesive as a team as well. As such, if one person cracks the nut the entire team was working on then great, but if that person goes to near superhuman lengths to do so, then the team learns a very different lesson instead.

## Do Not Allow the Team to Over-commit

If you feel the team is over-committing to a sprint, explain to them why they should not do that. It is better for them to finish the stories before the end of the sprint then ask for more from the product owner than get to the end of the time-box before finishing.

## Be on the Look Out for the Team's Strengths and Weaknesses

This is something you should establish early on in the development process. Knowing your team's weak and strong points will help you guide them; a good trainer knows how far the clients can go and works around that.

If you get to know what your team is capable, or not capable of right from the start of your work together, that will be your yardstick as to how much or how little you can push the team knowing very well they can or cannot handle what is on the table.

Knowing them better will also help you implement engineering practices like pairing because you will be in a position to know if these practices work with them or not.

## Show Respect and Trust to Your Team's Space

The scrum scenario gives everyone in the scrum team sufficient room to work to their full potential. You, the product owner, and the development team all have spaces linked to your roles.

Working together and collaborating will help you develop patterns that work well for you as a team and for individual roles; respect those, and the team will respect your station too.

Be sensitive to everyone's conduct so you easily know when someone thinks you are over-stepping your precincts because sometimes, you may do it without forethought or necessarily doubting your team's abilities.

## Respect all the Time Boxes

The aspect of time boxes is an important principle in scrum, and you as the Scrum Master and an expert should be a living example of good to time boxing. In scrum and everywhere else, time limits are in place to protect man against himself. We all have this tendency to keep going indefinitely and, without time constraints, we would not be as concise as we could be.

## Encourage Friendship

When people working together actually enjoy working together, the products they produce are of greater quality because they are in a comfortable work set up where there are no suspicions and no mistrust about each other.

As the Scrum Master, you cannot work miracles and get people to like each other, but you have it within your power to create an environment that fosters comradeship. Encourage the team to be a team and work as one. The team should be able to laugh with each other, have team time, encourage and motivate each other, as well as celebrate with a member who has achieved something. You will be surprised how big a difference this makes.

If there are disputes within the team, work to solve them by holding one-to-one, group discussions and particularly through the use of the retrospective. Remind the team that the retrospective is an excellent way to suggest improvements. This can often prevent frustrations from becoming a one-on-one argument because the load is shared between team members and discussed amicably without any finger-pointing.

## Encourage your Team to Aim Higher Limits

All of us occasionally need a push in the right direction. You should be that push for your team. Remind them they are capable of much better results if they open themselves up to possibilities.

Motivation is not a term reserved for those who are at low points in their lives; those who are doing well also need encouragement to keep on keeping on. You have studied your team and know if they are capable of more than they are letting on; if they are, encourage them.

There are no awards for mediocrity, and the difference between mediocrity and exceptionalism is the effort one puts in. Motivating and encouraging the scrum team should not be a one-man role; the team members can also do that. They can be answerable to one another in sticking to their commitments, hold each other accountable to high standards of work and even challenge each other to grow more and strive for more.

## **Create A Multi-Talented Team**

Producing software or innovative products cannot be a task for a team comprised of team members with similar skills. Those working on the same product/project should have the varying skills needed to get the product built to a high standard. This is a key principle of Scrum.

Your scrum team cannot comprise of Jacks-Of-All-Trades; however, as the scrum master, ensure a good mixture of skill sets. Each development process will have many parts to deal with; having the most knowledgeable team member will work in the team's favor.

Software teams usually need people skilled in fulfilling the role of QA tester, software developer, business analyst, designer, information architect and more. As a Scrum Master, you can be a key advisor to the management team to ensure that all of the skills necessary are covered by team members. You can also be involved in the recruitment process to ensure that the prospective team members are open to working on a scrum team.

### Educate your Team on Scrum Tools

Make use of original scrum tools and new web tools to make your work more efficient.

Use Scrum Master tools to make your work easier. Scrum is so much more than just the task board. You have got burn-ups chats that show the amount of work remaining in a project, velocity tracking that tracks each team's progress per sprint, and story mapping where the team can be occupied in an exercise of setting up the backlog on the wall.

### Always Facilitate One Team at a Time

Many Scrum Masters work with more than one team at a time and some even claim to be good at what they do for all those teams; for a Scrum Master to be effective in his or her duties, one team at a time is more than sufficient.

As you get used to the duties, it might not be challenging in the old sense, but the fact remains – a Scrum Master always has a lot on his/ her plate. Working with two teams at the same time doubles the work quantity, which is not a great idea.

# Conclusion

Thank you for making it through to the end of this book. I hope it was informative and that I was able to present you with all the resources you have to accomplish your objectives in learning Scrum methodology.

Try and integrate Scrum into your business or company! It's an amazingly useful process that can truly help streamline your work ethic. It can help you work on your communication skills, learn how to be a team player, and jump-start your creative side. It doesn't have to be used in a high-end company; it could even be used for running a charity event! It's a program that is extremely effective, flexible, and definitely worth doing.

Often, when new methodologies are being adopted, the temptation is to go in with a "big bang." Resist that temptation at all costs! Give yourself time to change to the Scrum framework and focus on attaining your team's set goals. Work towards following everything you have learned and try to avoid some of the common mistakes. Be consistent in the implementation of Scrum and you shall achieve your desired results regardless of the scope of your project.

Finally, no matter how good a system is designed, the effectiveness of its operation is highly dependent on the people using it. Therefore, it is essential that you truly understand and appreciate the working of Scrum and then dive in to partake of its many benefits.

CPSIA information can be obtained
at www.ICGtesting.com
Printed in the USA
LVHW050745181120
671953LV00031B/520